Vocabulary, Semantics, and
Language Education

CAMBRIDGE LANGUAGE TEACHING LIBRARY

A series covering central issues in language teaching and learning, by authors who have expert knowledge in their field.

In this series:

Vocabulary, Semantics, and Language Education

Evelyn Hatch

Professor Emerita
University of California, Los Angeles

and

Cheryl Brown

Associate Professor
Brigham Young University

CAMBRIDGE
UNIVERSITY PRESS

Published by the Press Syndicate of the University of Cambridge
The Pitt Building, Trumpington Street, Cambridge CB2 1RP
40 West 20th Street, New York, NY 10011-4211, USA
10 Stamford Road, Oakleigh, Melbourne 3166, Australia

First published 1995

Printed in the United States of America

Library of Congress Cataloging-in-Publication Data

Hatch, Evelyn Marcussen.
Vocabulary, semantics, and language education / Evelyn Hatch,
Cheryl Brown.
p.   cm. – (Cambridge language teaching library)
Includes bibliographical references and index.
ISBN 0-521-47409-4. – ISBN 0-521-47942-8 (pbk.)
1. Linguistics.   2. Semantics.   3. Lexicology.   4. Language and
languages – Study and teaching.   I. Brown, Cheryl, (date).
II. Title.   III. Series.
P123.H313   1995
410 – dc20   94-47083
                                                                   CIP

A catalog record for this book is available from the British Library

ISBN 0-521-47409-4   Hardback
ISBN 0-521-47942-8   Paperback

Contents

Contents

Contents

Preface

Vocabulary, Semantics, and Language Education was originally one of four manuals prepared for an introductory course in linguistics at the University of California, Los Angeles. Colleagues and graduate students who contributed or corrected many of the examples that appear in this book over the years include Roann Altman, Kirk Belnap, Frances Berdan, Dana Bourgerie, J. Donald Bowen, Patricia Boyd, Guy Butterworth, Cherry Campbell, Elizabeth Carter, Kory Collier, Susan Curran, Jeanine Deen, Carmen de Neve, Dan Dewey, Patsy Duff, Marietta Elliott, Michael Gasser, Van Gessel, David Hart, Barbara Hawkins, Joseph Huang, Larry Hunt, Ann Johns, Randall Jones, Tsuko Kato, Kathleen Kelly, Deborah Kitsch, Machiko Kuwahata, Carrie LaPorte, Anne Lazaraton, Rachel Locker, Melvin Luthy, Brian Lynch, Mohamed Marzouk, Toyotomi Morimoto, Leann Parker, Donald Parry, Evelyn Payne, Sabrina Peck, Sandra Plann, Karen Schlue, Joan Schwartz, Rina Shapira, Tomohiko Shirahata, Yasuhiro Shirai, Shu-yin Shyu, Raisa Solovyova, Steven Sondrup, Madison Sowell, Paul Stevens, Chantal Thompson, Paula Van Gelder, Masakazu Watabe, Vanessa Wenzell, Cheryl White, Mary Willis, Walter Whipple, Jeni Yamada, Midori Yoshida, and Asako Yoshitomo.

We are grateful to Charlotte Basham for her data from Navajo and Koyukon children. The graduate students at Temple University, Japan, supplied us with many metaphors of teaching and learning, and David Block, at ESADE in Barcelona, helped us better understand the role of metaphor in language. Students at the 1993 TESOL Summer Institute who contributed examples include Nora Bruce, Vita Chimienti, Fatma El Hindawy, Bruce Evans, Mamdouh Fouad Hassan, Jeanine Paul, Miyuki Shinohara, and Kristin Witt. Wherever possible, we have acknowledged contributions in the text.

Sergei Dobrichev at the Linguistics Institute in Barnaul, Siberia, Julia Veschitska from Zhitomir, Ukraine, and all the participants in the CIS-USIS seminar did their best to educate us about not only discourse analysis but also semantic and lexical analyses carried out by scholars in that part of the world. Håkan Ringbom, Esther Glahn, and Kirsten Haastrup generously helped us learn more about lexical research in the Scandinavian countries. We thank Louise Jansen and Michael Clyne for making us more aware of the important work in semantics and sociolinguistics that is ongoing in Australia.

Preface

To our many friends, students, and colleagues who gave us suggestions about ways to improve the materials we offer sincere thanks. We especially thank Brita Butler-Wall, Carmen de Neve, Patsy Duff, Cecilia Ford, Michael Gasser, Larry Hunt, Elite Olshtain, Sabrina Peck, and Vanessa Wenzell, who helped compile the original manuals for the UCLA introductory course in linguistics, and Dan Dewey and Barbara Jones, who helped check our references.

We thank Mary Vaughn, Sue André, and Jane Mairs at Cambridge University Press. Their suggestions have given this book a clarity and style that might otherwise have been lacking. We alone are responsible for any remaining errors.

Acknowledgments

The authors and publisher would like to thank the following for permission to reproduce copyrighted material:

Blackwell Publishers for Figure 3.1 from *Words in the Mind*, by Jean Aitchison, 1987, Figure 5.1, page 54.
Dr. Roger Brown for Figure 2.2 from *Social Psychology*, by R. Brown, 1965, Figure 7–1, page 307.
Cambridge University Press for excerpts from "Relations Models and Metascience" by W. Fawley, in M. Evens, ed., *Relational Models of the Lexicon*, 1988, pages 364–368.
Edward Arnold Publishers for Figure 10.3 from *An Introduction to Functional Grammar*, by M. A. K. Halliday, 1985, Figure 6–26, page 191. Reproduced by permission of Edward Arnold (Publishers) Limited.
Harcourt Brace and Company for Table 11.1. Table adapted from *Aspects of Language*, Second Edition, by Dwight L. Bolinger, copyright © 1975 by Harcourt Brace & Company, reproduced by permission of the publisher.
Harcourt Brace and Company for the list in Practice 11.3.1. Excerpt from *Fundamentals of Linguistic Analysis*, by Ronald W. Langacker, copyright © 1972 by Harcourt Brace & Company, reproduced by permission of the publisher.
Holt, Rinehart and Winston for the Ilocano chart of plurals on page 197. Table adapted from *Descriptive Linguistics*, Workbook, by Henry A. Gleason, copyright © 1955 and renewed 1983 by Holt, Rinehart and Winston, Inc., reproduced by permission of the publisher.
John Benjamins for Table 6.5 from "Words You Know: How They Affect the Words You Learn," by B. Laufer, in J. Fisiak, ed., *Further Insights Into Contrastive Analysis*, 1991, Table 1, p. 589.
Linguistic Society of America for Figure 1.1 from "The Structure of a Semantic Theory," by J. J. Katz and J. A. Fodor, in *Language, 39,* 2, page 186.
Routledge and Kegan Paul for Table 6.1 from *The Origin and Diversification of Language*, by M. Swadesh, 1972, pages 283–284.
TESOL for Figure 12.1 from "Some Issues Relating to the Monitor

Model," by S. Krashen, 1977, in *On TESOL '77: Teaching and Learning English as a Second Language: Trends in Research and Practice* (p. 149), edited by H. Brown, C. Yorio, & R. Crymes, 1977, Washington, DC: Teachers of English to Speakers of Other Languages, Inc. Copyright 1977 by TESOL. Reprinted by permission.

Introduction

It is a convention in textbooks to begin with a definition of the field of study. Linguistics textbooks begin with a definition of phonology as the study of the sound systems of language, syntax as the study of the systematic ways sentences are formed in language, and discourse analysis as the system shown in text formation. Unfortunately, there is no single term that we can define that includes semantics, lexicon, and vocabulary. Each has its own definition.

The term *semantics* refers to the study of meaning and the systematic ways those meanings are expressed in language. Part I of this volume is concerned with semantics and semantic analysis. The term *lexicon* refers to the overall system of word forms and, when we include *morphology*, the study of word formation in languages. The term is also used to refer to the way forms might be systematically represented in the brain, that is, the mental lexicon. Parts II and III of this book are used to discuss the lexicon and lexical and morphological analyses. The term *vocabulary* refers to a list or set of words for a particular language or a list or set of words that individual speakers of a language might use. Since vocabulary is a list, we might think that the only system involved is that of alphabetical order. Modern lexicographers, however, are concerned with much more than the alphabetical ordering of words in dictionaries; they, too, look for system. The notion of choice in vocabulary selection and methods used in acquiring and teaching vocabulary also form an important part of this book.

The selection and organization of information within each section of this book posed several problems. There are different ways of carrying out semantic analyses and lexical analyses, and many claims have been made about the acquisition and teaching of vocabulary. Deciding what to present sent us in various directions. This was similar in many ways to a teacher asking what we mean when we say, "I know that word," or when we say we want our students to acquire vocabulary in our language classes. Do we expect that we or our students will know the meaning of the word in all its contexts? Will students know, for example, that *just* means different things in "I *just* have to tell you what happened today!" "No one thought the verdict was *just*," and "There are *just* 360 shopping days until Christmas"? Do we expect our students to retrieve and use words or only to recognize them when reading? In knowing a word, must

1

we know something of its etymology? Do we need to know how to derive other words from it so that, knowing the word *shop,* for instance, we can derive "shopping days" or "Christmas shoppers"? As our students acquire vocabulary, do they also learn restrictions on the grammatical use of the words? We may teach words like *advise* and *suggest,* but will students automatically note that although "She advised me to study Japanese" is grammatically correct," "*She suggested me to study Japanese" is not? Words also join in loose to tight chains called collocations. If we teach *table,* will our students readily chain it in common collloctions such as "sit at the table," "tabletop," "reserve a table," "table the motion," "head of the table," "table mountain," "water table," "table of elements," "turn the tables on," as well as form the same types of association pairs (e.g., *table* and *chair*) as native speakers? Must we know the semantics of figurative use of words as well? If we teach common words such as *fall, jump,* and *walk,* will our students automatically know they may be used metaphorically for "fall in love," "jump to a conclusion," or "walk it off"? And, finally, will they know whether a word can be used in both written and spoken language and, if so, whether it will work equally well in stuffy talk, tough talk, and sweet talk? Knowing a word is not as simple as it might seem. Knowing what to include in this volume has also not been as simple as it might seem.

A second problem concerns the importance of hypotheses and the arguments that weigh in favor of or against the hypotheses. For example, there is agreement that semantics is the study of meanings and that we talk about semantics using words. Beyond that there is little agreement as to how meanings should be studied. Most linguists agree, however, that there is a difference between linguistic and conceptual systems (although we believe there is much overlap between linguistic knowledge and conceptual knowledge). An interesting example of the separation of cognitive and linguistic skills is shown in the data of Marta, a retarded adolescent studied by Yamada (1981). Marta's poor numerical concepts are reflected in inaccurate information given in linguistically correct responses. Marta can "count" and knows she should point to items as she counts them. However, she may assign two numbers to a given item or count the same item several times. In cases where she has correctly counted an array of items, she is not then able to say how many items there are, demonstrating a lack of the cardinal concept. In spontaneous speech, her temporal and numerical expressions fall within the appropriate semantic field: "I was like 15 or 19 when I started moving out o' home, so now, I'm like 15 now, and I can go." Marta has not grasped the 1-to-1 principle in counting nor the cardinal principle in telling how many items there are (a clear cognitive deficit), yet is able to produce numbers in appropriate places (and even to use ordinals such as in "second friend," "third school"). This leaves us with the problem of specifying the boundary line between cognitive and linguistic knowledge. That is, while there is agreement that differences in cognitive and linguistic skills related to semantics and the lexicon exist, linguists and cognitive psychologists are only now beginning to explicate this agreement in terms of the mechanisms which connect language and thought.

In linguistics textbooks, language is often defined as a *system,* and the task of the linguist is to discover and describe system (the sound system, the semantic system, the lexical system, the morphology system, the syntactic system, the discourse system, and their many subsystems). Conventionally, a linguistic system is made up of units and processes that operate on the units. In the chapters that follow, descriptions have been made in terms of units (structural description) and others have been made in terms of process (procedural description). For example, metaphor may be described in terms of structural categories such as simile and metonymy or in terms of a process that results in a system that links physical perception with metaphors of life and emotion. Lists of types of antonyms in a structural description may be followed by a process description that links antonyms to the ways we evaluate objects and actions that take place around us. Words may be described as nouns or as verbs in a list of word classes, but a process description may show how nouns can become verbs and vice versa. Linguists approach their task in different ways and, depending on their theoretical orientation, may stress one type of description more than another. We have included both structure and process wherever possible in our descriptions of semantic and lexical systems.

The chapters in Part I show a gradual shift in the kinds of questions linguists have asked about the semantic system. Chapter 1 begins with componential analysis, an analysis of the semantic features of words. For example, the meaning of *girl* is in part determined by the features ⟨+feminine⟩ and ⟨+young⟩. Features are also used in semantic field analysis, allowing us to distinguish among members of a family of lexical forms. Thus, a feature such as ⟨+serving⟩ might help us distinguish the meaning of a *ladle* from a *spoon* in the semantic field of cutlery. Chapter 3 moves to the more cognitive approach to semantics, represented in core semantics and prototype theory. We can use core semantics to analyze the central meanings of words and how meanings extend outward along particular dimensions. For example, if you visualize the concept *cup,* there are many ways you might change its shape, the materials from which it is made, and its functions before you must change the word *cup* to *glass, stein,* or some other form. In prototype analysis, we select the best exemplar for a particular concept. So, asked to name a tree, we might select *oak* as the best example. Chapter 4 looks at the relations among words that help to identify a concept. If we think of a frog, we may also think of *jump* as a typical action, *green* as a typical color, *croak* as a typical sound, and so forth. Chapter 5 discusses figurative language. Figuratively, a frog may be able to talk as Kermit the frog, or, in desperate circumstances, it may be changed into a prince with a kiss. Figurative language, in particular metaphor, is an extremely powerful process that only now is being systematically addressed in semantics. In Chapter 6 we consider the notion of universal concepts and the variety of ways in which linguists have described correspondences in conceptual terms across languages. The final chapter in this section, Chapter 7, is devoted to script semantics (the relation of concepts to larger pieces of the language), which we contrast with the conceptual structure hypothesis (where concepts are linked to sentence syntax).

Part II consists of two chapters on lexical processes by which the vocabulary of a language may be increased. Chapter 8 discusses borrowing, coinage, shifts, and conversions. Borrowing of word forms across languages is a common phenomenon – one with possible positive and negative effects for language learners – so it receives the most attention. Chapter 9 is about processes of word building, including additive lexical processes (e.g., compounding) and subtractive lexical processes (e.g., clipping). Again, additive processes are those of greatest importance for language learners, so they receive the most emphasis in the discussion.

Part III is concerned with word classes and morphology. Chapter 10 looks at traditional methods of classifying words into parts of speech and the problems that arise from such classifications. Chapter 11 turns to a discussion of morphology and word formation processes with derivational morphology. These processes are those that result in learner errors such as "The opposite of expand is *in*pand," or "This year is very activ*ity* year." The topic of Chapter 12 is inflectional morphology (e.g., verb tense and aspect). Inflectional morphology forms the basis of grammar-centered language instruction, although here it is discussed as a process that is part of the lexical system.

Part IV is concerned with vocabulary choices made in language use (discourse) and how that choice is influenced by a variety of social factors. Chapter 13 highlights variation in lexical choice owing to register, individual style, gender, age, and role differences. Sociolinguistic studies of geographic and social groups are also discussed. In Chapter 14 we consider the vocabulary of communication signals and the lexical choices available for particular speech acts.

Although every chapter of this book is related to language acquisition, language learning, and language teaching, Part V takes these topics as its major focus. Chapter 15 highlights the strategies and processes learners employ to acquire and use vocabulary. Chapter 16 considers more specifically how learners can be assisted in the acquisition process by teacher strategies and vocabulary pedagogy.

Because one can find information about the topics in other sources, our goal is to do more than just inform language teachers and language students about a wide and interesting array of topics which affect language learning. Therefore, we have selected examples from language learner data that demonstrate the structures and processes *and* the difficulties these pose for learners. Data in these examples come from learners of varying proficiency levels, ages, and first-language backgrounds. Examples of processes are drawn from many languages as well.

We believe that learning about any field is easier if the information presented is put into use, so, unlike other books on semantics and lexicon, this book encourages you to use the information. Each chapter includes Practice sections that make the connection between description and application more explicit. They give hands-on experience with data and offer suggestions for related research projects. At the end of each chapter is a Research and Application section. Here you will find brief summaries of research similar to that discussed in the chapter. You are not expected to complete every Practice item or answer all the questions posed in the Research and Application section. Rather, consider each one, and, after reading the summaries, select those that relate to your interests and carry out the suggested research or further investigate the questions posed.

This book will not give you specific techniques to teach vocabulary. However, it should help you make better decisions about approaches to teaching. You will find a wealth of ideas for teaching and for materials development in the descriptions and the research summaries. The book will help you to understand why you or your students successfully acquire some lexical processes and yet fail with others. That understanding should also enhance your teaching and learning.

Our overall goal in preparing this book has been to reveal system at the semantic and lexical levels of language and to relate that information to vocabulary acquisition and language education. This overall goal has been divided into several course objectives.

Objectives

1. You should understand the search for dimensions within componential semantics.

Evidence: Classify examples according to their semantic features (markers and distinguishers). Given data, perform a semantic field analysis. Discuss the strengths and weaknesses of this analytic approach.

2. You should be familiar with core semantics and prototype theory.

Evidence: Give examples to illustrate core versus peripheral meanings and to illustrate prototypes. Discuss the strengths and weaknesses of these analytic approaches.

3. You should be aware of the lexical relations among words and of relational models of semantics.

Evidence: Identify the lexical relation between pairs of words. Compare the goals of relational models with those of componential and prototype semantics.

4. You should understand the nature and pervasiveness of figurative language.

Evidence: (a) Give examples of literary and conceptual metaphor. Give examples of the use of metaphor in teaching and learning. (b) Given data, discuss the possible ease or difficulty of learning and using particular types of metaphor. (c) Illustrate ways that metaphors combine to form social models of reality.

5. You should be acquainted with the arguments for universal concepts and nonuniversal representation of concepts across languages. You should be able to make predictions about ease or difficulty in learning terms for concepts according to the correspondence between languages.

Evidence: (a) Give examples that argue for universality of concepts. Give examples that show differences in concept representation. (b) Given data that show contrasts in the way concepts are represented in two languages, determine the relative ease or difficulty of learning the terms.

6. You should be able to demonstrate the connection between script contexts and semantics.

Evidence: (a) Supply script components (actors, props, actions), links (ISA, HASA, DO, etc.), and inheritance features for a given script. (b) Illustrate differences in script construction across language groups and predict learning ease or difficulty on this basis. (c) Compare the goals of conceptual dependency theory and the conceptual structure hypothesis.

7. You should know the major word-building processes used to create new words in different languages.

Evidence: (a) Give examples of compounding, affixation, conversion, reduplication, root elaboration, borrowing, shifts, initialization and acronyms, clipping, collocation and idioms, portmanteau and euphemism. (b) Given an example of any of these processes in a language, predict learning ease or difficulty.

8. You should be able to identify major word classes and make predictions about the ease or difficulty of learning specific examples within each class.

Evidence: Given particular words, identify their part of speech and give a rationale for your prediction of ease or difficulty of learning.

9. You should understand what a morpheme is.

Evidence: Given language data, isolate morphemes and give their meanings.

10. You should be able to classify English morphemes as (a) lexical or grammatical, (b) derivational or inflectional, (c) bound or free, or (d) prefix, suffix, or infix.

Evidence: Given English language data, classify morphemes according to the categories noted.

11. You should understand that morpheme units may systematically change their shape (morphophonemic processes) when they occur with other morphemes. You should be able to determine how "normal" the process is and the possible difficulties such changes might present to learners.

Evidence: (a) Identify the changes in supplied data. (b) Comment on the difficulty of the process for language learners.

12. You should know that some morphemes are highly productive and others are not.

Evidence: Given a list of inflectional and derivational affixes, rank them on a scale of high to low productivity.

13. You should know that there are cognitive, social, and linguistic reasons why some morphemes are easy or difficult for child L1 learners and second and foreign language learners to acquire.

Evidence: Given a list of inflections, you should be able to predict ease or difficulty of learning.

14. You should know that much of meaning is determined by context and that lexical choice is determined by context.

Evidence: Give examples to show how word meanings change across contexts. Give examples to show how lexical choice is sensitive to dialect membership, formality, register, gender, age, and status difference.

15. You should know that words and lexical phrases are used as communication signals.

Evidence: Give examples of words and lexical phrases used in opening, closing, turn-taking, backchannel, bracket, and preempt signals. Give examples of lexical items used to meet Gricean norms and to achieve interpretable messages.

16. You should be aware that many speech acts are performed using lexical phrases.

Evidence: Given a particular speech act, you should be able to list lexical phrases used to perform the speech act.

17. You should know the basic steps necessary for learners to acquire vocabulary and recognize the kinds of errors or problems which result when all steps are not taken.

Evidence: Given examples of learner errors in vocabulary use, you should be able to explain what essential steps have not been used sufficiently.

18. You should be aware of compensation strategies used when learner vocabulary is limited.

Evidence: (a) Give examples of learner and native speaker strategies used to compensate for vocabulary deficits. (b) Give examples of strategies used in motherese and foreigner talk, and in talk to second and foreign language learners of different proficiency levels.

19. You should be able to evaluate teacher techniques and language teaching materials which promote vocabulary acquisition.

Evidence: (a) Give examples of teacher techniques and language teaching materials along with an assessment of their likelihood for success in assisting learners to acquire vocabulary. (b) Give a rationale for your evaluation of such techniques and materials.

20. You should find questions that interest you enough that you will want to carry out your own research project(s).

Evidence: Prepare a brief research plan or carry out a minipilot study to obtain data that would allow you to answer the question(s). This project should show your awareness of the theoretical and practical issues involved, include a statement of why you think the question is important and interesting, a review of some of the relevant research, and your own research plan (or minipilot).

These objectives have many relevant applications, in teaching and elsewhere. Think about each of the following situations. If you can match them to our objectives and to the topics listed in the table of contents, you will understand why it is important (and fun) to study this subject matter.

1. The librarian tells you that she has year-end funds to spend on dictionaries for your school. Because the users are mainly ESL students, she wonders if there are any special features she should consider in deciding which dictionaries to order. What can you tell her?

2. Your principal is upset because bilingual children in your classroom scored at a very low percentile on a standard English vocabulary test (Peabody Picture Vocabulary Test, English version) whereas they do well in the Spanish version of the same test. You don't understand this because the children appear to have the vocabulary needed for their schoolwork. The principal wonders how any child in this school could not know common words such as *lamp, bread, refrigerator,* and *stove.* How do you explain this? Does your explanation make any predictions as to what Spanish items the children might not know?

3. A fellow language teacher sighs and tells you that his students need a biology lesson, not a language lesson, because even very advanced students keep confusing *he* and *she.* Do you agree?

4. One of your international students says that Americans are too visually oriented. He claims that expressions such as "look it over," "give someone the eye," "private eye," and even the national anthem, "Oh say can you see," show this is the case. You are planning a cross-cultural communication class. Would this be something to include in your materials?

5. Teachers of advanced level courses complain that students are not taught the basics because they still leave off the *-s* ending for third person singular (e.g., *go* for *goes*). Teachers of the lower-level courses claim they have covered this grammar point. As the coordinator of courses, you must explain why this happens. You also want the teachers to work out a plan to solve the problem. What might you do?

6. A Korean student says that after *undergraduation,* she will study law. Another student writes that the computer is very *scientifical.* The teachers in your program keep a list of such creative examples in the hope that you will be able to see which are systematic (i.e., occur often enough to suggest you might want to prepare a self-access study unit). What do you predict?

7. Your first translation job is to convert a piece of technical writing from French into English. You have a bilingual dictionary for the Canadian technical terms in the subject field, and you complete the translation. Just for fun, you give your translation to a friend who is knowledgeable about the field. She returns the article to you saying she did not understand very much of your translated article. She understands the subject matter, so what could be wrong with your translation?

8. You have been asked to critique reading materials for child second language learners. The publisher says that vocabulary was selected on the basis of frequency and that each word is repeated a minimum of eight times in a book. You find the word *space* used for Sally

Ride's spacesuit, for blank spaces on a page, for a space heater, and the space a dog needs for exercise. Do you severely criticize the materials based on such observations?

9. You've noticed that science textbooks contain a large number of compounds (e.g., *seven-digit numbers, central facility, numerical analysis*). At the same time, you note that students almost never produce such compounds in their writing. Should you stress this kind of vocabulary in both reading and writing lessons?

10. In orientation, a foreign student asks you for help in identifying and locating the Coop, Ugly, and Cog-Sci. You explain that these are abbreviated forms for the Student Cooperative, the undergraduate library, and the cognitive science building. In dismay, the student asks if you can abbreviate all English words or just names of buildings. What do you reply?

11. A book publisher has asked you to write vocabulary notes for a novel which will be used by English majors in a university in Thailand. How will you decide which vocabulary items to annotate?

12. Your sister's infant is just beginning to talk, and she calls the dog, the cat, a furry jacket, a fuzzy pillow, and your bearded neighbor all *wau-wau*. She calls everything she puts in her mouth *kee*. Your sister is worried. Can the baby's utterances be normal?

13. A student asks you why people say *up* and *down* instead of *happy* and *unhappy*. You ask for an example, and he says "I'm really down today." What is your explanation?

14. You have taught a lesson on count and mass nouns. The students seem to accept your explanation about what is and what is not countable. Later you notice that we count noodle*s* but not spaghetti, onion*s* but not garlic, bean*s* but not rice, headache*s* but not flu. Did your explanation make sense?

15. Many languages have one word for the colors blue and green. Does this mean that they cannot distinguish between these two colors? Are dark blue and light blue really the same color?

16. Is it true that preschool-age bilingual children know fewer words than monolingual children? Your neighbor is using this claim as an argument against your use of two languages with children in your family. How do you respond?

17. A friend is from a part of the country where people say *slick up* for *clean*, *mulish* for *stubborn*, and *reckon* instead of *guess*. You claim she shouldn't be allowed near an English language class. She points out that other teachers say *chaps* and *mates* for *friends*, *queue up* for *get in line*, and *petrol* instead of *gas* and nobody objects. Can she keep her regional dialect when she teaches?

18. You have a difficult time saying no to invitations. You have been told that it's better just to say, "I'm sorry, I have other plans." Somehow this lexical phrase by itself does not seem to work. What other strategy might you use?

19. At an applied linguistics conference, the program includes titles with words such as *prototype, conceptual metaphor, scripts and schemas, cognates, loan translation, core semantics,* and a host of other terms that sound vaguely familiar. What is all this jargon?

20. One of your students tells you that even though he is not trying to be funny, his friends often *jiggle* when he speaks, telling him that he is very *humus.* He asks you if there are any exercises he might do to help him overcome his problem. What would you suggest?

21. The faculty members of your intensive language program are having a disagreement about whether you should use simplified or standard versions of classical literary works as reading texts. Those favoring simplified versions say that students cannot understand the standard versions. Those favoring standard versions say that the literary flavor of the texts is much better and that the difficulty of the books will help the students learn more words. What suggestions might you make to help resolve the conflict?

We can't promise that after working through this text you will react wisely to such situations, but we hope to introduce you to a wide variety of analytic methods that will give you the foundations to respond appropriately in these and similar contexts. You will notice that no objective asks you to trace the historical development of lexical and semantic analysis. And no objective asks you to give a history of techniques by which methodologists have enhanced learning of vocabulary. This means that you may complete this book without a real appreciation of the history of linguistics and language teaching methodology related to the lexicon. History is important and we believe that such objectives should be an integral part of any introductory course in general linguistics or methods of language teaching. Although we have treated such information in an implicit way throughout the book, we leave an explicit, detailed history to others.

As you look through the objectives and the table of contents, you may realize that your own goals and objectives differ from ours. As you draw up your goals, list them for class or study group discussion. Consider, too, how meeting your objectives might be useful when the knowledge obtained is applied to language learning, to materials development, language testing, or areas of second language evaluation and research.

Part I   Semantics

1 Semantic features and semantic feature analysis

One way of telling someone what a word means is to point to the item and say, "That's a shirt." However, we might also say, "Well, it covers the upper part of the body, it has sleeves, it usually buttons down the front," and so forth. This is a feature (or componential) method of definition rather than a pointing (or deictic) definition. The features or components help us to index the meanings of words, separate the various meanings of individual words, and help us to analyze relationships between similar words. Componential analysis originated with the work of Trubetzkoy and the Prague School of Linguistics, but it is perhaps better known now as semantic feature analysis.

Features

Semantic feature analysis is based on the similarities among sets of words. For example, look at the following list: Lady Macbeth, Ophelia, King Lear, Hamlet, Charlie Chaplin. Notice that all but one name are characters in a Shakespeare play. So we might say that Charlie Chaplin does not fit because his name does not share the [+Shakespearean character] feature. On another list we might find these names: Mae West, Stan Laurel, W. C. Fields, Shirley Temple, Charlie Chaplin. All of these people were movie stars, but, again, Chaplin would be separated from the group by a feature [+mime] because traditionally his were nonspeaking roles. Or, alternatively, Chaplin could be kept on the list and Shirley Temple eliminated on the basis of ⟨+child⟩.

A set of words such as *idea, newspaper, chair*, and *book*, present three ⟨+concrete⟩ nouns. We can actually point to a newspaper, a chair, or a book and say, "That's a newspaper," or "That's a chair," or "That's a book." We cannot point to an object and say, "That's an idea." *Idea* is an abstract noun, so it does not fit with those that are ⟨+concrete⟩. You may have noticed that some of the names on the first two lists are feminine and some masculine. In semantic feature analysis this is noted as ⟨+/−male⟩. This semantic feature has consequences for grammar. Nouns with this feature can be referred to by the pronouns *she* or *he*.

In another set of nouns – cheese, catsup, lettuce, carrot – the critical semantic feature is ⟨+count⟩. We can count carrots, but we usually employ other units for mass nouns: pieces of cheese, bottles of catsup, heads of lettuce, as opposed to three carrots. Count nouns take a plural *-s*. The feature ⟨+count⟩ is important in grammar because it determines the type of verb agreement required (e.g., "carrots *are* nutritious" vs. "lettuce *is* nutritious").

Features are thus helpful in two ways. General perceptual features help us distinguish among related sets of terms (as in the Charlie Chaplin examples). Other features are more grammatically based (e.g., abstract vs. concrete, mass vs. count). The problem for the linguist is to find a descriptive system that uses both types of features in a principled way.

The semantic feature analysis devised by Katz and Fodor (1963) illustrates an early attempt to do just that (see Figure 1.1). Their analysis describes the assignment of meaning to words in an additive fashion. To illustrate their system, they chose a polysemous word, *bachelor*, and diagrammed the features needed to account for its several different meanings. (Since all ⟨+human⟩ nouns must be animate, it is not really necessary to specify the ⟨+animate⟩ feature in the diagram. To do so would be redundant, and in linguistics redundant descriptions are not favored.) Notice that all but one meaning has the ⟨+male⟩ feature. In all probability, the academic meaning of *bachelor* also originally shared that feature.

Some of the features in the *bachelor* example (e.g., animate, human, male) are important in the analysis of meanings for large numbers of words. They are especially important because they have consequences in grammar. Only animate nouns can carry out actions such as sleeping and eating. Human nouns can carry out actions such as reading and talking. And male and female nouns are referred to by the pronouns *he* and *she*. The features that have consequences in grammar are called semantic *markers*. For linguists, in particular American linguists working within the generative school, these became the central features of interest. In this system, every word in the lexicon would include all the semantic markers that need to be considered in order to produce grammatical sentences.

Other features distinguish meanings for only a very limited number of words. That is, [+furry] is unlikely to distinguish meanings for a large number of words, nor does it have grammatical importance. In semantic feature analysis, these features are called *distinguishers*. We have used ⟨ ⟩ for semantic markers, those with grammar consequences, and [ ] for those that are distinguishers. Distinguishers are of much less interest to linguists. To semanticists and to language teachers, however, both types of features are important in analyzing the meanings of single words.

In a linguistic description that uses semantic feature analysis, then, a word like *sheep* would include semantic marker information such as word class ⟨+Noun⟩ and the features ⟨+animate⟩, ⟨−human⟩, and ⟨+count⟩. Thus, it could be placed in the noun slot (as a subject, an object,

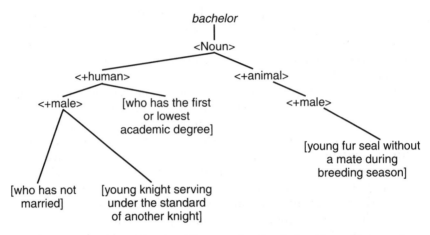

Figure 1.1 Semantic feature diagram for *bachelor* (from Katz and Fodor, 1963, p. 186; used with permission)

or in a prepositional phrase) of a sentence. Because it is animate, it could be placed as a subject before verbs such as *sleep* and *eat*. Because it is not human, it could not be placed as a subject before verbs such as *read* and *talk*. We know that we can count sheep, therefore, the entry would mark the noun as ⟨+count⟩ so that subject-verb agreement applies (e.g., "that sheep *is* white"; "these sheep *are* white"). However, we know that the plural for *sheep* is not *sheeps,* so we would need a special type of rule feature to tell us that this particular noun has a "zero" plural.

Information important to language learners and to semanticists would also include a set of distinguishers for each entry. For example, we would want to add a feature [+wooly] for *sheep*. We might assume, since the entry already says that *sheep* is animate and not human, that we would not need to enter a feature for [+four-legged]. Still, birds are animate and not human and have two legs, so in order to separate these, we need to add this [+/–four-legged] feature. Or perhaps we can use the [+/–wooly] feature or a [+/–feathers] feature to distinguish them.

Asked to define *sheep,* we are likely to say it is an animal with a wooly coat. The fact that we supply features when defining a word shows that features have some validity. Another piece of evidence used to validate the feature approach comes from slip-of-the-tongue studies. When we are tired, we may produce slips of the tongue where we utter a word other than the word we intend. The word we produce often shares many features with the intended word. Fromkin (1973) gives examples where speakers substitute one body part for another – "my *knee* hurts" where *ankle* was meant, and "on my *wrist*" when *finger* was meant. The intended word and the substitution share the features of [+body part].

There is also evidence of the importance of features in the acquisition of words. When we point to a book and say, "That's a book," we mean that the book is one of a class of items that we arbitrarily call *book*. This is a basic notion infants must master. Itard (1962) described his attempts to teach Victor, a "wild child" found at age 11 or 12 in the forests of Aveyron, France, such lexical items as book, key, pen, knife by associating word cards with the objects in this way. Victor became adept at "reading" the words on the cards and pointing out the corresponding objects. Itard was at first pleased with Victor's success. But when the door was locked to the room where the test items were kept, Victor failed. Given a card with the word *book* on it, he ignored the books in the room and tried to get into the locked room. "Thus every book which was not the one he had in his room was not a book to Victor" (p. 75). This was a teacher-induced error which fortunately could be corrected. Once Victor realized that a word like *book* referred to a class of items – books in general – he was faced with determining just how far the term could be generalized. For example, are large books, books placed in a case, or books with soft covers still *books*? Like child first language learners, Victor began to overextend the meanings of words according to the features of shape and use. He called pages, handfuls of paper, notebooks, newspapers, and pamphlets *books*. All straight, long objects made of wood became *sticks*. *Knife* became the term for anything that cuts.

Young children go through similar phases. Prior to two years of age, children may believe that words name particular objects (that *ball* refers only to the particular ball that they see roll under the bed) rather than to a class of objects. There is also a brief period, usually between 1½ and 2½ years, when children use a word appropriately for an object and then use the same word for other objects sharing some of its features. For example, in the famous study of his bilingual child Hildegard, Leopold (1939) notes her initial use of *wau-wau* for dog. Then she used the [+furry] feature of texture to allow *wau-wau* for furry slippers and a picture of a man wearing a fur coat. Lewis's (1951) child said *kotibaiz* for the bars of her cot and then used it for a large toy abacus, the toast rack (with parallel bars), and a picture of a building with columns. E. Clark (1973), in her analysis of such overextensions, shows they are primarily related to perceptual qualities of shape, size, movement, sound, taste, and texture.

Thus, there is considerable developmental evidence that learners do attend to semantic features in analyzing the meanings of words and assigning words to referents. Unfortunately, formal semantic feature analysis has not captured this as adequately as we might like. Most semantic feature analysis has been limited to markers that have grammar consequences and, as in arguments that support the validity of features, semantic markers do not appear as frequently as distinguisher features in research on slips of the tongue or developmental studies.

Practice 1.1

1. In each of the following sets of words, one word does not belong. Identify the feature(s) which unite the group and allow you to discard the "out" member. Which are semantic markers and which are distinguishers?

   cat, fur coat, bear, table
   clock, bathtub, gas meter, bathroom scale
   doctor, mayor, president, governor
   sing, accuse, blame, criticize
   happiness, talent, table, understanding
   corporation, thought, university, congress

2. Kelly, a 2-year-old, (data source: L. Hunt) used the word *bi* for the following objects: bean, bee, piece of gravel, cigarette butt, any insect, marble. What does *bi* mean?
3. Martin, a 3-year-old English speaker (Nemoianu, 1980, p. 489), gave the following definitions while playing with Sean, a German-dominant playmate. In each, determine which features Martin believes are important in the definition.

   Example A
   Sean: Who's Batman?
   Martin: He's the guy which has the thing on his back that flies. He's a, he's a, he's a man which has something on his back to fly up in the sky with.

   Example B
   Sean: What's a dis?
   Martin: It's an Exxon truck. It carries gas. It's an Exxon truck and they carry gas. I like Chevron better.

4. Here are some of E. Clark's (1973) examples of infants extending the meanings of words along features. (Clark drew these examples from the data in several classic diary studies in which a linguist-parent analyzed the language development of a child over an extended time period.)

   mooii (= moon) → cakes → round marks on windows → postmarks
   buti (= ball) → toy → radish → rounded stones
   bebe (= self in mirror) → photo of self → all photos → all pictures → all books with pictures → all books
   fafer (= train sound) → steaming coffee pot → anything that hissed or made a noise

> *bebe* (= baby) → other babies → all small statues → figures in small pictures and prints
>
> *fly* (= fly) → specks of dirt → dust → all small insects → his own toes → crumbs of bread → a small toad

In each example, identify and give a name to the feature used in the extension. Notice that two children gave extensions for *bebe*. Does your distinguishing feature differ for these two examples? If you can observe infants at a nursery, note examples of their extensions. Do they fit into Clark's perceptual categories?

Features in synonyms and antonyms

Synonyms are words that share meanings. Dictionaries traditionally provide a list of words that are more or less synonymous for each entry. A thesaurus, too, presents synonyms but it also gives words whose meanings are opposites (antonyms).

We assume that synonyms refer to the same entity. If all features are the same, the words should be interchangeable. However, native speakers will consistently select among them in similar ways. For example, we might assign the same features to *cease* and *stop* and yet realize that *cease* is most often selected in legal discourse. A mother is unlikely to say, "Cease that!" to a misbehaving child. Such words may be synonyms, but they survive in the language because there are differences in the ways and situations in which they are used.

Of course, synonyms do not usually share all of their features. We often use synonyms to make our lexical choices more precise. The expressions *or rather, technically,* and *more exactly* mark this use of a synonym for added precision. We may also use expressions to show that we cannot produce the precise term we wish to use: "in a manner of speaking," "sort of," "kind of." It is clear, though, that few (if indeed any) synonyms are synonymous in every respect. Some forms are better than others for a particular use in particular circumstances. And, so, they have slightly different features.

Although dictionaries list synonyms as words with similar meanings, the fact that X is a synonym for Y does not mean that Y is necessarily a synonym for X. For example, the *Dictionary of American Synonyms* lists *murder* as a synonym of *kill* but does not list *kill* as a synonym for *murder*. *Powerful* is listed as a synonym for *strong* but not vice versa. The *Dictionary of English Synonyms* lists *old, elderly,* and *senile* as its first three synonyms for *aged*. *Old* has *aged* and *senile* as its sixth and seventh choices; *ancient* is the first choice. The entry for *ancient* lists *old* as the first choice but does not mention *senile*. There is no entry for *senile* in this dictionary. *Elderly* is also not listed, although the synonyms for *elder* are *senior*, *older*, and *father*. Would this mean that it is only aged mothers who are termed senile?

One of the most important ways that we make text hold together is with the use of synonyms or chains of related words. For example, in talking about a problem at school, we might use *school, university, college, campus,* or other words interchangeably as synonyms. We might also select words that are not synonyms but which still refer to the same object. We might choose words that are related in features like *candle, flame, flicker, light* in describing candlelight. They all relate to *light* and, although they are not strictly synonyms, they share features and are used as though they were.

Antonyms, words which mean the opposite, present interesting problems for anyone seriously interested in semantic feature analysis. We can usually identify the feature on which the two words contrast. For example, *hot* and *cold* refer to the poles of a temperature dimension; one is positive and the other negative. *Long* and *short* refer to poles of a length dimension. *North* and *south* refer to direction in relation to a magnetic point, one pointing toward that point and the other pointing away from it. Thus, their meanings differ in terms of having or lacking qualities for a (distinguisher) semantic feature.

Many apparent opposites, however, are really extreme points on graduated scales. This is especially true of adjectives. *Hot* and *cold* may seem like opposites, but temperature is scaled, and we make our judgments as to what constitutes *hot, warm, cool,* and *cold* along that scale. The dimension is not just bisected into a plus and a minus value. In the same way, pairs like *big–small, many–few, tall–short, happy–unhappy,* and *long–short* are the opposite ends of scales. When we ask, "How long is your jacket?" "How unhappy is he?" "How tall is she?" "How many are there?" or "How small is it?" it is clear that there is no absolute point even at the poles. The terms are subjective and imprecise; they do not refer to an absolute place on the dimension. There is no obvious way semantic feature analysis can separate all these scalar points into plus or minus categories. (One could, of course, just change the dichotomies to scales.)

In language acquisition, researchers have found that semantic feature analysis is particularly helpful in understanding the acquisition of synonyms and antonyms. The research shows that one member of a pair of antonyms is more basic and easier to learn. The easier term in the pair is said to be *unmarked* and the more difficult *marked.* Positive (unmarked) terms are generally easier to learn than (marked) negatives. So *happy* is usually acquired before *unhappy; high* is usually acquired before *low.* To ask "How short is he?" assumes that the person is, indeed, short, whereas "How tall is he?" makes no assumption of whether the person is tall or short. *Tall,* the unmarked term, is easier and should be acquired first. If we ask "How unhappy is he?" we assume the person is unhappy, whereas "How happy is he?" makes no assumption. *Happy* is the more basic, unmarked form. This can be handled in a semantic feature approach by making the unmarked member of the pair the name of the feature so that the marked member would be minus for that feature.

Practice 1.2

1. Bolinger (1975, p. 195) gives examples of synonyms that cannot be separated using semantic markers. To *take back* and to *return* seem to be synonyms, but a feature of "belongingness" distinguishes the two. For example, what difference do you see between saying, "We took Tom back to the zoo," and "We returned Tom to the zoo"? A feature of "goal" seems to separate the verbs *go* and *head for.* What difference do you see between "I went home" and "I headed for home"? (Since so many such features seem to be necessary to separate the meanings of synonyms, Bolinger questions whether the entire lexicon can be accounted for using only a few hundred rather than thousands of features.)

2. Check a dictionary of synonyms for any two nouns, two adverbs, two adjectives, and two verbs. Select one of the synonyms for each entry and check its synonyms. Are they reciprocal with the original entry?

3. If you have access to a computer and a corpus of data, check the frequency of the following pairs of synonyms.

trip–journey	tell–relate	plan–scheme
hide–conceal	nearly–almost	fast–rapid
say–explain	book–volume	something–entity
attempt–try	end–conclude	location–place
munch–chew	go on–continue	talk–converse

   In your data, which item for each pair is more frequent? If you have an oral language data base, check the frequencies there as well to see whether they are the same for oral and written text.

4. Dittmar (1984) notes that a Spanish worker who spoke a pidgin form of German used the following forms: *nicht gut* (instead of *schlecht*), *nicht krank* (instead of *gesund*), *nicht lang* (for *kurz*), *nicht teuer* (for *billig*). Why should opposites via negation be easier to learn than antonyms? If the learner did not study German at school, would he actu-

ally have heard the forms he produced? How would you explain his use of these forms?

5. Here is an antonym list written by a third-grade Spanish-English bilingual child.

All the opeceves I now.
    up–down, in–out, boy–girl, small–larj, open–close, walk–fly,
    sit–stend, queen–king, rite–left, mom–dad, Mrs.–Mr., stop–go,
    sky–flore, happy–sad, man–woman, black–white, animal–
    person

(Data source: B. Hawkins & V. Wenzell)

Do you consider all these "opeceves" antonyms? List your own antonyms for each pair. Are they the same? If not, why not?

6. Chaudron (1982) discusses the types of synonyms and antonyms teachers and students use in classrooms. Here are a few examples:

Example A
T: What's his main point. . . . What's the main statement?

Example B
T: What does surrender mean?
S: Give up.
T: You give up. You stop fighting.

Example C
T: By temperance he probably means not drinking.

Example D
T: Kojak. . . . he's bald. OK? No hair.

Chaudron notes that in some cases the synonyms and antonyms were not clear. In some cases, teachers did not select common and familiar terms. Implicit correspondences are not as clear as those where teachers explicitly mark the terms as synonyms or opposites. Tape record your class (whether you are a teacher or a student) and transcribe the synonyms and antonyms. What makes the elaborations clear or confusing for students?

7. It has often been claimed that it is easier to learn antonyms than synonyms. Why should this be the case? What evidence from your teaching or language learning support this claim? Do you think synonyms change in difficulty depending on how proficient one is in the language? How might you research this question in your own classroom setting?

Features in definitions

When one of your students asks you for a definition of a word, you are likely to respond with whatever synonyms you can think of and a list of features that they share. Features are very helpful in giving meanings to words, but are some better than others? We know that some features are obligatory. For example, a tree must have a trunk and roots, but branches and leaves may be optional at different periods in a tree's life. In reality, though, people are more likely to define trees in terms of their branches and leaves than they are in terms of trunk or roots. The best definitions seem to be those which match what is most salient in perceptual terms.

One way researchers evaluate verbal skills of young children is by examining their ability to supply definitions for words or to give definitions as part of classification tasks. In classification tasks, children are given a series of picture cards and asked to sort them into piles and then explain why cards in each pile go together. Bruner (1966) found that the youngest children sorted picture cards by visual features (color, size, shape). This is not surprising, given E. Clark's (1973) work that shows children begin classification by using perceptual categories. Somewhat older children sorted cards according to visual features ("these all have holes in them") and by use ("you get dressed with"). By 8 years of age, children identified the common feature of their grouped cards ("all are tools," "you can eat them").

In tests where learners do not just name items but also give definitions, there is a good deal of controversy about rating responses. Cazden asks a very pertinent question: "Why are some definitions better than others?" (1972, p. 73). Why, she asks, is it "better" if the child defines wagon as a vehicle, rather than saying that you can ride in it? Yet in the literature on child language and in bilingual research, one way of judging a child's verbal abilities is to rate his or her responses in this way. The lowest rating is given to function definitions and the highest to a synonym, a word which captures shared features. Perhaps this is because first language learners seem to proceed through the developmental stages described by Bruner and others. If older children use fewer functional features in definitions, then these responses should be rated lower than definitions which use other types of features. Yet in some very complex fields, such as physics, function definitions are considered best. And in poetry, functional definitions abound as in this opening to a verse of Gaspar de Alba's poem "Beggar on the Cordoba Bridge":

> Domingo means scrubbing
> our knees for church.

(1987, p. 7)

Or Frost's poem "The Death of the Hired Man":

> Home is the place where, when you have
> to go there
> They have to take you in.

(1969, p. 165)

Practice 1.3

1. Replicate Bruner's card-sorting task with your students. Do they all sort cards in the same way, or are there differences according to first language background? What comments or definitions do they offer in explaining why each pile forms a group?
2. After reading Cazden's remarks (1972, p. 73) on definitions, decide how you would scale children's definitions and those of your students. Then score the card-sorting comments and definitions in Practice 1.3.1 according to your scale. Would you obtain different results if you followed a methodology that gives a very low rating to function definitions?
3. Snow et al. (1991) used the Wechsler Intelligence Scale for Children – Revised vocabulary subtest as one measure of verbal abilities of children in grades 2, 4, and 6. Because the vocabulary test is the one test that did correlate with home and school variables, it is important that the test be valid and reliable. Look at the test and critique the items and scoring methods.

Semantic features and grammar

So far we have talked about semantic features that may guide us in differentiating the match between words and meanings. We would need a very large number of features to do this work, however. Linguists believe that a much smaller number of features would be needed in writing grammar descriptions Many nouns, for example, have special requirements regarding subject-verb agreement and this requirement would be listed as a feature of the noun. It is unlikely that [+furry] would determine anything about subject-verb agreement or pluralization in a language, but ⟨+/−count⟩ might. It's unlikely that [+wings] would have grammatical consequences, but ⟨+/−human⟩ might very well determine which nouns can be subjects of particular verbs.

Semantic markers that have grammatical consequences are of special importance for linguistic descriptions. Not all of these features are universal. Most languages have arbitrary classification schemes. That is, they classify objects in some way and then use grammar markers to reveal the classification. Although the classification may seem arbitrary, generally speaking, languages have a series of binary oppositions, such as singular vs. plural or masculine vs. feminine, and then various agreement rules that relate to the oppositions. Some of the most typical noun oppositions are the following:

singular vs. plural
count vs. mass
human vs. nonhuman
animate vs. inanimate
male vs. female
vertical vs. horizontal
rigid vs. flexible
liquid vs. solid

In some languages, of course, these are not simple dichotomies, but rather three-way contrasts. For example, you might find:

singular–dual–plural
male–female–neuter
liquid–viscous–solid

Distinctions such as ⟨+/−human⟩, ⟨+/−count⟩, ⟨+/−animate⟩, ⟨+/−concrete⟩ have important consequences for English, and in many European languages as well. However, this does not mean that all languages will necessarily attend grammatically to the same features.

Gender is an important feature in many languages. If our first language does not use this distinction, it can pose a serious problem in second language learning. In a diary study, Kenyeres and Kenyeres (1938) described the reaction to noun gender of Eva, a Hungarian 7-year-old learning French. Hungarian does not mark nouns for gender. In January, Eva enumerated new words: "*La* chaise, *la* table" and then corrected herself to "*le* table," because the table was the papa while the chair was the little girl. Then she continued, "*la* fleur, *le* jardin – no, *la* jardin," because it was the mother of flowers. Later that month, she decided all things good and beautiful must be feminine, but soon found that this did not work. She was indignant to find that *oiseau* had only one gender and that one did not consider the mother of the birds and the babies as different. Yet she also wanted more system. If one would say "*un* oiseau," then all birds should be marked with *un*. Learning noun gender continued to be difficult for Eva. Given that adjectives agree with nouns in gender and number, you can predict the consequences of this problem.

Even in cases where languages do make the same typical oppositions, we cannot say learning will be trouble free. Many languages, for example, distinguish count vs. mass as a noun feature, and yet the things which seem to be mass or countable differ across languages. In English, the word *money* can't be counted. That is, we cannot say "one money," whereas in American Sign Language *money* is countable. ASL students of English may put money into the count category, writing questions such as "How *many* does it cost?" Other ESL students frequently speak of *luggages* or *homeworks*. ESL teachers themselves sometimes become confused when they have to remember differences across dialects; for example, that *math* is a mass form in American English but *maths* is countable in British English. So there are differences in what is and is not countable even across dialects of the same language.

Although such distinctions can be problematic for language learners, the system can be described by linguists. Semantic feature analysis has been a useful way of linking these descriptions to the identification of features that would be needed for a theory relating semantics to grammar.

Practice 1.4

1. Navajo has 11 noun subclasses which require different kinds of agreement rules. Devise a +/− feature title for each of the following groups on the basis of whatever semantic similarities you see within them.

   rock   book   bottle   hat   coin
   pencil   pole   cigarette   rod
   snarled hair   tangled string   loose hay
     wispy clouds   fog
   mud   tar   mortar   beat-up felt hat
   sheet of paper   animal hide   blanket
   burden   load   body of water   storm clouds
   rope   string   hair   any unknown object

2. Dyirbal noun classes were the inspiration for the title of Lakoff's (1987) book *Women, Fire, and Dangerous Things*. Read the section of the book (pp. 92–104) that deals with Dixon's (1968, 1982) descriptions of these noun classes. What semantic basis is reflected in Dyirbal noun classes and why does Lakoff find this so interesting?

3. The ⟨+/−count⟩ feature for nouns which can or cannot be counted has important consequences in terms of articles or other determiners. Mark with an asterisk (*) the unacceptable combinations in the following lists.

enough syrup	many syrup
some kerosene	a few sugar
fewer jewels	less sugar
enough letter	much letter
some dime	a few letters
fewer concerts	less letters
too much sugar	too much bean
two chairs	a few letter
fewer luggages	less luggages
one foliage	one leaf
two furniture	fewer letters
fewer jewelry	less syrup

Which quantifiers can be used with ⟨+count⟩ nouns, and which go with mass ⟨–count⟩ nouns? The distinction between mass and count nouns is usually presented early in English language teaching textbooks. If you teach advanced learners, check your materials to see what kind of follow-up is done with this distinction.

4. Japanese has something similar to our quantifiers. Identify what unifies the following nouns that can be quantified by *hon:*

   hon with long thin objects, rope, hair, dead snakes, dried fish, baseball hits, shots in basketball, serves in volleyball

   If you cannot find a Japanese speaker to check your answer, read the section in Lakoff (1987, pp. 104–109) that talks about Downing's (1984) analysis of *hon.* If this is not possible, try this alternative activity: List the kinds of quantifiers used in English (e.g., *heads of, pieces of*) and illustrate the noun categories with which they can be used.

5. Most languages have singular and plural forms. Still, what needs to be pluralized will not always correspond across languages. For example, *vacation* can be singular or plural in English but always has the plural form *vacances* in French. Many languages have a distinction between count and mass nouns. Again, what is countable is not always the same across languages. For example, *information* is a mass noun in English. To count *information* we would use "*X* pieces of information." If you are a speaker of another language, translate these terms and see whether they correspond. Or, if you teach international students, note which students say "I went for *vacations*" or "I need some *informations.*" Ask them for the corresponding terms in their first languages.

Evaluation of semantic feature analysis

As you may have realized already, the dividing line between semantic features that have grammatical consequences and those that do not is often unclear. This is one of the basic criticisms of semantic feature analysis. For example, features such as [+small] or [+dear] are needed to account for the diminutive /i/ applied to many nouns (e.g., *kitty, horsie, mommy*), but these are not included in the list of marker features with grammatical consequences. If we use only features that apply to many items (such as ⟨+animate⟩) and do not use distinguishers, our linguistic description will not tell us that *sheep* can be combined with verbs such as *baa* or *bleat*, while *horse* cannot. It will not tell us that *bird* can combine with *fly* but *snail* cannot. Further, we will not even be able to disambiguate words like *bachelor* in sentences without the use of distinguishers. Both types of features must be used or some more sophisticated cross-reference rules must be given if we want our linguistic descriptions to yield sensible interpretations of sentences.

A second problem pointed out by Bolinger (1965) is that of redundancy. We know that there are many markers that have consequences in grammar. The question is whether all of these need to be shown for every entry. For example, a feature such as ⟨+solid⟩ is needed so that we do not create sentences such as "she walked right through the bachelor." A feature ⟨+pliable⟩ is needed to prevent "he broke the bachelor in two." And a feature ⟨+organic⟩ is needed to disallow "she welded the bachelor." These markers are part of being or not being human and of being an animal. Should every dictionary entry include these along with ⟨+human⟩ and ⟨+animal⟩? If we put them in, the analysis method suffers from redundancy. If we do not, nothing (except the oft-cited "world knowledge") prevents construction of anomalous sentences. The analysis does not tell us precisely how this problem would be solved.

A third problem has to do with the naming of features. Bolinger argues that we should make a serious effort to find terms that are abstract enough to cover all the possible correspondences under it. The distinguisher [+/−old] is not a good term for a feature if we consider all the different objects that might have that particular feature. Bolinger suggests the use of an early–late feature because it can be used with any item that adjusts to a temporal scale:

	Early state	*Late state*
living being	young	old
humanity	primitive	advanced
perishable product	fresh	stale
other product	new	old
lunar phase	waxing	waning

	Early state	*Late state*
tide	flood	ebb
fruit	green	ripe
growing things	immature	mature

(Source: Bolinger, 1965, p. 4.

A fourth obvious problem for semantic feature analysis is that the features are presented as dichotomies when, in fact, we know that something may be somewhere in-between. In the early–late dichotomy, there has to be room in the middle. We know *teenager* is ⟨+human⟩. We also know that it has the feature of youth. But, while it is more young than old, it is not exactly young. If we assign it [+early], then what separates it from *child* and *infant*? We know that *nasty, mean, small-minded,* and *petty* are all [+pejorative] words. To separate the terms, we can't just label them all as [+pejorative]; we need to use a scale. Many features are scales, not dichotomies.

A fifth difficulty has to do with the use of markers when we interpret words metaphorically. Bolinger diagrams the meanings of the word *soup* as given in the Merriam-Webster dictionary. They include the meaning of an edible liquid food, but *soup* is also used to talk about thick clouds in "flying through the soup," where diffuse clouds are made to appear dense. When the [+dense] quality of soup is taken over to change diffuse clouds to something dense, the marker is being used metaphorically. We have said that markers are supposed to be features of a word. They either are or are not characteristics of the word. The analysis says nothing about using them across a range of words for metaphorical purposes. That puts the analysis "in the soup."

Modern linguistics has set these and other issues aside in the hope that they can be addressed at some later time after much more work has been done on the syntax (sentence grammar) of languages. At this point, the features that allow grammatically correct (if semantically strange) sentences are used. Those who study semantics must decide whether or not their major task ought to be that of determining how semantic features relate to grammar description.

Semantic feature displays, such as that given in Figure 1 for *bachelor,* have also been criticized. In tree displays, the feature listed at the top of the hierarchy will be the most general and most important feature, and each split after that will also be hierarchical in nature. There is often no clear rationale for arrangements that are used, however – the hierarchy is not always clear. And there is less evidence that humans actually categorize polysemes in this way. In the case of *bachelor,* if you were given a set of pictures of seals, knights, college graduates, and swinging bachelors and asked to divide them into two piles, it is likely that the first cut would be in terms of ⟨+/–human⟩. If asked then to divide the people pictures into two groups, and if the pictures included women in college caps and gowns, it's probable that ⟨+/−male⟩ would be the next category. If there were no women in the pictures, this wouldn't happen, and the pictures of knights would probably be the next to be excluded. In other words, the hierarchy seems logical but it is difficult to find direct evidence that people actually break down terms into these components or that they would arrange them in the same hierarchy if they did.

Practice 1.5

1. List as many words as you can that end with *y* (as in *kitty*). What feature(s) do they seem to share as a consequence of the *y*? What label would you give to the feature(s)?
2. How might you use Bolinger's early–late feature to teach words that contrast on this dimension?
3. Although it is not difficult to make assertions about the underlying features of words, what evidence is there that learners pay attention to such things? Do we actually add up the features in order to arrive at a meaning? Does anyone consciously say, "Okay, this is +noun, +animate, +human, +male, +unmarried, so it must be *bachelor*"? Whorf (1936) informs us that Hopi has one noun that covers everything that flies except birds. So a flying insect, an airplane, and even its pilot might be called *masa'ytaka*. Surely this seems no stranger to a Hopi than our use of *bachelor* to mean an unmarried man, an unmated male seal, a holder of the B.A. degree, or a knight in training! When we think of a bachelor friend, do we superimpose the seal or whatever else on our image of that person? Does the Hopi speaker consider flying insects and airline pilots as similar in some way? Do developmental evidence and slip-of-the-tongue evidence outweigh such questions, or could the use of semantic features be nothing more than an analytic device?

In this chapter we have introduced the notion of semantic features and discussed some of the strengths and weaknesses involved in semantic feature analysis. Linguists working within other theoretical frameworks have tried to incorporate feature information (both distinguishers and markers) in their descriptions in more comprehensive ways. We will discuss these alternative approaches in subsequent chapters. First, however, we will look at semantic field analysis, a methodology which shares many aspects with the semantic feature approach.

Research and application

1. Gillis (1987) traces the necessary move in child language from identification of individual objects by name to the comparison and the search for other exemplars. Language learning would be an impossible task if every object had its own name; the child must realize that deictic definitions (pointing: "it's a shirt") do not name individual items but rather refer to a class of like objects. Consider how Gillis's work might apply to children in a bilingual situation.

2. Wierzbicka (1991) demonstrates that English nouns are not simply singular or plural. She considers some nouns as dual, meaning that they form a semantic class of objects which have two identical parts, joined together and performing the same function. This dual noun class takes the quantifier "a pair of." The semantic class includes *scissors, tongs, tweezers, forceps,* and clothing (*slacks, undies, pajamas*). Prepare a research plan to investigate each of the groups she discusses using data from another language. You might consider using nonsense word items for bipartite objects to see whether children consistently use an *-s* form for one of each of the objects.

3. McCawley (1975) lists a number of examples where very similar nouns differ as to whether they are countable (or show *individuation*). For example, *noodles* can be counted in English but *spaghetti* cannot (though it can be in Italian). Other examples include *garlic* vs. *onions; rice* vs. *beans; fruit* vs. *vegetables; cold, headache* vs. *flu, diarrhea, tuberculosis.* McCawley claims that mass nouns are neutral as to individuation, whereas count nouns specify individuation. In the dictionary, *noodle* is defined as a thin strip of food paste, while *pasta* is defined as dough or paste made of flour and water. So dictionaries also recognize individuation. Check each of the terms (*garlic* vs. *onions,* and so forth) in another language to discover whether they are classified as mass or count in a way that corresponds or contrasts with English.

4. Miller and Charles (1991) investigated the type of contextual information that determines whether or not two words are semantically similar (i.e., synonyms). First, pairs of words (e.g., *car–automobile, coast–shore, noon–string*) were presented to native speakers, who judged the similarity of each pair of terms on a five-point scale. Second, they were asked whether each member of the pair could be used in the same context. To test this, Miller and Charles collected sentences that included the first word of the

pair and then collected sentences that included the second word of the pair. Then they deleted the pair of words and printed the resulting sentences on cards. The challenge for the participants was to sort the sentences according to which word fit. They found that pairs of words where either could be used in sentence contexts were also the pairs that were judged most similar. There were some items, however, judged as synonymous (e.g., *car–automobile*) that were not easily substituted for each other within certain sentence frames. If you teach a specific purpose English (ESP) class, select sets of words which have been presented as synonyms in course materials. Read Miller and Charles's study and design a study that would test the degree of semantic similarity of these terms. How would you apply the results to your teaching plans?

5. H. Buckingham, Jr. (1980) found that patients suffering from Wernicke's aphasia often substituted related words for the words they meant to utter. Look at the following examples and attempt a feature analysis of the substitutions (it will be difficult).

husband → *wife, south* → *north, hot* → *cold, nose* → *ear, hear* → *talk, hear* → *see, showed* → *saw, eat* → *drink, write* → *read, green* → *red, small* → *big, sister* → *brother, hotter* → *colder, summer* → *winter, Easter* → *Christmas, sons* → *daughters*. "I *sawed* (← *showed*) you the picture, didn't I?" "I wish that girl would come back and see how my *lights* (← *hearing aid*) are *reading* (← *working*)." "The girl that was *reading* (← *fixing*) it, I wonder if the thing is *reading* (← *working*)."

Such data are used to validate the psychological reality of semantic features. If this topic interests you, review Fromkin's slip-of-the-tongue examples (1971, 1973). Would error data from second or foreign language learners be useful as supporting evidence for this approach? Justify your answer.

2 Semantic field analysis

In the preceding chapter, we introduced the notion of semantic features. Initially, such features were used primarily to clarify polysemic meanings of words as in Katz and Fodor's (1963) famous example *bachelor*. The analysis, however, has been extended and challenged in descriptions of semantic fields.

Semantic fields

Semantic field analysis uses features to show the relationship of lexical items within a field or domain. For example, if we studied the word *iron*, we would also look at *toaster, vacuum cleaner*, and other items in the household tools domain. Or, we would study it along with *copper, zinc*, and other items in the metal domain. Because each field is examined separately, polysemy is not an issue (as it is in semantic feature analysis). *Bachelor* (as an unmarried man, a graduate with a B.A. degree, a person who serves a knight, or a sea animal) would be considered four different words and each defined within its own domain.

The classic example of semantic field analysis is that of kinship terms, an analysis which dates at least to the work of Kroeber (1909). He identified the following components in classifying kinship systems: generation, relative age within generations, consanguineal vs. affineal (sister vs. sister-in-law), lineal (father–child) vs. collateral (aunt–uncle), gender, kinsman and linking kinsman terms, and condition (alive–dead). This particular semantic field is especially important to field anthropologists in understanding and classifying family structures.

To illustrate the arguments about how semantic fields should be described, let us look first at a semantic feature description of the relationship among members of an immediate family. We know that some terms are ⟨+female⟩: *mother, sister, daughter*, and others are ⟨+male⟩: *father, brother, son*. So gender is an important feature. Some terms are related according to generation: *mother* and *daughter* illustrate an ascending or descending generation feature. Figure 2.1 is a semantic feature diagram illustrating the field (we have arbitrarily used ⟨ ⟩ brackets in the diagram). To follow the diagram, note that the items that are + for a feature branch to the left and those that are – for the feature branch to the right.

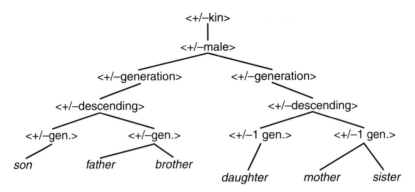

Figure 2.1 Tree diagram for family relations (adapted from Kroeber, 1909)

There are several problems with Figure 2.1. First, it is unclear how the hierarchy of features is determined. Is gender the highest, most important feature in determining the place of items within the field? Or is the arrangement more a matter of aesthetic arrangement for the diagram? If the meanings are additive, then we would start at the bottom of the tree and add each feature in turn to obtain the meaning of, say, *daughter*. A daughter is +1 generation, +descending, +generation, −male, kin member of the family. A *sister* is a nongeneration female kin member of the family. The sum of these features does not give a simultaneous interpretation that could be obtained by a more traditional list:

father	mother
brother	sister
son	daughter

Brown (1965) uses three components to analyze eight kinship terms and places them in a diagram (Figure 2.2).

Displaying family organization in charts and then identifying terms for relevant relationships has the potential for misinterpretation if we hope to compare kinship groups across languages. For example, we have no separate terms for male and female *cousin,* yet we certainly view the distinction as important. Many other languages have distinct terms for male and female cousins. In Arabic, according to Marzouk and El Hindawy, there is also a special kinship term for two brothers who marry two sisters: They are *'adaayil.* One brother is *'adiil* to the other. The sisters are *salaayif* and one is the *silfa* of the other. When brothers marry sisters in the United States, they frequently get married on the same day, and their pictures are in the local newspaper, but there is no special vocabulary to distinguish them. The lack of a term does not make their relationship any

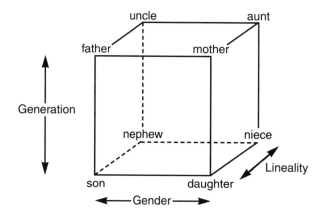

Figure 2.2   Box diagram of family relations (adapted from Brown, 1965, p. 307; used with permission)

less close than it might be in an Arabic-speaking society. The number of divisions, then, is determined by the languages being described.

Practice 2.1

1. There are numerous anecdotes of young children asking for clarification of kinship terms: "What's a girl nephew?" "Spot's puppies, are they my sisters?" One child identified a cousin as someone you play with and who lives far away. When his best friend moved away, he asked, "Joe's my cousin now, isn't he?" Piaget's (1928) "brother" experiment addresses the issue of how children work through kinship terms. At stage 1, the child believes that *brother* and *boy* are synonyms and that *sister* and *girl* are too. Stage 2 children exhibit awareness that *brother* as a kin term requires that there be a sibling (a brother cannot be an only child). At stage 3, children not only realize that *brother* is a male sibling, but that the relationship is reciprocal. If you work with young children, prepare a research design which would help you elaborate on these findings for other terms in the kinship field. If possible, include bilingual children in the project (or observe children who are native speakers of another language) so that you can see whether the stages are the same across different languages.

2. Ask young children of different ages for their definition of *family.* It is generally claimed that age and gender terms

are important in the child's categorization of kinship terms and that only later does the child turn to family functions such as eating together. What do their definitions show you about the way these children view family and kinship terms? You might want to carry out a cross-cultural or cross-linguistic study by adding other groups.

3. Second language learners may also search for kinship terms as in this example from Butterworth and Hatch (1978, p. 429). Ricardo is a teenaged Spanish speaker newly immersed in an American high school.

Example A
Ricardo: My uncle and esposa?
GB: and wife.
Ricardo: and wife and ninos?
GB: Oh, and children.
Ricardo: Yeh.

Example B
Ricardo: Brother of my, how do you say, my my uncle woman you know.
GB: Your uncle's wife.
Ricardo: Yah . . . woman is my uncle.
GB: Oh, your aunt. Aunt.
Ricardo: My aunt husband.

Look at your language textbooks. What kinship terms are taught? How many different terms are included, and how are these sequenced?

4. Prepare a self-instruction unit for yourself on these terms for the language you are learning. As you begin to use the terms, check to see whether they are actually used in the same way as they are in your first language. Are they used as terms of address or only to refer to members of the family when talking to people outside the family? Does it matter if the relation is on the mother's side or the father's side? Does age make a difference in the terms used, for example, for older and younger brother? Is the relation term used alone or with a first name or family name? Are the categories strict or flexible? For example, is "aunt" used to refer to all female friends of one's mother or only to the sisters of one's mother or father? Is "brother" used as a general term of address for all comparable age males of the group?

5. Select a workplace and list the work relation terms. How many levels are there in the job title hierarchy? On what other dimensions do the titles differ (male/female, young/old, experienced/novice, etc.)? When are job titles used as terms of address? Are they used more often in speaking of the person than as terms of address?

Semantic field displays

Placing forms in a chart or a box of plus and minus features gives the description a very static quality. It also creates the impression that the words themselves contain these features rather than the impression that we assign words these features in order to comprehend or produce the terms. Linguists using semantic feature analysis traditionally employ trees, changing the table into a diagram that illustrates hierarchy. Compare Table 2.1 and Figure 2.3 for the semantic field of table settings.

TABLE 2.1   FEATURES FOR TABLESETTINGS

	Silverware	Dishes	Glasses	Linens	Setting	Serving
Knife	+	−	−	−	+	−
Ladle	+	−	−	−	−	+
Plate	−	+	−	−	+	−
Platter	−	+	−	−	−	+
Wineglass	−	−	+	−	+	−
Wine carafe	−	−	+	−	−	+
Napkin	−	−	−	+	+	−
Tablecloth	−	−	−	+	−	+

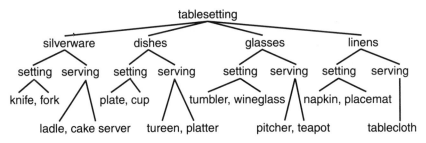

Figure 2.3   Tree diagram of table setting (adapted from Cruse, 1986, p. 147)

TABLE 2.2   TABLESETTING

Silver		Dishes		Glasses		Linens	
Set	*Serve*	*Set*	*Serve*	*Set*	*Serve*	*Set*	*Serve*
knife	ladle	cup	platter	glass	pitcher	napkin	tablecloth
spoon	cake server	plate	tureen	tumbler	teapot	placemat	
etc.	etc.	etc.	etc.	etc.	etc.	etc.	etc.

The tree diagram gives us a better picture of the relationship of the terms within the field. In truth, though, it is a taxonomic arrangement, rather than an additive one. You do not add +setting +silverware to arrive at the meaning of *fork*. Instead, the tree diagram is probably interpreted as shown in Table 2.2, where a spoon is a kind of silver setting in a table setting and a pitcher is a kind of glass serving item in a table setting. The meanings are not additive. Instead, the taxonomy provides the logical basis for inclusion or exclusion in each category.

An example from Tyler (1978) may make these differences in approaches to analysis clearer. According to Tyler, we do not decompose words in a field into semantic features. We learn that an oak is a kind of tree (probably because someone pointed out a tree and said, "That's an oak"). We do not think, "Let's see, an oak is a kind of tree because trees have trunks, and roots, and leaves, and are big, and an oak has a trunk and leaves and roots and is big, therefore an oak is a tree" (p. 194). All we need is to know that there are oak trees and have someone point one out to conclude that oaks are a kind of tree.

Another example of a semantic field is shown in Lehrer's (1969) comprehensive chart of the relevant features of culinary semantics (Table 2.3). A simplified version appears in James (1980, p. 93) with some of the semantic components for English and German. In the table, 0 means the feature does not apply distinctively one way or the other.

Although the semantic field is set up to look like a series of +/– semantic features, it is really a taxonomy, where the "kind of" relation is more fully specified. For example, frying is a kind of cooking that involves the use of fat in contact with a flame and it is not usually gentle.

The ultimate in taxonomy, however, occurs in classification in science, where it is important to give one, and only one, term to each distinct item and to place it in a hierarchical organization. Synonyms and homonyms are not acceptable in such systems. The systems people use do not follow those of science, so there is endless overlap and fuzziness in common terms for wildflowers, for birds, and for fish. The easiest way to drive a taxonomist crazy is to refer to all blue birds as bluebirds or all yellow flowers as daisies. Members of the Audubon Society who keep track of

TABLE 2.3   SIMPLIFIED CULINARY CHART

	C1 *with water*	C2 *with fat*	C3 *in oven*	C4 *contact with flame*	C5 *gentle*
Cook	0	0	0	0	0
Boil	+	−	−	+	−
Simmer	+	−	−	+	+
Fry	−	+	−	+	0
Roast	−	−	+	−	0
Toast	−	−	−	+	0
Bake	−	−	+	−	0
Kochen1	0	0	0	0	0
Kochen2	+	−	−	+	−
Kochen3	+	−	−	+	+
Braten	−	0	0	0	0
Rosten	−	−	−	+	0
Backen	0	0	+	−	0

Source: Adapted from Lehrer, 1969.

the types of different birds they have sighted go into shock each time a decision is made to change the names of birds. When two formerly different birds like Bullock's oriole and the Northern oriole are considered one bird (the Northern oriole), birdwatchers go through their record books and change the designations. And when one bird designation becomes two – the brown towhee split to become the California towhee and the Canyon towhee – birdwatchers are delighted because it means they can add to their life list total one more bird they've seen!

Practice 2.2

1. Table 2.4 shows some of the words for footwear. Mark each footwear word as +/− the set of features. What problems do you find if you interpret the table as an additive semantic feature analysis? As a taxonomy? Can you show hierarchy in either case? Can you show a basis for logical inclusion or exclusion in the overall structure of the field?
2. Do a short field analysis for various types of shirts: dress shirt, T-shirt, blouse, singlet, and so forth.
3. Cruse (1986, p. 85) illustrates the contrasts between English and French in expressions for the semantic field of perceptions: The visual experience line for English uses

TABLE 2.4   FOOTWEAR CHART

	Boots	Sneakers	Sandals	Booties	Slippers
Foot mostly covered					
Made of leather					
Made of rubber					
Waterproof					
For use indoors					
Raised heel platform					
For use in sports					
For infants only					
Covers foot and lower leg					

TABLE 2.5   PERCEPTUAL VERBS IN ENGLISH AND FRENCH

English			French		
see	look at	watch	regarder	regarder	regarder
hear	listen to		entendre	écouter	
smell	smell		sentir	goûter	
feel	feel		sentir	toucher	

look at for a static visual field and *watch* for a changing visual field (Table 2.5). What other English terms can you think of for this semantic field? What correspondences do you find for these terms? If you are teaching or learning another language, prepare a similar chart. Then note how these terms are presented and taught (if they are) in your course materials. Is this a semantic field?

4. Rhetoric manuals teach students to define by giving the term (e.g., "an oak"), then the class to which it belongs ("is a kind of tree"), and then its distinguishing features ("with. . . ." or "which has . . ."). Write a definition for each of the five footwear terms in Practice 2.2.1. Does the definition make use of the features listed in the chart or are other features more appropriate?

5. Consider how you might draw a semantic field analysis of plant terms. Where would *weeds* go? It's been said that weeds are just plants that we don't want but get anyway. In French and Spanish weeds are called *mauvaises herbes* and *malas hierbas* (bad grasses). German uses

Unkraut (nonplant, not noncabbage). Do all languages (at least those that you can investigate) separate plants according to whether or not they have the feature ⟨+wanted⟩?

Evaluation of semantic field analysis

Semantic field analysis uses features to identify the relationship of lexical items within a field, with the goal of discovering how terms within the field or domain differ from each other. In semantic feature analysis, by contrast, the primary goal is to find those features that are distinctive, that have consequences for the grammar of the language, and that help to clarify the various meanings of a single word.

Since semantic field analysis uses a feature approach in relating items within a semantic field, the analysis inherits the problems we have already discussed for semantic feature analysis. First, are the features always either present or absent (plus or minus)? The problem of features that are present only sometimes is even more complicated in semantic field analysis. In semantic feature analysis, which is tied to the discovery of distinctions that have grammatical consequences, the features can more easily be described as plus or minus (though there are still problem areas). In field analyses, the features are distinguishers since they seldom have grammatical consequences. Even so, the features used in defining semantic fields are not always true dichotomies. Table 2.6, for example, shows *buildings* as a semantic field; many of the categories are not plus-or-minus dichotomies. Depending on the school, it may or may not be a business. A mosque is a religious building, but it may or may not also be an education building. These can be left as neutral values, or some proportion might be assigned to plus and some to minus. Notice, too, that there is no feature in this chart that separates *high school* and *institute*. Another feature must be added as to level of instruction. No feature on this chart separates mosque and synagogue, so one more feature must be added. This highlights another difficulty with feature analysis: the number of features needed to remove ambiguity from building terminology would have to be very large indeed. (For some semantic fields, the number is only one less than the number of items being disambiguated.) If parsimony is a criteria for theory, then this type of analysis suffers. In application rather than theory, however, such a detailed analysis of differences might be useful.

We have considered ways in which meanings are indexed first as general semantic features (distinguishers), semantic markers that relate to grammar, and finally semantic fields. As we have seen, the analysis in each case is basically taxonomic. Yet there are two problems with taxonomies. The first has to do with determining the hierarchical arrange-

TABLE 2.6 BUILDINGS CHART

	Business		Entertainment		Religious	Gov't	Education
	Wholesale	Retail	Performance	Social			
Factory	+	−	−	−	−	−	−
Shop	−	+	−	−	−	−	−
Theater	−	+	+	−	?	?	?
Pub	−	+	−	+	−	−	−
Mosque	−	−	−	−	+	?	?
Synagogue	−	−	−	−	+	?	?
Courthouse	−	−	−	−	−	+	−
City hall	−	−	−	−	−	+	?
High school	−	?	?	?	?	?	+
Institute	−	?	?	?	?	?	+

ment of items in the field. Given the building domain, should the terms first be split into private and public buildings? Should they be organized by size (small buildings, multistory buildings, skyscrapers), or should they be organized according to building materials (the three little pigs' straw house, stick house, brick house)? The initial and subsequent cuts are determined by our view of the domain. Many believe that taxonomic approaches just create lots of file drawers or pigeonholes into which forms can be slotted. This creates a feeling of order and neatness but leads to a second problem in that it obscures the process learners actually use in understanding words. In order to highlight a more process orientation, to get away from the put-it-in-a-box approach, linguists prefer to use tree diagrams. These diagrams suggest that the classification is not static but a series of choices made by the speaker to express meanings.

This use of trees to suggest a series of choices has been criticized as well. The analysis may be descriptively interesting, and it may be diagrammed in a way that seems to reflect choice in language production, but there is little evidence that speakers actually process items by breaking them down into their component features. It seems quite unlikely that we match +human, −degree holder, +male, −married to arrive at *bachelor* or that we determine *city hall* as the right choice of the building semantic field by checking off the plus and minus categories listed in Table 2.6. We are not arguing that we never decompose words into their features in making lexical choices. We may do so in dealing with problematic use of words and we certainly do in giving definitions. Indeed, adult second language learners who approach learning in an analytic way may find such analyses very useful in determining not only the vocabulary of a domain but also the distinctions that are made in selecting one rather than another term in the semantic field.

These criticisms are not meant to negate the value of semantic field analysis. It is extremely important to begin an analysis with a listing of terms for a field. Once such a task is undertaken in a serious manner, the field may be divided into domains of related terms within the field. For example, Lehrer (1983), in examining how people talk about wine, found that experts and novices used a wide variety of terms that could then be grouped into a series of dimensions related to taste. These included acidity, astringency, age, body, balance, smell, finish, and whether it was active (still, gassy, sparkling, etc.). Terms that show an overall general evaluation included those of high praise (*subtle, delicate, elegant, fine, complex*), low praise (*clean, refreshing, simple, sound*), mildly derogatory (*insipid, bland, ordinary*), and strongly derogatory (*off, ghastly, awful*). By linking these various dimensions, the entire field of wine terms as used by a variety of people in many areas and of many levels of expertise, can be categorized and described.

Beyond the hierarchical arrangement of domains within a field, however, Lehrer's work is especially interesting because she shows, first, that contrary to popular opinion, there are many terms related to taste. Second, she demonstrates how the terms are negotiated in conversational interactions. For example, one group described a wine as:

A: Earthy!
H: Mossy – like moss smells and tastes.
E: Kind of flinty – that would be earthy – Chablis.
H: Yeah.
E: Makes you think of pebbles or stones or something.
S: Minerally?
. . . .
E: Flinty.
I: I don't know about flinty.
H: It's like metal.
D: Metallic? It's not metallic.
N: It has corners?
E: Smell of an unburnt match?
H: Smell of somebody's cellar, in a wet place.
D: Musty or something.

(Lehrer, 1983, p. 108)

The negotiation continues at length, as the tasters not only offer taste terms but terms that affect taste (the smell, the feel of it in the mouth, and so forth). Lehrer's work, therefore, goes beyond field analysis to the relation of terms within a field.

Other researchers have proposed very different ways of describing the semantic relations among terms for a field. Lewandowska-Tomaszczyk (1990) uses a three-tier system to illuminate the characteristics that separate meanings. The tiers list features that are necessary, central, and typical of the terms. For example, *human* would, of necessity, be a mammal. Central to the concept *human* is the ability to think, and the ability to talk is typical. For families of terms, such as *furniture*, the division into tiers might be:

Necessary condition: artifact
Central condition: [function] for people to sit on, keep things in, etc.
Typical condition: HAVE [surface]

> to sit on = *stool, chair*
> to lie on = *bed*
> to sit or lie on = *couch*
> to put things on = *table, desk*

HAVE [container] to keep things in

> with shelves for books = *bookcases*
> with rod or hooks for clothes = *wardrobe*

This method bridges the work in semantic field analysis with that of cognitive psychologists such as Langacre, Clark, and Lakoff. Lehrer's extension of field semantics to relations overlaps the work of linguists and lexicographers who use relational models. We will turn to the more cognitive approaches in the next chapter as we discuss core semantics and prototype theory. Relational models will be discussed in Chapter 4.

Research and application

1. Southworth and Daswani (1974, pp. 191–194) present diagrams of English, Hindu-Urdu, and Tamil language kinship groups. If you are interested in family structure, select another language, prepare a kinship chart, and show how similar or dissimilar it is to each of these languages.
2. Wu (1990) examined the use of kinship address forms by speakers of Mandarin Chinese with non-kin. Although it has been said that speakers use these terms in addressing older people, Wu found they were also used in addressing juniors and even strangers. Prepare a research plan to investigate the range of languages in which kinship terms are extended beyond the family. Is English in the minority in this regard?
3. In the following excerpt (transcribed according to the conventions of conversational analysis), H is a Persian and M a Japanese student of English.

H: Do you–do you spend uh (.4) some drugs =

M: Mmhmm

H: = In your food?

M: Mm hm (.2) ye:s =

H: = Like saffron, or salt, or pepper something like that?

M: Mmhmm oh: I: see. Yes mm (1.0) Japanese?

H: Yes, in Japanese food.

M: O:h in Japanese food mmm Japanese food no:t spi-cy: (.2) almost =

H: What does it mean? spicy?

M: Spicy means uh mm (1.0) mm mm mm not-do you know spice?
(.2) spicy meaning uh sometimes with seed with uh tree seeds
or uh: nuts.

H: Yes

M: mm example umm tabasuko? An uh, muhstad mm and pepper.

H: Yes, I got it.

M: Not spicy Japanese food. (.2) Very soft taste.

(Data source: Schwartz, 1980)

Are spices a semantic field? Do the examples given in this excerpt
match those you would supply? Why is *drugs* not an appropriate
cover term for these items? What is the semantic relation between
spice and *drug*?

4. Henley (1969) investigated the semantic field of animal terms (20
   terms) using five experimental tasks (free listing, pair ratings for
   similarity, triad ratings, verbal association, and paired associates
   learning). Using multidimensional scaling techniques, she found
   that size and ferocity were the most important dimensions in the
   groupings of the animals. Why is this finding important as counter-
   evidence to a semantic feature hierarchy or a semantic field
   display approach? You might want to replicate her study in a language other than English to see whether a cross-linguistic task
   would obtain the same results.

5. Korfeld (1975), in a case study of a retarded individual, discusses
   the responses of retarded individuals to commands such as, "Put
   the book on the chair." Instead of placing the book on the chair,
   they responded by picking up the book and sitting on the chair.
   What might this say about the power of the furniture semantic
   field? What other interpretations might one give for such a
   response?

6. Car terms are now said to be the most discriminated field in the
   United States. That is, asked to name cars, people can think of
   more names than they can for, say, vegetables or schools. Aronoff
   (1985) shows that the semantics of any American car name relates

to its position relative to other kinds of cars – each depends for its meanings on the other words in the semantic field. After you have read this analysis, select another product semantic field (perhaps refrigerators, washing machines, bicycles, dolls) and carry out your own analysis.

7. In working on taxonomies it has been noted that while *seat* has the subcategories of *chair, bench, stool,* and so forth, there is no similar cover term for things we climb on, such as *ladder* and *step stool.* There is no cover term for things that hold items together such as *staples, paper clips, glue,* and so forth. There is no word for things with teeth such as *combs, rakes,* and so forth. However, even without a cover term, we are easily able to group items together that go together. People can still sort cards into stacks that reveal the categories. Barsalou (1983) discusses the number of categories that we create on short notice: what to take out of the house in case of a fire, what to do on the weekend, or presents to take to a party. None of these have cover terms. Check these categories in another language. If you find a language that does have a cover term, design an experiment to compare how well speakers of this language carry out a card sort task compared with native English speakers.

8. To collect data on the lexicon of wine (and the ways people talk about wine), Lehrer gathered experimental data as well as conversational data during wine-tasting sessions. If you have found a lexical field that you wish to investigate, you might examine her methodology and analysis in detail. Can your data also be broken into domains (if so, what might they be)? Do you believe that experts and novices talk about the lexical field you have selected using very similar or very different sets of terms? Would your findings be useful to a language teacher? If so, specify how they might best be used.

3 Core meanings and prototype theory

Katz and Fodor, as shown in their analysis of the word *bachelor*, used a feature approach in examining the ways in which words with the same form but slightly different meanings are related. The intent of such analyses is to identify features that are critical, especially grammatically critical, in determining meaning. However, if you ask people for a definition of *bachelor*, it is unlikely that they will think immediately of an unattached male seal. Because no special weight is given to primary meanings in semantic feature analysis, we need another way to talk about meanings that will capture the notion that some meanings of a word seem to be more central than others.

In trying to understand the ways in which we assign meanings to words, cognitive psychologists and linguists use two terms: core and prototype. *Core* (as opposed to periphery) relates to meanings of a particular word which are most central, primary, or invariant. The core meaning of *break* is that of breaking an object such as a cup, not the breaking of waves on the shore. A *prototype* is a best instance example of a concept. Thus, *robin* might be a prototype best instance of the concept BIRD and *oak* might be a prototype best instance of the concept TREE.

Core meanings

Labov (1973) asks us to decide when we call a cup a *cup,* what the core meaning of *cup* is, and under what circumstances the core meaning is missing and the object is judged to be something other than a cup. If a cup has no handle, is it still a *cup?* If it is tall and made of clear glass and you serve Irish whiskey in it, is it a *cup?* If you drink tea in it, does that change your choice or is it now a *glass?* What if it is square and has no handle, but you drink coffee from it? What if it is tall, made of styrofoam, but has no handle? For most Americans, the core representation for *cup* is a handled container, about three inches high with slightly curved sides (width to height taper), made of earthenware china that is used to serve coffee. If we vary these dimensions or change the material from which it is made, use it for some other function (e.g., if we put flowers in it or hand it out as a prize at an athletic event), add a lid, or remove the handle, we have moved away from the core to a more peripheral representation. Beyond some point, we may need to use a different word – *glass, teacup, stein, vase, wine glass*. When do we decide to use a different word? And are the dimensions and the cutoff points the same across languages?

Although most concepts used in discussing core meanings relate to objects, there are core meanings for verbs as well. For example, the word *break* has several meanings, but if you ask people to produce sentences with the word *break,* they will use the core meaning of an agent breaking a physical object such as a cup. If you ask people to produce sentences with the word *put,* it is likely they will use an example where an agent transfers a physical object to a flat surface. Core meanings of verbs are connected to their propositions.

Kellerman (1978), in his now famous study of *breken* in his comparison of Dutch and English and Dutch and German, has demonstrated that second language learners, once presented with the word for *break* in a new language, are more likely to believe that those meanings closest to the core ("the cup broke," "he broke his leg") are those to which the new word can apply. They are less likely to believe that the same word could be used for more peripheral meanings such as *strikebreakers* or *icebreakers*. Here are the sentences that Kellerman used in his experiment. To determine which meanings were most central, he presented native speakers of Dutch with cards on which the following sentences (but not the translations, of course) were printed:

1. De golven braken op de rotsen.   (The waves broke on the rock.)
2. De lichtstralen breken in het water.   (The light rays refract in the water.)
3. Hij brak zijn been.   (He broke his leg.)
4. 't Kopje brak.   (The cup broke.)
5. Na 't ongeluk is hij 'n gebroken man geworden.   (After the accident, he was a broken man.)
6. Zij brak zijn hart.   (She broke his heart.)
7. Hij brak zijn woord.   (He broke his word.)
8. De man brak zijn eed.   (The man broke his oath.)
9. Welk land heeft de wapenstilstand gebroken?   (Which country has broken the ceasefire?)
10. Sommige arbeiders hebben de staking gebroken.   (Some workers have broken the strike.)
11. Nood breekt wet.   (Necessity breaks the law - a saying)
12. Dankzij 'n paar grapjes was 't ijs eindelihk gebroken.   (Thanks to a few jokes, the ice was finally broken.)
13. 'n Spelletje zou de middag enigszins breken.   (A game would break up the afternoon a bit.)
14. Zij brak 't wereldrecord.   (She broke the world record.)
15. Zijn stem brak toen hij 13 was.   (His voice broke when he was 13.)

16. Zijn val werd door 'n boom gebroken.   (His fall was broken by a tree.)
17. Het ondergrondse verzet werd gebroken.   (The underground resistance was broken.)

The native speakers of Dutch sorted the cards, ranking them on the centralness of the meaning of *breken*. This procedure allowed Kellerman to be sure that his own intuitions of coreness were correct. Next, he asked Dutch learners of English whether they thought the English word *break* could be used for *breken* in each sentence. Dutch high school and university students studying English or majoring in English read the Dutch sentences and predicted whether *break* could be used for *breken* in each. All learners were willing to use *break* when the meanings were closest to the core. Kellerman found a U-shaped curve where beginners and advanced students were most willing to use *break* in instances further from core meanings. Intermediate learners were less willing to use *break* in items far from the core. To explain this U-shaped curve, we might claim that advanced learners may have been exposed to the full range of meanings for *break*. Perhaps beginning students are more daring while intermediate learners are more cautious because they have found that expecting similar words in two languages to correspond can lead them into error.

Polysemy and homonymy in core semantics

Polysemes are the many variants of meaning of a word where it is clear that the meanings are truly related. The verb *break* has many different variants which are related in meaning. The verb *put* also has an array of polysemes. Homonyms (sometimes called *homographs*), on the other hand, are variants that are spelled alike but which have no obvious commonality in meaning. The classic example is the word *bank*, which could mean a financial institution or the bank of a river or a tier or row of objects (such as a bank of seats at a baseball game). These meanings are not noticeably related and therefore would be listed as three separate or distinct words with different meanings in dictionaries.

Jakobson (1972) claims that there is something invariant – a *Gesamtbedeutung* (a general meaning) that links even these separate entries. Jakobson uses the example of *bachelor*, as so many linguists had, to show that all of the meanings have in common the idea of an adult male (unless the context specifically specifies otherwise as in *bachelor girl*) with one item lacking in his life.

One question regarding core research is whether or not polysemes such as those shown in the *break* example really are the same word (whether there is some invariant *Gesamtbedeutung* that links them) or whether some should be listed as separate lexical items. The *break* of "break a cup," "heart broken," and "icebreakers" share meanings. Some of these meanings are more central or corelike than others. The problem, then, is to work out some way of showing how central or corelike the meanings are and how they vary as they move out from that core. This has required the use of dimensions (we will turn to ways of talking about dimensions in the next section).

Polysemes and homonyms are of special interest in cross-dialect and sociolinguistic studies because some of the meanings of polysemes or homonyms may occur in only one of the dialects or be used by only a specific group in society. For example, when someone offers you a biscuit, are you being asked if you'd like a cookie or a baking-powder quickbread (a *scone* in British English)? *Biscuit* is a cross-dialect polyseme. An example of a cross-argot homonym would be words such as *horse, snow,* and *tea* when they are used in drug cultures to refer to drugs. These meanings are not, as near as we can tell, immediately related to their more common meanings.

Practice 3.1

1. Graham and Belnap (1986) used a technique similar to that of Labov involving pictures of various objects (cups, glasses, bowls, chairs, stools, benches, shoes, and boots) with varying heights, widths, and details (with or without handles, with or without shoelaces). They then asked native speakers of English and Spanish to name the objects in the pictures. The native speakers of Spanish, who were learners of English as a second language, were also asked to name the objects in English, with a week's time between their performance on the naming task in the two languages (half of the subjects did the task first in Spanish and half did it first in English). You might be surprised to learn that the dividing line for switching from one name to another (such as from *cup* to *glass*) was not always the same for the speakers in their two native languages, and the dividing line for the switch in English as a second language was often much closer to the native Spanish dividing line. Try this experiment with the same objects in another language that you or your students know. What features (size, shape, details) seem to determine the point at which a switch to a different word is used for the item? Do learners seem to change their dividing point when using their second language?

2. Prepare a research plan to replicate Kellerman's procedure, but select some other lexical item, perhaps the verb *stop* or *drop*. Once you have drawn up a series of sentences containing different meanings for the word, ask native speakers to rate them in terms of core to noncore meanings. What core meaning(s) do you think you will obtain for the word? Which do you predict will be judged as far from the core? Now find a word in another language that corresponds to this core meaning. Does that second language word correspond to the English word in all the examples? Write out your plan for administering the items to English speakers learning the language. If you want to see if the U-shaped curve obtains for learners at different levels, what proficiency levels would you select? (If you decide to develop this exercise into a paper, you will want to read Shirai's [1990a] comments on methodology in his analysis of *put* and Jordens's [1977] study comparing core and peripheral meanings of words along dimensions.)

3. Look at various collections of contrasting lexical items in American English and British English. Decide which are cross-dialect polysemes and which are homonyms. Are polysemes more confusing to language learners than homonyms? Justify your answer.

4. Examine various monolingual dictionaries that you or your students use. See how the dictionary lists polysemes and homonyms. What factors did the editors use to separate polysemic meanings from homonyms? Find several examples of words in the dictionary with both polysemic listings and homonym listings. Would it be easy for language learners to recognize the reasons why some meanings are listed under one main entry and others are listed under a different main entry? Justify your answer.

5. Is it enough to say that if no shared meanings are present, the word should be listed as a separate entry? Consider various jokes that play on polysemy or homonymy. Elephant jokes are a good source for these ("How do you get down from an elephant? You don't. You get down from a swan.") Other sources are newspaper titles ("Council puts brakes on bike path") and bumper stickers ("Education kills by degrees"). After you have collected several examples, determine whether homonymy is required for all such jokes.

Prototypes

The research literature in psychology (e.g., the 1983 research of Rosch and associates) shows that we definitely have shared ideas about what is the most prototypic instance – the best example – for many concepts. We all know what the color red looks like though we may find it difficult to describe. Given a series of color chips ranging in shades from purple to orange, we all could pick out the prototypic red chip, the best instance of red. And the chip we select would agree with that chosen by most other people as well. This is true across all language groups, even those that may not have a word for red (though almost all languages do). It appears that we interpret categories in terms of their clearest cases. Four claims have been made about processing and prototypes:

1. Items judged to be typical members of a concept can be categorized more efficiently than atypical ones.
2. Typical members are learned first by children.
3. Prototypes are named first when subjects are asked to give examples of members of a concept.
4. Prototypes serve as cognitive reference points.

In the discussion that follows, you will see that these claims are generally true but that in some instances they can be questioned.

If you think about the concept BIRD, your best instance may have a different name depending on where you live, but it will capture most of the features that you associate with the concept. For most Americans, the prototypic bird is a robin (which is actually a thrush, quite different from the much smaller European robin). In this case, the prototype or best instance will vary from area to area. Obviously, the American robin is not a prototypic bird if you live at the South Pole. Yet, penguins would be very far from prototypic for most Americans. Thus, some prototypes are based in the human perceptual system (as in primary color terms) while others depend on location and cultural norms.

Whereas prototype research works with sets of words for a given concept, the discussions of findings vary as to whether we make an all or nothing judgment (i.e., an ostrich is or is not a bird), whether we make a graded judgment (i.e., an ostrich is a bird to a degree), or both (i.e., an ostrich is a bird but not a very good example of that concept). The latter appears most likely. Evidence in support of this can be drawn from other parts of the language. For example, we may use adjectives to show that a particular instance of an item varies from the prototype. *A tall woman* is a woman who is taller than our usual prototype picture of *woman*. We might also use adverbs. If we say, "The boy threw the ball gently," the prototypic notion of force in *throw* has been weakened. So, we might consider forms such as compounds (*compact car*) as similar to other vocabulary choices (*convertible*) that vary away from or toward the prototype.

Dimensions with prototypes and core meanings

Linguists and cognitive psychologists are concerned not just with identifying the prototype of any lexical entry, but with the *dimensions* along which others that fit in the concept group vary from the prototype. Similarly, researchers in core semantics have tried to identify the dimensions on which the secondary or peripheral uses of a word vary from that shown in the core or primary meaning. Perhaps this is why there is so much confusion of the terms *core* and *prototype*. Researchers within each tradition are looking for dimensions that capture variations from central meanings or central representations.

Many of these dimensions that have been identified have to do with natural experience, in particular with perceptual dimensions such as shape and size. The dimension of size and shape is shown in Figure 3.1 for the concept BIRD. This circle shows that the robin is the central prototype for bird. If we look in the next ring out we see birds of the same approximate size: sparrows, bluebirds, and so on. As we move toward the outer circles, size and shape change so that penguins and ostriches are judged much less birdlike.

There is at least one piece of evidence that validates relationship among items in the circle. Rips (1975) asked whether diseases could pass from one bird group to another. When the direction was from a more prototypic to a less prototypic bird, the answer was *yes*. When the spread of disease was to be from the less toward the more prototypic birds, the answer was *no*.

While others used circle or wave diagrams to illustrate the range from most to least prototypic exemplars of a concept, Rosch et al. (1976) categorized meanings along two axes. The vertical axis arranges things from the most abstract form to the most specific: for example, *tree* to *oak* to *California live oak*. The horizontal axis arranges objects of the same level of abstraction by their attributes. In the following example, *oak, sycamore, magnolia, pine,* and *aspen* would all be on the same horizontal line. On the vertical axis, the point where objects share the most attributes is called the basic level. The levels above and below the basic level are called superordinate and sub-basic.

Superordinate:	tree
Basic:	oak, pine, maple, elm . . .
Sub-basic:	California live oak, Lodgepole pine, Norwegian maple, Dutch elm . . .

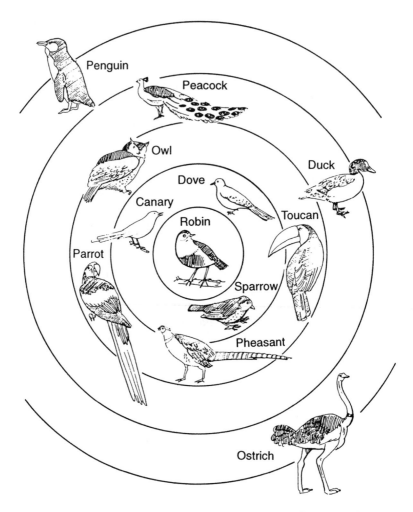

Figure 3.1 Circle diagram for the concept BIRD (from Aitchison, 1987, p. 54; used by permission)

A basic-level object name can usually be inserted into a sentence that contains a superordinate-level term and vice versa. For example, we can use the word *sparrow* for *bird* in the sentence "There are about a hundred birds on the telephone line." If we took a word from the sub-basic level to replace *bird*, however, the results might seem strange. "There are about a hundred golden-crowned sparrows on the line" seems odd because the focus is no longer birdness but rather the astonishing fact that so many of these particular birds should be on the line. Obviously, our prototype of birdness includes the fact that prototypic birds sit on electric lines. *Turkeys, penguins, eagles, hawks* do not do this, of course. If we took an item from an even higher superordinate level, say *animal*, we would be unnecessarily ambiguous. "An *animal* on the line" could be a squirrel just as easily as a bird.

Again, this shows us that not everyone agrees on which dimensions are most important in determining prototypes. That is, visual similarities in size and shape may not be the most critical dimension in determining prototypes for all items. The most important dimension might be functional (a glass is something we drink from whereas a vase is not). They may involve motor activity (getting off a *stool* vs. getting up from a *chair*). They may involve purpose (we may sit on either a stool or a chair when writing). And variation from the prototype may be along a combination of several such dimensions.

Superordinate, basic, and sub-basic levels

It has been suggested that learners acquire general basic-level items first. This has been contested for child first language acquisition. It is true that children learn the word *cow*, for example, before *animal*. But children also often learn the more specific sub-basic term before either the basic or the more general superordinate terms. Prior to learning *pet*, they are likely to learn *dog*. Prior to learning *dog*, however, they may learn the name of their particular family dog.

Nonetheless, evidence that basic forms may be easier can be found in evidence from language arts classes for young children. Hatch and Hawkins' (1991) data show that it is not difficult to get young bilingual children to use less general, more specific noun choices. In writing down oral stories, these children revised, clarified, and specified their noun and adjective choices. They had great difficulty, though, in deciding if and when more specific verbs were called for. *Strutting, shuffling, marching,* and *wandering* are all more specific words for the central notion of walking; they mean a certain kind of walking. Children did not use these on their own, nor did they respond to suggestions that when they said "We *ran so fast* to the end" they could write "We *sprinted* to the end."

There are also examples of second language learners who have acquired highly sophisticated, sub-basic level terms for some concepts but who do not know very common, superordinate level vocabulary items even though they may be used in everyday speech. In studies of second language lexical development, we find examples of children learning specific level vocabulary very quickly if the terms cover an area of interest to them. For example, Miki, a 3½-year-old Japanese child acquiring English in the United States, used terms like *hovercraft, submarine, and ambulance*. According to Yoshida (1978), Miki was fascinated by vehicles, wild animals, outdoor objects, and names of food and drinks. He used *fence, bridge, ladder, parachute, cliff,* and other sub-basic level terms. But, on the Peabody Picture Vocabulary Test, Miki was unable to name common objects that were possibly not interesting to him, items like *dress, skirt, ring, lamp* – all basic level terms. Kenyeres and Kenyeres (1938) also noted with surprise that Eva, a Hungarian child becoming bilingual in French, acquired many unusual words yet did not know some of the most common French words.

If learners acquired basic level vocabulary first and highly specific vocabulary or superordinate terms later, we might logically expect them also to forget more quickly the highly specific and also the superordinate terms and to retain basic level words longer. Olshtain (1986), looking at the language loss of her child after they left the United States and returned to Israel, comments on the substitution of general for specific terms and gives the following examples of what the child said:

There's a lady going (= walking) in the park.
The baby is putting (= holding) up a spoon.
I'm gonna wear hot (= warm) clothes today.
She's walking to (= toward) the chair (= bench).

Our definitions of superordinate, basic, and sub-basic, however, are rather fuzzy, so it is not clear whether these are truly examples that support a levels hypothesis. We can argue that *walking* is *moving* in a particular way, a way that is neutral rather than goal-directed. It is a basic level term for movement. *Going,* too, is a basic level term under the superordinate term of *moving;* however, it is a goal-directed type of movement. What has been lost might be the distinction between goal-directed (moving toward a place) and nongoal-directed motion. *Strolling* would be the sub-basic term, perhaps, for *walking.* In each of these examples the terms used during this period of language loss are less specific than the target forms, but they also show the problems involved with trying to make the three-level dimension work for all descriptions. It still is not clear whether word loss is related to any of the preceding models. As Olshtain suggests, the kinds of vocabulary a learner acquires or forgets must depend, in part, on age, the learner's interests, methods of teaching, the amount of reading the learner does, and the amount and type of social interaction experienced.

Practice 3.2

1. What level is the word *educator*? List as many other terms as you can for each of the three levels of this concept. How do they relate to each other? (Or do this for another word, perhaps *sports, fruit,* or *English.*)

2. Hawkins (Hatch and Hawkins, 1991) asked young bilingual children to consider alternatives for *said* in the stories they first told and then composed in writing lab. Noting their intonation in telling the story, students readily changed *said* to *yelled* or *laughed,* but did not use other forms such as *exclaimed.* One student was also unsure whether he could write, "But Long *worried* (said), 'There's a dog in the hall.'" What forms do you predict your students would use in a similar exercise? Work out a research plan to investigate related questions such as whether students revise their essays toward more precise vocabulary. If so, is this more obvious in the changes in nouns, adjectives, or verbs?

3. Sometimes it is difficult to decide what constitutes a basic level. Consider all the different types of words you might use for *seats* (e.g., *chair*). Then list all the more specific terms for each of your words (e.g., *high chair*). That gives us three levels. However, we might think of a yet higher level, *furniture.* What would the basic and superordinate terms be for this term? If we can change levels (make *chair* a basic item for *seat* and a sub-basic term for *furniture*), does this still support the hypothesis about what is learned first and best retained? What solution can you propose?

4. If you have data from a language classroom, look at the kinds of simplification teachers do in terms of vocabulary choice. When misunderstandings seem imminent, does the teacher switch to a basic-level item, a superordinate term, or a sub-basic term? When teachers give definitions, do they use a superordinate term to define a basic-level term or offer another basic-level synonym? Compare your findings with other "foreigner talk" papers (see Chaudron, 1983, 1988).

5. Oxford's (1990) list of compensation strategies used by second language learners includes "adjusting or approximating the message" and "using a circumlocution or synonym." Listen to or record your learners as they speak in natural circumstances. When they do not seem to know a term, do they compensate by using a superordinate term and distinguishing characteristics of the thing they are trying to explain, do they try another basic-level term, or do they give several more specific sub-basic terms? Give examples to support your answer. Does the compensation strategy used seem to depend on the level of word the learner is searching for?

Fuzzy categories, levels, and prototypes

Bolinger (1975, p. 205) said that "meanings are as elusive as a piece of wet soap in a bathtub." The same could be said about categories, levels, and even prototypes. The difference between prototype and core can be taken care of most easily. As explained earlier, the prototype meaning is the best instance, template meaning that speakers of a language think of when a concept is named. Prototype analysis is more psychological, perhaps, than linguistic. It is especially interesting when the prototype is universal, as it is likely to be if based on our perceptual systems as in the concept RED. An English speaker is unlikely to select a purple or a pink or a red-orange color chip when asked to find the central red chip. Core meanings, on the other hand, are those which are most central for a set of polysemes (words with the same form but slightly different meanings). Work in core semantics focuses more on finding dimensions on which core meanings can differ in the periphery while maintaining a common base. Researchers in prototype theory also look for dimensions, but usually they do so in terms of a hierarchy of superordinate, basic, and subbasic forms.

When we turn to specific examples with any of the analytic methods discussed so far, we encounter difficulty because words do not have meanings in and of themselves. The meanings are conventional, arrived at through consensus and context, and very "fuzzy." We have said that some terms, like color terms, are fairly consistent: the primary colors of red, yellow, green, blue, black, and white appear to elicit similar responses from people (responses which say something about our visual perceptual system). Of course, many languages have one name for both blue and green. This does *not* mean that they do not distinguish these two colors, but only that the distinction is not marked in the language. In some languages, such as Russian, there is a word (*goluboy*) for light blue and another word (*siniy*) for dark blue. It is difficult to believe the prototypic blue is dark blue, but we do not have a word for light blue, the color many people think of for blue. Even though we would use *blue* to refer to these two colors, we still are able to distinguish between them visually.

The boundaries that result from the fuzzy union of two or more primaries are not so clear and color judgments vary. One example is trying to distinguish various shades of red in identifying wildflowers. Flowers that have much blue in the red are often called *blue,* and those with much pink may also be called *blue.* In fact, photography books contain discussions about the difficulty in photographing certain flowers because the film will not register the full range of colors present but read several as the same. This results in some very unred and unblue pictures of flowers in the red and blue sections in wildflower identification books.

Many languages distinguish between warm colors – such as yellow, orange, red, white – and cool colors – such as blue, turquoise, green. Others oppose dark colors, such as black and green, to light colors such as white and yellow. Ornstein and Gates (1964) note that cool vs. warm is an important distinction in Chinese for colors (and that there are different words for colors and for dyes). *Ch'ing* is the word for the cool colors: blue–green, grey–black. However, the color also comes from the words it is used with. Thus, *ch'ing sky* is blue, *ch'ing mountains* are purple, *ch'ing grass* is green, *ch'ing cattle* are black, and *ch'ing horses* are grey. The point here is that once we get beyond the primary color terms, the meanings of terms become fuzzy. The question, then, is whether it is the terms or our perception of reality that is imprecise.

This problem of dealing with fluid categories extends to semantic feature analysis. When we talked about opposites such as *day* and *night* in Chapter 1, we noted that it is only convention that sets the boundary line. Everyone knows that even very precise terms such as a *minute* can mean sixty seconds, but when used in an expression such as "wait a minute," it can be a lifetime. Baldinger (1980, p. 32) gives us a Spanish example of many resulting jokes about time. A philosopher says, "To me, 1,000 years is just a minute." Amazed, a peasant asked, "And 1,000 pesos?" "Like five centavos," the philosopher replied. "Then, sir," the peasant smiled, "please lend me five centavos." And the philospher replied, "In a minute."

Scientific, legal, and medical fields have struggled in the past to insist on precise terms. (Today, however, science is accepting more fuzziness. See Kosko and Isaka's article on "fuzzy logic" in the July 1993 *Scientific American,* for example.) You can see that in legal cases, pairs such as *life–death* must be defined with great precision. Because there is no consensus, however, we struggle with each term. During confirmation hearings for the United States Supreme Court, nominees are asked about their interpretation of natural law – law which is based on the notion that there is consensus about right and wrong – and the meanings of many such terms. Terms used by the United Nations and in international treaties must be precisely defined so that nations know to what they have or have not agreed. For example, what does *aggression* mean? What does *open sea* mean? Decisions which can threaten the world, one's life, or one's health depend on definitions having precise consensual meanings.

Finally, there is fuzziness in what constitutes the dimensions on which words vary in meaning from the prototype concept. We have already noted that the prototypic bird might be a penguin at the South Pole and a robin in the United States. The prototype for tree might be a palm tree in Hawaii, but not in the rest of the United States. The prototype for a musical instrument may be a *guitar* for a teenager or a *harp* for residents of heaven. The variability and the fuzziness of changing prototypes are sources of fascination for all of us who love languages and language learning but a source of frustration for those who would prefer meanings, like bars of soap, to hold still long enough for us to capture them.

Practice 3.3

1. List as many words of physical geography as you can think of (from little mounds to the highest mountains) in a language of your choice. Diagram them in some way. Once you have decided on your diagram, give the words in random order to native speakers and learners of the language. Ask them to rate them in terms of height, volume, and whatever other features seem to be important. How much agreement do you find? Then, make up a sentence-level multiple-choice test offering the three closest choices from your list. How fuzzy are the boundaries when the words are put in sentence context?

2. Italian, Japanese, and Arabic all have three different terms for the color *blue,* one for light blue, one for royal blue, and one for navy blue.

	Light blue	*Royal blue*	*Navy blue*
Italian:	celeste	azzurro	blu
Japanese:	mizuiro	ao	kon
Arabic:	labany	azra'	koḥly

(Data source: V. Chimienti, M. Shinohara, and F. El Hindawy)

Perhaps these different words reflect the color of the sky, water, and night. Add examples from other languages you might know. Are these categories fuzzier or more precise than our light blue, medium blue, and dark blue?

3. In the Olympics, scores for events such as diving, figure skating, and gymnastics are computed to three decimal points, and winners may be separated by as little as .012. This makes the ratings seem like precise scores. It is possible, too, to grade students' compositions in this way, turning grades into precise numbers. How fuzzy are such ratings in reality?

4. List as many words for dwellings as you can. It is said that people agree that *hut, house,* and *mansion* clearly differ, but the boundary line for words between each term is fuzzy. How clearly can you separate all the words you have listed? Repeat this exercise in another language of

your choice. What comparisons can you draw in terms of clear or unclear boundaries?

Research and application

Core meanings

1. In Chapter 1, we noted that children use perceptual features such as shape, texture, and sound before others such as function. Andersen's (1975) study showed that children younger than 6 years of age use shape and material to identify cups and glasses. Later they discriminate these items according to function. Validate this study with children acquiring a different first language or a second language.

2. Dillon (1977) claims that young children learn the word *hammer* via both form and function and wonders whether they transfer this double form and function categorization to all tools. He also notes that *polish* is a difficult word for young children to learn because its meaning is primarily that of function. Young children often call shoe polish *paint*. If you are able to observe young children, work out a research plan to investigate this division of function and other formal features in the acquisition of lexical items.

3. K. Williams (1991) analyzed the Hausa words *ci* (eat) and *shaa* (drink), which are used for a much wider range of meanings than in English. Williams suggests that the extension of the meanings are radial in nature from the core meanings. *Ci* has a meaning in the sense of *consume* and we might use it in English in the way it is commonly employed in Hausa (e.g., "eat up the profits," "fire ate up the house"), but it also extends to a meaning of *seize* in winning a war, taking a town, or winning a race. After reading this article, try to find parallels in other languages for the nine extensions for *ci* and the four for *shaa*.

4. Coseiu (1967) demonstrates various ways of displaying relations among polysemes for the German word *Schall*. After reading this article, decide how each display gives slightly different information. Select a word from your own first language and diagram the relations in each of the ways demonstrated in this article. Decide why each method is or is not useful in teaching this vocabulary item to language learners.

Prototype meanings

5. Battig and Montague (1969) gave university students 30 seconds to list examples of words for 56 categories. They then took the most

frequent examples to be the prototype for the category. The prototype vegetable, for example, was carrot, pea was second, and corn was third. Read this study and replicate it with students of different first languages or with your ESL/EFL students. Analyze the data and compare your results with those of Battig and Montague. To update your paper, fit your results into a discussion of prototype research.

6. Rosch (1973) took six items that ranked from high to low in frequency in the Battig and Montague study and asked students to rank these on a seven-point scale of how well they exemplified the category. Thus, Rosch validated the notion that the most frequently mentioned item would also be the best exemplar or prototype for the category. After you have carried out the research suggested in item 1, you might also want to carry out this validation procedure.

7. Levenston and Blum (1977) found that their adult learners of Hebrew first acquired common basic-level terms. The basic terms cover a fairly wide field (*car* covers many types of cars). These Hebrew learners then overextended the basic terms to other levels (e.g., used the Hebrew equivalent of *car* for all vehicles). Is such overextension common for beginning language learners regardless of what language they may learn? How might you research this question?

8. Rips et al. (1973) showed that when people are asked to judge the similarity between all possible pairs from a set of animal concepts (e.g., *lion–dog, lion–hawk, dog–hawk*), the judgments have to do with distinctions such as species membership (fish are judged as similar to other fish and dissimilar to birds). However, people also make distinctions based on notions such as ferocity. A hawk might be judged similar to a shark because both are fierce. Such notions also help predict how quickly we can determine whether a stimulus word is a member of a superordinate category such as bird. Birds have a prototypic value for qualities such as ferocity. Those birds that most closely approximate prototypic values for these dimensions are more quickly assigned to the bird category according to McClosky and Glucksberg (1979) and Smith et al. (1974). Would second language learners make the same similarity judgments as native speakers? Are the prototypic values for critical dimensions the same across language groups? Barsalou (1985) found that when people were asked to assume a cultural perspective ("If you were American, African, or Chinese, . . ."), their ratings of birds shifted. Are the ratings of people who assume a perspective likely to be the same as members of that cultural group? How might you research these questions?

9. In Chapter 1, we noted that definitions giving functions are evaluated lower than those giving features of the word or a superordinate term. Thus, the definition of a tricycle "you ride on it" would
be rated lower than "it's a three-wheel vehicle." Usually skills
learned later are thought to be more advanced. In Andersen's
study (item 1), children did not use function to distinguish meanings as early as they used the perceptual features of shape, texture, and sound. Dillon's study (item 2) suggests that the words
themselves determine whether or not function will be used. What
do the studies suggest about the value of function in definitions?
How might you develop a rating scale to evaluate definitions in a
way that weighted superordinate- and subordinate-level information with attribute and function information?

4 Relational models in semantics

The goal of *semantic feature analysis* is to discover a set of features that make up the meanings of words. In this analysis, two lexical relations – synonyms and antonyms – are important because words related in these ways share features. Antonyms share features with the exception of one where the feature is negative rather than positive in value (e.g., *hot* and *cold* are related although they are at opposite poles of degree of temperature). Synonyms also share features, usually varying in terms of collocations or register rather than in meaning. (For example, *entity* is a formal synonym of *something*. We might say "bring something," but not "bring entity" or, conversely, "the entire entity" but not "the entire something.")

The goal of semantic field analysis is to arrive at meanings shared by a group of words in a domain. That is, all the words within the field relate to each other, yet differ in details, which are captured in the analysis. Thus, kinship and furniture are each a semantic field including a group of related words. The analysis reveals the structure of the semantic field.

In core semantics, the many meanings of a single word are related by defining the most invariant, central meaning and the spread of usage of the word along dimensions which move meaning from central to peripheral uses. Prototype semantics identifies the best instance word for a concept and then identifies other words that vary in some way from the prototype. The prototypic tree might be an oak. In terms of relations, a tree is a kind of plant, an oak is a kind of tree, and a black oak is a kind of oak. In prototype analysis, this relation is discussed in terms of superordinate, basic, and sub-basic levels.

Each of these analytic approaches highlights relations which are important in substantiating the analysis and ignores others. This lack of scope has been one of the major criticisms leveled at each analysis. In addition, each is illustrated with selected examples (e.g., *bachelor, kinship, break, bird*) rather than applied to all the words in the lexicon – again, a lack of scope. As soon as we broaden the scope to all words, other relations emerge as important.

The goal of *relational semantics* is not to identify meanings of words but to identify the semantic relations between them. Whereas other models treat relations in an implicit manner, the goal of relational models is to make the relations explicit. If you were given the word *farm* and asked to offer word associations, you would likely name buildings (*barn*), equipment (*tractor*), animals (*cows*), crops (*wheat*), and people (*farmer*). You might associate the word with other rural (*ranch*) or city (*town*) terms. You might produce clang responses – words that rhyme (*harm*) or words beginning with the same sound (*fun, fall*). Each of these associations relates to the word *farm* in some way. Relational models attempt to identify all the types of relations in meanings that can be obtained between words. (Therefore, they will not include clang responses since such words are related through their phonological form rather than through meanings.) Those interested in language teaching acquisition immediately want to know whether this approach can help us understand how learners build a network of meanings that can be easily changed over time. After all, understanding acquisition means understanding the ways we organize our semantic knowledge of the new language and how the information is reorganized to accommodate the new material encountered in each succeeding language lesson.

The relational approach has evolved primarily out of the work of Russian and Polish theoreticians, particularly that of Apresjan (1969), Ilson and Mel'čuk (1989), Mel'čuk and Zholkovsky (1970, 1984). These theorists believe that semantic theories must be encyclopedic (i.e., have coverage similar to that of a dictionary and a thesaurus). To give a better notion of their work, let us turn first to a few of the relations identified in relational models.

Types of relations

Converse relation

If you ask people to say the first word that comes to mind when they hear the word *teach*, they are likely to say *learn*. Such pairs are neither synonyms nor antonyms. The words have a converse relation. This important mutual relation is linked to the *script* or scene in which they occur (we discuss scripts in Chapter 7). *Teacher–student* are converse roles in a classroom script. *Teach–learn* are converses related to roles in that script. *Clerk–customer* are converse roles in a service encounter script, and *buy–sell* relate to these roles in the script. *Tenant–landlord* and *rent to–rent from* are converses in an apartment leasing script.

In some linguistic and logical analyses, the interpretation of a reciprocally related set of terms is rather strict. First, it is assumed that the converse relation is centered in verbs. *Borrow–lend, buy–sell, like–*

please refer to the same action, but the focus is on the borrower–lender, the buyer–seller, the person who likes–the person or object that pleases.

A second assumption is that one member of the pair implies the other (implicature). Thus, if someone buys something we can assume something was sold. If we say that we borrowed something, we imply that something was lent. In some cases, the reverse implication also holds. If we sold something, someone bought it; if we lent something, someone borrowed it. In these double implicatures, the meanings of the verbs reflect one and the same event. In a sense, they are synonyms for an act except that the form changes with the shift of focus to the person or object that carries out the action.

A third assumption in a strict analysis is that the converse actions take place at the same time or moment. Temporal unity is illustrated in *sell* and *buy.* The verbs describe the simultaneity of transfer of ownership. The same event is seen from two different perspectives, that of buyer and seller.

If we take this strict analytic stance, we are left with many pairs which seem to be converses but do not meet the criteria. Sergei Dobrichev (personal communication) suggests that we call such pairs pseudo-converses. Let's look at some of these pairs. The nouns *buyer–seller* are in a converse relation but they are not verbs. However, we can link each to the appropriate verb: the seller sells and the buyer buys at the point where money and merchandise change hands. We also see a converse relation between pairs such as *ask–answer* even though the actions do not take place at exactly the same time (e.g., asking and answering occur in succession, not simultaneously). We also want to classify *ask–answer* as a converse even though the implications about action and role focus only works in one direction. Answer presupposes that someone asked something. But ask does not automatically imply an answer.

If we discard the assumptions of strict analysis, we can list many pairs of words as having a converse relation. In doing so, however, we encounter new problems. For example, we may accept noun pairs such as *doctor–patient* as converses without being certain as to how they are linked. The converse relation of the roles seems to be that the doctor offers medical assistance to the patient and the patient receives the assistance from the doctor. We may also intuitively feel that *doctor–nurse* go together in a converse relation because the nurse assists the doctor and the doctor receives assistance from the nurse. However, since they are working together, rather than in a converse relation, to treat the patient, assigning a converse relation to their roles seems less than satisfactory. The relation is not between a pair (*doctor–nurse*) but among three roles (*doctor–nurse–patient*). In such cases, the relation may, indeed, be better labeled a pseudo-converse or assigned to a different relation (in some analyses it is called a contrast relation).

Hyponym relations

Another relation is shown in the utterance "Lupine *is a kind of* wild-flower." *Lupine* and *wildflower* are not synonyms. This "is a kind of" relation is called hyponymy. (In some relational models it is called generic or taxonomic.) Because lupine *is a kind of* wildflower, *wildflower* has a generic, taxonomic, or hyponym relation with *lupine.*

The hyponym relation is one that we have already seen in Chapter 3. In discussing Rosch's categories of superordinate, basic, and sub-basic levels, we noted that there may be more than three levels and that this is a problem for the superordinate–basic–sub-basic classification. Each level, however, can be defined in terms of the hyponym relation: a desert lupine is a kind of lupine, a lupine is a wildflower, a wildflower is a kind of flower, a flower is a kind of plant. In relational models, levels are not named; instead, the relation is identified as that of hyponymy. Desert lupine has a hyponym relation to lupine, lupine has a hyponym relation to wildflower, and so forth.

Verbs, too, can be related through hyponymy. Kastovsky (1990) notes that HIT has the hyponyms *kick, punch, slap.* But these words are also linked to specific instruments that do the hitting: *foot, fist, palm.* So, more than one relation is needed – an instrument relation along with the hyponym relation forming a network of semantic relations among the words. There are many other possible instruments for HIT verbs but most of them apply to *hit* (with a club, hammer, etc.).

The hyponym relation is an important relation in writing semantic descriptions, as well as in terms of memory for words. MacLeod (1976) asked students to learn number–word pairs, such as 56–car. Later, when students were asked to recall the pairs, some were forgotten. New words were then substituted for those that had been forgotten. If the new word related to the forgotten word, there was some residual memory (savings) of the first word although not enough to allow the student to recall it. The strongest savings were found when hyponyms were used. So if the original pair was 56–car, the students remembered the new pairs if they were 56–vehicle or 56–Buick. Buick is a kind of car and car is a kind of vehicle. Little recall was found for antonyms or synonyms (56–car and 56–auto) or associates (56–car and 56–truck).

Part–whole relations

Most discussions of the part–whole relation identify it in terms of examples like *chapter–book* or *wheel–bicycle.* Iris et al. (1988) did a KWIC (key word in context) search of definitions in the computerized version of *Webster's Seventh Collegiate Dictionary* and found many part–whole relations in definitions. Examples such as "Pedals (wheels, handlebars) are part of a bicycle" show a relation where the part contributes to the whole, not just as a structural unit but as an essential element for the purposeful activity of the whole. Iris et al. found that this functional part–whole relation was by far the most common part–whole relation in definitions.

Some examples drawn from these dictionary definitions emphasize parts which can be detached quite easily (though the unit will no longer function): "drum is a part of a machine," "disk is a part of a plow." Other part–whole examples, such as "flame is a part of fire" and "flesh is a part of fruit," are not pieces that can be readily detached. Iris et al. found that some part–whole relations are temporal sequences ("hour is part of a day," "episode is part of a series"), some are spatial sequences ("front is the forward part or surface," "height is the highest part"), and still others are evaluative ("fat is the best or richest part"). Given the variety of part–whole relationships, one could argue that this relation might need to be subdivided according to type.

Grammar relations

In word association literature, we often find responses that are grammatically related. Young children are said to go through a stage where they treat word association games as though they were requests to complete the sentence. Therefore, a stimulus word such as *brush* might be responded to with *teeth*, the stimulus word *black* might be responded to with *horse*. Responses that are related in this way are called syntagmatic responses. Adults are much more likely to give paradigmatic responses, responses that are the same part of speech (e.g., black–white, brush–broom).

Words may also be lexically related in ways that seem to be syntactically motivated. The words *sing* and *singing* are lexically related; the words *sing* and *song* are lexically related in ways important for syntax. Language learners, especially those in the early stages of learning, are likely to give syntagmatic responses and related forms of the same word. Meara (1978, 1982) has shown that language learners give more syntagmatic responses, more lexically related words, and more clang responses to words than do native speakers. This has led to the claim that word associations of foreign language learners are similar to those of child first language learners. This hypothesis is not well substantiated once we look at the associations of bilinguals or advanced language learners (see Singleton & Little, 1991, and Söderman, 1993, in the Research and Application section).

In semantic feature analysis, we noted that linguists were primarily interested in features that have consequences for grammar. Relational models do this by including a separate description of grammatical patterns (see the next section). However, they also highlight lexical relations among words (as in the *sing–song* examples) and semantic relations that work along with the grammar component. The semantic relations that are related to syntax include such relations as imperative, permission, causative, and minus-and-plus relations.

In Mel'čuk's system, Imper is the lexical relation imperative. We know what imperative means in terms of grammar. We are less aware, perhaps, of imperative as a semantic relation between words. The lexical relation of the words *care* and *watch out!* or between *quiet* and *shut up!* is one of imperative. As you can see, the Imper relation is not assigned like a feature to a lexical item; rather it identifies the relation between the words. Perm is the relation of permit or allow. The relation between *go* and *let* is one of permission. Caus is the lexical function of cause. The words *sit* and *set* are lexically related by Caus. That is, *set* relates as causing to *sit*.

Some relations have to do with quantity and quality. Quantity and quality are important in grammar because they determine forms used in comparatives and superlatives. In semantic relations, however, it is the relation between words that is important. Quantity and quality are shown by the relations Plus and Minus. *Grow* is a verb with a Plus relation to *joy* (e.g., "Her joy grew by leaps and bounds") and *drop* is a verb with a a Minus lexical relation to *temperature* (e.g., "The temperature dropped").

Many other relations would be needed to ensure the type of encyclopedic coverage that relational models hope to demonstrate. As researchers work on enumerating these, two problems emerge: the need to label the relations consistently and to identify correctly the total number of relations required. While each researcher is free to label relations as he or she wishes, some consensus is evolving on terminology. The number of relations also varies from description to description, and if there are a large number, then the enumeration is of little value for theory. (Remember that in semantic feature analysis, linguists concentrate on semantic markers, those with importance for grammar, because it would be impossible to identify all the features needed to distinguish the meanings of words.) In relational models, the claim is that only some small number of relations will be found. The question still holds: Will it be possible to find a small set that can account for the semantic connections among all words in a lexicon?

Practice 4.1

1. List your first four word associations for the following
   words: *book, piano, table, magazine, teeth, blackbird.*
   Identify as many relations as you can among each set of

four words. How many have a synonym relation? How many have an antonym relation? Because we have just discussed three semantic relations (converse, hyponym, and part–whole), your responses may have been biased by that discussion. How many of the words show these relations?

2. List a word with a converse relation for each of the following roles: *coach, speaker, host, author, prosecutor.* Identify the verb action that relates each pair of terms. Now translate these roles to another language. Are the associated converses the same across these languages?

3. *Doctor* and *patient* are converse roles because the doctor offers treatment and the patient receives treatment. *Doctor–nurse* is a pseudo-converse because, although the nurse offers the doctor assistance and the doctor receives the assistance from the nurse, both are really treating the patient. We could make up a scenario where *judge* and *jury* would be converses (e.g., the judge instructs the jury and the jury is instructed by the judge.) However, the judge and jury together judge the person accused of a crime. The first two members in each of these examples is a pair in relation to the third member. Can you think of other examples where this type of three-way relation holds?

4. What is the relation of *junk food* and *potato chips*? Of *ice skates* and *skates*? How does the relation differ from that of synonymy? List additional examples for this relation.

5. Iris et al. identified a part–whole schema where the relation implies the removability or divisibility within a segmented whole. Examples include "a slice of bread," "a piece of pie," "a handful of sand." In the first two cases, the part has a predetermined size and shape, but in the third it does not. List three additional examples of this type of part–whole relation. Can the same partition of the whole be found for these examples in another language?

6. Taxonomies carry all the information we described earlier with tree diagrams and graphs as field semantics. Examples of items related in this way include *meat* (*beef, pork*), *fruit* (*apples, oranges*), *vegetables* (*peas, beans*), all of which are subsets of *food.* Iris et al. assign such examples to the part–whole relation. Do you agree with this classification? Reread the section on the part–whole relation and Practice 4.1.5. What subgroupings would you use for all the examples given by Iris et al. for the part–whole relation? Justify your answer.

7. Channell (1990) believes that it is more important to teach language learners paradigmatic associations (words that are the same part of speech such as *pencil–pen, wash–soak, important–crucial*) than to offer syntagmatic associations such as *pencil–write, wash–clothes, soak–stains, important–date, crucial–point*). Do you agree? Justify your choice.

8. Meara (1990) and others have described the mental organization of L2 words as more phonologically organized. Learners give more clang responses (e.g., *farm–harm*) than native speakers. They also offer associations that show they mistook the stimulus word for a phonologically related word. English students studying French, in French–English word associations, might respond *animal* to the stimulus word *béton,* confusing *béton* with *bête.* Or they might respond *essayer* to *traire* (to milk) based on its similarity to English *try.* Meara also notes that learners give more syntagmatically related forms (*wash–clothes* type responses), and that their responses are more loosely organized (they give a wider range of responses than L1 speakers). Assuming this is true for beginning and intermediate students, how might you use such insights to prepare vocabulary materials for these learners? Which relations would you emphasize (grammar relations, sound-alike words, words loosely organized around a topic)? Beginning and intermediate learners also give synonyms, antonyms, converses, and so forth just as native speakers do. Would you therefore want to emphasize these more than the syntagmatic, clang, or loosely associated relations? Justify your answer.

Relational models

In the United States, relational models have gained importance as computer scientists have tried to find ways to help computers "understand" text. To do this, computers need to understand the overall "script" or "scenario" and the organization of text within that script. They also need to understand the semantic relation of words within the text. Computerized dictionaries already exist. The problem of how to make the dictionary one that will allow for automatic reading of relations of meanings in text, however, is immense.

It is not surprising that the most promising semantic analysis for computer scientists would be one that tries to work with relations among all words of the language rather than analytic methods that only use illustrative examples. The problem is finding a complete set of relations and a dictionary that uses such categories. Different researchers use different terms for the relations, and most make no claims about the completeness of the set of relations they use. Because it is the most complete, many computer scientists involved with natural language processing have adopted the relational models of language of Mel'čuk and Zholkovsky (1970, 1984) and Apresjan (1969), who regard the dictionary as the basic foundation of theoretical linguistics. For them, language *is* the lexicon, the inventory of its words and relations and ways of combining them. (Within this view, grammar is primarily a means of expressing generalities that arise from the lexicon, a convenient way of decreasing the bulk in the lexicon. The view of most American linguists is exactly the opposite; that is, the function of the lexicon is to support the grammar and reduce the length of lists of exceptions to grammar rules.) Mel'čuk, Zholkovsky, and Apresjan call the theory they work with the Meaning-Text Model (MTM) of language. The theory attempts, first, to cover relations among all the words of the language. Mel'čuk believes that this can be done with just fifty-two relations.

In Mel'čuk's model there are fifty-two different relations. Some are relations typically found in dictionary and thesaurus entries – synonyms, antonyms, and converses. A sample of Mel'čuk's relations is shown in Table 4.1. We have not included all fifty-two relations because some of them are lexical rather than semantic relations (e.g., *dog–doggy, song–sing, fear–fearfully*); such relations are covered in Part II of this book. Other relations include both semantic and syntactic information (e.g., the relation Labor is a relation which requires the entry to be a secondary object: Labor (*esteem*) = *hold*; i.e., "X holds Y in esteem"). Only relations that are clearly semantic in nature are included. The list is adapted from Frawley's (1988) discussion of relational models and metascience (a similar list with different examples appears in Evens et al. [1980, pp. 74–77]).

Although identification of relations is the first goal of the analysis, the MTM model goes beyond the exhaustive identification of relations to deal with the issue of choice among synonyms in particular contexts. The theory addresses differences in denotative and connotative meanings, in evaluative meanings, and in kinds of associations or in emphasis among synonyms. The MTM model also considers kinds of similarities that exist between synonyms (i.e., exact similarity or neutralization of differences in certain contexts), an issue of particular importance for language translation.

It is difficult to believe that only fifty-odd relations will be needed to provide all the information relevant to the semantic relations among words (other linguists working with relational models have proposed somewhat different numbers and types of relations). These theoreticians

TABLE 4.1 SAMPLE RELATIONS WITH EXAMPLES

A	typical adjective for a participant A(suspicion) = full of	Mult	a regular aggregate of Mult(paper) = ream
Ant	antonym (exact or near) Ant(happy) = sad	Nocer	to harm, injure, or impair Nocer(access) = cut off
Bon	standard praise for entry Bon(advice) = sound	Obstru	to function with difficulty Obstr(justice) = obstruct
Centr	center of Centr(city) = heart	Perm	permit or allow Perm(go) = let
Contr	nonantonymic contrast Contr(chair) = table	Plus	more of Plus(distress) = grow
Conv	conversive Conv(buy) = sell	Pos	positive attributes of participant Pos(game) = skilled
Culm	culmination of Culm(ability) = peak	Propt	preposition for "because of"
Degrad	degradation of Degrad(marriage) = fall apart	Prox	Propt(greed) = out of to be on the verge of Prox(disaster) = on the
Epit	standard epithet (representing part of entry) Epit(body) = physique	Qual	brink of highly probable qualities of participant
Excess	excessive function of Excess(eyelid) = flutter	S	Qual(thief) = sneaky typical noun for a numbered entry
Fact	verb meaning "the realization of," Fact(suspicion) = confirm		S1(crime) = robber, S2(crime) = victim
Figur	metaphor of the entry Figur(love) = fire	Sinstru	typical instrument
Fin	stopping by Fin(fly) = land	Sloc Smed	typical location typical means
Gener	generic word Gener(blue) = color	Smod Sres	typical mode typical result
Germ	the core of Germ(problem) = crux	Sing	Sloc(house) = yard one instance of
Imper	the command associated with Imper(care) = Watch out!	Son	Sing(paper) = sheet to emit a typical sound Son(frog) = croak
Incept	the beginning of Incep(fly) = take off	Sympt	to be a physical symptom of
Liqu	the elimination of Liqu(group) = disband	Syn	Sympt(fire) = smoke synonym or near synonym Syn(happy) = glad
Magn	intensity Magn(hatred) = deep	Ver	true, correct, or proper Ver(ruling) = fair
Minus	less of Minus(wind) = slacken		

Source: Adapted from Frawley, 1988, pp. 364–368; used with permission.

are developing the model in a practical way, through the development of special dictionaries.

Practice 4.2

1. Identify the name of the relation – Anti, Minus, Pls, Conv, Syn, Perm, Sres – between each pair of lexical items.

temperature	drop
wax	wane
notice	announcement
excuse	leave
fire	ashes
teach	learn

2. Give an additional example for each of the following relations between lexical items. Which of the relations do you think are important for grammar and which for other semantic categories?

   A (*typical adjective*) suspicion–full of
   Bon (*standard praise for word*) advice–sound
   Centr (*center of*) city–heart
   Excess (*excess functioning of item*) eyelid–flutter
   Incep (*the beginning of*) fly–take off
   Fin (*the end or stopping of*) fly–land
   Mult (*regular aggregate of item*) paper–ream
   Prox (*to be on the verge of*) war–on the brink of
   S (*typical noun for participant*) crime–victim, burglar
   Son (*to emit a typical sound*) bird–tweet

3. Select a paragraph from a reading in one of your language teaching textbooks. Circle three words in the paragraph and identify the relation between each word and another word in the paragraph or another word in the dictionary (that applies to the meaning of the word in the text). If you were asked by a student to supply a meaning for each of these three words, how might your definitions make these relations explicit?

4. Now list three different words from the same reading and give a possible synonym. Are the meanings exactly the same or are there certain contexts where only one of the pair would be acceptable? What differences can you identify in terms of denotation and connotation for the terms? How important would these differences in denotation and connotation be if you were to translate this passage into

another language that you know? In your own words, explain why it is important that the MTM theory include denotation and connotation information for synonyms.

5. Practice 4.1.8 focused on the types of relations you would emphasize if you were preparing vocabulary materials for beginning or intermediate students. Review the list of relations given in this section and identify those relations which you would include in such teaching materials. Justify your selection.

6. Some relational semanticists divide relations into minor and major groups. The major groups include taxonomy (hyponomy), modification, synonymy, antonymy, and grading. These semanticists found that the part–whole, cause, and space and location relations were used somewhat less in their data. Does this information change or reinforce your view of which relations should be included in instruction?

Relational models in dictionaries

Piotrowski (1990) cites the *English–Russian Synonym Dictionary* (Rozenman et al., 1980) as a beginning attempt to develop and test the MTM theory of lexical relations. The dictionary includes an appendix that discusses theoretical issues within the MTM framework. It has 400 items drawn from *Webster's New Dictionary of Synonyms,* including only abstract words – those that have to do with processes, states, properties, situations, and activities. Thus, the focus is on verbs and adjectives which are, perhaps, the most difficult to define – a good test for the model. The synonyms are presented in groups, and each group is discussed in five sections: definition, meaning, collocations, grammar, and illustration. A typical entry might be four pages in length.

The definition section includes only the meaning that is shared by all the synonyms in the group. This meaning is called the semantic invariant. (Because this is a bilingual dictionary, the definition is followed by a list of Russian equivalents so that it is possible to do a rough comparison of synonym groups in the two languages.)

Next, the similarities and differences in meanings of particular synonyms are given in terms of semantic relations. The differences and similarities follow the theory by answering the question of whether there are differences in (a) denotation meanings, (b) evaluative meanings, (c) kinds of associations or connotations, and (d) in emphasis, and what kinds of similarities (exact similarity or neutralization of differences in certain contexts) exist between the synonyms.

Third, the kinds of common groupings, in phrases or sentences, (collocations) are shown for each of the words. This is followed by a discussions of similarities and differences among the synonyms regarding the grammatical constructions for each. Illustrations are also included.

Piotrowski (1990) includes a more detailed description of this dictionary and its relation to theory; he also evaluates several other attempts to implement relational models in practical dictionaries of Russian and English. For further information on the model and its use in lexicography, refer to his work as well as to Mel'čuk and Zholkovsky (1984).

Practice 4.3

1. Much relational information is already present in most dictionaries and need only be made explicit. *Promise* and *pledge* may be listed as synonyms, *hot* and *cold* as antonyms. Hyponyms appear in definitions with words such as "a kind of" ("a cat is a [kind of] mammal"). A causal relation is shown in a definition such as "to send means to cause to go." Evens (1988), who uses slightly different relation terms than Mel'čuk, suggests that these relations can be abbreviated very simply in word–relation–word triplets such as

promise	SYN	pledge
hot	ANTI	cold
lion	TAX(onomy)	mammal
to send	CAUSE	to go
cygnet	CHILD	swan
petal	PART	flower
Monday	SEQUENCE	Tuesday

(Data source: Evens, 1988, p. 3)

Select three definitions from a dictionary and list the relations in triplets following Evens's example.
2. The verb *make* has so many meanings that it is difficult to see how it might be defined independent of the words that surround it. Piotrowski (1990) gives an MTM treatment to this verb by noting first its "independent" meanings: "to make tables (bricks, wine, machines, dinner, breakfast)" and "to make a list (a note, notes, a report, a law, one's will)." This is followed by meanings wholly dependent on the words with which it collocates. Some of these are lexical – "to make money (profit, a livelihood, a living)," "to make friends (enemies, an ally of somebody)" – whereas others are more grammar-bound – "to make somebody do

something," "to make oneself understand." Next, partial loss of lexical meaning is shown (e.g., "Two and two make four," "Will you make one of our party?" "to make a jump, move, start"). This is followed by phrasal verbs (e.g., "make do with") and idioms ("make up your mind"). Using *make* as an example, discuss what advantages the MTM approach would have in a dictionary for language learners or language translators.

3. Meara (1990), in an article on how to help learners move passive vocabulary to active status, uses graphs to show the relations among items. He notes that associations are sometimes unidirectional. For example, *cabbage* → *white, green,* but not *white, green* → *cabbage.* Such graphs might be useful in showing why some words are harder for learners to retrieve than others. How might a relational dictionary reveal such information (as well as other information on relations) without becoming too cumbersome for learners to use?

4. The words "explanatory combinatorial" in the title of a dictionary implies that the dictionary uses relational theory. It is explanatory in that it explains all the relations between all the words in any given semantic field. It is combinatory because it also gives all the acceptable word combinations and information on syntactic patterns. Could any of your dictionaries qualify as an explanatory combinatorial dictionary? If not, what would need to be changed to make it approach these two aspects of such dictionaries?

Applying relational models

Although most of the work on relational models has been done in eastern Europe or in Montreal (where Mel'čuk is located), there are lexicographers and cognitive psychologists in the United States who have adopted many of Mel'čuk and Apresjan's methods in order to show the semantic relations between words. This group of relational semanticists is often identified as working with semantic networks, with natural language processing in computer science, or with relational lexicography. We will discuss their application of semantic relations in more detail in Chapter 6.

Relational semanticists are bridge builders; that is, they are open to using research done within other semantic models. For example, they often incorporate insights of prototype theory and semantic feature analysis in their work. They do this by using the notion of intension and extension in model building. Extension is the things which a term names. The extension of the term *tree* would include individual trees such as elm, oak, pine, and so forth. The term *oak* would encompass California live oak and black oak among others. Intension is the set of attributes or features that characterize the term. The intension of *tree* would include root, trunk, branch, twig, leaf, and so forth. Still, individual researchers may emphasize the relations that are used for one type over the other. Computer scientists, for example, seem to work primarily with extension relations, and linguists often emphasize intension relations.

There are also linguists and cognitive psychologists who have used insights from relational models to interpret their research. For example, Markowitz (1988) asked adults to sort cards showing pictures of various birds, pieces of furniture, clothing, and so on, into categories – a typical prototype semantics task. She then analyzed the comments people made as they carried out the sorting task. Markowitz first compared her results with those of Rosch, Labov, and others, showing that the perceptual shape/size dimension was important in determining whether or not an example fit into a stack. If a kitchen utensil became too large, it was put into an appliance stack; if tools became too large, they were put into a machine stack; if birds were very small (e.g., hummingbirds), they were grouped with insects; and small trees were separated into a bushes group.

Markowitz, however, found that people sorted the pictures into groups according to other criteria as well. Some people named the eagle as the most birdlike of the bird pictures because it was "so American." Gourmet cooks named *stove* as the best example of a kitchen utensil, while others placed it in appliance or furniture stacks. Some objects were related to the people associated with them. For example, a broom was not a good example of a kitchen utensil because janitors use them; chess was not a good example of sport because older people play it, and tape measures were not good tools because women use them for sewing. (Obviously these participants had not had much experience with female carpenters, electricians, or plumbers.)

Markowitz applied a relational model of the lexicon in classifying the types of dimensions in her data set. The relation she found most important in decision making was that of function (e.g., "a bulletproof vest isn't clothing because it's to stop bullets"). Size and shape were important, but so was the part–whole relation (e.g., "a snake isn't a good example of an animal because it has no legs"; "a turtle isn't a good animal because it has a shell"). The locative relation also was important ("eyes are not good examples of body parts because they are part of your face"). The relational analysis allowed Markowitz to categorize and explain the comments of participants in this study.

Iris (1984) also pointed out that knowledge of local events and social or cultural factors should be considered when looking at the development of types of relations in child language. She asked Navajo children to talk (in Navajo) about a set of forty picture cards of different animals. They named the animals, described them, and sorted the cards into groups that "go together," giving a rationale for the sorting. Although previous studies had shown that adults used the hyponym relation in such tasks, the children did not. Rather, they talked about the animals in terms of actions (e.g., "it eats hay, it bucks, it kicks, it runs, it sings"), locations (e.g., its home, habitat), and physical properties. In addition, they talked about possession (things the animal has), communality (something the animal does with others, as "the sheep go around together"), emotions (e.g., "the bull gets mad"), and functions (e.g., "horses are used to rope a bull"). After examining the data from individual children in detail, Iris suggests that, instead of assuming that as children mature their definitions become more complex, we consider that as children mature they move toward greater consistency in giving definition and a better integration of information across items within a lexical domain.

Iris used the relational model to investigate lexical organization of monolingual children. Although no one has done so to our knowledge, applying relational models to the data would give new life to research on bilingual word associations. Word association research has a long history in psychology, and it has been an area of interest in bilingualism where researchers wish to understand how the lexicon of two languages might be represented in the brain. Most of these studies use the storage metaphor. One expectation in this research is that if words in two languages for the same concept are stored together, then all the data about the concept would also be shared by both languages. We would expect the learner to give similar word associations for a given stimulus in each language. Kolers (1963) had university students who were native speakers of Thai, German, and Spanish carry out a word association task under four conditions: first language associations to first language stimuli; English associations to English stimuli; first language associations to English stimuli; and English associations to first language stimuli. Sample responses for the Spanish speakers included:

L1–L1		*English–English*	
mesa	silla	table	dish
muchacho	hombre	boy	girl
rey	reina	king	queen
casa	madre	house	window

L1–English		*English–L1*	
mesa	chair	table	silla
muchacho	trousers	boy	niña
rey	queen	king	reina
casa	mother	house	blanco

The bilingual students in this study gave very similar word associations to those of native speakers as long as the stimulus word was a concrete noun and in particular if the object could be handled and manipulated as well. They gave fewer similar associations when the stimulus word was abstract or emotion-laden. Politzer (1978) also found that Americans studying French gave word associations similar to those of native speakers but also gave syntagmatic and clang responses to some words.

If we think about word association responses in terms of relations (rather than in terms of whether or not the words from each language are stored together with the concept), we find that bilinguals do not simply give the translation in the opposite language. Rather, the relations are often those of nonantonymic contrast, hyponyms, or part–whole. Such findings have led to speculation as to whether translations are synonyms or identical (i.e., the same concept with different forms).

We mentioned earlier that the MacLeod (1976) study showed that greater savings of meanings occur in tests of recall in the hyponym relation than in the synonym relation. Turning to bilinguals, MacLeod investigated whether the same results would occur for direct translations of items. He asked French–English bilinguals to learn a list of 20 number–word combinations. Five weeks later they were asked to recall the word in response to the number. All the missed items were then relearned under four conditions. The word paired with the number was either (1) the same word as before in the same language, (2) a different word in the same language, (3) the same word in the other language, or (4) a different word in the other language. The participants were then asked to count backward by threes from 100, and then were retested. The findings showed, not surprisingly, that savings occurred under condition 1: the same word in the same language. However, the same amount of savings was shown for condition 3: the same word in the other language. This led MacLeod to view the two words for the same concept as identical rather than as synonymous.

There are a wealth of studies on bilingual word association, studies which have been carried out to address a wide array of research questions. Much of this literature might now be reviewed with the question of how it connects to work on relational models of semantics.

Practice 4.4

1. In Markowitz's study, some people put all pictures of ugly insects in one group and all pretty ones in another. Some people separated cultivated flowers (such as roses) from wildflowers. What dimension(s) would cover this card sort? Do you think your dimension(s) are important in determining the most prototypic instance of most objects?

2. Markowitz's study is especially interesting because it uses both numerical data and qualitative data. As participants sorted cards into groups, they were asked to explain the stacks they made, as well as their ratings of how good an example each item in the stack was. Because the items, the procedure, and the analysis are all very clear, this might be a good candidate for a replication study using participants from another language group. By doing the replication and publishing the results, you may also contribute to work on relational models of the lexicon.

3. Parker (1985) reported on a pilot observation of two teachers giving definitions during reading lessons to third-grade classes that consisted of many Chinese and Hispanic students. The following extended definition sequence links many words to the word *spring*. List the relations you discover to the word *spring* in the data. How useful do you think relational models would be in analysis of classroom data?

T: What's a spring, Tessa. I explained it to you. Just a few minutes ago.

Tessa: It's a um um puddle of water. That's underneath the ground. That um . . . it is . . . that is fresh.

T: It's fresh water that you can drink. It's a small . . . amount of water. It's not like a big lake or something. Okay. And you can for –

Tessa: The dirt's in the water. Then it's yukky.

T: Well, the dirt is heavier than the water so it's gonna settle to the bottom of the water, and if you scoop off scoop off the top, you're gonna get clean water. Because dirt is heavy. So it's not gonna stay on the top.

Tessa: Well how big is it?

T: It could be . . . it could be big enough to let his family live there for a long time, like up in xxx my husband's family has a spring. There's a lot of water. Like for one person. But you couldn't feed a whole city with it . . . very long. Okay? They . . . It it's just underground water. Sometimes it's a large amount. Sometimes it's not.

Tessa: Is it about this big or so? (*uses arms to show size*)

T: That's why he was saying, he – Well, it could be. Well, it could only be (*circles arms for dimensions*) On the top it could only look like this big, but it can

be so deep, that it could have so much water in it,
that you could use it for a long time.

S: It doesn't look deep but it is.

T: Right. And that's what they did in the desert. When
the springs dried up, and they couldn't get any
more water, they had to move on. Okay? That's
why Abu never had a home.

Tessa: Well why did Abu start digging in that other place.

T: Well that's further along. We'll find out.

(Parker, 1985)

4. In both the Markowitz and Iris studies discussed in this
   section, the authors emphasize that social and cultural
   knowledge must be considered when we carry out research on both acquisition and use of relations. For example, Iris points out that a Navajo man used many relations
   in talking about certain animals, but when talking about
   cow, bull, horse, and donkey, the items were all linked together using the rodeo activities of roping, kicking, and
   bucking. The Navajo word for man, *hastiin,* was linked to
   these animals by the activities of riding, roping, and clown-
   ing that are typically carried out at the rodeo. Given this
   cultural context, the responses and types of relations were
   much more consistent for these animals. Provide an example of a context that would shape the types of responses
   and relations for yourself or for your language students.

5. If we analyze a semantic field, we organize the items
   within the domain in some logical way. For example, the
   field of animals might be organized by biological species.
   However, it might also be classified in terms of pets, live-
   stock, and other animals. Or it might be classified according to whether the animal was bovine (eats grass), canine,
   or feline. Consider how these terms would be handled in
   relational models of semantics. What are the advantages
   or disadvantages of each method for data analysis? What
   advantages or disadvantages do you see for application to
   teaching?

There are many different relational models, all of which identify lexical
relations (but disagree on the number of relations). The models are proposed primarily by lexicographers working with cognitive scientists in an
attempt to build computerized natural language processing systems.

Lexicographers have long criticized work in semantics as being illustrative; that is, it describes only a few examples (such as *bachelor*). They

believe that semantic theories must be encyclopedic (i.e., coverage similar to that of a dictionary and a thesaurus). They believe that relational models are a step in the right direction. Relational models of the lexicon are, indeed, important if computer models of scripts are ever to move beyond limited examples to more encyclopedic coverage. We will return to this topic in Chapter 7.

Research and application

1. Singleton and Little (1991) used a C-test to collect data from learners of French and German. (A C-test is similar to a cloze test, where students supply words that have been deleted from a text.) In Singleton and Little's C-test, students restored words from the text where only part of the word was deleted. The French passage began: *Aujourd'hui la communication entre la jeunesse et le monde des adultes est devenue presque impossible. Les adu_____ s'efforcent d_____ se mon_____ tolérants, ma_____ les po_____ sont bri_____*. Singleton and Little then analyzed the responses of the students against the background of word association studies (especially Meara and Söderman's work on paradigmatic and clang responses). They found that when students made errors, the errors were predominantly semantically related to the missing word. Some interesting creations occurred. For example, in a slot that should have been filled in with *auteur* (author), a learner used *autrice* assuming probably that there should be a feminine form for author and linking the form *auteur* to like forms (*acteur–actrice; médiateur–médiatrice*). After reading the article, construct a C-test for another language group. Administer the test to five people who are learning the language. Instead of linking your analysis to that of syntagmatic vs. paradigmatic responses, analyze the responses using a relational analysis.

2. Söderman (1993) reports on the most comprehensive word association tests of foreign language learners based on responses written by Finnish students at different levels of English proficiency (seventh grade, high school, university, and highly proficient language majors) to the Kent-Rosanoff word association list. Her data challenge the assumption that a shift in types of responses is just a matter of age and language proficiency. To study this further, she compared the responses of very proficient learners of English and native speakers on very frequent and relatively infrequent words. Both groups made more syntagmatic responses to infrequent items. Söderman suggests this may be because it is often difficult to think of a synonym or antonym for less frequent words. If you are interested in research on the bilingual lexicon, this study is es-

sential. As you go through the experiments, consider how the study might be recast in light of relational models of the lexicon.

3. Iris et al. (1988) comment on the acquisition of part–whole relations by children. The early acquisition of spatial expressions reflect the claim that all relations are originally derived from physical knowledge of the world. These part–whole relations are then extended to nonphysical examples. Iris et al. claim the child gradually expands but does not necessarily replace the spatial with class, superordinate, and taxonomic structures. The earlier relations are retained to be used when needed. Part–whole is then not one relation but a whole family of overlapping relations. Iris et al. propose four general part–whole schemata: functional, segmented, collections and members, and sets and subsets. Other lexicographers have claimed that there are more than four types. Chaffin and Herrmann (1988) claim there are at least six. Read each of these articles and decide how developmental data (or data from second language learners) might support each claim.

4. In Practice 1.2.4, we noted the use of *nicht* rather than an antonym in the data of a German learner. Duff has analyzed the data of an adult learner of Chinese who also used negation but in a slightly different manner. In this case, the learner did not know the term *near here* or *nearby* and said: "Ta zhu zai nar. Bu yuan bu yuan." (She lives there. Not far not far.) The native speaker then asked if the person lives at school, to which the learner replied, "Bu shi xue xiao. Ta- ta de fang jian bu yuan." (It's not school. Her- her room is not far.) Using these examples, show how one might use relational models in the analysis of the circumlocutions or other strategies that learners use when they do not know or cannot recall a lexical item.

5. Sternberg and Powell (1983) asked high school students to read passages that contained unknown words and then to write sentences using the words. Eight types of context cues that occurred in the passages seemed to influence the students' ability to write definitions. These included time, space, description of physical properties, functions, worth or affect, cause, class membership, and equivalence. Determine the relation for each of these eight types of cues and then reinterpret the study in terms of relational models. You might wish to replicate the study with your international students, relating your findings to this study and to relational models of semantics.

6. Ilson and Mel'čuk (1989) discuss the network of relations among the various senses of the concept BAKE. They note that BAKE has three senses: (1) dry heat in cooking, (2) dry heat making something hard, and (3) dry heat as it affects people. Example sen-

tences include "Potatoes bake well." "John baked the potatoes." "The rolls baked quickly." "John baked the pot in the kiln." "This oven bakes excellent bread." "The mud on the shore baked hard." "Boston was baking in a heat wave." Semantic relations are given to illustrate each of the senses for BAKE and illustrations are given of other expressions (baked Alaska, baked beans, sun-baked) that also need to be treated if the coverage is to be encyclopedic (for their explanatory combinatorial dictionary). Compare and contrast this analysis with the discussion of cooking terms in semantic field analysis in Chapter 2.

7. Riegel (1970) used a relational approach to study changes in definitions of children as they mature and of those of the elderly. In general, he found an increased use of multiple relations, which he believes mark cognitive reorganization throughout life. If you are interested in ontological and gerontological issues, read this volume. Do you agree with Riegel's categorization of relations into four groups? How might you apply this study to your own research on vocabulary acquisition and attrition?

8. Casagrande and Hale (1967), as part of a study in dialect variation, collected folk definitions from one speaker of Papago (an American Indian language) for 800 terms. The definitions were then reduced so that a definition of the Papago word for wolf was "they are like coyotes, but big." The definition includes two relations – comparison (like coyotes) and attribute (big). The types of relations used were then listed by frequency (along with English glosses of the definitions). Finally, the types of relations used by this individual were compared with those that appear in traditional English word association lists. Werner, Manning, and Begishe (1983) and Iris (1984) follow a similar method looking for relations in the definitions given by Navajo speakers. How might you use this methodology to carry out a similar study? If you are interested in the differences in contrasts between the types of relations used to organize information in different languages, you could use the methodology, first collecting folk definitions in one language and then in the other. If you decide to develop this topic, be aware that relational semanticists have cautioned that more precision is needed in identifying relations within folk definitions (and that working from the English glosses can lead one into error). As you develop your research plan, decide which set of relations (Mel'čuk's or others) you will use and be sure that you can identify each in a consistent manner.

5 Semantics of figurative language

Pervasiveness of figurative language

As shown in the previous chapters, linguists have searched for ways of describing the semantic structure of words and how they relate or refer to concepts or to semantic fields. These descriptions were evaluated in terms of how well a taxonomy distinguished related terms in a semantic field. Their research demonstrates quite clearly that referential semantics is an important field of inquiry. However, only since the late 1970s and early 1980s have we begun again to realize how important and pervasive figurative language is. Metaphorical processes are as fundamental as literal reference in semantics.

In Chapter 4, we noted that relational models treat figurative language as just one of more than fifty semantic relations. Taxonomies, as we have already seen, can be useful but, in this case, they hide the pervasive nature of metaphor as a cognitive and social *semantic process*.

We will return to taxonomic descriptions, but first, to show what we mean by the pervasive nature of metaphor, consider some ordinary, everyday language examples from Lakoff and Johnson's (1980) *Metaphors We Live By*. In this seminal work, Lakoff and Johnson note that we often talk about abstract concepts using the terms for more concrete concepts. We use terms from a concrete *source* field to talk about an abstract *target* field. For example, IDEA is an abstract concept. It is difficult to give a precise definition of the word *idea*. So, we turn to other source fields. We may talk about ideas as though they were plants, food, or people:

Source → *Target*
Plants → Ideas
    Ideas are planted
    even in a barren mind
    ideas grow from seeds
    ideas bud, flower, or die on the vine
Food → Ideas
    cook up an idea
    idea smells fishy
    stew over an idea
    swallow an idea
    a half-baked idea

People → Ideas
    idea is someone's brainchild
    idea still in its infancy
    idea needs to mature; what an adolescent idea!
    the idea died but was resurrected

As you have noticed, we do not select only one source and use it metaphorically in talking about the target. We often use multiple layers of metaphor. Several sources may be used for one target concept:

Source → *Target*
Building → Argument
    lay a foundation
    build the argument brick by brick
    provide a scaffolding for our side
War → Argument
    shoot holes in my argument
    take aim at a premise
    attack an argument or point of view

A second basic point established by Lakoff and Johnson is that metaphor is common and pervasive not just in English but in all languages and across all dialects and that it appears in literary as well as everyday language. One of the basic metaphors in Western societies is PEOPLE are MACHINES. Lakoff and Turner (1989) call our attention to its use in poetry:

> At the violet hour, when the eyes and back
> Turn upward from the desk, when the human engine waits
> Like a taxi throbbing waiting.
> (T. S. Eliot, "The Waste Land")

The same metaphor occurs in everyday language. In a note, for example, a friend wrote, "I'm running out of steam. I think my gears are stuck." Lakoff gives an example in which the metaphor works both ways: "The computer is punishing me by wiping out my buffer." Here the machine is a person who punishes and the person is a machine containing a buffer.

The issue of the system behind such metaphors will be discussed in detail later, but before we do that, we want to review the more classical method of identifying and classifying types of figurative language.

Practice 5.1

1. Look at each of the three source-to-target metaphors for IDEA. Add as many examples to the list as you can. Then

search for similar terms in a language you are learning or teaching. How universal are these particular metaphors (IDEAS are PLANTS, IDEAS are FOOD, IDEAS are PEOPLE)?

2. Are the metaphors reversible? Can we talk about plants as ideas, food as ideas, and people as ideas? In the PEOPLE are MACHINES metaphor, we noted that it is possible to reverse the metaphor to MACHINES are PEOPLE (i.e., machines can be personified). Do you believe the source-to-target relation is more often unidirectional? Give examples to support your opinion.

3. Here are some examples of metaphor from political campaign rhetoric. Everyday metaphor: "A much better *shot* at *carry*ing the state." Original metaphor: "The White House isn't a Waffle House." Is it possible to determine the source and target fields for each? In these examples, is metaphor used to talk about abstract concepts? If not, why is metaphor employed?

Categorizing figurative language

Traditionally, figurative language has been described in terms of categories: simile, metaphor, allusion, personification, and so forth. We will look at each of these categories briefly.

If one turns to traditional treatments of figurative language, two major categories stand out: *simile* and *metaphor*. When we use a simile we call attention to the fact that we are asking the listener or reader to consider X as similar to Y. We do this with the phrase "X is like a Y." We make the comparison explicit by asking that there be a transfer of characteristics of Y to X. We find many examples of simile in literature, poetry, and everyday talk. In his poem "A Dream Deferred," Langston Hughes wrote

> What happens to a dream deferred?
> Does it dry up like a raisin in the sun?

and we visualize a strong, vital dream dying and drying up into a shriveled, ugly raisin. Or consider Robert Burns's poem, "O, my luve is like a red, red rose," and we transfer the characteristics of a red, red rose to a woman. When we read Shapespeare's satiric sonnet 130, "My mistress' eyes are nothing like the sun," we again transfer characteristics from a source field to a target field.

We find similes in everyday talk, too.

This heat! It's like the Fourth of July!
The noise is like a waterfall. How could it be just a flood?

In contrast to simile, metaphor does not say that something is like a source field; it uses the source field to define the target. Emily Dickinson writes "Hope is a thing with feathers that perches in the soul." Here the distinction between *is like* and *is* appears marginal. However, when Carl Sandburg writes, "The fog comes on little cat feet. It sits looking over harbor and city on silent haunches and then moves on," the metaphor is clear. Fog *is* a cat; it is not just like a cat.

In poetry, we are aware that similes and metaphors are being used. Yet, we may be unaware of the pervasive nature of simile and metaphor in everyday talk.

Two additional terms, *synecdoche* and *metonymy,* describe different categories (though, perhaps, not different processes) of figurative language. *Synecdoche* covers those cases where we use a part for a whole or the whole to talk about the part. *Metonymy* is the category where something closely connected (but not a part) is used to refer to the whole. Thus, in synecdoche, "ten sails" may be used to refer to ten ships in describing a sailboat race ("Ten sails can be seen rounding the buoy"), or "gray beards" might be used to refer to old men ("We need some gray beards to help us out"). Examples of metonymy include "the crown" to refer to a queen, "the bench" for a judge, or "the balcony" for the people in the balcony of a theater. Another delightful example reported is "The ham sandwich is a lousy tipper." The ham sandwich is not part of the person who ordered it but is related to him, a clear case of metonymy. Lakoff and Turner (1989) use a slightly different categorization: in metaphor, a "whole schematic structure is mapped onto another whole schematic structure." Metonymy, for Lakoff and Turner, has only one conceptual domain and two things belong to it. So part–whole relations are metonymy. Examples from Lakoff and Turner of part for whole include "We need some new blood in the organization" and "Mrs. Grundy frowns on blue jeans." They also consider *face* for person ("We need some new faces around here") and object for user ("The buses are on strike") as examples of metonymy. In Lakoff and Turner, no distinction is drawn between synecdoche and metonymy.

Personification is another category of figurative language. We talk about objects as though they were people, asking the listener to assign the qualities of humanness to objects. For example, we talk about the health of our relationships as though relationships could take on the characteristics of people ("a healthy/sick/tired affair"). Newspapers, books, and other texts are commonly personified; they can talk or perform other actions just like people ("the paper said," "books tell us," "the experiment shows us"). Personification is so common that we are scarcely aware of how powerful a process it is.

High school literature classes learn the three As, a mnemonic device to remember the terms antithesis, allusion, and apostrophe. In each of these, we illustrate a concept by referring to something or someone else. Apostrophe allows us to address inanimate things or historical personages as though they were alive. Edna St. Vincent Millay provides us with an example when she begins a poem, "Oh world, I cannot hold thee close enough." Allusion allows us to refer to persons, places, or events (real or imagined) to illustrate or add to a statement. A friend on a whale-watching trip alluded to the poet Robert Frost, saying "and whales to see before we sleep," and a retired friend alluded to Tennyson's "to rust unburnished, not to shine in use," saying old folks need to "shine in use, not to rust unburnished on the shelf." By doing this, we ask our listeners or readers to bring knowledge from the source and apply it to our target point. Sometimes the allusions are a bit obscure. For example, the news commentator Daniel Shorr once described the inaction of our government in meetings with NATO and the UN as reports from the Dithering Heights. The allusion to Wuthering Heights seems obscure and not particularly apt though it has a nice ring. Antithesis allows us to connect drastically opposing ideas. The connection is usually in opposing phrases like "You're coming, I'm going." The classic example is "Give me liberty or give me death!"

If you consult a source for a list of literary devices you may find other methods mentioned which also connect a source field to a target field. Some other strategies include irony (e.g., "He's a real winner" said of a klutz) and oxymoron (e.g., a "fun run" is an oxymoron for anyone who hates running). Also listed are understatement (e.g., "a trifle cold" said of a 5-below-zero-degree cold front) and hyperbole ("a sea of despair"). Although antithesis connects drastically opposing ideas, paradox opposes conflicting sources. For example, the snake is a symbol almost universally associated with the sky and celestial phenomena. In North American mythology it is the symbol for rainbows, lightning, and rain; water is the source of life. But, paradoxically, it is also the symbol of the underworld, darkness, and death.

The identification and listing of categories of figurative language may be useful, for when we read research about figurative language, we need to know which types of metaphor are included under the umbrella term. Nevertheless, with metaphoric language, whatever the type, we utilize the same underlying process: the speaker or reader applies some aspect or similarity from a source in order to talk or write about a target.

Practice 5.2

1. Nash (1985) in his book on linguistics and humor, gives one formula for jokes: *X* is like *Y*. "Living in Pearblossom *is like* watching a plank warp." Is this a simile or a metaphor?

How many jokes can you think of that fit this formula? Are any of them funny if you change the form to a metaphor?

2. Ragevsky (1979) does not separate metonymy and synedoche. Instead, metonymy is divided into six types. Add an example to each of Ragevsky's.

   a. sign for signified thing: grey beard
   b. instrument for agent: best pens of the day
   c. container for thing contained: drank a cup
   d. name of organs: play by ear, ready tongue
   e. whole or genus for part or species: the poor creature that is man.

   We would expect hyperbole to run rampant (yes, that is a metaphor) in advertising. However, Ragevsky gives us examples ("a thousand and one cares," "haven't seen you for ages," "flood of tears," "millions of reasons," "world of effort," and even "skyscraper") that occur in everyday talk. Collect examples of hyperbole. In what circumstances are they used? Do you use them?

3. Advertising is full of oxymorons such as "genuine imitation leather" and "real manufactured gemstones." "Free gifts" offered in promotions are seldom free. Government is also guilty of confusing us with terms like "value added tax." No value is added by the tax; in fact, the value of the item once the tax is paid is less, so the tax should be called a *value subtracted tax*. Collect your own examples of oxymorons. In one sense, such oxymorons are humorous, but they could also be harmful. Are your examples harmless or harmful?

4. A favorite example of paradox is the biblical passage from Ecclesiastes 3:7–8.

   a time to rend, and a time to sew . . .
   a time to love, and a time to hate
   a time of war, and a time of peace.

   In this case, is it clear which is source and which is target? Or is the entire passage a source which is to be applied to an overall target?

5. In the Navajo belief system, many of the powers, with the possible exception of Changing Woman, are both good and bad. Is the paradox relation common in the belief systems of many cultures? Give examples if you can. If paradox is important in belief systems, what might this say about the role of figurative language in human thought?

91

6. There are many types of correspondence used in analogies. Supply the missing member in the second set.

branch: tree	→	page: _____ (component: object)
tree: forest	→	book: _____ (member: collection)
slice: cake	→	piece: _____ (portion: mass)
aluminum: airplane	→	wood: _____ (stuff: object)
paying: shopping	→	chewing: _____ (feature: activity)
Los Angeles: California	→	Cairo: _____ (place: area)
adolescence: growing up	→	memorization: _____ (phase: process)

We can use such analogies, asking listeners or readers to apply the characteristics of a source to a target. So we might refer to a search for a book in the library as looking through a forest in hope of finding one special leaf. In forming such analogies, we may employ synecdoche, metonymy, or even personification. Give an example of your own for each of the analogies listed. Then use each in a figurative way by applying it to a target.

7. What would you think if, in an article on the acquisition of metaphor by second language learners, all the examples of metaphor happened to be personification? If you were designing a special research "caboose" for a proficiency exam, what range of types of metaphor would you want to include in order to feel confident that the results could speak to the issue of learners' comprehension of all types of figurative language?

Metaphor as a universal process

In the remainder of this chapter, we use the term *metaphor* to refer to the process of applying or using a source to talk about a target. The identification is not through ordinary, literal reference but rather via this transfer of meaning from one area to another.

The cognitive psychologist H. Clark (1973) noted that we talk about many things in a less than literal way. For example, we talk about understanding as though it were a visual phenomenon ("oh, I see, I see!"). We use directional prepositions *up* and *down* to talk about how we feel ("I'm feeling up." "That lifts my spirits." "He's really down."). In his research, Clark found that many of our ordinary ways of talking about our experience relate to our human perceptual system and our experiences with the real world. This is quite clear in the many visual metaphors in the English language.

To explain the *up–down* metaphors, Clark related their use to the three physical reference planes and three associated directions. The normal encounter in conversations is face to face. Our eyes, ears, and feet all point to the front. The first of the three physical reference planes, when we are standing, is ground level. Everything that is aboveground and seen is up and positive. Things unseen, down, belowground are negative. This use of *up* and *down* as positive and negative in value is then applied to a variety of targets. We talk about our conscious and unconscious states as up and down (e.g., "wake up" vs. "fall asleep"). When we talk about control, we use up and down for being subject to control (e.g., we are "held down" or we "rise to the occasion"). Status, too, is related to whether one is up or down ("high on the ladder" vs. "fall from office," "low man on the totem pole"). Rational and emotional terms are contrasted in terms of up for rational ("keep the discussion on a high plane") and down for emotions ("fall in love") and in politics ("They were shouting at each other. It was so dirty. A low-level debate in every respect!")

The second physical reference plane is to the right and left as we look "out" in standing position. Both directions are positive but are viewed as distracting from what is straight ahead. So we talk about "side issues," "side talk," and about "having to take sides" – all are viewed as distractions to our normal straight ahead orientation.

The third physical reference plane is the front-back vertical plane. Things in front are positive ("look ahead") while those behind are usually less positive ("don't look back"). This third physical reference plane is the basis of many of the metaphors we have for life because we use this spatial reference plane to talk about time. We view time as though we are moving ahead along a highway. We talk about future time as "coming events" ("I'm looking *forward* to your party"). We say that time comes and goes by us ("This week really *rushed by*. Before I knew it, the week *flew by*"). We talk of "trouble *ahead*." We worry about being early or late, "ahead of time" and "behind schedule," as though time and space relate to our physical reference planes.

Examples such as these led Clark to believe that much of everyday metaphor in language has a perceptual basis, and since humans all have the same perceptual mechanisms, he hypothesized that these same metaphors would occur across languages. They are universal.

Lakoff (1987) and colleagues (Lakoff & Johnson, 1980; Lakoff & Turner, 1989) have provided a more comprehensive argument that metaphor is perceptually based. They have demonstrated that metaphor is both a perceptually based system and a socially based system. Before looking at metaphor as a socially based system, we will look at three important questions that Lakoff and colleagues have addressed regarding metaphor as a perceptually based system. One question has to do with system within sets of metaphors. Can such a system be discovered? A second question is whether some metaphors are more basic (and acquired earlier) than others? A third question has to do with the distinction between everyday metaphor and literary metaphor. The first two questions may be more cognitive in nature than the third, but the research and the claims regarding each question concern the universality of the process.

System in perceptual metaphor

To illustrate the notion of system in perceptual metaphor, we will begin with an example of metaphor of emotions. Emotions are abstract feelings and so it is only natural that we would use other source fields to talk about the target field of emotion. However, in emotional states, we do have perceptions of tension, of heat or chill, or perhaps agitation. These perceptions are clear in the metaphors we use for love and anger. Kövecses (1986) gives us many examples for the emotion of anger. We feel body heat, pressure, agitation; notice the redness of skin that results; and perhaps our anger even interferes with normal perception (see examples below). Notice that the feeling of heat leads us to a FIRE source as a metaphor for anger. In our agitation, we may take on our opponent and that agitation becomes a source metaphor for anger. The examples of anger interfering with our normal perceptual processes (adapted from Lakoff, 1987, pp. 380–397) gives us the metaphor of anger as insanity:

Body heat
    hot under the collar
    all hot and bothered
Pressure
    burst a blood vessel
    have a hemorrhage
Redness
    scarlet with rage
    flushed with anger
    red with anger
Agitation
    shaking with anger
    hopping mad
    quivering with rage
    all worked up
Interference with perception
    blind with rage
    seeing red
    couldn't see straight

ANGER is FIRE
    inflammatory remarks
    add fuel to the fire

ANGER is an OPPONENT
    struggle, battle, fight, wrestle with, overcome
    surrender to, come to grips with

ANGER is INSANITY
    drives me out of my mind
    drives me nuts/bananas
    go crazy, berserk/bonkers

Kövecses then looked for system within metaphors of emotion. A basic notion is that we contain our emotions inside our bodies. This builds on the BODY is a CONTAINER metaphor. Lakoff and Johnson give us many English examples that fit this notion ("she is filled with love"; "she was filled with anger"). Kövecses suggests that the intensity of the emotion has to do with how filled the container becomes. We talk about the *depth* of our love as a measure of its intensity. When the container becomes filled, the emotion *overflows*. We *pour* out our feelings as our emotions overflow.

Turning to anger, Kövecses and Lakoff see stages in the degree or amount of anger. According to Lakoff and his colleagues, we can capture this information on emotions in a systematic way if we begin with metaphor of the physical body as a container.

BODY IS A CONTAINER
    filled with anger, love, despair, loneliness
    contain my joy
    brimming with happiness
Emotion is the heat of a fluid in a container
    Why are you so cold? an old flame
    You make my blood boil
    Simmer down! keep cool
    reach the boiling point
Emotion increases, the fluid rises
    anger welled up
    building up inside
    in a towering rage
    felt her gorge rise
It produces steam, pressure, explosion
    all steamed up, fuming
    She blew up
    blew a gasket (piston), erupted (volcano), blew a fuse (electricity), on a
        short fuse, set me off (explosive, bomb)
Part of container goes up in the air
    blew my stack, flipped her lid, hit the ceiling, went through the roof
The fluid comes out
    poured out her love, oozed sweetness, smoke poured out his ears, she
        had kittens, had a cow
                (Adapted from Lakoff, 1987, pp. 380–397)

These metaphors all relate to the human perceptual systems, to the way we perceive the world around us and the feelings within us. Some of the metaphors are more prototypic than others. For example, we can talk about "cold anger," but the use of heat and fire for anger would be more prototypic than cold. "Cold anger" seems to be anger that is very tightly controlled, unable to surface but stored in an intense form for later retaliatory use.

All humans have the same perceptual system, so it follows that many of these metaphors should be universal in nature. Shyu (1989) and Kelly (1989) investigated the issue of universality by comparing the system of metaphors of love and anger in Chinese and Turkish with those of English. The word for anger in Chinese is *ch'i,* which also means any kind of gas, odor, or air, as in the atmosphere. It also means "the breath of life," a form of energy. Although *ch'i* is invisible, Chinese medicine claims that health is mainly determined by whether the ch'i can circulate well in the body. *Ch'i* combines with adjectives to describe emotions such as "joyful air" (*hsi ch'i*), "angry air" (*nu ch'i* or *yuan ch'i*), and "haughty air" (*ao ch'i*), meaning joy, anger, and pride, respectively. Normally, the *ch'i* inside the body stays calm and unnoticed. However, when someone is irritated, the air appears ("his chest is full of angry air"), the pressure grows within the container ("he is bearing pent-up air"), and the angry person may be warned to calm or cool the air. But if the air increases, it results in aggressive facial behaviors ("his air caused his face to become green, purple"; "his air caused his green blood vessels to pop out, he suddenly changed color") and then escapes ("the angry air caused the smoke to pour out of his seven holes [mouth, nose, eyes, and ears]"; "his air caused his eyebrows to become straight and his eyes to become white"). As you can see, there are strong similarities to the system of metaphors of emotion that begins with the body as a container. In English, the building of anger is the change from a liquid, to heat, to steam. In Chinese, it is air which becomes heated and rises to be released as steam. Despite differences in details, the overall system appears to be the same.

Turkish metaphors are also similar to those of English although, as Kelly (1989) demonstrates, anger is often referred to as nerve: *sinirden titriyordu* (he trembled from nerves) and *siniri oynadi* (his nerves are dislocated, meaning really mad). Anger produces heat: *kizma* (don't get hot) and produces a color change: *sinirden mosmor oldu* (from nerves he became purple), *renk vermemek* (not to give color, meaning to hide one's feelings). Anger is also fire: *ates sacmak* (to scatter fire, which is to lose one's temper), *burnundan ates fiskiriyordu* (fire spouted out from his nose, showing extreme anger). Anger is seen as affecting the senses: *Sinirden gozu hic birsey gormuyordu* (from nerves, his eyes don't see anything, meaning he was blind with anger); and anger is insanity: *Delirtmek* (to send someone crazy). The body-is-a-container metaphor is also seen in Kelly's data. *Yuregi sinirle dolu* (his heart was filled with nerves) identifies the heart as one of the first parts of the container. *Girtlagina kadar sinirle doluydu* (he was filled up to his throat with nerves) shows anger building up to the moment before it explodes, *bardagi tasiran son damla* (the last drop that made the cup overflow) is the straw that broke the camel's back, and *sinirlerim bosaldi* (my nerves are emptied) shows the release once the container overflows.

Since the social worlds in which we live differ, we would expect to find some differences in the metaphors across languages. For example, most of the love poems in Arabic use metaphors that link the desert and thirst with longing for love. Our folk models or commonsense models of our social world might lead to quite different types or different uses of metaphor. The issue of universality and language or culture-specific metaphors needs much more detailed research.

The metaphors we have listed here for emotions are so common that some scholars have suggested that they are dead metaphors. However, it is clear that we draw upon these metaphors in order to express our feelings in new situations. In 1992, Los Angeles was the center of civil unrest. In a press conference from a White House Rose Garden meeting, concerned leaders said:

The temperature across the country, it's hot. It's at the boiling point.
Boiling. It's boiling over in L.A.
After things cool off, what will [President] Bush do?
We're feeling the heat in L.A.
It was just bottled up anger and it exploded in violence.
They were venting the anger they felt. They're still simmering over the verdict.
Rodney King lit the match and now we're burning.

And in Los Angeles, community leaders went on TV to speak to those who were rioting:

Hey, cool out. Back off. Move down.
Chill out, folks. We're all outraged.
They short fused. It's a flare up, unleashed fury but you gotta cool down.

So, the issue of whether or not such metaphors are dead is of little importance. Metaphor permeates all of language and reflects the way we perceive our worlds, and, thus, helps others understand us.

Practice 5.3

1. In terms of reference planes, right and left are both said to be positive yet there are many expressions in English that suggest that right is positive and left is less so. *Right,* meaning correct, is positive. "My right-hand man" is a person who gives unquestioning support (originally it referred to male secretaries who sat to the right of the boss, and little attention is paid to the person who sits in that location), while a "left-handed compliment" is qualified support. List as many other examples of *right* and *left* expressions as

you can. Are they equally positive or negative? Do the same expressions appear in another language you may be studying or teaching?

2. In a language you know, list examples for anger which parallel or differ from those offered by Kövecses and Lakoff. Do your examples support the claim of a universal conceptual basis for metaphors of emotion?

3. In Arabic, the emotion of love is commonly linked to water. Enani (1993) offers us translations from Arabic of lines such as "I kissed her mouth, holding her locks on both sides of her head, and drank deeply as a thirsty man drinks from the cool water of a pond," or the less elegant (in English) lines that describe unattainable love "like camels in the desert, nearly dying of thirst even while carrying water on their backs." Poets write of longing and desire as stages in the "need for water." Are such terms used widely in most desert cultures? How widespread is the love-as-thirst metaphor in English? Give examples to justify your answer.

4. Examples of metaphors for the emotion of love include heart, often used (metonymy) to refer to the emotion of love. Thus, love becomes an object which can be given to another ("I gave him my heart"; "he held my heart in his hands"). It is a solid object but it can be broken ("she broke his heart"). The object is a commodity ("I paid a lot for so little love," "I treasured this love"). Love is also seen as a plant that grows ("Our love flowered. Our love grew. I don't know why it died." Shu-ing Shyu (1989) reports a Chinese expression, "this red apricot blossoms outside the wall," as a metaphor for a married woman who is having an affair – the flower is outside the house). The lover may be talked about as food (honey, sugar, hunger for your touch). Love is insanity ("I'm crazy about her," "he's driving me wild") and causes us to behave as animals (wolf, tiger). Lovers are birds (turtledoves, my little chickdee, love nest). For some, love is a game ("can't get to first base") or even war (conquest, shot down, war paint, dressed to kill). How similar are the metaphors of love in the language you used for item 2?

5. U.S. President Clinton has talked about "growing the economy." He has also said, "We've been in the basement so long, we don't know what it looks like up in the sunshine." Collect and analyze examples of his use (or that of some

other leader of your choice) of figurative language related to the economy.

6. When Clinton fired the head of the FBI for suspected misuse of perks, a commentator said that the FBI head was "not just under a cloud but out in the rain for six months." List as many metaphors of suspicion and shame as you can. Is it possible to group them as Lakoff and Kövecses have the metaphors of emotion?

Acquisition of metaphor

A number of conflicting claims have been made about the acquisition and use of metaphors, arising from two points of view about the nature of metaphor. The first point of view is that metaphors are higher-order uses of language: they are creative and occur mainly in literature. In this view, the types of metaphor discussed in the previous section are of little interest because they are dead metaphors and so are akin to clichés. The second, opposing point of view is that metaphor is a basic process in language and is ubiquitous. This second point of view states that metaphor, even newly created literary metaphor, cannot be entirely new; it must be based in our perceptual and social systems. If this were not so, we would not understand new and creative uses of metaphor in literature.

This conflict about the nature of metaphor is also reflected in claims about the acquisition of metaphor. If one believes that metaphor is a higher-order skill used primarily in literature, the claim that children do not acquire metaphor until well into their teens seems reasonable. On the other hand, if one believes metaphor is a basic process in language, claims that children produce metaphor at an early age are quite tenable. In addition, if one believes that metaphor relates to basic perception, then certain types of metaphor should be acquired earlier than others. There is research in the literature that takes each position.

MacKay (1987) hypothesized that spatial and personification metaphors should be the most basic since they relate most directly to perception. He surveyed the metaphors in 59 children's poems. The poems contained 864 "live" (newly created) metaphors, 43 percent of which were personifications. He then went on to look at an additional 177 nursery rhymes and found 111 live metaphors, 77 percent of which were personifications. Poets writing for young children must believe, therefore, that young children are able to understand personification.

Billow (1981) and Leondar (1975) studied the language of preschool children and found that they spontaneously produced metaphors (e.g., describing themselves as "barefoot all over," using "daddy hopper" for a large grasshopper, or saying that mint candy produces a "draft in the mouth" or that a chimney is "a house hat").

If we look at Chukovsky's (1968) collection of children's language in verbal play (translated from the Russian), we find some examples that young children take things quite literally. For example, a child became quite upset on hearing an adult ask for the lady fingers. He protested that they are not made out of fingers but of dough. Chukovsky suggests, in spite of the many examples in the book, that children only create novel metaphors by accident. Yet examples of such accidents are numerous. For example, one child asked, "What's a knife? The fork's husband?" After swallowing each bite, another child stopped and listened. Then he smiled and said, "It just ran down the little ladder to my stomach." Another child marveled at the process of digestion: "Isn't it wonderful! I drink coffee, tea, cocoa, but out of me pours only tea!"

Gardner et al. (1978) say that children can produce such metaphors but that they do not appreciate the metaphors of others nor can they offer a rationale for their own metaphors. Gardner et al. suggest there is a "U-shaped curve" for production of metaphors. Young children go through a "wild" stage where they do produce metaphors without true metaphoric capacity, followed by a period when they do not, only to rediscover metaphor at around 10 to 12 years of age. This position suggests that a child first learns literal meanings of words and only later begins to comprehend and use metaphor.

Piagetian theory suggests that children in the "preoperational stage" can recognize metaphors if they apply to physical objects, but only later at the "concrete operational" stage will they agree that metaphoric meanings can extend to people. According to this school of thought, the production of metaphor requires the child to think of an object as though it were another, to perceive similarities, and to wilfully override the boundaries. Marti (1987) claims that early metaphors are a result of the child's incapacity to differentiate identity, resemblance, and difference relationships.

In a series of experiments, Palmero and associates found that children aged from 3 to 10 years, given a context and task that is appropriate to their age, do comprehend metaphorical relations. For example, preschool children can act out metaphoric relations (e.g., tears as rain). In a study that involved the retelling of stories (metaphoric vs. literal versions of the same story), the children had no particular problem with metaphor. Palmero (1986) says, given that such studies demonstrate the ease with which young children deal with metaphor, it seems highly unlikely that children learn only literal meanings at first. The question, he believes, is when do children come to understand metaphors as adults do. "Thus, [Shelley's] 'my soul is an enchanted boat' may be understood only by an adult, whereas 'my yellow plastic baseball bat is an ear of corn' may be understood by child and adult" (1986, p. 15). While children would assign some meaning to "my soul is an enchanted boat," it might not be appropriate from an adult's point of view. Palmero believes then that while children are acquiring meanings of a word, "they are ready to extend that word or domains of words to metaphoric uses."

Practice 5.4

1. Palermo (1986) says that in the story retelling task, the only item which caused children problems was a metaphor revolving around yesterday (behind) and tomorrow (in front). Several children explained that one can see yesterday but not tomorrow, so yesterday is in front. This seems to conflict with Clark's notion that spatial orientation provides us with our metaphor for space = time. On the other hand, preschool children may not yet have learned that metaphor well. How would you design a project to research this question further?

2. Children begin pretend play at a very early age. They pour 'sand' tea and offer it to imaginary playmates. To the distress of their parents, they pretend their sandwiches are airplanes soaring through the air. Would you equate such nonverbal symbolic play with the use of verbal metaphor?

3. Teachers at a workshop reported the following metaphors used by very young children. A 3 year old looked at the moon and said, "Oh, it's a toenail moon!" Another child, seeing a parrot at the zoo, said "Look, a rainbow! A rainbow!" If you can observe young children, collect examples of their creative use of metaphor. Can you categorize your collection in terms of different types of metaphor? Which type is most common in your data?

4. Since so many words have different meanings and can, on occasion, be used in sentences which allow for ambiguity of meaning, *and* since so much of meaning in discourse is also ambiguous, we are constantly creating our own interpretation of meanings. Why, then, should interpretation of metaphor be a higher-order capacity? Try to relate your response to the acquisition research above. Do you agree with Ragevska (1979), who wrote that "metaphoric extension . . . is always at work in the acquisition of vocabulary and the development of thought" (p. 153)?

Literary and conceptual metaphor

Metaphor is a pervasive process in language, yet we believe that writers have special talents in the creation and use of metaphor. What, then, is the difference between literary and conceptual metaphor? Lakoff and Turner (1989) say it is a matter of degree and skill; others say it is in the aptness of the metaphors.

To investigate this question in depth, Lakoff and Turner compared metaphors used in poetry and literature with those of ordinary talk. The basic underlying metaphors appear to be the same, yet the skill with which they are used certainly contrasts. As an example, let us review their treatment of the LIFE is a JOURNEY metaphor in literature and ordinary language use. The basic parts identified by Lakoff and Turner for the metaphor are as follows:

LIFE is a JOURNEY
There is a traveler.
The traveler moves through a series of locations; one or more may be an intended destination.
Travelers with destinations choose paths to get where they want to go.
There may be impediments to travel (bumpy roads, quicksand).
The traveler needs provisions.
The traveler may require a guide.
Along the route, the traveler passes landmarks that help in gauging progress.
Along the route, the traveler encounters crossroads and must decide which way to go.

In ordinary conversation, we use these metaphors in talking about life and our activities during life (e.g., education, marriage, work). We say that we "still have a long way to go" to make our work perfect. We may get sidetracked ("I really got off the track"), encounter impediments on the way ("we're going over some rocky ground there"). We may need help ("without my friends I'd really be lost") and worry about the choices we make ("I shouldn't have taken this route").

Robert Frost's poem ("Two roads diverged and I, I took the one less traveled") and the Twenty-Third Psalm ("He leadeth me beside the still waters") exemplify literary use of these metaphors. Such metaphors are not different from or more apt than those of everyday talk. Rather, they are employed with great skill, and many (rather than just one) appear within one passage to produce a layered effect. Lakoff and Turner cite these examples along with many others to show the richness of metaphor in literature.

Other LIFE metaphors include LIFE is a DAY (see Dylan Thomas's poem "Do not go gentle into the night," where the end of life is the end of the day), LIFE is FLUID in the BODY (see W. H. Auden's "As I walked out one evening," where life is said to leak away as "the crack in the tea-cup opens"), LIFE is FIRE and LIFE is a PLANT (see the sonnet below). Lakoff and Turner not only illustrate the metaphors using the poems mentioned here, but they also discuss the combination of these metaphors using the standard example of metaphor in English literature: Shake-speare's sonnet 73. Literature teachers and writers on metaphor have long cited it as the supreme example of multiple metaphors for life within a single piece of literature.

> That time of year thou mayst in me behold
> When yellow leaves, or none, or few, do hang
> Upon those boughs which shake against the cold.
> Bare ruined choirs, where late the sweet birds sang.
> In me thou seest the twilight of such day
> As after sunset fadeth in the west;
> Which by and by black night doth take away,
> Death's second self that seals up all in rest.
> In me thou seest the glowing of such fire,
> That on the ashes of his youth doth lie,
> As the deathbed whereon it must expire,
> Consumed with that which it was nourished by.
> This thou perceiv'st, which makes thy love more strong.
> To love that well, which thou must leave ere long.

Lines 1 through 4 use the lifecycle year of plants (LIFE is a YEAR, LIFE is a PLANT) as a metaphor to describe life. As Lakoff and Turner point out regarding line 3, it is not cold, but wind that shakes trees; it is a person who is being shaken by the cold of approaching death. Lines 5 through 8 use the LIFE is a DAY metaphor; in lines 9 through 12 LIFE is FIRE, and the final lines (13 through 16) contain a plea for love that nourishes life (the traveler needs provisions).

Lakoff and Turner have selected an impressive collection of poetry to illustrate their belief that poets and ordinary people share models of the world, models which are represented through metaphor. Poets and writers are able to arrange and use metaphors in ways that have especial power and grace. Because we share the underlying models of life that are found in these metaphors, we understand and are moved by such lan-guage. Even when our models differ, we are able to recognize many of the metaphors of other cultures and appreciate the models revealed through them. Compare the Shakespeare sonnet with the English rendition of the following traditional Navajo prayer,

> In beauty may I walk. All day long may I walk.
> Through the returning seasons may I walk.
> Beautifully will I possess again
> Beautifully birds. . . . Beautifully joyful birds. . . .

On the trail marked with pollen may I walk.
With grasshoppers about my feet may I walk.
With dew about my feet may I walk.
With beauty may I walk.
With beauty before me may I walk.
With beauty behind me may I walk.
With beauty above me may I walk.
With beauty all around me may I walk.
In old age wandering on a trail of beauty,
lively, may I walk.
In old age wandering on a trail of beauty,
living again, may I walk.
It is finished in beauty.
It is finished in beauty.

(Rothenberg, 1982, p. 208)

Practice 5.5

1. Collect examples from oral language of metaphors of life in another language. Are they the same as those given by Lakoff and Turner?
2. Select one of the poems mentioned in this section and ask a speaker of another language to study it with you. Are the metaphors clear to both of you? If this poem were translated into the other language, would the same metaphors be used as effectively in that language?
3. Can you find passages similar to the Twenty-Third Psalm in the literature of other religious traditions? In what ways are the passages similar or different? Are there any examples of a guide that attempts to *mis*lead one on the journey? Are the passages that describe this less poetic in nature than that of the guide we can trust?
4. At his death, former President Richard Nixon was described as a giant, one who never traveled in the shadow of others but in whose shadow other political leaders labored. He left, it was said, giant footprints on the land, footprints that others might do well to follow. In American mythology, the giant Paul Bunyan and Babe the Blue Ox stride across the continent. They leave giant footprints which, when filled with water, form the Great Lakes. They carve the land, and the plowing they do directs rivers into their courses. Do all cultures use the metaphor of heroes striding out across the land, leading others to follow in their giant footsteps? What evidence can you give from mythology or from everyday use to support your answer?

Social models and metaphor

Although E. and H. Clark and other cognitive psychologists have been primarily interested in metaphor for what it can tell us about human cognitive processes, Lakoff and his associates have always considered metaphor to be both cognitively and socially determined. Kövecses (1986, 1988) talked about world models that are reflected in our metaphors. Though some metaphors are more central (or prototypic) than others, they are organized to reflect our common-sense understanding of life – a folk theory that acts as a standard for determining normality within a culture (D'Andrade, 1987). Thus, it is both a social and cognitive process.

Similar metaphors form the basis for understanding many areas of social life. For example, our understanding of politics is also organized around the journey metaphor. After President Clinton's 1994 State of the Union address, a yearly "state of the nation" speech, news commentators talked about his "leading" the country, his changing the "direction" of domestic policy, that Congress needed to "follow where he leads" so that the country avoids the danger of just "drifting along." They told us that Clinton needed to "lay out the map" so we can "see where we are going." Clinton himself used these same metaphors when he announced that with his 1994 budget proposal, "We have ended the drift and broken the gridlock of the past." While it may be difficult to visualize a gridlocked highway which simultaneously drifts, the journey metaphor is clear. In fact, if you look at the parts of Lakoff and Turner's LIFE is a JOURNEY metaphor, you see that these also apply to politics: POLITICS is a JOURNEY perhaps because it reflects the life of our country. The only difference is that the country rather than the individual is the traveler.

In Lakoff and Kovecses's scenario of anger, the folk theory of anger consists of five parts: offending events, anger, attempt at control, loss of control, and act of retribution. In Shyu's (1989) investigation of metaphors of emotion in Chinese, we find a similar model. In Chinese, however, the causes of anger include the lack of good manners and social restraint. Anger itself is seen as fire or hot liquid in a container in English but as heated air in a container in Chinese. Chinese also locates the spleen in the many expressions of "hot spleen air." Both languages have metaphors in which anger is a dangerous animal with which we struggle, but the personification of anger in Chinese is much more common and the person is expected to struggle valiantly to control anger. In Chinese, an angry person is very dangerous and should not be touched or provoked. The basic system of the metaphor is identical to that of English although the details show cultural differences: in Chinese it is air that heats, the person must fight fiercely to control the emotion, and, if that fails, the angry person is seen as very dangerous indeed.

The metaphors of love as an emotion are also very similar in these two languages but there is the added dimension of *yuan* (destiny) which differs from the English notion of *bond*. Shyu suggests that, despite differences in detail, one would expect strong similarities since so many of the metaphors are related to the physiological effects of the emotions. Looking at other metaphors (other than those associated with emotions) may reveal stronger sociocultural differences in the models revealed through metaphor.

Practice 5.6

1. Quinn (1987) gives evidence for a culture model of American marriage using the metaphors of young husbands and wives (11 couples), interviewed separately (approximately 15 or 16 hours each) about marriage. As you might imagine, marriage is seen as something which is built ("solid foundation," "building on the relationship," "a do-it-ourselves project," "using parts"), an ongoing journey ("through the good and the bad, unable to continue"), an investment ("afraid it may cost too much," "being short-changed in this relationship"), mutually beneficial ("for both of us," and "vice versa"), knowing and seeing ("I didn't know who he was," "I didn't see," "My eyes were closed") and physical obstacles ("uphill stretches," "stormy weather"). In her analysis of the metaphors given by each person, Quinn discovered eight propositions about American marriage: marriage is a joint enterprise, it may succeed or fail, it is risky, it is full of unknowns at the outset, it is difficult and effortful, it is mutually beneficial, and it is enduring. She shows how each of these propositions are cast in metaphor by individual speakers. For example, the speaker may state through metaphor that lack of knowledge about marriage leads to difficulty, which leads to divorce. If difficulties are "worked through" in a way that is mutually beneficial, then marriage is enduring. Speakers talk about the work and learning needed to make marriage "stick," about learning a lot, and they also ask where they would "go" if the journey failed. Where else will one find a spouse as a fitting or irreplaceable part, both joined and beneficial, unless marriage is jointly lived? Does the analysis seem to fit your folk model of marriage? Read and discuss the model with someone from another culture. How different is this model from their own?

2. Collect as many metaphors of WORK as possible. How might these be collapsed into statements that would form a model of work? Is the model culturally specific? Is it specific to some particular type of work?
3. A claim has been made that the United States is a violent and military culture. Reporters, as well as political leaders, often use WAR and GAME metaphors. One U.S. politician, for example, said, "We're out of the end zone but only at the thirty-yard line," making the event described into a football game. Another said, "With all the smoking mirrors being thrown up around us–." Is this a combination of "smoking gun" and "mirrors," or confusion with "smoke and mirrors," or is there an expression "smoking mirrors"? Collect examples from news programs that use WAR or GAME metaphors. Do these same metaphors occur in news reporting in other languages? Does your collection support the claim about U.S. culture?

Metaphors of teaching and learning

Thornbury (1991) suggests that there are a number of recurrent metaphors that teachers use to characterize teaching. Included are LEARNING is a JOURNEY, the LESSON is a MOVING OBJECT, LEARNING is a MECHANICAL or COMPUTATIONAL PROCESS, and LEARNING is PUZZLE SOLVING. We can easily find examples of each of these metaphors, which include groups of metaphors within them. Just as we found many other metaphors under the LIFE is a JOURNEY metaphor, there are many other metaphors within the LEARNING is a JOURNEY metaphor. Here are a few collected by graduate students at Temple University, Japan, from classrooms, from comments teachers wrote on students' papers, and from their reading of applied linguistics texts on methodology.

JOURNEY
We've covered a lot of ground today.
Didn't the discussion get a bit derailed?
Bring the idea home.
We have a long way to go on this topic.
I resent having to wade through all their homework.

NEED FOR A GUIDE ON THE WAY
This book is your guide to language acquisition.
The book is the instructor's companion in teaching.

107

IMPEDIMENTS ON THE WAY
It's articles that get in the way.
Writers still fall into this trap no matter what I do.

LANDMARKS TO GAUGE PROGRESS
Watch for signposts along the way.

The metaphors the graduate students collected far exceed those mentioned by Thornbury. They found many journey metaphors, metaphors of mechanical or computational processes ("processing input," "automatic production of well-constructed paragraphs," "language acquisition device," "adding new material to the lesson"), and puzzle solving ("clues to the question," "decode," "decipher," "keys to the puzzle"). But they found many other metaphors as well.

FOOD
Students are starved for challenges of any kind.
tasteless ideas, concoct something new
spice up your thesis
beef up your paragraphs
it all boils down to two points
chop it up into understandable thoughts

OSMOSIS and CONDUITS
It just won't sink in!
Students have to absorb what was said.

MINING
Dig out the answer.
break new ground today
just on the surface

BUILDING
nail down the argument
building basic language skills

THEOLOGY
Language teaching is a high calling.
to place redemption on the shoulders of the language teacher
awaken and revive in them a passion for learning

LAW
learning the laws of grammar
never arrive at the freedom to speak

SPORTS
The learner can now tackle much harder tasks.
Students engage in a cognitive wrestling match
competent coaching from the skilled teacher

WAR
need to combat the intrusion of the learners' native language
arm your students
experience, or arouse him to a defensive kind of learning.

MEDICINE or ILLNESS
this treatment is input
The cure for interference is simply the cure for ignorance.
learning was difficult and painful
blind to students' needs
turn a deaf ear to students' tantrums

PLANT
a seed of truth
a harvest of strange ideas
rooted in the first language

WEAVING
weaving of old and new information
the fabric of the talk that is being woven

ART
paint a broad picture
in black and white
your composition is out of focus

HOUSECLEANING
clean up your work
Clean work – it's organized

If we look through such metaphors, we see that many encompass reciprocal activies and roles such as teaching/learning, the teacher/the learner – doctors and patients, players and coaches, supervisors and workers. (Others emphasize the creative side of learning – weaving, painting.)

Block (1992) asked language teachers and learners what they think the role of a teacher is. Teachers supplied a number of roles: coordinator, facilitator, giver of information, disciplinarian, motivator, friend, coordinator, parent. Many of these imply corresponding student roles. Block also elicited the roles of students: worker, recipient of information, and so forth. He also surveyed the metaphors in a number of teacher-training texts. Block then compared existing models in the field of applied linguistics of teacher and learner roles to those offered by teachers and students.

Block's work is important to students and teachers, to researchers and teacher trainers, for we need to know what our folk model or folk theories (our shared commonsense ideas) about teaching and learning are. We need to know if the model(s) that emerge from our methods courses are the same as those of practicing teachers and students. We need to know whether these models of teaching and learning (and the metaphors that come from the model) are universal or whether they are culture specific. If we hope to bring about change in the teaching and learning process, then we need to see precisely where our metaphors contrast and how understandable and sensible our new metaphors are to those who might implement them.

Practice 5.7

1. Classify each of the following metaphors into relevant categories of the analogies listed above.

   Clean up your spelling errors and return.
   I wish I could just unlock the door for you but you must do it yourself.
   What makes this class tick?
   My ideas just won't take shape.
   Tie up the ideas in the conclusion.
   The chain of ideas isn't clear.
   Patching here and joining there will help it hang together.
   Let your impression germinate a bit.
   Write more economically.
   The linguistic framework entails construction of sentences which build basic skills.
   Polish up the first two paragraphs.
   This is rubbish, trash!
   The growth of bilingualism is slow indeed.
   Did you digest your teacher's comments?
   I'm really feeling my way with this assignment.
   I think I was left in the dark.

2. Select one methodology book and scan it for metaphors of teaching and learning. Do they fit into the groups you identified in item 1?

3. Collect teacher comments on student compositions. Do the metaphors for writing differ from those of other areas? Check the major metaphors listed by Tomlinson (1986), who looked at salient steps in writing and metaphors authors use: Looking for ideas, they dig and dredge or hunt, cast nets. In nurturing ideas, they seed, prune, and cultivate. In combining and revising, they brew up and stew over their writing. They hope for a yeasting or brewing process to occur, and they put it in the oven to encourage further change. One writer noted that the final revision is like

the step in cookbooks to "correct for seasoning." The choice of metaphor, in particular when writing becomes difficult, shows how writers think about their work. How do your metaphors fit into those listed by Tomlinson? Do teachers and professional writers differ in their use of metaphors to describe the writing process? How might you investigate this question further as a research project?

4. Program administrators often talk about "team spirit" as though staff members were playing a game. They may use military or religious metaphors, claiming the team has a "mission." Collect metaphors used by or for those in administrative positions. How do the metaphors differ from those of teaching or writing?

5. We have many metaphors for the ways words might be represented in the brain. Sometimes we talk about the brain as though it were a warehouse. We "store" vocabulary and "retrieve" it from storage. In this metaphor, we think of words as physical objects, which can be lost or found in the warehouse or organized in different ways. If we do not think of words as objects, but rather as forms produced by connections as various parts of systems are activated (the brain as electrochemical wiring), we cannot talk about just two things – word and concept – but rather of multiple connections at many different levels. There are, of course, many metaphors for the connection between words and their mental representations. In another language of your choice, determine what metaphors are used for the mental representation of words.

In this chapter we have said that metaphor is a basic process in language that reflects our perception of the world and our feelings, and is not a higher-order process (although skilled writers select and combine metaphors in a more artful manner than most of us can attain in everyday language use). The metaphors we use reflect our common-sense understanding of our worlds, and so they form a folk model or folk theory about life, about learning, and about our emotional experiences. Thus, it is much more than the relation *Figur* described in Chapter 4. The relation is a pervasive process in language learning and language use. This notion is not, perhaps, something new but rather something rediscovered anew. In 1912, Weekley wrote, "Every expression we employ, apart from those connected with rudimentary objects and action, is a metaphor" (p. 97).

Chapter 6 will consider another group of relations which were not included in relational models: the semantic relations that occur across languages rather than within one language. Chapter 7, the final chapter in Part I on semantics, will look at script semantics, another method that relates to our view of the world and our actions and interactions within it.

Research and application

1. In Terban's (1990) *Punching the Clock,* a book for children 8 to 12 years of age, drawings illustrate the meanings of funny action idioms. Ask children in this age group to explain the metaphors without the illustrations. Do children need to be taught what these expressions mean? The *Amelia Bedelia* books, a popular children's series by Peggy Parish, features a girl who takes everything literally. *The Stupid Family* is another children's book where metaphors are taken literally. Why are stories in which things are taken literally so popular with adults and children? In contrast, *The House is a House for Me* is filled with metaphor that is not to be taken literally. In each illustration in this book, the CONTAINER metaphor is invoked for house (e.g., "The mouth is a house for the tongue"). Plan a research proposal to test the comprehension of metaphor by young ESL learners or bilingual children using these or other children's books.
2. Ackerman (1983) says that children have more difficulty with metaphor than adults, but claims this is because adults have had more experience with the conventional use of nonliteral meanings. Adult language learners, however, also have difficulty in recognizing nonliteral meanings while native speakers can accurately interpret figurative vs. literal meanings of phrases just from the intonation. If Ackerman is correct, we can attribute it to lack of experience with culturally specific use of metaphor. Or, we might claim that learners need to study the intonation that marks nonliteral meanings of phrases in English. How might you research the value of each of these explanations?
3. Shyu's (1989) and Kelly's (1989) studies of metaphor in Chinese and Turkish agree with D'Andrade's (1987) study in which he found that the Ifaluk of Micronesia had very similar general frameworks as those of American-European cultures. All of these groups divided internal states into thoughts, feelings, and desires. However, D'Andrade found that the detailed expression of these thoughts, feelings, and desire are quite different from those of English. Shyu and Kelly also found important differences in the details of how the metaphors of emotion were formed. Given your knowledge of other language groups, what sort of research plan can you devise to look at differences and similarities across lan-

guage and culture groups. Might it be best to select some area other than those involving emotions for such a study? If so, why?

4. Paivio and Clark (1987) considered the role of imagery in the comprehension of metaphor using the terms *topic* and *vehicle* to refer to target and source. In the example "Divorce is the earthquake of the family," "divorce" is the topic (target) and "earthquake" the vehicle (source). The metaphoric comparison is that both are destructive. Paivio and Clark asked university students in introductory psychology classes to give the meanings of metaphors that were high and low in imagery and intelligibility, using 48 metaphors selected from the 204 poetic metaphors in Katz et al. (1985). The highest scores on meaning were for metaphors that were high in imagery for both topic and vehicle and high for intelligibility. Examples of the "high" group follow.

High in imagery in both vehicle and topic:

The stars are beads strung on one string.
Clouds are tossed pillows.
The body is a fading mansion.

Examples of low imagery that were difficult for the students follow.

Low in imagery of both vehicle and topic:
Contemplation is a transparent spider web.
Memory is a heap of broken images.
All prayers are the same grief flying.

Select an example from the high and low imagery metaphor groups presented in this article and replicate the study with one beginning, one intermediate, and one advanced language student. On the basis of this minipilot study, decide whether a full study of metaphor comprehension by language learners would be a worthwhile research project (is it feasible, are the questions interesting, and so forth).

5. Harris (1975, 1986) gives many examples of metaphor in technical writing. He notes that popular names for the small bones of the inner ear – *hammer, anvil, stirrup* – reflect their shapes and are the same as the Latin names *malleus, incus,* and *stapes.* He shows that the letters of the alphabet have been used metaphorically for shapes (e.g., A frame, C clamp, O ring, I beam). He also offers numerous examples where the terms of technology and science are derived from human anatomy (e.g., pipe elbow, eye bolt, mouth of a tunnel, fuel bladder, lip of a crucible, jaws of pliers, pipe nipple, steering knuckle). Shape images may also be drawn from animals or plants (e.g., saw horse, plumber's snake, watch stem, branch circuit, honeycomb construction). Design a way to see if similar

processes are used in technical writing in your target language. Then, decide if you should consider preparing special materials on metaphor for your language for a specific purpose class. Design appropriate materials and try them out with students.

6. Brownell (1988) describes studies that show that patients with right hemisphere damage display metaphor-specific dysfunction, and that patients with either right or left hemisphere damage perform poorly compared with normal control subjects on both metaphoric and nonmetaphoric language. These studies and others suggest that one possible role for the right hemisphere is the processing of metaphoric language. However, Glucksberg et al. (1982) believe (as does Lakoff) that the same language processes are used to understand literal and figurative language. So, both hemispheres may process metaphors, but the right hemisphere may play a role in responding appropriately (once both hemispheres have finished processing). If you are interested in neurolinguistics and the differences between the hemispheres in terms of language processing, read and critique the Brownell (1988) and Glucksberg et al. (1982) articles. Are you convinced by the experimental and anecdotal evidence? How would you interpret the findings? Do they support the assumptions of cognitive psychologists such as Lakoff (or Weekley, writing much earlier) that all language is basically metaphoric and that it is not necessary to posit separate processes for literal and figurative language?

7. Throughout history, writers have suggested that certain problems in science could not be solved until scientists had the proper metaphor. Harris (1986) quotes Emerson's essay on language (section 4 of *Nature*, published in 1837) to show that an awareness of the use of metaphor in science is not new. A metaphor can function as a helpful model for thinking about the problem, as in Harvey's sudden insight into the working of the heart as a result of seeing a fire pump. Or, Harris notes, the metaphor can impede progress, as in the persistence of the bird model hampering aircraft design in a number of ways. Consider the metaphors that are used for language and for language learning. How might they advance or impede our understanding of language and learning?

6 Semantic space across languages

In the previous chapters, we have discussed semantics in terms of features, semantic fields, core meanings, prototypic words for concepts, the basic semantic relations between lexical items, and figurative processes. Although we have highlighted cross-linguistic correspondences and differences as we discussed each of these analytic approaches, the question of universality of concepts and cross-linguistic correspondences has not been central to any of the approaches. The notion of universal semantic PRIMITIVES (i.e., basic concepts or meanings) is one of great interest to philosophers, psychologists, and applied linguists in their work on contrastive analysis, error analysis, and interlanguage research. In this work, the researcher attempts to find some small set of primitives that could be used to paraphrase or define all other concepts that occur in languages. The primitives would be universal and, thus, would give a basis for discovering the ways semantic space is divided in cross-linguistic comparisons. Miller and Johnson-Laird (1976) began their work by identifying those primitives that relate to perception. They identified almost 100 such primitives just to cover object recognition, including size, horizontal, vertical, top, bottom, rigid, straight. Lexicographers working in relational semantics protested that such primitives might allow one to identify perceptually, for example, a chair, but would not capture the meaning of *chair*. For that, they claimed, one must add relations such as those we discussed in Chapter 3 – for example, FUNCTION (a chair is to sit in) and HYPONOMY (a chair is a piece of furniture). Others claimed that the analysis should not begin with object identification but with action.

The basic criticism of each of these attempts has been that the number of primitives appear to be too numerous to be useful in describing meanings. Wierzbicka, a linguist who has devoted more than 20 years to the discovery of a fundamental set of semantic primitives, has shown, however, that while the task of defining primitives is exceedingly difficult, it is not impossible. She identified (1980) a set of thirteen basic semantic primitives that cannot be further divided and which allow one to paraphrase the meanings of all other concepts. These primitives and the combination of the primitives to form concepts in natural languages comprise what she calls natural semantic metalanguage. Wierzbicka's thirteen basic semantic primitives are *I, you, someone, something, world, this, want, not want, think of, say, imagine, be part of, become.* With these thirteen primitives and the names of natural species (e.g., cat, elephant, apple), she is able to paraphrase the meanings of concepts of natural language. She also illustrates how many of the problems of semantic analysis (such as circularity in definitions) can be solved using this method.

Because Wierzbicka's theory is the result of many years of careful analysis, it would not be fair to offer only a paraphrase of natural semantic metalanguage. Rather, we refer you to Wierzbicka's many books and articles for detailed study. However, the work relates directly to many of the sections of this chapter. In particular, Wierzbicka offers us a guiding principle in her translation of Apresjan's observations on elementary meanings:

> The more elementary a given meaning is, the greater the range of the languages in which it can be expressed by a single word: elementary meanings are apparently expressed by single words in most languages of the world. The diversity and lack of congruence of the semantic systems of different languages arise at the level of combinations of elementary meanings.
>
> (Apresjan, 1974, in Wierzbicka, 1980, p. 69)

In this chapter, we will look at some of the universal categories that have been proposed in cross-linguistic work and then consider specific types of semantic correspondences across languages.

Universal categories

Our semantic categories are based in our experiences with each other within our environment. Because all humans have the same basic perceptual apparatus, deal with the same spatial orientation to our environments, and share many other experiences, we expect that there would be some strong similarities in the structuring of semantic space across languages.

For example, one might suspect that all languages would have words for family groups, food classes, work groups, plants, and animals, and there should be universal categories of perception (see, hear), sensation (hunger, thirst), and emotion (love, hate). Yet, cultural differences are strong and the ways in which we divide up the world are often culturally specific. "The vocabulary of a language could be considered a kind of lexical map of the preoccupations of a culture" (Fowler, 1985, p. 65).

Given that we all have the same neural mechanisms for perception, we would expect that we would see or perceive reality in similar ways. Color perception is a good example of this notion. As we have already seen in Chapter 2, however, all languages do not have the same set of color terms. Yet, Berlin and Kay (1969) showed that color terms can be predicted.

Looking at 20 languages from different language groups, they found that if a language has only two color terms, they will be for white and black. If there are three, red will be added. Green and yellow are the next two color terms to be added, then blue and brown. Finally, terms for purple, pink, orange and grey may be added (in any order). Primary color terms predominate in terms of which colors are named in languages of the world. So, our shared visual apparatus does influence the naming of colors in languages. However, the number of colors named varies from one culture to another. Of course speakers of languages with few color names can perceive differences in color hues which are not named in the language.

Surprisingly few concept terms actually occur in all languages. You might not be surprised to learn that *louse* is one of them. Lice exist everywhere or at least speakers of all languages have them in their vocabularies! Swadesh (1972) first proposed a list of 200 concepts that he thought were basic enough to be universal. The list was then used to obtain data that would allow one to describe the lexicon (and the sound system) of another language and to trace the family relationships of languages. Once linguists began working with non-Indo-European languages, however, they found that all languages did not have terms for all concepts. The number of concepts linguists use to begin their analysis has now been reduced to 100 (Table 6.1). Because it is possible in English to misread the concept in the case of noun-verb homonyms, the fifty-four nouns have been italicized.

As a language teacher or language learner, you know that the words that represent each of these concepts differ across languages. Students, however, are often amazed to learn that speakers of other languages do not recognize their language (whatever it may be) as having the "right" words for concepts. We often act as if we believe at least partially in the naturalist hypothesis that there exists a natural connection between word form and meaning. We may think that "cock-a-doodle-do" is the natural word for the crowing of a rooster, but we know that other languages use other onomatopoeia for this same concept. We may agree that the Big Dipper is the right term for that constellation and be surprised that speakers of other languages feel that the word for plow or great chariot is a better match.

Words from other languages may just not sound right to us. A Danish-English bilingual child remembers being unhappy as a child when her mother insisted she call flowers *blomster.* The child associated the sounds with *bloomers* (a word for girls' panties used in her community at that time) not with blooming. How could a word that sounded like bloomers be the word for flowers? Sound symbolism is part of our feel for the appropriateness of the words we use for concepts. There seems to be something right about words like *glimmer, glisten,* and *glitter* with the initial *gli* sound.

TABLE 6.1   100 COMMON CONCEPTS

1. I	26. *root*	51. *breasts*	76. *rain*
2. thou	27. *bark*	52. *heart*	77. *stone*
3. we	28. *skin*	53. *liver*	78. *sand*
4. this	29. *flesh*	54. drink	79. *earth*
5. that	30. *blood*	55. eat	80. *cloud*
6. who	31. *bone*	56. bite	81. *smoke*
7. what	32. *grease*	57. see	82. *fire*
8. not	33. *egg*	58. hear	83. *ash*
9. all	34. *horn* (animal)	59. know	84. burn
10. many	35. *tail* (animal)	60. sleep	85. *path*
11. one	36. *leather*	61. die	86. *mountain*
12. two	37. *hair*	62. kill	87. red
13. big	38. *head*	63. swim	88. green
14. long	39. *ear*	64. fly	89. yellow
15. small	40. *eye*	65. walk	90. white
16. *woman*	41. *nose*	66. come	91. black
17. *man*	42. *mouth*	67. lie	92. *night*
18. *person*	43. *tooth*	68. sit	93. hot
19. *fish*	44. *tongue*	69. stand	94. cold
20. *bird*	45. *claw*	70. give	95. full
21. *dog*	46. *foot*	71. say	96. new
22. *louse*	47. *knee*	72. *sun*	97. good
23. *tree*	48. *hand*	73. *moon*	98. round
24. *seed*	49. *belly*	74. *star*	99. dry
25. *leaf*	50. *neck*	75. *water*	100. *name*

Source: Swadesh, 1972, pp. 283–284; used with permission.

There is also something right about the /i/ ending which many languages use to show affection or small size (as in our *baby, Buddy, granny, dolly*). Fonagy (1963) found that Hungarian children thought words ending in /i/ were quicker, smaller, prettier, and sounded more friendly. Words ending in /u/ were thicker, hollower, darker, sadder, blunter, and even sounded bitter. The /i/ and /u/ sounds take on a meaning of their own through sound symbolism.

The mnemonist described in Luria (1968) was extremely sensitive to the sounds of words. For him the Russian word for pig, *svinya*, was not "right":

Now I ask you, can this really be pig? Svi-n-ya – it's so fine, so elegant. . . .
But what a difference when you come to khavronya (sow) or khazzer (Yiddish for pig). That's really it – the kh sound makes me think of a fat greasy belly, a

rough coat caked with dried mud, a khazzer. . . . But take the word samovar. Of course it's just sheer luster – not the samovar, but from the letter s. But the Germans use the word Teemaschine. That's not right. Tee is a falling sound . . . so how could Teemaschine mean the same thing as samovar?

(Luria, 1968, pp. 87–88)

Although most of us are not quite so sensitive to the sounds of words, it is true that some words in our language seem to be just right. Still, we know that there is no best word for any object. A table could as well be called a *batel* (or *mesa, bord, tabla, tarabeeza*). The choice is arbitrary, as long as it fits the sound patterns of the language.

Monolingual children (as compared with bilinguals) find it difficult to believe that it is possible to call a dog anything but *dog*. The word, for them, is inseparably linked to the concept. An adult friend who had never traveled outside the Midwest, returned from a trip to Mexico, claiming to be amazed that people there called a cow *vaca* when everyone knows it's a cow. According to the Bible, Adam was given the privilege of naming things before Eve appeared on the scene. But, Mark Twain (1905) wrote, once there, Eve knew that there could only be one possible name for each. She saved Adam from making mistakes on several occasions. "When the dodo came along, he thought it was a wildcat – I saw it in his eye. But I saved him. . . . I just spoke up in a quite natural way of pleased surprise. . . , 'Well, I do declare if there isn't a dodo!'" Twain's Eve was wrong about there being only one possible name for things; word forms are arbitrary. There is no systematic, direct correspondence between sounds of words and concepts.

Some languages may have many words for certain concepts. For example, English has one basic-level word *dog,* but many words to identify different types of dogs. We have one basic-level word *tree,* but different words for each type of tree. (Can you imagine how difficult it might be for a linguist to point to a tree and have the informant give the word for that specific tree, a different word for the next tree, and so forth. It is not always easy to get the term that you want!)

If the lexicon is a map of the preoccupations of a culture, we would expect to find differences in the degree of specialization of forms. For example, North American English has numerous terms for types of cars (see Aronoff's 1985 study of automobile semantics). Eskimo languages are often reported to have a very large number of words for *snow,* although this is denied by most linguists, who point out that there really are only two root forms from which the other terms are derived.

Not only do languages differ in the number of terms they use for a concept, but the range of meaning of each term may cover the concept in different ways. For example, the English verb *eat* can be done by any animal. People eat meals, cows eat grass, fish eat bait, and so forth. That is not the case in German; *essen* is restricted to people and *fressen* is the

119

form for animals. *Drink* is restricted to liquids in English, but in other languages (e.g., Arabic and Japanese), the word for drink is also used with cigarettes. *Bathroom,* in American English includes a toilet, a sink, bath, and shower. Nakao (1989) points out that the Japanese equivalent, *furo(ba)*, is a place to clean and warm oneself, but it does not contain a toilet.

Every language learner has embarrassing memories of errors made in assuming that some word carries the same range of meanings in another language as in the first language. For example, the notion of a watch "working" is ridiculous in Spanish. In German, *gehen* means to go by foot, not in a vehicle. So you can't use *gehen* to say "Do you plan to go to America?" If you do, everyone will laugh.

Contrastive analysis

Linguists have carried out lexical comparisons across languages for two basic purposes: to discover family relationships among languages and to locate the correspondences or lack of correspondence between lexical items in languages.

Although all languages have prototypic meanings for the central concept in polysemes (e.g., that the *break* of "break a leg" is more central than the *break* of "coffee break"), the range of correspondence in polysemes does not correspond across languages. Still, we expect languages that are closely related to each other (like German and English) not only to have words which may be very similar to each other for a concept but also to extend the meanings outward from core to peripheral in similar ways. We do not expect this to be the case when we compare words for a concept across very different language families (e.g., English and Hungarian).

The languages within the Romance language group do, in fact, have many related words for concepts and the range of meanings of the words is often very similar. Nehls (1991) contrasts the designation of spherical objects in five languages, discussing his findings in light of prototype semantics (Table 6.2). Romance and Germanic languages all belong to the Indo-European language group. The examples show the close similarity of forms in the three Romance languages (French, Italian, and Spanish) in contrast to the two Germanic languages (English and German). Still, the similarity among all the languages for the word globe and, for English and the Romance languages for sphere is because English was heavily influenced by French at different periods in its history. Examples of less prototypic uses include those in compounds (Table 6.3).

Consider, now, the word *head,* one of the basic concepts on the Swadesh list. The prototypic meaning must be that of a person's head, but there are many other meanings for the word. If we look at the extension

TABLE 6.2   SPHERICAL OBJECTS

Feature	English	German	French	Italian	Spanish
not elastic	ball	Kugel	boule	palla	bola
elastic	ball	Ball	balle	palla	pelota
bounces			ballon	pallone	balon
shooting	bullet	Kugel	balle	pallotola	bala
projectile					balin
model of earth	globe	Globus	globe	globo	globo
geometric figure	sphere	Kugel	sphère	sfera	esfera

Source: Adapted from Nehls, 1991, p. 330.

TABLE 6.3   COMBINATIONS WITH SPHERES

English	German	French	Italian	Spanish
ball bearing	Kugellager	roulement à billes	cuscinetto a sfera	cojinete de bolas
ballpoint pen	Kugelschreiber	stylo à bille	penna a sfera	bolingrafo
snowball	Schneeball	boule de neige	palla di neve	pelota de nieve

Source: Adapted from Nehls, 1991, p. 332.

of the word for this concept across language families, we see that neither the range of meanings nor the forms for the items is the same (Table 6.4).

The core meaning of table must be that of a dining room table. This central meaning of table as a piece of furniture used during meals is shown in the primary word association, *chair*. If the core meaning for *table* was that of a chart, then *chart* or *numbers* might be the first word association offered. All cross-linguistic word association tests show that Spanish-English bilinguals associate *table* and *mesa*. The relation, however, does not correspond in other collocations (i.e., *mesa* is not used for a table of figures). The correspondences shown by Robinett (1965) are:

English	Spanish
table	mesa
tablecloth	mantel
timetable	horario
table of figures	tabla
turn the tables on	volverse la tortilla

When languages are not closely related, we expect there to be fewer correspondences in the way that the semantic world is segmented. A

TABLE 6.4   CORRESPONDENCES FOR *head*

English	French	Arabic
(of a person)	tête	raas
(of a coin)	face	turra
(of a bed)	chevet	raas siriir
(of a match)	bout	raas (kabriit)
(of a table)	au bout	raas (tarabeeza)
(of an organization)	directeur	mudiir *or* ra'iis (*or* el raas el kabiir)
(of beer)	mousse	—

Data source: Mackey, 1965, and F. El Hindawy.

lexical contrastive analysis reveals the similarities and contrasts between languages. Such information can help us to predict which lexical items will be easy or difficult for our students or ourselves as language learners.

Practice 6.1

1. Note the color terms included in Swadesh's list. Why are these colors included and others excluded? A number of writers have given an "experience" explanation for the predominance of color terms (red is the color of blood, yellow is the color of the sun, blue is the color of sky, black is the color of night, white is the color of the light of day, brown is the color of earth, and so forth). Others have claimed that it is our visual system that determines the dominance of primary color terms. Cazden (1972) makes no claims about the order of acquisition of color terms by young children, but she offers "archaeological" evidence of children's color preferences. Boxes of crayons (black, red, green, yellow, blue, brown, purple, pink, and orange) were issued to children at the beginning of the school year. As children used up the crayons, new boxes were issued and the leftover bits collected for general use in a single container. At the end of the year, the container became packed with unused pieces of two colors, purple and orange. How does this evidence relate to Berlin and Kay's (1969) findings? The bilingual child Hildegard (Leopold, 1939, p. 688) was very interested in colors but found them difficult. *Rot* was her first color and was used for other colors as well. *Blau* was second, followed by *white* and *weiss*. Next came

orange. How does this evidence relate to Berlin and Kay's findings? How might you account for the early appearance of *orange*?

2. Notice that terms for days of the week and for months are not on the Swadish list. How do you account for this? Do all languages have seven-day weeks? Does the week start with the same day in all languages? What about months? Prepare a chart that shows differences across languages to justify the omission of such terms from the list.

3. Russian has a word for each of the two days on each side of today while in English we use primarily phrases once we get beyond *tomorrow* and *yesterday.* The Russian words (supplied by G. Browning) are *poslezavtra* (day after tomorrow), *zavtra* (tomorrow), *segodnia* (today), *vchera* (yesterday), and *pozavchera* (the day before yesterday). Collect as many terms for days on each side of *today* as you can across languages. Display these in chart form.

4. Sometimes there is no matching term for an English concept we want to express in another language. Or, if there is, it does not include exactly what we want to say, or it includes things we do not want to say. Wierzbicka (1990a) says that the Russian word *toska* is a unique blend of melancholy, sadness, and indefinable yearning. The English word *sadness* does not capture this blend. *Sadness* may be translated as *grust'* and *pecal'* and a number of other terms in Russian. So, again, the correspondence in ways these emotional concepts are lexicalized is quite different Give an example of your own that illustrates this lack of correspondence. What solutions might translators use when there is no direct correspondence?

5. In another language, elicit the words for ball, head, and table and the other forms as shown in the examples in this section. What similarities and differences do you find? Can the equivalent for head also be used for "head of a pimple" (*raas dimmil* in Arabic)? Is the word for "head of an organization" more often modeled after the French "directeur"? Is *head* used for "head of lettuce"? Is *table* used in an expression equivalent to "table the matter"?

6. Miller (1991) looks at the different meanings of the noun *board.* He divides these into hierarchies of concepts rather than hierarchies of words:

The word *board* {board, committee} is a hyponym of the concept {social group, group of people}; the word *board* meaning {board, plank} is a hyponym of the concept {lumber, sawed wood}; the word *board* meaning {board, blackboard, chalkboard} is a hyponym of the concept {writing surface}; and so on. . . . In another language, each *board* might be expressed by a different word. (1991, p. 187)

Elicit the words for these concepts in as many languages as you can. Prepare a chart that shows the correspondences and contrasts. Prepare a research plan (perhaps a match-the-lists test) to see if beginning learners from these different language groups make errors in using these forms in English.

7. The Japanese word for *drink* is used as it is in English for drinking liquids such as water. It is also used for consuming soup, cigarettes, and medicine. It is also used for the in-breath of surprise and (perhaps metaphorically) when one is unwilling but finally accepts a condition. In some theories all of these would be listed as terms for INGEST. Check to see whether this use of one term for so many uses is common in other languages. If you teach students whose first language is Japanese, ask them whether this distinction between English and Japanese has caused them any difficulty. If you are studying Japanese, is this difference difficult to remember?

Acquisition and error analysis

In identifying the thirteen semantic primitives of her natural semantic metalanguage, Wierzbicka (1980) noted that the primitives combine in basic ways to form propositions like:

I'm thinking of someone
I'm thinking of something
I imagine something
I (don't) want this something
I say something
A part of this something is this something
I'm thinking of you
I'm thinking of a world
This someone wants something

She notes that similar combinations appear very early in a child's first language acquisition. For example, Halliday's (1975) Phase I of child language includes the following expressions that fulfill basic functions:

Functions	Lexical forms
Instrumental	I want, I don't want
Regulatory	Do as I tell you
Interactional	Me and you
Personal	Here I come
Heuristic	Tell me why
Imagination	Let's pretend
Informative	I've got something to tell you

(Note that the lexical forms can be reduced to the primitive propositions. "Do as I tell you" can be paraphrased as: I want you to do something; "Tell me why" can be paraphrased as: I want you to tell me something.)

However, a child learning a second language must be able to deal not only with elementary meanings in the first language but also with differences in semantic organization across two languages. McLaughlin (1984) proposes a three-stage model. At stage 1 the bilingual child works with an undifferentiated system where the lexicon is not separated for the two languages. At stage 2, the child differentiates the two systems but may mix lexical items occasionally. At stage 3, the two systems are differentiated. Mixing might still occur, but the child would know that the term is from the other language, would use it for special purposes, and mark it as mixed.

One question of concern for many parents and teachers is whether having to do this extra work places the child at a disadvantage. Numerous studies show that there is no difference in the number of words learned by bilingual and monolingual children. However, since the bilingual child is not only learning two words for the same concept but also must begin working out all the extensions of the words in the two languages as well, it is not surprising to find that the number of words for the bilingual child refer to fewer concepts. Pearson, Fernandez, and Oller (1993) note that the bilingual children in their sample had fewer different words within each language than monolinguals but, adding the words from the L1 and L2, the totals were equivalent to that of monolingual children. So the oft-cited notion that there is a lag in vocabulary development is not strictly true.

The question of when a bilingual child is aware of the fact that lexical items from two languages are being learned is addressed in a number of diary studies. Ronjat's (1913) child, Louie, learning French and German, called this talking "comme papa et comme mama" and at the age of eighteen months asked for translation equivalents for concepts. He continued to elicit translation equivalents in a manner reflective of many field linguists. At 3 years: "Mama, purée de pommes de terre, wie heisst?" to get "Kartoffelbrei." After the mother named a dish "Gefüllte Tomaten," he asked his father, "Comment tu dis, toi?" to get "tomates farcies."

125

Pavlovitch's (1920) study of a child learning Serbian and French showed an awareness of lexical differences by age two. Leopold (1939), studying his daughter's acquisition of German and English, claimed a growing awareness of separation of lexicon between ages 2 and 3½ years.

Older children adding a second language, of course, are immediately aware of the differences in the way languages carve up semantic space. Eva, the 6-year-old Hungarian and French bilingual child studied by Kenyeres and Kenyeres (1938), was astonished that *seven* and *week* were not the same word in French as they are in Hungarian. And she found it hilarious that French should have the same word for *tongue* and *language*. Adults, too, find amusement, joy, and frustration in lexical correspondences and contrasts between languages they are learning. Our favorite example of this comes from Ringbom (1987) where an adult Finn says, "He bit himself in the *language*" (Finnish *kieli* means both language and tongue). Every language has its own way of dividing up semantic space and then extending meanings outward in interwoven nets.

McLaughlin's three-stage model gives us a broad picture of how learners separate the lexicon of the languages they learn. When we are tired or under stress, however, keeping all the information separate or retrieving the right pieces is not always picture-perfect. Many people who travel overseas find that it is not native language terms (or even those of their best known second language) that come out when they are trying to produce the target language. Rather, the terms are from other languages. For example, at the end of an extended trip, an applied linguist stopped in Mexico City for the TESOL conference. Exhausted, she decided to take an afternoon merienda. As she sipped soothing hot chocolate, even such simple expressions as "thank you" came out in French, Arabic, and even Swahili before the Spanish forms!

Although McLaughlin's model considers acquisition in terms of processes, many linguists look instead at the correspondences among L1 and L2 items and attempt to predict difficulty or ease of learning in terms of the correspondences. We will discuss these in the next section on loan translation and cognates.

Practice 6.2

1. Pearson, Fernandez, and Oller (1993) looked at the reported vocabulary of 25 simultaneous bilingual and 35 monolingual (22 English; 3 Spanish) toddlers and infants, using the toddler and infant forms (Spanish and English version) of the MacArthur Communication Development Inventory. The parents looked at a list of words typical for children in these age groups (679 toddler and 395 infant words on the English list and 732 toddler and 428 infant

words on the Spanish list) and identified those that the child used – parental recognition of words used rather than recall. If you were working in a bilingual kindergarten, would this be a useful way of measuring the language development of your students? Justify your answer.

2. McLaughlin (1984, pp. 181–182) claims that bilingual children initially transfer the meanings of lexical items in the first language to those of the second language. Thus Hildegard, Leopold's English–German child, used "Mommy alle," transferring the English *all gone* meaning to German. Standard German does not apply *all gone* to people in this way. Vihman's 3-year-old Raivo said that he could read and demonstrated this by counting, for in Estonian, *lugema* is used for both *read* and *count* (Vihman & McLaughlin, 1982). Give examples of your own (or ask your students for examples) that illustrate this phenomenon.

3. Shanon (1991) asked bilinguals to recall instances where they had made a faulty shift from one language to another. Examples included a speaker who had a conversation in English and, on leaving, meant to say good-bye in English but switched instead to Hebrew. Shanon also gives examples of students in foreign language classes, called on to respond in Japanese, answering instead in Russian, the previous language studied. How might such errors fit into McLaughlin's three stages of acquisition of lexicon?

4. Ringbom (1987) gives many examples of Finns using Swedish words in their English utterances. Consider your own language learning experiences, read through Ringbom's list, and then explain whether this is different from lexical language mixing.

Error analysis, loan translation, and cognates

There are many problems learners experience with seeming correspondences in lexical items across languages. Once we have learned a word for a concept, we often find that we can extend the use of that word to the same contexts as its corresponding term in the our first language. For example, once we have learned that *alto* is the word on stop signs in Mexico, we may try to use *alto* in all the situations we might use *stop* in English. If we try to translate "stop it" directly into Spanish (*alto este*), the result will not be Spanish. Loan translation is a common lexical process in second or foreign language learning that often leads to error. Ringbom's (1987) error analysis data illustrates this. Having learned the

English word *ball* and the verb *fly*, a Finnish speaker produced the form *flying ball* which is a direct translation from the Finnish word for volleyball: *lentopallo*. The Swedish *barnvagn* means buggy (British English pram) and accounts for the loan translation error *child wagon*.

Cognates are words which have the same or very similar forms in two languages. In fact, if languages share many cognates, there is good reason to believe that they are related languages. As we saw in the *ball* example (Table 6.2), Romance languages share many cognates. A classic example is the word for flour: *harina* in Spanish, *farine* in French, *farina* in Italian, and *farine* in Romanian.

When we find cognate forms in a language we want to learn, we are usually delighted. It makes the language seem familiar and offers us a break – we already know the new vocabulary item. In Kotsinas' (1983) study of the early Swedish vocabulary learned by Katrina, an immigrant from Poland, and Dimitri, an immigrant from Greece, 50 percent of Katrina's words were cognates with Polish and 40 percent of Dimitri's were cognates with Greek.

Kotsinas does not believe that cognates are always as helpful as they may seem. Learners may overuse and extend these cognates instead of acquiring other more precise synonyms. For example, *gangster* was used for any unpleasant person and *problem* was used as a word for bad. The Swedish word *fråga*, meaning *ask*, was used for the Swedish forms of tell, talk, discuss, say, and explain. The Swedish word *komina* (come) was used for the Swedish words come, go, travel, begin, start, and understand.

Forms that sound the same, and therefore appear to be cognates may, however, have very different meanings. Using them can have disastrous consequences as in Nash's (1978) title example: "Don't *molest* [bother] me now, I'm busy." These are called false cognates (or false friends). The form is very similar in the two languages but the meanings differ.

Ringbom (1987) collected a very large corpus of lexical errors of Swedish and Finnish learners of English. His analysis of false cognates in Swedish and English shows three different types of correspondences:

1. Cognate form but completely different semantics for the forms.

   The unsure youth is made the *offer* (Swedish for victim) of fashion.
   Sugar is *gift* (Swedish for poison) and full of calories.
   I have also *proved* (Swedish = tried) few times smoking.

While the forms of these words in the two languages are similar, their meanings are quite different.

2. Cognate form with very limited similarity in semantics.

   He had 80 years birthday in this month so he is very *actual* person.
   (aktuell = current, topical)

I *spring* and swim (springa = run).
He should learn how to *handle* in the right way (handla = act)

Here the forms have some limited semantic relation to each other though not that intended by the speaker.

3. Cognate form with partial semantic equivalence.

Engineers plan more and more *ways*. (vag = road)
I could work what I *will*. (vilja = want to, sometimes will)

The word *way* is used for road in English in expressions such as "highway" "byway" and "along the way," but would not be used in this context.

Another interesting utterance that might fit in this category is "I have a car and my man has also a car." Man, a Swedish cognate with English, means husband in Swedish. In many English dialects it also can mean husband, but usually the phrase "my man" has a special intonation when it means husband.

Ringbom's detailed, rigorous work in contrastive lexicon gives us a useful taxonomy of many different types of transfer errors. His data come from learners of English with two very different first languages – Swedish, which is quite closely related to English, and Finnish, which is from a very dissimilar language family. Ringbom has looked at differences in error type in relation to the first language, as well as at the effect of third language learning on lexical transfer and interference. For example, if a Finnish speaker has studied Swedish and German and then begins English, will there be stronger transfer from these languages or from Finnish? However, Ringbom has not articulated hypotheses as to the relative difficulty of each type of correspondence in his taxonomy. For that, we will turn next to hierarchies that have been proposed in the literature of contrastive analysis.

Practice 6.3

1. Leopold (1939) notes that Hildegard produced such blends as *Butterfliege* for *Schmetterling*. How is this related to loan translation? Celce-Murcia (1978) notes that her daughter Caroline also produced blends like *piedball* for football but attributes this blend not to loan translation but rather to Caroline's difficulty with the fricatives. The fricative /f/ sound of *foot* is more difficult than the stop /p/ sound of *pied*. Check the literature on loan translation and try to determine whether phonological difficulty plays a major role in forms used by learners.

2. In the language textbooks you use, what position has the materials developer taken regarding cognates? Are they used extensively or are they avoided? If the materials are written to be used by students from many different first languages, do the authors make any direct reference to cognates between languages?

3. Nash (1978) suggests seven questions that we need to seriously consider when introducing cognates in language teaching:

   a. Is the relative frequency of the term the same in each language?
   b. Are some synonyms of higher frequency than the cognate word?
   c. How many shared senses are there for the cognate forms?
   d. Are there splits in either or both languages and, if so, are they the same? (For example, *concerto* in English and *concierto* in Spanish are cognates but the Spanish *concierto* splits into *concerto* and *conceit* in English.)
   e. Are cognate nouns also cognate in terms of taking a plural form? (For example, *vacances* in French is plural, whereas the English form *vacation* can be singular or plural.)
   f. For cognate verb forms, are they cognate in terms of acting on an object (transitive) or not (intransitive)?
   g. Do verb cognates allow an animate or inanimate subject?

   Which of these is the most important in terms of development of language teaching materials? Justify your choice.

4. Examine each of the following Spanish/English cognate examples from Nash. How might they fit into Ringbom's classification of false cognates?

   Smoking is not *convenient* for your health.
   Some *type* was acting silly in the bar.
   The *material* of today's lecture is conservation.

   If you teach (or are learning) Spanish, collect examples of false cognates that you believe should be identified in language teaching materials (ESL or SSL) to help learners avoid these problems. Do you think that pointing out false friends may discourage learners from making use of cognates which have similar distributions in the two languages?

5. The following examples are from a special university program in Mexico designed to prepare scientists to read chemistry materials in English. Although students were not expected to produce English, they were asked to write a brief essay on their program. Circle the cognates in the following example data. How much do the learners appear to be using cognates? What are the possible advantages and disadvantages to using cognates?

a. The activitys that a chemical engineering student do in the school are so different I can mencione with culturals until cientific research.
b. The environmental are very nice, everybody we're good brothers. The installation are so very old; our school have 52 years old. The teachers are goods (except somebody about 10%), thus the nivel is good in all the country.
c. The project only is aplicated in this faculty for to see the results. The form is analized: preview, analisis of vocabulary, comprehension of text, parcial translate.
d. The escencial point is for read of english. The text are estudied in one week generally.
e. A estuding of ciences chemical is destacated to razoned for he. The teacher of the ciencies chemical destacan in many ideas what to do, reaccioned to the estudent in the problems what have the student in the class. The actividites is not concenter also the memory in sheer razoned.

6. We often find that cognates that initially seem equivalent have different connotations. This is an especially important issue when translating passages. English has many cognate forms originally borrowed from French. English speakers use the French word *régime* to refer to a government in a negative way, but it is a neutral term in French. Consult an English-French bilingual dictionary to see whether this difference is shown. How useful do you believe the dictionary you consulted would be to someone engaged in translating?

Predicting difficulty

Using contrastive analysis and error analysis, linguists have made predictions about difficulty of learning. Some of these predictions, as we have seen, have to do with universality of concepts. Others have to do with core meanings of lexical items. Others have been discovered by looking at correspondences across languages.

The types of correspondences each linguist considers depend on the goals of the research. The goal may be linguistic in nature – for example, a contrastive analysis of a particular lexical set. There are several studies that have looked at the ways in which languages express the concept TO PUT ON various articles of clothing. Japanese, according to an analysis by Backhouse (1981), uses *haku* for putting articles of clothing on the lower body, *kaburu* for putting things on the head only, and the more general term *kiru* for the upper body (or for articles of clothing such as a jumpsuit that would cover more than one area). English does have more than one term but none of these (don, slip on, slip into, get on, get into) are required for putting clothing on specific parts of the body.

The goal might be one of lexicography. Snell-Hornby (1990), for example, is primarily interested in finding correspondences between languages in order to prepare dictionaries that would allow for accurate translation. Snell-Hornby divided the L1 and L2 relationships into the following groups: (1) terminology or nomenclature (oxygen: *Sauerstoff*), (2) internationally known items and sets (typewriter: *Schreibmaschine*), (3) concrete objects, basic activities, and stative adjectives (chair: *Stuhl, Sessel*; cook, boil: *kochen*; technical: *technisch, fachlich, Fach-*), (4) words expressing perception and evaluation which are often linked to sociocultural norms (clout, thrill, bustle, bleak; *keifen, kitschig, gemütlich*), and (5) culture-bound elements (haggis, wicket, drugstore, Pumpernickel, *Privatdozent, Sechselauten*). Snell-Hornby believes that it is easier to find equivalents between languages in the first two groups with less correspondence for parts of group 3 (as we have seen in the comparison of cooking terms in Lehrer's 1969 work), and little hope of finding direct correspondences for groups 4 and 5. The work of lexicographers, thus, has been one source of prediction about difficulty in learning. That is, if we assume that the more direct the correspondence between lexical items in two languages, the easier the items will be to acquire, and terms for concrete objects, basic activities, and technical, internationally recognized terms should be much easier than those that are more culturally bound.

The goal may be pedagogical. That is, the contrastive analysis may present teachers with information about what will be the easiest or most difficult types of correspondences in learning. The goal is to predict difficulty of *types* of correspondence. Laufer (1991, p. 589) suggested that we can categorize the kinds of lexical correspondences between languages which would facilitate or impede learning (Table 6.5).

Thus, cognates (similar to the L1 in form and meaning) would facilitate learning while false cognates (similar to L1 form with difference in mean-

TABLE 6.5   LAUFER TABLE OF CORRESPONDENCES

Facilitating factors	*Difficulty inducing factors*
Similar to L1 in form and meaning	Similar to L1 form with difference in meaning
Overlap in semantic grids between the word in L1 and L2	Incongruencies in gridding: one to many correspondences, partial overlap, metaphorical extensions
Similar connotation	Different connotation
Meaning relation: hyponymy, antonymy, converseness	Meaning relation: synonymy
	Similarity in sound to other words in the language

Source: Adapted from Laufer, 1991, p. 589; used with permission.

ing) would induce difficulty. If all the meanings of the words used for a concept are the same (overlap in semantic grids), learning should be facilitated. If, instead, the form in the first language becomes two or more forms in the second, there may be problems. So, Spanish speakers learning English might forget that two different verbs are needed for *lo conociamos* (we knew him) vs. *lo conocimos* (we met him). In partial overlaps, the Spanish word *esquina* is similar in most ways to the English word *corner* except that it means only the outside corner, not the inside one.

Cultural connotations can also make for easy or difficult learning, depending on the match. For example, *iglesia* means church, but it does not bring to mind the white wooden building with a steeple that is typical of churches in the Northeast and Midwest parts of the United States. And, finally, when meaning relations are those of hyponymy (*X* is a kind/ type of *Y*: *chocolate mousse* is a type of *dessert*), antonymy (*X* is the opposite of *Y*: *humble* is the opposite of *proud*), and converseness (e.g., *sell–buy*), Laufer believes these will be easier than synonyms. Tables such as Laufer's are useful, but they do not make predictions as to which of the factors facilitate the most or induce the most difficulty in learning.

Stockwell, Bowen, and Martin (1965) in their contrastive analysis of Spanish and English made a series of hypotheses about the difficulty of acquisition of phonological forms depending on the degree of similarity between the two languages (Figure 6.1). The same hierarchy is perhaps less successful when applied to semantic correspondences.

Learning a new item is difficult in phonology (a level-4 difficulty), but a new lexical item will not cause the same level-4 difficulty that it does in phonology. A split category, however, will be difficult. Think of the difficulty young children have in distinguishing *borrow* and *lend*. These two terms are often covered by one term (in Dutch, *lenen*), and such splits

133

Ease–Difficulty (0–5)	Category	Relationship Native Lang.	Target Lang.	Process
4	*Overdifferentiate* new category	0 →	1	learn new item
3	split category	1 ⇶	1 2 3	make new distinction
2	*Underdifferentiate* absent	1 →	Ø	avoid production
1	coalesced	1 2 3 ⇶	1	overlook distinctions
0	*Parallel* no difference	1 →	1	transfer
3	reinterpret shape or distribution differs	1 →	1	give familiar item new shape or position

Figure 6.1 Hierarchy of difficulty (adapted from Stockwell, Bowen, and Martin, 1965, pp. 282–291)

are definitely more difficult than it appears from the chart. Learning to avoid production when a term does not exist in the L1 or learning to collapse several forms to one form in the L2 is not always an easy task. Learners keep looking for the missing terms. For example, in Japanese, the words for jaw and chin are both covered by the term *ago*. Americans learning Japanese say having only the one term just doesn't seem right to them. In German there is just one word, *Uhr*, for watch and clock. Again, English speakers learning German are likely to search for ways of making *Uhr* more specific, perhaps via their invented compound *Armbanduhr*.

Even when we accurately identify splits, splits may not all be equally easy or difficult. For example, the split of English *know* into French *connaître* vs. *savoir* or German *kennen* vs. *wissen* would be listed as a 3 on the difficulty scale. The distinction between knowing people (*connaître, kennen*) and knowing information (*savoir, wissen*) is semantically transparent and therefore relatively easy. It probably is not that difficult to acquire. Sharpe (1989), however, shows that the split of *know* to *shiru* and *wakaru* in Japanese is less transparent. The difference is usually explained as between knowing and understanding, but this rule alone does not work. Additional pragmatic information on status and politeness needs to be considered in making a choice between *shiru* and *wakaru*. In this case, learning which verb to use might be much more difficult.

The differences in connotative range show that even when terms appear to have one-to-one correspondences, native speakers do not interpret pairs in the same way. For example, Stockwell, Bowen, and Martin point out that *policia de transito* means traffic cop, but it is doubtful if drivers on the Los Angeles freeways interpret traffic cop in the same way as Spanish speakers might interpret *policia de transito*. It's not surprising, then, to find Spanish speakers in Los Angeles mixing "traffic cop" and "cop" into their Spanish. *Policia de transito* wouldn't have the same ring.

Connotation covers all the cultural associations called up with a word, whereas pragmatics deals with when and how items are used. Stevens (1991) found that both conflicting connotations and conflicting pragmatic norms need to be taught along with terms. He gives examples where English speakers who have learned Arabic continue to misunderstand the pragmatic or cultural associations that go along with the use of such terms as *ma-a'lish,* which translates roughly into "never mind" or "it doesn't matter." However, *ma-a'lish* is also used for "sorry." You can imagine that such learners would continually interpret *ma-a'lish* as "never mind" or "it doesn't matter." In English these are used as a way of accepting an apology, not as a way of offering an apology. And Americans frequently become annoyed ("Whaddaya mean 'never mind'?") when someone says "ma-a'lish" as an apology.

As Stockwell et al. point out, it is impossible to work from such a chart as Figure 6.1 because differences in cultural connotations and pragmatic use must also be considered along with form and semantic correspondence. Therefore, Stockwell and colleagues analyzed the correspondences in lexical items across languages in several ranges: syntactic, morphological, denotative, connotative, and circumstantial. An example of contrasts in denotative range is shown in Figure 6.2. Such examples show how difficult it is to talk about simple splits in the way we can for contrasts in the phonological systems of two languages.

Nevertheless, the Stockwell, Bowen, and Martin hierarchy (Figure 6.1) is helpful in conceptualizing possible difficulties for learners in very broad outlines. But the correspondences, especially if we include idiomatic and metaphoric uses, are much more complex than those presented here. Nevertheless, it is useful for comparative studies and in planning lexical choice in materials development. (For a table with more complex relations, see Stockwell, Bowen, and Martin, 1965, p. 284, and the examples following the table.)

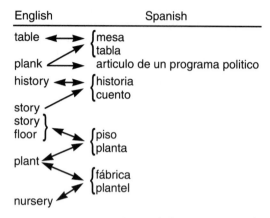

English	Spanish

Figure 6.2   Spanish-English contrasts (adapted from Stockwell, Bowen, and Martin, 1965, p. 284).

Practice 6.4

1. According to J. Deen, a pocketbook, meaning a purse or handbag, is *een (hand) tasje* in Dutch. *Een pocketboek* can only mean a paperback book. How might you visually diagram this correspondence? A calendar that we use to note appointments (*diary* in British English) is *een agenda* in Dutch. In English and in Dutch, *agenda* can be used for the agenda of a meeting. *Een kalender* is used for the calendar that hangs on the wall. Consult Figure 6.2 for help with a diagram for this correspondence.

2. The French word *aussi* can be translated as *therefore, consequently,* and *also. D'autre part* can be translated as *moreover* or *on the other hand.* Can you determine when you use each of these English connectors? Would it be easier for a French speaker or for an English speaker to learn these forms in the other language?

3. When we dress, we *put on* our clothes. Korean has several forms for the meaning of *put on: Sinta* is put on the foot, *kkita* is put on the hand, *ssuta* is put on the head, and *ipta* is used for everything else. According to the hierarchy of difficulty, how difficult would it be for native speakers of English to acquire these terms? Compare the Korean system with the Japanese system for *put on.* Who should learn the Korean system quicker, Americans or Japanese students of Korean? McCawley (1970) claims that it is the manner of putting on items (not the items or the part of the

body they are put on) that determines the form. As evidence, he says that if you put socks on your hands or use a necktie to hold up your slacks, the Japanese term will be determined not by the article of clothing but by the manner in which it is put on. Do you agree with this analysis? Would this explanation help in teaching the Korean or Japanese terms?

4. According to Gasser (1988), the Japanese word *mizu* means water, while *yu* refers to water that is warm or hot. So if one wanted to say, "You put too much water in the tub," *yu* would be the appropriate terms (unless you like icy baths!). When temperature is not an issue, *mizu* would be selected. So, a Japanese speaker complained in English, "The faucet's broken." And, in response to the question "Which one?" replied, "Water" – meaning the cold water faucet. Draw a diagram similar to that illustrated for *table* ↔ *mesa* by Stockwell, Bowen, and Martin (Figure 6.1). How difficult would it be for you to fluently produce the appropriate Japanese terms? How difficult would the correspondence be for Japanese students of English?

5. Stockwell, Bowen, and Martin note there is no form for *minister* in Spanish. The cognate form *ministro* refers to a cabinet official. The word *misionero* is used for a Protestant minister. How difficult would it be for English speakers to learn to suppress *ministro* to refer to a minister? Do you believe that all of the following lexical splits would be equally difficult? *Be* becomes *ser, estar; for* becomes *por, para; you* becomes *tu, usted.* If you think they are not equally difficult, give examples to justify your predictions.

6. In Spanish or another language, what verb would be used for *pass* in the following expressions: "He passed a red light." "He passed me on the road." "They passed a law." "Pass the potatoes!" "She passed the course." "They passed the dividend on to their shareholders." According to your analysis, how difficult would it be for an English speaker to learn the forms in the language you described?

7. Stockwell, Bowen, and Martin use the term *circumstantial range* to talk about differences among forms according to pragmatic circumstances. They point out that there is no direct correspondence between such politeness forms as *perdón, lo siento, con permiso,* and English "sorry," "excuse me," "pardon me." List the types of exchanges where each of these forms are appropriate for English and then where the politeness forms are appropriate for Spanish (or

    another language of your choice). What is the correspondence between the use of these terms in the two languages?

8. Stevens (1991) outlines the pragmatic contrasts between English and Arabic for time expressions. In English, we can say "in a minute" without really having the pragmatic force of a promise or firm commitment. However, if time expressions are used in other circumstances, they usually do have this force. If we ask a clerk when merchandise will be ready, and the reply is "tomorrow," we interpret this as a firm commitment. In Arabic, *bukra* is the term for tomorrow. However, in this same circumstance in a store, it might be a real promise, some vague tomorrow, or even a polite refusal to have the merchandise ready. If one wants to be sure of the degree of promise, some negotiation must be done. Another time expression in the utterance gives more commitment to the time frame (e.g., the equivalent of "tomorrow, God willing, in the afternoon"). The pragmatic force of promise or firm commitment is different in the two languages. While English speakers are often frustrated in this situation, frustration of Arabic speakers is no less common in the face of the rudeness of Americans who think a promise is a promise (when no promise or even a refusal had been signaled). Check to see whether the pragmatic meanings of *tomorrow* in another language are closer to those of English or of Arabic. How might you include pragmatic information when teaching such terms?

Lexical transfer and interference – the study of cognates and of borrowing of items across languages – are all important issues which appear in subsequent chapters. Examples are given here to show that these are semantic issues as well as lexical issues. Since borrowing is such an important lexical process, it is treated separately in Chapter 8.

Research and application

1. Lehmann (1977) identifies the functional distribution of *say, speak, talk,* and *tell* in English and compares the distribution to the German *sagen, reden,* and *erzählen:* In English, *saying* can be attributed to text ("the directions say," "the brochure says"). This is not possible with *sagen. Speak* is used to refer to faculty ("he speaks six languages") and quality ("he speaks well; he is a

good speaker"), but "talk" is used for quantity ("he talks a lot; he is a great talker"). In German, *reden* can be used for quality and quantity. The English word *tell* is used to give information ("he told us the answer"), to command ("he told the kids to be quiet"), or entertain ("he told a joke"). In German, *sagen* is used for information and commands and *erzählen* for entertaining. How might you diagram these correspondences between languages using the hierarchy of difficulty? Alternatively, select another language (preferably a non-Indo-European language) and chart the correspondences for these related words. First, determine the words used for the general TALK concept. Then try to elicit as many synonyms as you can in the language. Finally, attempt to discover whether it is only the categories Lehmann described which account for the shift in terms. How closely does the distribution parallel that of English and German?

2. Ameka (1990) looks at four types of "experiences" which are linked to the roles of actor or undergoer. These include perception (see, hear, perceive, etc.), psychological, mental, or emotional experience (love, hate, anger, fear), sensation (hunger, thirst, itch, pain), and activity (eat, work). Languages often use grammar to show whether the experience is one in which the person acts or one in which the person receives or benefits from an action, or whether the speaker undergoes the experience. Ameka demonstrates this for Ewe (an African language). After reading his article, determine whether this is the case for English or another language of your choice.

3. Nilsen and Nilsen (1975, pp. 121–123) list verbs of experience. Use the groups of verbs categorized as psychological events (those that show a positive or negative reaction to experiences). Using this list as a starting point, design a research project to compare emotion terms cross-linguistically. (For a very different approach to the study of emotions, you might also wish to read *Australian Journal of Linguistics 10* (1990), an issue devoted to the semantics of emotions which use Wierzbicka's natural semantic metalanguage as a basis of cross-linguistic comparisons.)

4. Zubin and Svorou (1984) compared spatial terms in English, German, Korean, Mandarin, Peruvian Spanish, and Egyptian Arabic. They use plots to show the correspondences (Figure 6.3). For example, the comparison of English *wide* and *far* shows that *wide* has a much broader range than *far* and that the two words overlap. The distribution for German is quite different. Draw a comparison diagram for the language you teach or are studying. Compare your diagram with those in Zubin and Svorou for an ex-

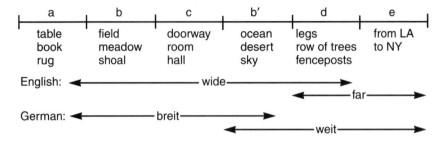

Figure 6.3

tended cross-linguistic comparison. What predictions can you make about how easily these terms will be acquired depending on which language is being learned by speakers of one of the other languages. Are diagrams such as these useful in language teaching? If so, design a short lesson where you use such diagrams (or have your students produce them). How might you evaluate the effectiveness of the materials? If you are interested in these terms, compare Lehrer's semantic feature analysis of the German terms *lang, kurz, breit, hoch, niedrig, gross,* and *klein* (1974, pp. 123–124). Which type of analysis do you think is more useful in illustrating cross-linguistic comparisons?

5. To our knowledge, there has been no attempt to use relational models (discussed in Chapter 4) for the analysis of split categories across languages. However, it is possible to draw comparisons across languages using relations. For example, Durrell (1988) contrasts the following set of English and German terms:

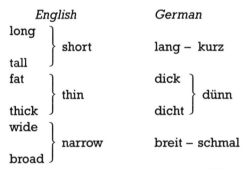

(Source: Durrell, 1988, p. 238)

Given pairs of terms like *long–short, tall–short,* we immediately relate them as antonyms. But we relate long–short as qualities typical of certain objects and tall–short as qualities of others – the relation between the quality and the object, A(typical quality), and the quantity relation of Minus or Plus. Thus, it might be possible to analyze splits using relational models. Review Durrell's examples of contrasts between English and German. How might relational models clarify the lexical relations within each language and then between the terms in the two languages?

6. Stative adjectives refer to inherent properties such as size, shape, and substance (tall, circular, liquid). Snell-Hornby (1990) notes that these should be easier than dynamic adjectives. Dynamic adjectives are not inherent but are temporary or changeable or based on value judgments. The value is relative to some implied norm set by the speaker or imposed by the social environment and implicitly accepted by the speaker (e.g., *vulgar, naughty*). The notion of dynamics can also apply to verbs (*gleam, bustle, waft*) and nouns (*hag, thug, hovel*). Snell-Hornby states, "In language learning and translation, dynamic adjectives, descriptive verbs and nouns with dynamic evaluation are a notorious source of difficulty and error – and they are at the same time given unsatisfactory treatment in bilingual dictionaries." Snell-Hornby argues that perception verbs are especially difficult to represent across languages. Consider her example of the perception of light and heat, starting with the word *gleam*. Gleam is light that is stable, though it may be perceived only briefly or temporarily; the light may be soft and subdued but not lacking in intensity. The light may be emitted and reflected with warmth (evening sunlight, light reflected on gold, on hair, on brass). She then sets up a chart for English and German:

flash	← twinkle	← shine	
	sparkle	│	
	shimmer	gleam	→ glow
	glimmer	beam	smoulder
glisten	← glitter	│	
	glint	glare	
		│	
		blaze	
	flicker	← flame	
		│	
		flare	

(continues)

(Snell-Hornby, 1990, p. 220)

First, how might you research the hypothesis that stative adjectives are easier to learn than dynamic adjectives? Note that Durrell's examples in item 4 are stative adjectives, yet they are predicted to be trouble sources for learners. Do you think the lack of correspondence between the two languages for the terms of perception of light will cause more problems for German learners of English or for English learners of German? Check to see if all the terms listed are included in a bilingual dictionary under the word *shine*. Do the entries adequately identify the differences in this lexical field?

7. Ard and Homburg (1983) compared Spanish and Arabic ESL students' performance on the vocabulary section of a language test. Spanish students had higher scores since, by recognizing cognates, they could guess meanings. Arabic students did not score as high. After reading this article, analyze the general proficiency or placement tests that are used at your school. Are the test items biased in favor of any particular language group. If they are, justify your own decision as to whether the items should or should not be rewritten.

8. Dole (1983) lists examples of transfer or interference from a second to a third language. Examples of interference from French in the English of a native speaker of Polish include the following:

Urgency entrance of the hospital
. . . wants a piece of *glace*
We should buy a *pamplemousse.*
I can't *assist* the meeting.
Then I worked for the *ambassade.*

Examples from French to English in the speech of a German include:

Serve yourself. (*Sers-toi* in French and *Bediene dich* in German)
You must ask him for an *explication.* (explanation)
You *inscribe* for the course. (register)

142

French to English for native speakers of Spanish included:

They're not too *pressed* to send the forms. (*pas tellement pressé, no tienen prisa*)
The trip *arrived* the same week as my trip to Chile.
I'm going to *pass* a month in Majorca. (*voy a pasar*)

It is sometimes difficult to know whether to say that interference is from the second language or from the first when the native language and the first foreign language are as closely related as French and Spanish or German and English. Compare the errors of the preceding Polish speaker with those of the Finnish speakers in Ringbom's study. Do you see resemblances? Design a research project which would parallel Ringbom's with another language which is not in the Germanic or Romance language families.

9. Bentahila (1975) examined the interference of French on the learning of English by Moroccans. Ulijn, Wolfe, and Donn (1981) studied the effect of French as a second language on the English of Vietnamese immigrants to the United States. Ringbom (1987) discusses the role of the second language, Swedish, on the English of Finns. Review these studies and any others you discover. (Another unpublished study is that of Gasser, described briefly in Hatch, 1978, p. 450). Wimmi, an adult native speaker of Punjabi who also spoke Hindi and English, moved to Ethiopia and began to use Amharic immediately in her hospital work as a nurse. She learned the Amharic word that means to visit. She then extended it to the meanings of the act of seeing since, in English, we often use *see* for *visit*. Prepare a research plan to look at the effect of second languages on lexical learning in a third language.

10. Using Wierzbicka's natural semantic metalanguage, Dineen (1990) draws cross-linguistic comparisons between English discomfort terms *embarrassed, ashamed,* and *shy* and their Danish "equivalents" *flov, forlegen, ilde berørt, pinlig,* and *skamfuld.* The differences shown reflect, in part, the Danish willingness to talk quite openly about things which are semi-taboo in English. They discuss their bodies quite openly, feeling that bodies cannot cause one discomfort though people can. The concepts of shame and embarrassment seem to be different in the two languages. To illustrate that cultural values, even for groups as similar as Danish and English, are important, Dineen compares two phrases, "to be past shame" and *have bidt hovedet af al skam,* phrases which appear to be equivalents. To say one is past shame is a terrible judgment in English while *have bidt hovedet*

af al skam is praise in Danish. It means one is willing to put aside shame or embarrassment in a situation one would normally avoid for the good of others. Harkins (1990) writes about the concept of shame as used by Aboriginal speakers, a use in which a person has been singled out for any purpose (whether scolding, praise, or attention) and thereby loses the security and anonymity of the group. This concept is shared by many cultures and is problematic for many teachers whose cultures and languages do not lexicalize this concept in the same way. If you are from (or teach students from) another culture, compare the concept and lexicalization of shame and embarrassment with that found in these studies. In what way would this information be of practical use in the classroom?

11. Lehrer (1974, p. 65) compares American English and Scottish terms for bakery products using semantic features (e.g., +/–yeast, +/–sweet, +/–soft). She also compares cooking terms in French, German, Farsi, Polish, Japanese, Mandarin Chinese, Jacaltec, Navajo, Amharic, and Yoruba (pp. 155ff.). Select either bakery products or cooking terms and, after you have read her descriptions, add another English dialect or another language and carry out a similar analysis. What splits, collapses, and other correspondences have you discovered? What advantages do you find to combining semantic field analysis and cross-linguistic comparisons?

12. Szalay and D'Andrade (1972) found that Americans and Koreans held different connotations for many words. To find the connotations, they asked each group for word associations to many words with social content (e.g., social, to cooperate, equality, socialism, pride, faith). The associations, and thus the connotations, for the terms differed. For example, *educated* held connotations of learned school knowledge for Americans, while the first Korean association for the term was *polite.* Yamamoto and Swan (1989) also found that foreign teachers of English in Japan had very different connotations for descriptive adjectives used in their study. For example, *naive* was thought of as a negative term by most of the foreign teachers but was more neutral for the Japanese teachers of English. These studies show that social terms or descriptive adjectives might be a good place to begin to study differences in connotations across language groups. Read and critique these and other articles as preparation for a research project of your own.

7 Script semantics and conceptual structure

In this chapter, we will attempt to incorporate many of the analytic methods discussed in previous chapters. As applied linguists, language teachers, and language learners we know we must somehow relate concepts, the vocabulary for concepts within the language we use in speaking and writing of our experiences. Cognitive psychologists, lexicographers, linguists, and researchers in artificial intelligence who attempt to model natural languages on computers are also faced with the problem of connecting concepts, the words representing concepts, and text.

As models have been proposed and refined by these psychologists, computer scientists, lexicographers, and linguists, a new field has evolved, known now as cognitive science. In the field of cognitive science, we find that language and semantic memory are envisioned as 'networks' and these networks are formed and activated in terms of some larger overall organization of events.

In this chapter we will consider two theories of what these networks might look like. First, we will review Schank's conceptual dependency theory, a theory that is action-based but which also relates concepts to the language of everyday activities represented in scripts. Then we will very briefly introduce Jackendoff's conceptual structure hypothesis, a more linguistic solution to the problem of relating mental concepts, lexical items, and sentence syntax but, in this case, without appeal to any larger context.

Scripts

The notions of scripts and schemas, which has influenced our work for decades, is the theoretical basis of much research on reading and composition. In script theory, we extend the notion of prototype beyond that represented by words. You might think of a script as a general prototype or template for an event. Concepts are part of the script for an event and the vocabulary for the concepts is 'activated' along with the script. And, as we have seen in previous chapters, the vocabulary for concepts becomes the source vocabulary to be used as metaphor across scripts to new target concepts.

With the script theory presented here, we will attempt to bring together much of what we already presented about semantics. While there are many different theories of script representation, we will combine that of Schank and his colleagues (1977, 1984), a theory sometimes called conceptual dependency theory, with that of Anderson (1983), particularly his work on augmented transition networks (ATNs). Once we have presented the general theory, we will look at how it relates to semantic theory in detail.

Although the following description oversimplifies this approach, at least a general outline of scripts is necessary in order to understand how semantics and lexicon are viewed within it. If you think of a language classroom, you realize that there are people who play established *roles* within the classroom script. TEACHER, STUDENT, TEACHER'S ASSISTANT, PRINCIPAL, and CUSTODIAN are examples of such roles. (These roles are placed in capital letters because they represent concepts, not vocabulary items.) In a courtroom, the roles include those of JUDGE, DEFENDANT, and so forth. In the hospital, DOCTOR, NURSE, PATIENT, and other roles are found. The vocabulary (*teacher, student,* and so forth) that represents these role concepts can then be activated for the script. This is formalized with an ISA link so that "*teacher* ISA TEACHER" shows that the lexical item *teacher* is an instance of the concept TEACHER. "*Cheryl* ISA TEACHER" shows that Cheryl is an instance of TEACHER and inherits all the characteristics of that role.

In some scripts where the role has dress requirements, "JUDGE HASA ROBE" and "NURSE HASA UNIFORM" would also be inherited by whatever name is placed in the judge or nurse role. Roles also have particular PROPS assigned to them. TEACHER HASA DESK, JUDGE HASA GAVEL, and NURSE HASA CHART are examples of props assigned to these roles. Notice that the relation of props and clothing are formalized with the HASA link. (The attachment of props to roles explains why we use a definite rather than an indefinite article for props: both roles and props are "known" items once a script is activated. We wouldn't say "A judge raised a gavel" in describing a courtroom scene. Instead, we would use definite articles even though neither judge nor gavel have been given previous mention: "The judge raised the gavel.")

In addition to having props, role players carry out actions within the script that are usually in a temporal order. If you place all the actions that take place in the classroom in chronological order, you might have a set of acts similar to those a teacher or student normally does. These actions, the actions of all those who have roles in the script, form the backbone of the template script.

Some of the actions are physical. For example, the teacher may walk about the room. MOVE is a volitional act. The concept MOVE may be actualized in a variety of different vocabulary items. The choice of items for a concept field forms a *schema*. As you can see, the schema relates to the earlier discussion of synonyms (Chapter 1) and semantic field analysis (Chapter 2). Thus, we can incorporate semantic feature and field analysis into script theory. There are many words that mean to move in a certain way as shown in Figure 7.1. We can also relate the choice of items in the concept field to the categories of superordinate, basic, and sub-basic levels discussed in Chapter 3. Given what we know about superordinate, basic, and sub-basic levels, the lexical item most often selected would mostly likely be *walk*: "The teacher walked around the room."

The teacher may also, for example, move books from a table to a desk. This move is a physical transfer of material, a concept called PTRANS. The actual movements within this general concept for moving items are then further specified (i.e., the teacher must KNOW where the object is, PROXimate or locate it, and take CONTrol of the object). At the lexical level, prototype theory would give us such words as *pick up* (for the GRASP move in taking CONTrol of an object) and *put* (for the PTRANS of an object to a flat surface) as the most basic lexical choices, yielding, "The teacher picked up the book" and "The teacher put the book on the table."

Teachers hand papers back to their students. In this case, the PTRANS of moving the object from one place to another is accompanied by a ATRANS move. ATRANS refers to a transfer of ownership schema. The lexical relation converse (from Chapter 4) is shown in the choices *give to* and *take from*, or *give* and *receive*. These are typical verb choices for the transfer of ownership concept.

In classrooms, we hope that there is a healthy exchange of ideas. Ideas are not objects that can be picked up and moved from place to place yet, as we saw in the Chapter 5, we typically refer to them as such via metaphor. MTRANS is the concept for mental transfer of information. Possible converse vocabulary for this concept include *teach* and *learn from*, or *explain* and *understand*. If, instead of MTRANS, we use a metaphorical extension of PTRANS where ideas are talked about as though they were physical objects, we might use the converses of *give* and *take–receive*. In neither case is there a transfer of ownership for the information is now shared, not the property of only one or the other.

There are other action concepts that, for simplicity, we will label as DO. For further explication, see Schank (1984). DO is just a prototypic verb concept; the actual concept would have to be specified in further detail in any analysis.

The notion of EVALUATION is another important part of every script. As we carry out the actions of any script role, we constantly determine the "goodness of fit" to our mental model of how this script should play out. If we are at a restaurant, we evaluate the event by matching the meal, its presentation, the service, and so forth, to each part of the script template;

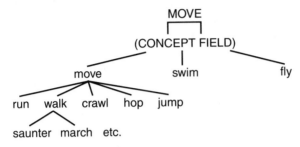

Figure 7.1   MOVE schema

we also evaluate the event in terms of how well it meets our goals in participating in the script (Are we still hungry?). The motives that go with roles are also important in evaluation. Very often we judge motives according to the role played rather than the person playing the role. So, if the teacher holds up her hand, we do not expect a student to interpret this as a signal that the teacher wishes to answer. Instead, the sign is recognized as a call for attention and quiet. The motive for the action is bound up with the role. Actions we cannot assign motives to can be quite disturbing because we do not know exactly how to interpret them within the script.

In another script, the person who plays the TEACHER role may now be a PARENT. Although some characteristics of the two roles are similar, others are not. Or, the STUDENT, out of the classroom and now on the playground, may change roles to those of STAR ATHLETE, BULLY, or LEADER. We play a wide variety of roles as we change from script to script. We hope that in each script, we will not be seen as that role, but rather as the person who defines self through the ways in which we play a multiplicity of roles. Nevertheless, it is difficult not to assign motivations to people in terms of actions of the roles they play in other scripts. For example, if we know someone is a star athlete, we are apt to judge that person's motivations in other scripts as though he or she were still playing that role. We judge teachers in the same way. Or we simply think they are absorbed into the blackboards at the end of the day to re-emerge the next – that is, they have no other roles in life.

Practice 7.1

1. Berko-Gleason and Weintraub (1976) described the trick-or-treat sequence of Halloween. The child's goal, when first taken on this traditional venture, may not be very clear. The goal may be to have fun or to get candy or to

dress up and scare people. The child may not know the "trick or treat!" opening demand or the "thank you" that comes at the end of the script. Parents or older siblings walk the child through the script from beginning to end many times during the evening. Select another traditional script (e.g., 5K race, wedding reception, Super Bowl party, pancake breakfast fund raiser) and list the obligatory roles, props, and actions. What prototypic vocabulary might be used for some of the concepts you have identified? What stereotypic utterances are used by people playing some of these roles?

2. If you work with very young children, document the amount of script teaching that adults or older siblings do. For example, do they give the child a toy phone and instruct her to "Say hello to Daddy"? Are they the ones who link actions to motives or states ("Oh, he went back to sleep. Guess he's tired.")? In your examples, is the teaching directed at the script components or at the language needed for the script? Do older children coach, model, or teach younger children the specific language needed for the script?

3. How often do children pretend to be (i.e., play the roles of) mother, father, older sibling, or pets? What role attributes do they assume in this play? If you observe children of different ages, do they refuse to play the role of BABY at a certain age? When? Is the age of refusal different for girls and boys?

4. What scripts do young children practice: ironing, cleaning house, going to the store, going to the doctor, driving the car, chasing robbers, going to school, playing teacher? Do they also use correct gestures or other nonverbal signals that go with the role? Von Raffler-Engel (1977) has studied the early emergence of language and culture-specific gestures in young children. For example, a 27-month-old Japanese child playing with a toy phone bows to her listener. If you have observed similar language-specific gestures in the play of young children, do these gestures go with particular stereotypic utterances or specific vocabulary items?

5. Being able to play roles in second language scripts is often judged as a mark of good language learning:

Example
Observer: Do you guys want to play doctor?
Juan: I wanna be the doctor.

Carlos:	(*on phone*) Allo doctor, I'm sick.
Juan:	Come.
Carlos:	OK, I be right there.
Juan:	Bye.
Carlos:	(*hangs up phone and pretends to knock at the door*)
Juan:	Come in.
Carlos:	(*turns to observer with a proud grin*) Hey, he knows a lotta English!

(Data source: Wong-Fillmore, 1976)

Look at the example and list the roles, props, and actions for the script. What are the prototypic utterances that go with the actions of the script. In what way do they differ from those given by these child language learners? What other phrases might they have used to show their script competence?

6. Some people learn particular second or foreign language scripts very well. A colleague was judged to have excellent colloquial Arabic because of her ability to play the customer bargaining role very well at the market. Are there special scripts in which you or other language learners either excel or fail? How do you account for the variability across scripts? Is it a matter of not knowing the script components, the prototypic utterances that go with the roles, or the right lexical choices for the nuances needed to show status or politeness conventions within the script?

7. Videotape your students (or yourself as a learner) in a role play of your choosing. What special script language do the learners use? What other choices of lexical items, phrases, or utterances might be used instead for a more successful performance?

8. In Chapter 5, we noted the ways we talk about teachers and learners via metaphor. In scripts, we also must specify the attributes of script roles. What attributes would you list for the TEACHER role in the classroom script? What attributes would you assign to the STUDENT role? What range of lexical items can be used for each attribute? Are there special attributes that need to be assigned to the bilingual classroom teacher and to the bilingual student?

9. How might a teacher create a new type of student role for students with special attributes? For example, consider the child who has lived in another country – say, China – and then returns and enrolls in a Chinese foreign language

class. The learners' Chinese, acquired in that country, might be more fluent and colloquial than the teacher's. How might such attributes change the student and teacher roles in the classroom script?

Scripts and semantics

How does script theory relate to semantics? First of all, the script specifies concepts, which then activate lexical items associated with the concept. Thus, once a service-encounter script, say, grocery shopping, is called up in response to the goal of obtaining food to satisfy the need of hunger, all of the typical roles would be activated: SHOPPER, CLERK, and so forth. All the prop concepts would be called up: GROCERY CART would be connected to the shopper as a temporary ATRANS of ownership. REGISTER (some sort of computer, register, adding machine) would be connected to the CLERK. The SHOPPER actions (MOVEing down the aisles, PTRANS of objects from shelf to cart) lead to CLERK actions of PTRANS of objects from cart to bags or boxes. The ATRANS of ownership of the items is carried out through a CHARGE PAY (give and receive payment) exchange. These concepts are not words. The actual words are viewed as instances of the concept. There are also stereotypic sets of phrases that go with particular roles. "Have a nice day" is a formulaic closing utterance for the clerk; "I now pronounce you husband and wife" is a formulaic utterance of the minister role in the marriage script; "Time to turn in your papers" is a formulaic utterance for teachers in the classroom script. The lexical items, whether utterances, phrases, or individual lexical choices are activated as we move from concepts to the words that express them. Although much of the language is predictable, each instance is sensitive not only to the script but also to the motives of the players. In each instance of playing a role in a script, we are also sensitive to evaluation.

Second, there are many terms available for every concept. The diagram for these terms is often called a concept schema. Traditionally, we have called the choices in the schema synonyms, but they are not really synonyms within a script. The scripts themselves restrict the vocabulary choices that can be made. For example, Figure 7.1 shows some of the choices for the concept MOVE, but is unlikely that the words *swim, fly,* or *crawl* would be activated in a classroom script.

We mentioned that EVALUATION is ubiquitous in scripts. We constantly evaluate our performance and the performance of others in creating a new instance of any script. In evaluation, the choice of lexical items, whether you prefer a field semantics approach of taxonomic boxes or tree diagram options, would be along a scale rather than synonymic.

Third, lexicographers using relational models highlight synonym, hyponomy, function, attribute, and various types of part-whole relationships among lexical items. In script theory, this is handled by listing the attributes of roles and props. For example, roles are most often played by HUMANs. Human beings have bodies and these bodies, in turn, consist of parts such as head, neck, trunk, arms, legs, and so forth. These parts are further divided into parts so that fingers, thumb and palm are parts of the hand. The hand, forearm, and upper arm are parts of the arm. These can be specified by HASA and ISA links for concepts. HUMAN HASA BODY; BODY HASA PARTS; HEAD ISA PART; TRUNK ISA PART; ARM ISA PART; ARM HASA PARTS; HAND ISA PART. The hand is then redefined according to its parts. Each time a human is activated, these attributes are there. Speakers or writers need not explicitly mention attributes of roles nor the connections among them; they are already given or presumed present.

Earlier we noted that lexical relations include not only synonyms and antonyms but also the mutual relation of converses, which are tied to our notion of script. *Teacher* and *student* are not really opposites; rather, they are roles with reciprocal functions within a script. The roles involve the converse actions of *teach* and *learn*. Since we learn as much, if not more, from our students as they do from us, the actions of teaching and learning are, in actuality, not tied to the role of teacher and student. Rather, the roles and actions are reciprocal. That is, we can change teacher and student roles within any classroom script. Nevertheless, the typical template assigns teaching (and the authority that goes with the role) to the teacher and learning to the student. In other scripts, the roles might be SELLER and CUSTOMER who SELL and BUY props in the script. Again, in bargaining, there is a reciprocal shift as the buyer becomes the offerer of a potential price. The seller shifts from offering the merchandise to considering whether or not to "buy" the offer. The actions of players of these roles reciprocally build the script in each new instance of playing the roles.

Professional office visits also demonstrate the reciprocal nature of actions attached to ROLES. The doctor or dentist or lawyer or teacher QUESTIONS the patient, client, or student regarding SYMPTOMS and offers REMEDIES. The actual building of an advice-giving event, however, is negotiated by the people playing the roles. There are cycles of evaluation and negotiation throughout the script. The advice seeker and the advice giver listen, accept or reject, and evaluate symptoms and remedies. The script is much more complex than a simple LIST-symptoms and LIST-cures set of actions.

We mentioned that scripts that share much in common can be grouped together into a larger class. For example, all scripts that involve a contract of exchanging money for service (shopping scripts, entertainment scripts, professional-office-visit scripts, and so forth) might be grouped together as service-encounter scripts. Vocabulary searches can then easily be run across all the scripts within a group of like scripts. There are case study examples where language learners report doing just that. Zernik (1987) reports hearing the term "rip you off" as part of a description of a service encounter with a garage mechanic. Given the negative intonation, Zernik realized the meaning had to be a negative evaluation term. He hypothesizes that a learner would then check evaluation terms for contracts: service (not done, poorly done) relative to charge for service. The lexical item *cheat* might spring to mind and the learner could then begin to listen for contrasts between *rip off* and *cheat* throughout all service encounters.

This grouping of similar scripts also lets us relate the notion of source and target transfer of meanings in metaphor. If metaphor is as basic a process as Lakoff and associates claim, we would expect to find a great deal of metaphoric transfer across scripts that are related. Indeed, this is the case. Remember the many metaphors that teachers used in talking about teaching and learning mentioned in the previous chapter. We can group together creative-enterprise scripts such as weaving, painting, writing, and teaching and metaphorically transfer terms from one script to another with ease. Or we can group together various treatment-of-problems scripts such as medicine, engineering, teaching, and theology and transfer terms of cures, treatment, and reawakening across them all. Thus, metaphor can be incorporated into script theory.

The nature of semantic networks are being specified in greater and greater detail as computer scientists attempt not only to model scripts but all the relations that exist between words. The hope is that an on-line dictionary might be added to script models – an online dictionary that gives information on such relations as types of synonyms, antonyms, converses, part-whole correspondences.

In our discussion of scripts, we said that ISA is a link that joins exemplars to concepts. However, the nature of the ISA link would have to be more specific once the model is enlarged and a relational dictionary is added. For example, when an ISA relation is called up, the relation might be IS A KIND OF ("An oak is a tree"), the generic or hyponym relation. The ISA might be IS THE SAME AS ("intelligent is smart"), the synonym relation. It might be an attribute, IS AN ATTRIBUTE ("a rock is hard"), or IS MADE OF ("a lens is made of glass"), the typical adjective or quality and labor relations. While all of these are considered ISA relations, they obviously differ in terms of type of relation. In our discussion of scripts, the part-whole relation was labeled as the HASA relation where props are part of a role (judge HASA gavel) or where parts of an object are named (body HASA parts, arm ISA part). Many semantic networks use HASPART or PART-OF for this second type of relation.

There are many different relational models, all of which identify the lexical relations (but disagree on the number of relations) needed to make it possible for a computer to "parse" and understand scripts (see Chapter 4). Some of these models have been proposed by lexicographers working with cognitive scientists in an attempt to computerize natural language processing systems.

So far, we have demonstrated that script theory allows us to bring together the many seemingly separate notions we have described in this section on semantics. Relating semantics to scripts solves some of the problems that semantic feature analysis alone cannot solve. We can show, for example, that the problem of plus vs. minus dichotomies are better presented as scales. The choice of an item on the scale relates to the particular script selected and to evaluation within the script (and of role motives and register differences that go with the particular script instance). As relational models are added to scripts, we will have an even more powerful way of bringing together much of the information about semantics described in previous chapters.

Practice 7.2

1. Baldinger (1980) lists the following change of possession terms: *give, steal, accept, deliver, lend.* What other terms can you think of? How do scripts influence the choice of lexical item?
2. Each of Baldinger's terms in item 1 has many meanings, some of which do not signal a change of possession. Look at the following list of expressions and determine whether or not a change of possession is signaled by the verb *give:* "give him a book," "give him fits," "give him your hand," "give him a gold medal," "give him a cold," "give him a test," "give him a beer." Do you think that the change-of-possession meaning is the prototype meaning for give?
3. Verbs of motion like *chase, follow,* and *pursue* are also tied to scripts. If a police officer chases a suspect, the meanings of these verbs differ from their use in a classroom script. Think of a variety of scripts that might use these terms. The choices of mental transfer (MTRANS) terms (*tell, ask, warn, explain, answer, show*) also differ across scripts. In what ways are the meanings of the terms the same or different depending on the script? Give examples to support your answer.
4. Some of the choices for the PTRANS concept are *take, move, bring, put, send,* and *remove.* List as many other terms as you can. Find parallels for these terms in another

language. What similarities and differences do you find in how these terms show the physical transfer concept?

5. In the "rip off" example for car repair, Zernik hypothesized that a learner would compare the uses of *rip off* and *cheat* across service-encounter scripts. In which service encounters would you be more likely to use *cheat* than *rip off*? Is the choice a matter of the type of service-encounter script? Or is it a matter of intensity of evaluation? What would be the result if the learner generalized *rip off* as a synonym for *cheat* across all service encounter scripts?

6. The connection between scripts and lexical items is sometimes so strong as to be dangerous. Osgood (1978) writes, "A man can freeze to death for lack of kindling wood and yet be found with a pocketful of wooden pencils – because pencils are coded to write with, not to make fires with." In creativity workshops, participants are encouraged to think outside scripts. One exercise to encourage creative thought is, "Given a common item, how many things can you think of to do with it?" Select an item and list as many uses as you can. Can you arrange the uses in terms of a hierarchy of scripts? Is your hierarchy based on the frequency or the importance of the item for each script?

7. In neurolinguistics, there is a set of symptoms that are sometimes called *thought disorder.* Patients exhibit what might be called nonscript-bound use of lexicon. Prototypic words for a script are called up, but the organizing framework of the script quickly disappears and the person continues talking with vocabulary "activated" by a lexicon associated not with the script but with individual vocabulary items. The result sounds similar to that of stream-of-consciousness writing or certain types of poetry:

    a. My mother's name was Bill and coo. St. Valentine's Day was the start of the breedin' season of the birds.
    b. Looks like clay. Sounds like gray. Take you for a roll in the hay. Hay day. May day. Help! I just can't. Need help. May day.
    c. I had a little goldfish like a clown. Happy Hallowe'en down.

(Data source: Chaika, 1985)

Think about what this might mean in terms of theory. In the introduction, we cited J. Yamada's research to show that conceptual and linguistic systems are separate systems. How could we use the Chaika data to claim that script systems and semantic systems are separate as well? Or could we claim that language is an integrated cognitive-social-linguistic system, but that at places in that system, processes may be short-circuited, producing what only appear to be separate systems? (If you can articulate this well, please let us know your answer!)

Script semantics, language teaching, and testing

There are many areas of script analysis that have direct counterparts in language teaching. For example, consider the teaching of languages for specific purposes. Students training in hotel or restaurant management have specific purposes in mind for studying languages. If they hope to attract tourists from Japan or if they hope to create a Japanese ambience in a Japanese-style restaurant in another country, then it is important to know the Japanese script for hotels or for restaurants. The language for the variety of scripts within this profession are limited so the language instruction can be directed toward those specific scripts.

Special courses for nurses, doctors, and other medical personnel also highlight script learning and the vocabulary necessary for medical purposes. The acquisition of vocabulary in medicine can also be related to script theory. It is not uncommon in some countries for shopkeepers to have mastered their particular special purpose scripts in many different languages. They need to be able to do the script in English at one moment, and be ready to replay it in French, German, Italian, Spanish, or Arabic the next. You might believe that this learning has little scope, but if you think of the range of service encounters, you realize that the language needed for these scripts can be generalized and refined across many different situations. The vocabulary needed in contract negotiation is transferable to many different scripts.

If you think of most survival courses in languages for new immigrants and travelers, you will see that they are organized around scripts (e.g., going to the market, going to the doctor, getting a driver's license, using public transportation). Although these courses are not usually considered specific purpose instruction, they relate to script theory. The vocabulary taught in each unit is script-bound to a large extent.

Finally, in language assessment, the vocabulary of domains is often tested. This domain includes all the vocabulary that is used by persons playing specific roles and using specific props in the home situation, for example. The vocabulary of this domain could be subdivided into that of semantic fields (i.e., kinship terms, eating utensils, cooking terms, furniture terms, clothing and personal adornment terms, names of toys, and so forth). The vocabulary of the school domain would include that of actors,

156

props, and actions of the school script (i.e., role terms like student, principal, teacher, security guard; prop terms like books, pencils, chalkboards, basketball hoops; and the action terms discussed earlier in this chapter). The language and the vocabulary of domains is very much script-bound.

Practice 7.3

1. Prepare a list of vocabulary words that you believe a 7-year-old child should know for the home domain. Check your items against the Peabody Picture Vocabulary Test English, French, or Spanish versions. Did you list all the key words included in this test? What scripts from the home domain are reflected in the test items? Select the items that seem most important to you and administer the test to both monolingual and bilingual children. Are the bilingual children able to give you the vocabulary in each language? How would you explain your findings? What strengths and weaknesses do you see in the test and your own items in terms of testing the general vocabulary of young children? In how many domains and how many scripts must one be able to operate before one can be judged "bilingual"?
2. Prepare a list of school terms that a bilingual child would need to know by the end of the first year of instruction. Administer this test to both monolingual and bilingual students. Can the bilingual children give you terms for these items in both languages? How would you explain your findings?
3. In elementary schools, the curriculum often includes mandated units. California missions, space and space exploration, and computers are three units in a fourth-grade classroom we observed. Consider the importance of the vocabulary in each of these units for the bilingual child. What words might be included in a test of fourth-grade academic vocabulary?
4. Survival courses are meant to prepare adults for everyday interactions in their new language in a variety of scripts. After this first level is completed, what other script areas listed in this section might one select next (and what types of vocabulary would need to be learned)?
5. If you have taken a specific purpose or survival course in another language, what types of scripts and vocabulary did you hope to learn? How did you go about dealing with the

inadequacies in the number or types of scripts and vocabulary given in the class?

6. There are a number of theories about the best ways to promote infant bilingualism. One of these is the "one language–one person" principal where one person, parent, or caretaker consistently uses one language while the other consistently uses a second language. This has been extended to a "one language–one environment" principle where one language is used consistently at home and the other at school. Another model in bilingual education is the alternate days' use (on Monday, it's Spanish; on Tuesday it's English). How do these principles relate to script learning and to the acquisition of language by domains?

Thematic and conceptual structure theory

Because linguists are primarily interested in the acquisition of the syntactic system of language, it is not surprising that most linguists criticize script theory as lacking information about how the meanings in scripts are related to syntactic structure. For them, script knowledge is just part of "world knowledge" and, as such, has little relation to linguistic theory.

Even at the sentence level, however, linguistic theory must include some characterization of semantic meaning, and it is this level of representation that is of interest to linguists. Fillmore, Chomsky, Gruber, and Jackendoff, among other linguists, consider roles important in clarifying the relationship between semantics and syntax. The roles, however, are not tied to scripts but to sentences, and the relation differs significantly in these writings. A brief summary is offered below. (More technical arguments about the relation of semantics and syntax can be found in the writings of each of these theorists.) Following this short summary, we will turn to Jackendoff's proposal that semantics be included within a more general conceptual structure. We will attempt to show how his conceptual structure hypothesis relates to conceptual dependency theory.

If you think about the roles that persons or objects play in sentences rather than scripts, you can see that parts of meanings can be derived from those roles. Fillmore (1977) identified a number of roles important for semantic-syntactic relationships. We will only touch on his classification of roles here (see Part II for a detailed discussion). If a person intentionally and willfully carries out an action shown in a verb, the person has a special role of *agent* of the action. In English, agents commonly occur in subject position. However, if the person or object is acted upon, the role is less active in meaning. This role is called *patient*. The patient is typically a direct object. If the action is carried out using another object, that object has an *instrumental* role. Roles typically occupy certain positions in sentences. Thus, in the sentence "John cut the wood with a band saw," *John* has an agent role and is in subject position; *wood* has a patient role and is in object position; *band saw* has an instrumental role and is a prepositional phrase. The *recipient* role is that typically assigned to indirect objects (e.g., "Miss Rodriguez [agent] taught Bob [recipient] Spanish [patient]"). The relation between these theme roles and syntactic position, however, is not strictly predictable. In the sentence "The band saw cut the wood," *band saw* is still in an instrumental role but it now serves as subject of the sentence. In the sentence "The wood was cut by John," the patient and agent have been switched so that the patient is in subject position and the agent in object position. The order of recipient and patient can also be changed: "Miss Rodriguez taught Spanish to Bob."

Such case or theme roles also appear in Chomsky's theory of government and binding where they are called "theta roles." In Chomsky's 1981 *Lectures on Government and Binding,* he notes, "It has traditionally been assumed that such notions as 'agent-of-action,' 'goal-of-action,' etc. play an important role in semantic description" (p. 35). He proposes that theta roles can be assigned a "theta-position" in syntax. Because Chomsky did not completely specify theta roles, the MIT Lexicon Project (Levin, 1985) set as its goal the defining of the inventory of theta roles (how many roles are needed and how are they best characterized) and criteria for determining how these roles relate to the functions of verbs and nouns within sentences. The MIT Lexicon Project's position is that there is a direct correlation between thematic structure and semantic classes and syntax.

Jackendoff's work (1985), however, differs in that he claims that there is a correlation between thematic roles and meaning but not necessarily between theme roles and syntax. Instead of limiting his description to theme roles, he proposed a conceptual structure hypothesis. Conceptual structure does not contain script information but it does contain information that comes from perception (visual and sensory information) and motor information. Conceptual structure must, then, give some description of the concepts described as MOVE or PTRANS in script theory since they involve motor information. A description must be given of the concept MTRANS since this involves perceptual information, and of EVAL since evaluation relates in some sense to sensory feedback. In Jackendoff's work, this description would be part of conceptual structure, a separate level of description which brings together perceptual (visual, sensory, etc.) information, information from the motor system, and pragmatic information, as well. Thus, in Jackendoff's theory, semantic structure is part of conceptual structure. It is relevant to, but independent from, strictly linguistic phenomena.

As an example, Jackendoff's proposed description (as presented by

Wilkins, 1994, p. 123) for the verb *put* includes syntactic information that it is a verb and that it is preceded by a subject noun phrase and followed by an object noun phrases and a prepositional phrase.

PUT
[–N, +V]
NP_i _____ NP_j PP_k

This is followed by the conceptual structure, which here consists of two tiers. A thematic tier shows that *put* is an event where a thing goes from one location along a path to another location:

$$[_{EVENT} \, GO \, ([_{THING}\alpha]_j, \begin{bmatrix} [FROM \, ([_{PLACE}]_i)] \\ PATH \, [TO \, ([_{PLACE} \, \tau])]_k \end{bmatrix})]$$

An action tier shows that the act of putting involves causality where one entity acts in a volitional, causal manner on another:

$$[_{EVENT} \, CAUSE \, ([_{THING}\beta]_i, [_{EVENT} \, ACT \, ([_{THING}]^\beta, [_{THING}]^\alpha)])]$$

The thematic tier in this theory is related to perception (and involves thematic roles such as location, source, etc). The action tier is related to a theory of events and involves such roles as agent, patient, and so forth. Thus, the conceptual structure hypothesis contains within it the notions introduced earlier by Fillmore (1977) and adopted as theta roles by Chomsky (1981). In this hypothesis, however, these roles do not directly determine syntactic structures. The link between the semantics of conceptual structure and syntax is accomplished by a system of subscripts.

The subscripts in Jackendoff's formal notions are used to tie the description together. The identify of *i, j,* and *k* are the same at each level of the description. So in the syntactic description, the subscript *i* would identify the subject *Susie* in the sentence "Susie put the baby in the chair." In the thematic tier, *i* is the source at which the movement begins (i.e., the baby moves from Susie to the chair). In the final action tier, the subscript *i* shows that Susie is the agent that carries out the act that causes the movement of the baby to the chair.

The MOVE concept in script theory is described more completely in Jackendoff's theory (as presented by Wilkins). For example, the conceptual structure thematic tier for ENTER as a verb of motion is described as:

$$[_{EVENT} \, GO \, ([\alpha], \begin{bmatrix} FROM \, ([_{PLACE}\beta]) \\ PATH \, TO \, ([_{PLACE} \, IN \, ([\gamma])]) \end{bmatrix})]$$

This concept structure shows that something goes from someplace along a path to another place. Notice, though, that the sentence "Susie entered (*from the hall) (*into) the office" is not acceptable in English. The English verb *enter* has included the PATH and PLACE functions within it and only expresses the final location. The Spanish sentence *Susana entró en la oficina* is acceptable. Wilkins (1994) explains that Spanish does not include the PATH and PLACE function in the verb and so these must be supplied syntactically. According to Jackendoff (and most linguists), the same conceptual structure is shared by the two languages, but the lexicalization of the concept differs and this information is reflected in sentence syntax.

As you can see, Jackendoff's conceptual structure descriptions are much more complete than the concept labels of scripts. To show this, we have contrasted his more detailed description of one type of PTRANS, the concept PUT, and one MOVE concept, ENTER. With separate tiers of description for conceptual structure (theme and action and a temporal tier not presented here) and tying the conceptual tiers to syntactic information, Jackendoff's description also allows us to pinpoint the contrasts in lexicalization of conceptual structures across languages.

Practice 7.4

1. Nilsen and Nilsen (1975, p. 111) list four classes of motion verbs: transportation (e.g., *walk*), transfer (e.g., *throw*), exchange (e.g., *reimburse*), and communication (e.g., *explain*). Add one more example for each class. Explain how Schank's conceptual dependency theory and Jackendoff's conceptual structure hypothesis differ in the way they would include such verbs in their respective theories.

2. Talmy (1980) shows that there is a difference in the ways that Spanish and English lexicalize the path part of the concept SWIM. Can the following sentences mean both that the swimming took place under the waterfall and that a path was crossed from one side of the waterfall to the other?

   Ben swam under the waterfall.
   Benjamin nadaba debajo de la cascada.

   Which theory, conceptual dependency theory or conceptual structure theory, best accounts for this difference? Select two other languages and determine whether both readings are possible for the words for SWIM.

3. Shirai (1990a) notes that it is perfectly acceptable in Japanese to say the equivalent of "I put the book" or "He finished talking and put the receiver." Jackendoff's conceptual structure for the concept PUT is the same for both languages. What part of the conceptual structure is lexicalized in a different way in the two languages? (Recall

161

Wilkins's explanation of lexicalization of ENTER in Spanish and English.)

4. American Sign Language often includes location in verb signs. Using a sign for move, for example, it is possible to show the starting point and the ending point. To show that I will give you a book, the sign might start at the location of the book and move toward you. If you know or are studying ASL or another sign language, explain how location is lexicalized in such signs as LOOK AT, BRING, and other signs of your choice. Think of the ways that size, shape, manner, and intensity are lexicalized into verbs such as RUN, EAT or other signs. Would Jackendoff's conceptual structure hypothesis be useful in analyzing American Sign Language?

5. Each of the following verbs marks a change of state that occurs only if an instrument can be used. If you were writing a conceptual structure description, how might you characterize the CAUSE of the change in state for these verbs? Explain how parts of the description might be 'subscripted' to show this. You don't need to write a formal description, though you may if you wish.

Verbs of change of state (instrument)
dampen, douse, dye, electrify, flood, freeze, season, shock, spice up, turn off–on, wash, wet down

6. Some verbs that relate to a change of state reflect an internal change, whereas others are caused by another person (agent). Identify which of the following states would require a separate agent in the description. In some of the examples, does something else need to be specified (i.e., do all the verbs seem to relate to the change of state in the same way)?

State or change of state: "Be/become X"
educated (teach, learn)
dead (die, kill)
aware (remind, remember)
risen (raise, rise)
forgiven (apologize, forgive)
knowing (see, show)
set (sit, set)

Select another language and check to see whether similar pairs of verbs relate to the change of state.

7. In collections of humorous quotes, we may label the humor as coming from oxymorons, strange conversives, or other misplaced relations. It is also possible to view the errors as examples of mistakes in conceptual lexicalization. For example, "I collided with a stationary truck coming the other way" is wrong because the verb *come* has a conceptual structure for movement which is impossible for a stationary truck. What errors of lexicalization can you discover in the following quotes said to have appeared on insurance claims?

My car was legally parked as it backed into the other vehicle.
An invisible car came out of nowhere, struck my vehicle, and vanished.
A pedestrian hit me and went under my car.
The telephone pole was approaching fast. I was attempting to swerve out of its path when it struck my front end.
A stop sign suddenly appeared in a place where no stop sign had ever appeared before. I was unable to stop in time to avoid the accident.

Summary of Part I

The goals of cognitive psychologists and linguists are not always the same and their descriptions of the semantic system differ. Linguists need a semantic description that will fit into their overall conception of language. Componential analysis fit into the theory current at the time it was first proposed. Semantic features and phonological features met the same perceived need to break units down into still smaller components, which were meaningful for transformational descriptions of language. Psychologists have been more interested in the relation of perception and language and so their descriptions include features that have a less central impact on the grammar system of the language. Still, core vs. periphery and prototype analyses are important in both psychology and linguistics since core or prototype exemplars are more basic and should, therefore, be easy to learn. Our perceptual system also seems linked to our use of everyday conceptual metaphor, and for some cognitive psychologists this is a crucial area of research on semantics. In conceptual dependency theory, Schank and his associates have attempted to link the structure of everyday events (scripts) and the concepts activated with the scripts. Computer scientists, however, cannot build natural language processing systems that are large enough to handle all the possible scripts of real life without figuring out how to build larger and more detailed lexicons. Lexicographers working with relational models of semantic networks hope to build such models. Linguists like Jackendoff, however, attempt to link cognitive concepts and the ways the words that lexicalize these concepts are used to create sentences. Applied linguists find all of these approaches to semantics of interest. However, the theories – whether natural semantic metalanguage, conceptual dependency theory, relational models, semantic feature analysis, prototype analysis, or analysis of metaphor – must apply across linguistic systems. Therefore, much of their research has examined the value of each analysis across language systems and the potential of each analysis in explaining variability in second language learning.

Not surprisingly, linguists criticize cognitive psychologists for ignoring syntax and cognitive psychologists criticize linguists for ignoring any structured language beyond the sentence. Lexicographers criticize both linguists and psychologists to the extent that each ignores the centrality of the lexicon in language theory. Each has limited the scope of description because the phenomena to be described are so complex and the description is so difficult. There is no reason, however, that the strengths of all of these approaches might not one day be joined into a coherent theory of language. Since our presentation of the methods of semantic analysis in Part I has also simplified these approaches, we encourage you to read the major writings of each approach to understand better how cognitive and linguistic descriptions relate to the study of meaning.

Research and application

Semantic relations in cognitive models

1. Collins and Quillian (1972) developed a network model of semantic relations that has been popular in cognitive science. They used reaction times as a measure of connectedness: if the pause before response was short, it was assumed that the information was in the network. If the pause before response was longer, Collins and Quillian assumed the information was not in the network and had to be constructed or inferred. Their relations include:

    a. superset–superordinate   frequently used and less used supersets exist (e.g., a bear is a kind of animal)

    b. subsets   most important, easiest strategy (e.g., trees include oaks, pines, and maples, among others)

    c. similarity   properties of one concept applied to another via inference, providing a basis for distinguishing (e.g., a lamb is like a sheep only smaller) or grouping (e.g., a tri-

cycle is like a bicycle because
they both have wheels)

d. part   especially useful for geography,
anatomy, and architecture

e. proximity–adjacency   especially useful for geography
and anatomy

f. consequence   especially useful for history and
(causality) and   science
precedence

g. parent   for kinship

Since Collins and Quillian identify certain relations as being especially important for a particular field of study, you might use this system as background for developing lessons that stress particular lexical or semantic relations between words. Which relations would you select? How does the choice differ from that you identified in Chapter 4 on relational models?

2. Rumelhart, Lindsay, and Norman (1972) developed "maps" as visual displays of how "pathways" between words are represented. The network that is revealed is a pictorial network. Look at the diagrams and maps they develop and decide whether you might be able to use one or both in teaching particular types of semantic relations. If you believe they would be useful, develop a short presentation using the method and evaluate its effectiveness. Share your findings with other teachers at a staff meeting or conference.

Scripts

3. Nilsen and Nilsen (1975, p. 111) give lists of lexical items for four classes of verbs of motion. How might you differentiate among these via scripts?

4. Bermudez and Prater (1990) used brainstorming (where children call out words they associate with a particular topic) and clustering (where they then group the words into categories) techniques with limited English proficient writers to develop elaboration. The teacher acted as scribe, writing words and phrases suggested by 16 third- and fourth-grade bilingual children on a topic. The words were written on a transparency and shown on an overhead projector. Concepts that were related were circled on the transparency. Two days later, the children wrote about the same topic. The children in this group that used brainstorming and clustering wrote more elaborate compositions than children in the group that did not. How would you explain the results of this study with script theory? Since the children could activate

165

the vocabulary associated with the script and could group the words into concept areas, why would these techniques be needed to improve their writing about the script topic? Design a research project that would test the effectiveness of brainstorming and clustering techniques with adult students. Would you predict the same results (more elaborate writing)? What areas of writing other than elaborateness might be related to this technique?

5. Many studies have shown the comparative strengths and weaknesses in vocabulary for bilingual children by domain. Bilingual children may know the vocabulary of the home (names for furniture, dinnerware, clothing, food) or of school (recess, playground, teacher, math, social studies) in one language but not the other. These differences may not be evident in a general vocabulary test but might be detected if children are tested by domain (see Fishman et al., 1971). Legaretta (1979) also developed a series of tests that elicited vocabulary by domains as part of a larger evaluation of types of bilingual programs. Locate as many instruments as you can that test vocabulary by domain. After you have critiqued the available tests and test methods, devise and try out a pilot procedure of your own.

6. Review the survey of word association tests in Albert and Obler (1978, pp. 47–58). The results of these tests are related to the notion of compound vs. coordinate bilingualism or of balanced bilingualism, language dominant bilingual, or second language learning. How might script semantics across domains relate to the findings?

7. Demers and Farmer (1986, p. 177) give lists of words with emotive meaning. We have suggested the selection of items on the scales might be related to script roles in particular settings. Here are some of the scales: places: tavern–bar–dive, women: fairer sex–female–broad, automobiles: car–jalopy–heap, relationships: separate from–walk out on–desert, talk: uninteresting–nonsense–baloney. How would you answer a student's question as to when you use each choice on the scale? Prepare a research plan to test whether your students or native speakers of the language make a consistent choice when multiple-choice test items illustrate different scripts.

8. Erickson and Mattson (1981) and van Oostendorf and de Mul (1990) show that adults answer questions such as "How many animals of each kind did Moses take on the ark?" without noticing the Moses–Noah error. They attribute this to the semantic similarity of Moses and Noah. Both are male biblical characters; they are both leaders, involved with water, and so forth. How might

this finding relate to script theory and spreading activation across scripts? Do you think that second language learners experience more or fewer such semantic oversights? How might you go about testing your answer?

9. Brinton and Gaskill (1978) used edited videotapes of news broadcasts in teaching EFL in Germany and ESL to adults in Los Angeles. The article describes the procedures used in each environment (e.g., vocabulary glosses, prelistening and guided listening activities, follow-up activities). They list the benefits of broadcasts in the classroom:

   a. They are timely and relevant.
   b. The recycling of vocabulary is more consistent, in particular in news items which reappear over a period of several weeks.
   c. News items provide the student with a more useful core vocabulary, which enables the student to more readily participate in the type of conversations he or she is likely to encounter in a social situation.
   d. The cultural asides gleaned from news broadcasts provide the student with a broader knowledge of the target culture.

   Tape a newcast about one topic from National Public Radio news over several days. Is there a script for the news reports? Select key vocabulary for two of the news items and prepare a gloss for each. What prelistening and guided listening activities would you use? What follow-up activities? Ask students to rate the usefulness of the newscast lesson in terms of the four benefits listed by Brinton and Gaskill.

Sentence-based hypotheses (case, theme, conceptual structure)

10. Miller et al. (1990) describe the types of relations in WordNet, an on-line lexical database, including ISA relations, which are called hyponyms in WordNet. Miller says that the hyponym inherits the features of the more generic concept and adds at least one feature that distinguishes it from its superordinate term. What feature would distinguish *July* in JULY ISA MONTH? WordNet also includes HASA relations, which are called meronymy in the WordNet system. This relation is symmetric as in A HASA X (the book HASA page) and X ISA PART OF A (a page ISA part of a book). The system also includes synonymy where one item can be substituted for another without changing the truth value of the sentence. Similarity judgments may also be given of the type that X IS SIMILAR TO Y means that Y IS EQUALLY SIMILAR TO X ("New

York is similar to Chicago"; "Chicago is similar to New York").
Read this introduction to WordNet and consider how an on-line
lexical database of this sort might be linked to script theory.

11. The *Oxford Advanced Learners' Dictionary* (Hornby 1989) uses semantic headings for polysemous verbs that reflect those of case
grammar descriptions. The most common verbs in English are
those that have the most meanings (have, be, run, make, go, take,
set). The meanings are separated by headings such as performing an action, receiving or undergoing action, producing, causing or allowing something to happen. Check other dictionaries to
see if they use case descriptions to separate the meanings of
common verbs. What other case headings might you add if you
were designing a dictionary that used a conceptual basis?

12. Fillmore (1971) analyzes many different lexicalizations of the concept JUDGE, including *accuse, blame, criticize, credit, praise,
scold, confess, apologize, forgive, justify,* and *excuse.* Read this article and integrate Fillmore's analysis with a script approach.
Which verbs go with what roles in which scripts? Alternatively,
look for instances of these verbs in the classroom script and see
how they relate to teacher, student, and principal roles.

13. Miller (1972) describes the outcome of card-sorting tasks for a
group of verbs of motion including *go, stride, walk, stroll, tiptoe,
sprint,* and *jog.* The analysis revealed that the verbs were
categorized along two dimensions: speed (slow to fast) and foot
orientation (heel to toe). Prepare a research plan to investigate as
many verbs of motion as you can. You might try several options: a
contextual analysis based on a computer search for the forms in
data such as the Brown corpus, a variety of displays (semantic
field boxes, tree diagrams, relational model descriptions), and a
script analysis. You could carry out the project in a language
other than English or as a cross-linguistic comparison of terms
from two languages.

Part II   Lexicon

8 Adding to the lexicon

There are many ways in which the lexicon of a language can be enlarged. We will discuss four in this chapter: borrowing words from other languages; creating new words (coinage); using the names of people or places to refer to a related object; making shifts and conversions where meanings of words or their parts of speech change. In Chapter 9 we will look at additive and subtractive processes used to create new terms for meanings.

Borrowing

All languages borrow words from other languages. English borrowed an extremely large number of lexical items from French during the occupation period which followed the Norman Conquest in 1066. Legal occupation meant that terms for the court, law, and property would enter English from French. And so, while English terms like *king* and *queen* survived, French provided the new words *sovereign, crown, state,* and *government. Thief* and *steal* are English terms but *burglar* comes from French, along with such law terms as *accuse, plea, fee,* and *attorney general.* Because the French took military control, we find *enemy, danger, soldier,* and *guard* added to the lexicon. The influence of the church brought new terms, too, like *religion, service, virgin,* and *trinity.* And, of course, the language of food also changed. As has often been noted, Sir Walter Scott in *Ivanhoe* popularized the saying that while the names of many animals in their lifetime are English (e.g., *cow, calf, sheep, swine, deer*), they appear on the table as French (e.g., *beef, veal, mutton, pork, bacon, venison*).

All cultures that have contact are likely to borrow vocabulary from each other. English has words borrowed from almost every language of the world. Immigrants from many parts of the world have brought their languages to enrich our own. Many words in U.S. English have a Spanish origin, which should not be surprising since Spanish has been an important language of the Southwest for long periods of our history. In other parts of the world, borrowing also occurs primarily between neighboring languages (as in the heavy borrowing from Arabic in many Afro-Asiatic languages). Or at a particular time in history, a language may borrow mainly from one language (as in the Japanese borrowing of English words in the past 40 years).

Borrowing is a sociolinguistic process which is not always appreciated by all members of the language community. In countries that have a language academy, there is usually an attempt to keep the language "pure" by prohibiting borrowed words. For example, France, by law, has tried to prevent the use of English words in French. AGULF, an acronym for the society of users of the French language, successfully sued TWA, the Paris Opéra, and *Le Monde* for using English words to sell or promote products. Nevertheless, things such as *le parking du building* are heard frequently, and a quick perusal of French popular magazines shows that even law cannot stop the process.

Borrowed words may be marked as such by keeping the original pronunciation and spelling of the word. However, if the word is used for any length of time, changes begin to occur and the pronunciation and spelling become closer and closer to the borrowing language. For example, in U.S. cafeterias that serve a variety of food from other countries, students order Mexican breakfasts pronouncing *desayuno de carne, tacodillas,* or *huevos rancheros* in a decidedly English-sounding fashion.

Some languages have affixes which help to nativize borrowed words. For example, Japanese uses *suru* (a marker similar to our *do* auxiliary) for borrowed words such as *memorize suru* and *touch suru.* When English adjectives are used, a *na* marker may be used, as in *intellectual na benkyoo,* or *cool na nominomo.* German often uses *-i(e)ren* so that English *ruin* becomes *ruiniren, publish* becomes *publiziren,* and Italian *capire* becomes *kapieren.* Russian uses *-ovat* so that *publish* would become *publikovat* and *figure* would be *figurirovat.*

Frequently, borrowed words are used for only a specific meaning. For example, the word *pink* might be borrowed although the language already has a word for pink. The English word might be used only for a lipstick color, whereas the native language word would be used for all other items. *Hotel* might be borrowed and used for Western-type hotels, and the native language word would be used for those not Western. In Japanese, for example, the word *request* has been borrowed and nativized as *rikuesuto,* but it is only used as a request for a band to play a certain song. The word *mansion* has been borrowed and nativized as *manshyon* to refer at first only to high-rise condos but now can be used even for a one-room apartment. In the Nepali language (Acharya, 1990), the English word *impression* is used but only for printing; the word *cabinet* is borrowed but only used to refer to the government. A *calendar* is only the kind hung on the wall. *Paper* is used only for newspapers and *fire* is only used in the sense of firing bullets.

The meanings of borrowed words may also be extended to other new meanings which do not obtain in the source language. For example,

Stanlaw (1982) writes that the words *wet* and *dry* both appear as loans in Japanese. But *wetto* has been extended to include the meaning of sentimental or soft-hearted, and *dorai* can mean businesslike.

Borrowed words can become an unintended source of humor. For example, *Agua Dulce* ("sweet water" in Spanish) is the name of a city in California where building is now prohibited due to contaminated ground water. Bolaq, a district in Cairo, is an adaptation of *beau lac,* though there is no lake to be seen. Similarly, Lake Los Angeles, located in the desert, has only a dry lake bed. (The Chamber of Commerce hopes to persuade voters to change the name to stem the deluge of calls from fishermen, boat owners, and swimmers looking for a new vacation spot.)

Restaurants often use French words to create effect, but novelists also use borrowed words to create ambiance. Herbert, in his *Dune* series, borrows heavily from Arabic. *The Clockwork Orange* is famous for its use of borrowed lexical items from Russian. In each case, a special time-warp or sinister effect is achieved.

A distinction needs to be made here between lexical borrowing and language mixing. In borrowing, the words become part of language and are used by the speakers of that language as though they were native lexical items. We all use terms like garage (French), confetti (Italian), vodka (Russian), goulash (Hungarian), and robot (Czech) without much thought of their origin. There are, of course, stages in assimilation of borrowed words. They may be marked with special affixes; the pronunciation of the words may gradually shift until they fit that of the native language. The end result is that the words are treated as ordinary words of the language.

In language mixing and switching, the words are momentarily borrowed by individual speakers in order to create certain effects. The novelists mentioned earlier borrowed words from other languages into English in a manner that made them appear to be part of that language within the world of the novel. This is quite different, say, from Peter's (1983) delightful Amelia Peabody, a heroine who switches from English to Arabic with ease, thereby adding to our appreciation of Peabody's many intellectual accomplishments.

The dividing line between borrowing and mixing is fuzzy to say the least. We usually think of borrowing as a long-term process within the language of a social group and mixing as a momentary individual phenomenon. However, within bilingual communities the distinction is less clear. Members of such communities may use either the L1 or L2 when speaking with monolinguals. In their own social communication, however, they may use the L1 with heavy borrowing from the L2. Although it is almost always possible to determine which language is basic, the amount of mixing is great. Some linguists claim that the mixed language spoken by the bilingual social community is a separate L3.

Practice 8.1

1. We mentioned a number of ways that languages "nativize" loan words (such as adding *-ovat* to make the borrowed word more Russian). In the languages you know, what sorts of markers are used?
2. Borrowing words becomes more complicated when words are borrowed into a language that marks gender. One solution is to assign all borrowed words arbitrarily to one gender. Sometimes, however, the borrowed word is given the same gender as the closest corresponding word in that language. For example, here are some English words used in Texas Spanish (Tex Mex): *una bike (una bicicleta), el dress (el vestido), al shopping center (al centro).* Does *los egg whites* fit this pattern? If you know a language that marks gender, see how it solves the problem of assigning gender to borrowed terms.
3. As borrowed words become nativized, the pronunciation has a better fit to that of the native language. Look at the following list of borrowed words in Japanese. Say the word aloud several times so that you can identify the English source word. There may be cases where you can supply the English words but are not sure of the meaning. Check these with a native speaker of Japanese.

mega hon	bakku miraa	enjin kii
gaado man	makaroni uesutan	doraibu mappu
neku tai	tabako	maikuro basu
famiriisaizu	poppu koon	shoppingu sentaa
jogingu	saundo torakku	beebi buumu
depaato	iji oodaa	sukin shippu

(Source: Morimoto, 1983)

Acharya (1990) gives examples from Nepali where *vote* becomes *bhoT, plate* becomes *pilet,* and *orderly* becomes *ordali.* What do these Japanese and Nepali examples tell you about the differences in phonology in the languages?
4. Crane et al. (1981, p. 45) list words borrowed from French into English. They also note that borrowing results in synonyms of the original English term and the borrowed French term, such as *help–aid, hide–conceal.* Select ten words and check their synonyms in a dictionary of synonyms. Trace the etymology of the synonyms in an etymological dictionary. How many of the synonyms can be accounted for in terms of borrowing?

5. American Sign Language borrows words from English. Ordinary fingerspelling is not considered borrowing, but when fingerspelled words take on other attributes of signs (place, movement, and palm orientation) they take on the phonology of ASL and become integrated into the sign system. The fingerspelled word A-L-L is now used with different movements, and can mean YOU-ALL, ALL-OF-THESE-THINGS, ALL-OF-US, ALL-OF-THEM (small group close), ALL-OF-THEM (large group far away), ALWAYS-SO-FAR, EVERYTHING-LISTED, and others. The fingerspelled D-O can be made with different movements and orientations to mean "What am I supposed to do?" "What are you doing?" or "I've been doing lots of busywork." If you know ASL, give additional examples of the ways in which words borrowed from English are made to fit the sign system.

6. For many years, languages borrowed technical and scientific words from either Latin or German. Now, much technical vocabulary is taken from English. List examples of technical vocabulary that have been borrowed into another language you know. Have the words been changed in any way to make them fit the language? How important is standardization of terms in scientific writing?

7. We have noted that Japanese has borrowed many English words and nativized the forms to fit Japanese phonology. If you teach (or are learning) Japanese as a foreign language, how useful are these borrowings in language learning? Should these borrowings be made explicit for learners? Conversely, some languages have contributed only a few items to English. If you teach in a multicultural school, would you highlight these borrowings as a way of stimulating multicultural awareness? Explain your reasoning.

8. If you are interested in the relation of politics and language, investigate the language policies of Turkey or Nepal. Turkey is an especially intriguing case with regard to lexical (and structural) borrowing. If you believe the policy has been successful, how do you account for the borrowing that has occurred? Nepal (Acharya, 1990) is presently embroiled in a controversy as to whether items should be borrowed from Sanskrit or from English. Despite the controversy, lexical items continue to be borrowed from both and from Hindi, Urdu, Persian, and Arabic. This is an important issue as the country moves toward making Nepali

the language of instruction, where new terms must be introduced for academic purposes.

Coinage

Every language has words that have not been borrowed from other languages but that have developed with the language over time. These are called native words. But what happens when a new word is needed, no appropriate borrowed word is available, and there is no native word? There are a number of options, but one obvious one is to coin a new word. Derek Smith, the Louisville basketball player, is credited with creating *high-five,* a word first used as a celebratory gesture, a slap of right hands by players, high over their heads. Since then, it has become a general celebratory term (e.g., "Market upswing brings high-fives to Wall Street").

In the introduction to this book, we said that words are arbitrary, but we know that is not strictly true. The form of the word must fit the phonology of the language. If we were to discover a new product, we would not name it Sbmeyt or Wnhrat because neither fits the sound patterns of English. Depending on the image we hoped to evoke for the product, we might try for combinations of sounds that somehow seem to exemplify that characteristic. If we wanted to emphasize the endearing qualities of the item or its small size, we would likely end the word with the letter *y, i,* or *e* – letters used for the /i/ sound. If we wanted to emphasize the sheen of its surface, we might well begin the word with *sh-,* as in *shimmer, shine* and so forth. So a new wax product might begin with *sh-* or *gl-* (if we prefer *glitter, gleam, glisten*). Companies spend a great deal of money trying to find exactly the right sound and letter combination for their particular product. The car name Acura is said to be an example of an excellent choice bacause it sounds as though the engine has the perfect engineering of a Swiss watch. Miyata is supposed to have an appealing ring to it so that, even though it carries no meaning, it would appeal to a worldwide market. The car itself does but it is doubtful if Spanish speakers find its name all that sporty, fun, and appealing. Still, it is said that Mist hairspray sells well in Germany even though *mist* means filthy in German.

Practice 8.2

1. How do you think the makers of the product *Kleenex* arrived at that name? Why do you think the brand name became the word for facial tissues? Kodak is another example of a brand name that has become a general synonym for camera. List as many other brand names which

have become general terms as you can. Why have they been incorporated into the general lexicon in this way?

2. Potter (1971) lists many words which were coined by individuals and then became common. Many of these people, however, either based their new words on Latin or other languages. For example, George Bernard Shaw is credited with introducing the word *superman* (and starting the fashion in *super*-words) based on his translation of Nietzsche's *Ubermensch.* Can you think of other examples of individuals who have coined words for the language?

3. *Astroturf* was a word created for the grasslike synthetic covering on sports fields. On National Public Radio news, a U.S. senator talked about *astroturf* as mail from his constituents that did not reflect grass-roots opinion on an issue but rather the efforts of lobbyists who get people to sign form letters. How quickly do you think that new words are used metaphorically? Can you supply additional examples?

4. Select two recent words and compare their treatment in two dictionaries of new words (e.g., J. Green, *Neologisms: New Words Since 1960,* S. Tulloch, *Oxford Dictionary of New Words,* or Ayto, *Longman Register of New Words, 1989*). Which dictionary would a language teacher find more useful? Justify your choice.

Names of people and places

The names of inventors of products or people associated with particular products have often become the words for the products themselves. Such words are called eponyms. For example, the word *maverick* came from the major of San Antonio who refused to brand his cattle. Maverick then became a term for unbranded cattle, and later for anyone who took an independent stand.

The word *boycott* is also based on the name of a real person, Captain Boycott, a retired British army captain who oversaw estates in Ireland and refused to give humanitarian concessions to his Irish tenants. They hated him so much that they ostracized him and boycott became a synonym for rejection and isolation.

Many who use Tupperware plastic containers are unaware that they were named for the inventor, a chemist at DuPont. A favorite eponym is *poinsettia* – a Christmas plant named for the ambassador to Mexico who introduced it to the United States. Not only inventors or famous people from long ago have their names used in this way, for new eponyms are formed constantly. For example, in computer talk, a *sagan* means a large quantity of anything, after the astronomer Carl Sagan's famous "billions and billions" talk. So one might say the United States spends sagans on the military. The eponym *gerrymander* was recreated in Japanese when Prime Minister Hatoyama divided areas in Japan in a way that favored his political party. This action was called a *Hatomander.*

The opposite type of relation also exists. Many family names are taken from ordinary words, in particular words for occupations, making names like Smith, Miller, Farmer, Baker, Cooper, Wright, Potter, Fisher, and Hunter very common.

Names need not refer only to specific people. They may simply be used in a metaphoric fashion to refer to someone else who happens to exhibit the same traits as the person named. For example, "She's the Madonna of our neighborhood," or "He's completely Ollie North."

Place names can become common words, too, although they remain as the name of the place. Almost any place name can be turned into an adjective. There are Hollywood jeans, Parisian nights, and Santa Ana winds. This doesn't mean that the jeans, the nights, or the winds come from these places but rather that some quality of the place has been used as an attribute of the words they modify. Place names have also become nouns. Camembert (cheese) and limousine are named after places in France. Charleston, the dance, is also the name of an American city. Tabasco (a sauce) is the name of a river in Mexico. Diseases are often named for the place in which they first occurred (Rocky Mountain spotted fever).

Some names may have multiple origins. For example, it's not clear whether a name such as Bower means someone who makes bows, if it compares the person to a flower bower, if it comes from the German *Bauer* meaning farm laborer, or perhaps some other source. Children may be named not only after famous people but also after places and even natural disasters. Mamdouh Hassan writes that after the Cairo earthquake, one child was named Mohamed Zelzal (*zelzal* = earthquake) and there are similar reports of San Francisco babies being given the middle name *Quake.*

Ordinary words can also become the basis of place names. The town of French Lick, Indiana, is located in the Ohio Valley which was once covered by an inland sea in which salt accumulated. The salt springs in the valley are called licks because the cattle, buffalo, and deer would lick the earth to get at the salt. So there are towns called Elk Lick, French Lick, Salt Lick, and Blue Lick in that area.

Place names can usually be traced through the history of an area. Many place names along the California coast came from Hokan (the language of the Chumash Indians): Ojai, Lompoc, Point Mugu, Pismo Beach. *'Awhay* is the word for moon; *Lompo'* means stagnant water; *Muwu*

177

means beach; and *Pismu'* means tar. Nobody goes to view the flower fields in Lompoc thinking that they are going to an area of stagnant water. Place names in California also reflect the mingling of its two major colonizing forces. In the southern part of the state, Spanish-speaking explorers used their calendar of saints' days to name places (San Bernardino, San Jose, San Juan Capistrano). In the northern part of the state, the Argonauts provided names reflecting characteristics of their mining camps (Brandy Flat, Rough and Ready, Dead Horse, Fiddletown, Poker Flat, Last Chance).

In science eponyms abound, and a definite etiquette governs how eponyms are used from field to field. In astronomy, comets are named for the first person who observes them. In other fields, scientists can only hope that their colleagues will memorialize their work in this way. Botanists and ornithologists have been so honored by colleagues; plants and birds carry the names of important researchers. In medicine, eponyms are often used to identify diseases (leading to the humorist S. J. Perelman's quip, "I have Bright's disease and he has mine").

Practice 8.3

1. Look up the following names of people that have become names of objects: blanket, bloomer, sandal, zinnia, souboise (sauce). Who were these people?

2. In another language you know, look for eponym examples. How powerful a process do you believe this might be as a source of new vocabulary items across all languages?

3. In an essay on eponymous science, Eisenberg (1993) says that place names are favored eponyms in mineralogy and chemistry. She notes that Ytterby, Sweden, appears in the names of four elements – yttrium, terbium, erbium, and ytterbium. She also discusses the use of nonpossessive form when the eponym is from a location (Lyme disease) or from a patient's name (Duffy blood factor) and the use of the possessive form when the eponym is named for its discoverer (Bright's disease). Given that eponyms are common in science, would you point them out to students in science classes? Should they be included in ESP science classes for multilingual students? If so, who should research and provide information on the eponyms to the class, the teacher, the students, the ESL specialist, or the science specialist?

4. The names of important educators and linguists have been used to identify certain hypotheses about language (e.g., the Whorfian hypothesis) and language learning or cogni-

tive development (e.g., Piagetian stages). Are these eponyms ever used in the possessive form? When two names are mentioned, is the eponym then always hyphenated (e.g., the Sapir-Whorf hypothesis)?

5. It's been suggested that religion exerts an influence over name giving and when this does not happen, individual taste may run wild. Some names coined by parents are beautiful (as in the name Autumn Brown), and others are humorous or even weird. While working in a personnel office, a friend came across many strange combinations. Our favorite was an employee named Crystal Shanda Leer. There were many Ima's and Iva's with funny last names. One governor of Texas actually named his daughter Ima Hogg. Parents also give way to their patriotic feelings; one of our students was named Love America. We have had friends whose real names were Sunny and Poopsie. (Teachers were always insistent that these couldn't be their real names!) As children we played with children nicknamed Buddy, Sonny, and Sissy. Ask your grandparents if they have a copy of their high school yearbook. If not, go to your library. Check the names (and any nicknames) of students from two generations ago. Compare these with those in a current yearbook. How have the names changed? How do you account for the change?

Conversion

Conversion is a process which allows us to create additional lexical items out of those that already exist. It is also a process in language change. We like a word so much that we decide to use it in new ways. So, a saw is used to saw, a bag is used to bag, a file is used to file. A flirt flirts, a snoop snoops, and a spy spies.

This process is not limited to one-syllable words. Shovels are used to shovel snow. Bottles are used in bottling and butter for buttering. An umpire umpires a game, a star stars in a film shown at a theater where an usher ushers. Nor is the process limited to the creation of verbs from nouns. For example, one hears complaints that the student bookstore upped its prices again.

New conversions are constantly being created. Chick Hearn, the sports announcer for the Los Angeles Lakers, says that Kareem abdul-Jabbar used to "vacuum it in and sky hook, it for two," meaning that he pulled in the ball and got it in the basket. He says that a running player "greyhounds it down the floor," that Magic Johnson "cross-courts the ball, but it's fly-swatted away." A woman says that she'll "microwave the chicken." A teenager says he will "flea our dog." An invitation to an art gallery opening says, "We will of course quiche and perrier you." People talk about "zip-coding their letters," "trashing papers," "carpooling people." They say they will "Haagen-Daz" or "pizza a bit" before they "freeway" on home.

Ankist (1985) classified noun-to-verb conversions according to patterns. These included such things as applying or removing what the parent noun denotes (e.g., "newspaper the shelves"; "flea the dog"); to go to or perform an activity at a place denoted by the parent noun (e.g., "to youth-hostel Europe," "to jacuzzi"); to apply duration or time as denoted by the parent noun (e.g., "to Christmas in Hawaii"); to behave or take the role of the parent noun (e.g., "to John Wayne it," "to zombie out"); to cause to resemble whatever the parent noun denotes (e.g., "carpool the people," "to trash the neighborhood"); to produce the process or activity denoted by the parent noun (e.g., "to suction the ear," "to conference"); to perform actions usually performed by means of the parent noun (e.g., "to RV across America," "to scissor the material"). Thus, it appears that conversions can be used for location, duration, agent, goal, and instrumental functions.

Practice 8.4

1. Give a sentence for each of these types of conversion.

   Instrument: David removed the snow *with a shovel.*
   (He *shoveled* the snow.)
   saw, hammer, rake, mop, brush, comb, label, elbow

   Goal or destination: The cowboys led the horses *to the corral.*
   (They *corraled* the horses.)
   jail, dock, bag, bottle, can, house, stack, bale, file

   Theme: off or away – She removed the dust off the chair.
   feather, pit, peel, scale, weed, shell
   into or onto – Sue put butter on the bread.
   pepper, salt, water, plaster, oil, saddle

2. There is evidence that conversion is a process in the language of children. A 5-year-old said:

   a. Mommy, I didn't want you to trash it out yet.
   b. Daddy, can you match this for me? (*holding up a plastic bracelet she wanted to have fixed by melting the ends together with a match*).

Another child picked up a worm and, when it wiggled, threw it down, saying, "It wormed on me!" If you work with young children, classify their conversions. Are they all nouns to verbs?

3. Can all nouns be converted to verbs?

4. To *stonewall* is a conversion used in talk about politics. List as many examples as you can of conversions that seem to be used primarily in special domains (e.g., offices, movies, hospitals). How might these be related to script semantics?

5. Here are some additional examples of conversion. Categorize each using Ankist's system: "We've *axed* the price." "We don't want to *scapegoat* anybody." "We have to *wait-list* some passengers." "Don't forget to *cc* (= carbon copy) this to everyone." "C'mon, *seatbelt* yourself!" "They *rotten-egged* him almost" (= the audience almost threw eggs at a speaker). "You forgot to *pickle* the hamburger." "The team *summered* in Colorado." "Careful you don't *onion* your eyes." "We have to *accordion* the curtains more." "They want to *champagne* this reception."

Shifts

The meanings of words themselves may shift over time. The classic examples are *knave,* which once meant a young lad and now means someone rather nasty; *deer,* which once meant wild animals in general (so bears could be considered deer); and *couth,* which meant known or familiar and now survives only in *uncouth.* We can find examples of shifts in progress even now. The word *broadcast* meant to scatter seeds, but now it is used primarily to refer to scattering words on radio and television. *Drive* originally referred to driving cattle but is now mainly used for driving cars. Clearly, what a word once meant is not always what it means now.

An amusing example is the word *virtue* which, according to Greenough and Kittredge (1901, pp. 241–242) is related to the Latin *vir,* meaning man. *Virtue,* then, originally meant something like "manliness" in general. Later it came to stand for warlike prowess. Still later, as it passed into French and then to English, it meant power, even magical strength, and it meant a noble quality. One wonders, then, how it came to be applied primarily to women (when it originally meant manliness) as in "may all your sons be brave and all your daughters virtuous."

Shifts may expand, limit, or replace the original meaning of words, in the process either elevating the value of the word or lowering it. For

181

example, the word *lust* did not always describe moral depravity but once meant pleasure. *Lewd* meant ignorant. Now these terms have much less favorable meanings, and other words have become more exalted. For example, *minister* used to mean servant, a *constable* was someone who cleaned horse stalls, and *angel* once merely meant a messenger.

Shifts may occur in one dialect of a language and not in another. For example, in standard Italian the word for parents is *genitori*. Influenced by the English word *parents,* the American Italian dialect uses *parenti* (Danesi [1985]). The word *parenti* in Italian is used for relatives rather than parents.

Changes in meaning differ across dialects of English as well. For example, the use of the word *lumber* to mean planks of wood sold in stores is uncommon in England, where *timber* is used instead. In the United States, *timber* refers to logs and even lumber before it reaches the market. The meaning of the word *corn* differs in British and American English, referring to grain in British English but to a particular grain crop in America. (*Corn* seems to be shifting in British English, however, perhaps owing to the influence of the American use of the term.)

Meanings of words also shift as they are borrowed from one language into another. According to Sonoda (1975), the meaning of loan word *raisu* in Japanese is restricted to cooked rice ready to be served. The borrowed word *feminisuto* (from *feminist*) refers to a man who is sentimentally fond of women. *Antena* (from *antenna*) is sometimes used to refer to a tall, thin person. In each of these cases a shift in meaning has taken place as the word is borrowed into the language.

Some words, of course, are so stable in sound and meaning that linguists can use them to group languages into related families. For example, the English word *hand* is very similar in meaning and sound to the word *Hand* in German. The Dutch, Danish, and Swedish words for hand are *hand, haand,* and *hand,* respectively. When we find many such cognates, we can surmise that these words were not borrowed from one language to another, but rather that all of these languages evolved from a common language that was spoken in the past.

Linguists estimate that Proto-German, the common ancestor language for all languages in the Germanic group (which includes English), was spoken more than two thousand years ago. Knowing that certain lexical items seldom shift meanings or sounds has also allowed linguists to look at how languages in the Germanic group are related to other groups that branched off from Latin, like the Romance language family (Spanish, French, Portuguese, Italian, Romanian).

By looking at highly stable basic vocabulary across these languages, linguists have been able to show how they and other families – for example, the Celtic family (Irish, Welsh, Breton), the Slavic family (Polish,

Russian, Bulgarian), and Greek, Albanian, and Sanskrit – relate to an even more ancient language family, Indo-European. Of course, the further back words are traced, the more difficult the task becomes.

We have already talked about cognates in Chapter 6. For linguists, cognates are important in discovering the family relationships of languages. For learners, cognates are important and, so long as meanings do *not* shift, helpful. Bantu (1981) argues that students should be encouraged toward "intelligent guessing" when they encounter cognates. Learners clearly hope to find true cognates and borrow when their limited lexicon fails them. When shifts occur in meanings for words with similar forms across languages, however, learners have to deal with false cognates. There are many examples of the negative effect of such cognates on lexical learning (see the Ringbom and Nash examples in Chapter 6).

Practice 8.5

1. McLaughlin (1970) lists pairs of phonetically similar but semantically distinct words that were derived from a common source word. Use your dictionary to see what details you can discover about when the following splits occurred and why. How do such splits relate to shifts?

to–too	mettle–metal
human–humane	gentle–genteel
urban–urbane	travel–travail

2. Select a short scene from your favorite Shakespearean play and note words for which meaning shifts have occurred. How important is it that audiences interpret the words you list correctly? If you were teaching this scene to ESL or EFL students, would you point out these shifts in meaning? Why or why not?

3. Hasselmo (1976) studied the vocabulary of Swedish immigrants to America. In the Swedish of Americans who had immigrated to midwestern America, words were found which are now archaic in Sweden. For example, in Bishop Hill, Illinois, Swedish-Americans used the following terms:

Bishop Hill Swedish	Swedish	English
blistra	vissla	whistle
dimpa	falla	fall
stoka	sköta	take care of
tymla	tumla	tumble
tappa	öppna	open

Vocabulary, semantics, and language education

TABLE 8.1 CORRESPONDENCES TO AMERICAN ITALIAN

Standard Italian	English	American Italian	Meaning
macchina fotografica	camera	camera	bedroom
fotografia	picture	pittura	painting
scantinato	basement	basamento	pedestal (art)
mobilia	furniture	fornitura	supplying (work)

Data source: Based on Danesi, 1985.

Which forms are closer to English, those used by Swedish-Americans or those used in Sweden? Why do you suppose these shifts took place in one environment and not in the other? Does your explanation work for the Danesi's *parenti* example as well? If not, how would you explain it?

4. Table 8.1 presents additional data from Danesi (1985). In standard Italian, *macchina* and *fotografica* both mean camera. Italian Americans shifted to *camera,* a form closer to that of the English word. However, in standard Italian, camera means bedroom. Why do such changes take place? Is it important to learn the standard (rather than the American Italian) forms.

5. Bantu (1981, p. 136) says that with "due caution" the German instructor can introduce cognates and loan words as part of language instruction in such sentences as:

Ich gehe zu einem Meeting, zu einer Sitzung.
Welche Mannschaft, welches Team hat gewonnen?
Hast du ein Auto, einen Wagen?
Er sucht einen Job, eine Stellung?

The teacher must know that *Auto* and *Wagen* are acceptable substitutes in most instances whereas *Job* and *Stellung* are not. Still, Bantu argues that false cognates account for only a few dozen examples while there are literally thousands of helpful pairs. Do you agree with Bantu? Give examples to support your reasoning.

In this chapter, we have begun to look at ways that languages enlarge the lexicon by borrowing from other languages, using words for new functions and meanings through conversion, or shifts. In Chapter 9 we will continue this theme by looking at additive and subtractive processes used to obtain new forms for meanings.

Research and application

Borrowing

1. Romaine (1986) gives examples in Punjabi of the use of markers with borrowed words in what she calls "code-mixed compound verbs." She notes that Kachru (1978) has also written about a similar phenomenon in Hindi where *karna* is used to demarcate borrowed verbs, as in the example *to pity*, which has a Sanskrit borrowed form, *daya karna*, a Persian borrowed form, *raham karna*, and a borrowed English form *pity karna*. Read this article and compare the examples with those for Japanese (with *suru*). Which of Romaine's explanations do you believe best explain this phenomenon? Justify your decision. If you find this topic of interest, use the information collected for Practice 8.1. by your classmates. Are pronounlike verbs (e.g., *suru, hacer,* or equivalents of *do* or *make*) used for this purpose over many different languages? If the data look promising, you and your classmates might develop this as a publishable research paper.

2. Hall (1964) shows the derivation of words from source languages in Malanesian Pidgin, Chinese Pidgin, Haitian Creole Taki-Taki. Read this article and others of your choice on the lexicon of pidgin languages. What interesting theoretical issues regarding semantics and lexicon are raised in the study of pidgin languages?

3. Haugen (1950) categorizes four major types of borrowing. Hybrid loanwords result from the blending of words from two languages. The word pronounced /blaUmschwapaɪ/ is from Pennsylvania German *blaUm* (plum) and English *pie*. Loan translations are another form of borrowing where the word is directly translated into the native language form. Examples like English *skyscraper,* French *gratte-ciel,* and Spanish *rascacielos* are also sometimes called *calques*. A third type of borrowing is the semantic loan. Haugen gives the example of the American Portuguese form *humoroso*, which has taken on the meaning of the English word *humorous* instead of retaining the meaning of capricious which it has in Portuguese. Loan homonyms are also exemplified in American Portuguese. The Portuguese word *grosseria* means a rude remark. The English word *grocery* sounds similar, so now *grosseria* is used for both a grocery and a rude remark. Relate these categories to Ringbom's (discussed in Chapter 6). Prepare a preliminary methodology for classifying data that you might obtain in your own research on errors, loans, and borrowed words used by language learners.

4. Otto Jespersen, the famous Danish linguist, wrote about borrowing as part of his classic book, *Growth and Structure of the English Language* (1938). A short excerpt, "Borrowing from the Normans," is reprinted in Laird and Gorrell (1971). How do you account for the fact that borrowing from French did not increase immediately after the Norman conquest but only later? Give as many reasons as you can for why this delay should be expected. In what types of cases would you expect no borrowing to occur?

5. Loanwords have been extensively studied in Japanese. More than twenty dictionaries related to loanwords were published from 1912 to 1935, and a journal on loanwords was published between 1932 and 1938. More current dictionaries list from 6,400 very commonly known to 16,000 newer loanwords, and books offer suggestions for correcting errors in the use of loanwords and for utilizing loanwords in learning English vocabulary. Review the history of English loanwords in Japanese (or in another language of your choice).

6. Stoffel (1991) examined the ways in which immigrants adapted loanwords borrowed from English into Serbo-Croatian. This adaptation included pronunciation changes and adding Serbo-Croatian grammatical and gender markings. This study is special since data were obtained from different areas of migration: the United States, Canada, and New Zealand. Stoffel found uniformity in the ways the borrowed words were treated by immigrants in all three areas. Identify immigrant communities that you might use if you were to replicate this study with other language groups.

7. The Quackenbushes (1974, 1977) have shown how Japanese makes English loanwords fit the Japanese sound system. Shibatani (1990) also describes the processes of narrowing meanings (e.g., using the English loanword *stove* as *sutoobu* but with reference only to a room heater rather than a cooking stove), extending meanings (e.g., using the English loan word *register* shortened to *reji* for cash register and then extending that to a term for the person who operates the cash register), shifting (e.g., the English *feminist* as *feminisuto,* which is a man softhearted toward women or one who treats women kindly with illicit intent), and pejoration or downgrading (e.g., *boss* as *bosu* means a mob boss and *madame* as *madamu* is a female owner of a bar). Read and critique this research as background for a study of your own on lexical borrowing in other languages. Can you show the same sound changes and the four types of processes in that borrowing?

8. Kimura (1989) found that Japanese students of English were better able to offer definitions for English words if there were corre-

sponding loanwords in Japanese than if no loanword existed. After giving the definitions, the students were also asked to rate their confidence in the definitions. Again, they were more confident of the definitions that they had given for words for which there were corresponding loanwords in Japanese. Kimura therefore asserted that teachers of English to Japanese speakers ought to give special attention to loanwords in instruction. How might you integrate this issue into your response to 7?

Person and place names as lexical items

9. Marmaridou (1989) examined both the referential and connotative use of proper names in communication. Collect examples of names used in a connotative or metaphoric way. What patterns do you see in their selection and use?

Meaning shifts and conversion

10. Select one language of your choice and trace its family classification. If you select one of the Old World languages, consult Ruhlen (1987). If you select one of the American languages, consult Greenberg (1987) or Campbell and Mithun (1979). Greenberg has also written on African language families. Give example words that show how the language classification was obtained. How important is shift vs. stability in this kind of linguistic analysis?

11. Sometimes words are borrowed and pronunciation changed so that items that can be thought of as polysemes in English become separate words. Morimoto (1983) gives several examples. The word *iron,* for example, has been borrowed into Japanese but has two different pronunciations according to meaning. The pronunciation /aian/ means a metal-headed golf club, but /airon/ means the device to press clothes. The word *strike* is also represented differently. The pronunciation /sutoraiku/ is used for a strike in baseball and bowling whereas /sutoraiki/, with a different final vowel, is used for a labor strike. He found that the katakana transcriptions of these words substantiate the claim that these have become separate words in Japanese, not polysemes. Consider loanwords with polysemous meanings. Has the pronunciation changed as these are nativized into the language? Would you agree that they have shifted enough to be considered new words?

12. Walsh (1993), in an article on the publication of *Le Dictionnaire Québécois d'Aujourd'hui,* notes that the government runs tele-

phone hot lines offering tips on how to avoid anglicisms like *le shopping,* which is used frequently in France. (*Le magasinage* is the preferred term in Quebec.) Jean-Claude Boulanger, a lexicographer at Université de Laval, estimates that about 90 percent of the words in the dictionary are standard international French; the rest are unique to Quebec. Examples include *pantoute* for *pas du tout; cave,* the French word for basement but used to mean an *idiot;* and the clipped form *char* from the French *chariot* to mean a car. It also includes entries marked as Anglicisms (*le fonne* for fun, *le free for all,* and *triper,* which means to get excited about something or have a trip about it). Boulanger says the dictionary will not lead to language deterioration, as critics claim. As a lexicographer, he defends the dictionary against those who would eliminate all Quebecois forms: "I can't leave out such words. It would be as if I didn't like the word *table,* so I just left it out." Why do English-speaking countries not establish hot lines to prevent shifts and borrowed forms from crossing from one dialect to another? (Actually, the British Broadcasting Corporation does circulate lists of American forms that should be avoided by their news commentators. If you can obtain a copy, comment on the words selected for this special treatment.)

9 Processes in word building

Shifts and conversions, coinage, eponyms, and borrowing help us increase the word stock of languages, yet there are other processes that do this in even more powerful ways. These are additive and subtractive processes that result in simple and complex word formations. Weinreich (1969) said that it would be helpful to have a simplex dictionary and, in order to locate all words, a "complex dictionary in which would be entered all compounds, complex words, idioms, phrases, and sentences familar to speakers of the language." We will discuss each process for obtaining complex forms and some that subtract to form shorter, more simple forms.

It seems almost arbitrary that some meanings are held in single words and others in several words. *Telephone* is a single word but *call up* is two. *Once* is one word but *one time* is two. A word in one language may be two in another. *Cheap* is *bon marché,* two words in French. *Last night* is two words in English, but one, *anoche,* in Spanish. Whether one word or two, each stands for a single meaning. The variety of ways in which single meanings are built up out of two or more words include both additive and reduction processes. First we will consider additive processes, which create compounds, reduplications, phrasal collocations, idioms and proverbs.

Compounding

For English, compounding is perhaps the most powerful word building process. The most common compounds are two nouns combined to create a meaning which differs from that of each of its parts, as in *fire engine* or *toothbrush*. However, compounds can be quite lengthy. Ads proclaim a "no-cost-to-you gift" or an "absolute money-back guarantee"; statistics books talk about the "b-slope regression line"; and we listen to songs with lyrics that say "I've got those God-why-don't-you-love-me-oh-you-do-I'll-see-you-later-Blues" (from Sondheim's *Follies*). One would think that there must be some cut-off point where the length of the compound makes processing difficult. However, it is not uncommon to find three-, four-, or five-part compounds (e.g., garbage can

189

collector, map-making geography class, affirmative action/equal opportunity employer).

Some linguists have tackled the problem of defining a compound in English. One test has been that if word stress falls on the first part of the compound, then it is truly a lexical compound. This would make *armchair* and *working paper* compounds, whereas *rough draft* and *chocolate cake* would be classified as phrases made up of nouns modified by adjectives. However, *chocolate cake, cherry pie,* and the *New York Times Magazine* (though they carry stress on the final noun) are all recognized as meaningful objects in and of themselves. So for us, these will be considered compounds, too.

A second test is whether the traditional patterns for adjectives can be used – can *very* or *rather* precede the compound? According to this test, *tall man* is an adjective plus noun, not a compound word. We probably would all agree that *spacecraft* is a noun formed from two nouns, but what about *flying spacecraft*? *Flying* behaves internally like a verb but here it looks like an adjective. Yet we cannot modify it with *very* (*"a very flying spacecraft") so according to the second test it is a compound. Verbs can be modified by *very much*. "The story interested me very much" can be changed to "a very interesting story." But "the spacecraft flew very much" cannot be changed to "a very flying spacecraft." So, it's not clear that *flying* in "flying spacecraft" is either a noun or an adjective. So, for now, we will call forms such as *flying spacecraft* compounds.

Frequently we can see how compounds evolved by grouping them according to a similar underlying semantic relation. A brick wall is a wall that contains bricks. A chocolate cake is a cake that contains chocolate. Ice water is water that contains ice. A picture book is a book that contains pictures. However, the pattern does not fit all such compounds. *Family man, rattlesnake,* and *ice cream* do not fit the pattern.

If we look carefully at compounds, we see that there are many different lexical relationships behind the compounds. Miller (1991) lists several relationships:

Cause: tear gas, sleeping pill
Have: bull's eye, picture book, writer's cramp
Make: rainwater, daisy chain
Use: waterwheel, steam iron
Be: whitecap, target site
In: house cat, country club, hillbilly
For: ashtray, fish pond
From: fingerprint, sea breeze
About: tax law, book review

Notice that these all meet the linguistic test for true compounds – the stress falls on the first part of the compound.

While we have noted that many compounds are made up of pairs of nouns, all types of combinations are possible. *Killjoy* combines a verb and a noun. *Greenhouse* combines an adjective and a noun. *Windbreak* combines a noun and a verb, *make-believe* combines two verbs. *Runoff* combines a verb with an adverb, and the reverse combination is shown in *downpour.* Two adjectives can be combined, as in *redhot.* It appears that almost any combination is possible.

Of course compounding is not limited to English. Italian has many verb-plus-noun compounds. For example, *portacenere* combines the Italian words for *carry* and *ash. Stuzzicadenti* combines *pick at* and *teeth.* German has even longer examples of compounds than English. It is said that the longest compound in German is *der Donau / dampf / schif / fahrts / gesellshafts / kapitän / anwärter,* a Danube steamship travel company captain applicant.

You might wonder why we create compounds when it is possible to say the same thing without the compound. After all, we can say, "I like cakes that are chocolate"; we don't have to use *chocolate cake* to convey that information. Compounds are useful ways of condensing information and they add variation to the way we refer to concepts in discourse. For example, in a composition we might begin by talking about *cuts in education* and then later refer back to this as *education cuts.* On a campus having fiscal problems, we can say that students have organized a protest against hikes in their *tuition fees.* Later in the discourse, we might refer back to this with the compound *tuition fee hike campaigning.*

Compounds allow us to condense information that has already been presented. Dressler (1985) gives examples of compounds serving similar discourse purposes across languages. Here are his examples from Italian and German literature:

First mention of topic:

che l'aveva piantata dopo due anni per andare a combattere nei Marocco stufo di litigare con lei
(her husband who left her in the lurch in order to go fighting in Morocco, weary of quarreling with her)

Topic resumed three pages later:

nel corso dei loro litigi pre-Marocco
(in the course of their pre-Morocco quarrels)

First mention of topic:

Nur eine Jungkuh ging auf das Eis
(Only a baby cow went on the ice)

Later reference:

Die *Eiskuh*
(The *ice cow*)

Compounds provide us new ways to refer to the same information, as well as condense the information. They are for that reason often used for newspaper headlines and advertisements and announcements, where space is at a premium.

Practice 9.1

1. As a review of Chapter 4, assign relation labels (using Mel'čuk's classification terms) to the relations shown in Miller's list.

2. Can you fit each of the following compounds into one of Miller's patterns? If not, what other relations would you suggest? Are these covered in Mel'čuk's list?

blackboard	growing pains	swimsuit
cable car	playboy	lie detector
landslide	piggybank	birth control
eyestrain	chocolate chip cookie	loudmouth
daredevil	sweet talk	freeway report

3. Patterson and Cohn (1990) list a number of innovative original compounds produced by Koko, a lowland gorilla who is being taught American Sign Language. Can you fit each of the following examples into one of Miller's categories? Would you say that Koko can produce metaphors?

Item	Compound sign
celery	lettuce tree
frozen banana	fruit lollipop
tapioca pudding	milk candy
stale sweet roll	candy rock

4. In rapid reading, we may misjudge the stress pattern and at least momentarily read a compound as an adjective plus noun, or vice versa. The *San Francisco Chronicle* (November 1, 1991) listed a group of heroes including "Wilbur J. Wetzel, 42, of San Jose, who pulled a fallen woman from train tracks, June 11, 1990." List examples of ambiguity with compounds (and the humor inherent in many such examples). Why would you expect to encounter more of these in reading than in listening comprehension?

5. Collect examples of compounds from newspaper headlines. In this section, we talked about the use of compounds to refer to earlier information in text. In the case of

newspaper headlines, however, the compound sets up information which may then be elaborated in the following text. For example, the headline "Woman Drowns in *River Plunge*" was collected by van Dijk (1985, p. 122). The text then goes on to say that her car "plunged 15 feet down an embankment into the rain-swollen River Severn." Give examples where the compounds are or are not later clarified in the text. What reason can you give for the cases where no explication is offered?

6. English compounds can be a source of wordplay. For example, Nilsen and Nilsen (1982, p. 274) have a rhyming game for compounds where students make up new names for their courses:

Course name	Rhyming name
Physical Education	Socks & Jocks
Plant Biology	Weeds & Seeds
Field Biology	Bag 'em & Tag 'em
Human Biology	Cuts & Guts

Are the names of your courses all noun compounds? Is it easy to find rhyming synonyms for them? Could you do the same thing in another language you know?

7. Although English and German use many noun–noun compounds, French does not. Newmark (1988) asks student translators how to translate *nerve cell* into French (can a cell be nervous?) and *travail musculaire* into English (can work be muscular?). Add an example from another language to each of the following correspondences. How many are noun–noun compounds? Is the form you supplied more similar to French or to English and German?

heavy labor, travail musculaire, schwere Arbeit
runaway (galloping) inflation, galoppierende Inflation, l'inflation galopante
government securities; effets publics; Staatspapiere (Staatsanleihen)

Acquisition of compounds

There is disagreement as to whether compounds are acquired as single lexical units or whether compounds are created from their parts. In her famous study, Berko (1958) asked young children why compounds like Thanksgiving and Sunday have the names they do. Children who were

193

quite competent in creating new compounds (they could, for example, create the term *wughouse* for the home of an imaginary animal) did not, in turn, analyze compounds in terms of their parts. They didn't think *Thanksgiving* had anything to do with giving thanks but rather with eating turkey. And, for them, Sunday is called *Sunday* because that is when you go to church.

Even though many languages use compounding to create new words, second language learners often find these forms difficult. Learners are not always sure whether the compound is possible. For example, an American Sign Language student describing the collection of sap from rubber trees wrote, "Every day, one times a line. So then that's thing is like water. Rubber water, maybe." If the L1 and L2 both use compounding extensively, learners may try to translate the L1 forms directly to the L2. Nemser (1991) gives examples of such loan translations: *ill car* for ambulance from the German *Krankenwagen; Alp dream* for nightmare from the German *Alptraum;* and *sidejump* meaning an extramarital adventure from *Seitensprung.*

A second problem for learners relates to the order in which the parts of the compound appear. There are pie apples and apple pies, there is gum-chewing (often used as an adjective to describe a person) and chewing gum. This, undoubtedly, is confusing to an L2 learner as shown in word order errors:

I planning to get master's degree in *engineering economics.*
Another course is *making decisions.*
All time I have my *book map* in my car.
AAA is very useful for the *stranger people.*

(Spanish L1. Source: K. Schlue, 1976)

Prince married *shoes girl.*
Soldier have a *glasses shoes.*

(Japanese L1. Source: T. Shirahata, 1988)

Near *Washington George Bridge.*
We eat in *room banquet.*

(American Sign Language L1. Source: L. Hunt)

Such errors suggest that learners do not learn all compounds as single new items but rather put the parts together to create the compounds. In doing so, they may use the typical word order of their first language. Another possibility is that they place the words so that the meaning on which they want to focus comes first and then the modification or comment part is added.

It is also possible that students are unaware that compounding is a very general process in English. This would account for the relatively low appearance of compounds in the compositions of international students.

They may also want to avoid as many errors as possible, and low production may reflect this avoidance.

Case studies show that learners who once produced correct compounds later make errors in word order. For example, Olshtain once told us that her children, returning to their home in Israel after a period in the United States, began to produce errors such as chip chocolate, pin hair, and tape scotch. Again, this gives some support to the notion that compounds are not initially stored as single lexical units. It is also possible that word order of the native language might either promote or reinforce such errors.

Case studies also show strategies beginning learners use when unaware that compounding is a possible choice. For example, Ricardo, a teenage Spanish speaker learning English (see Butterworth & Hatch, 1978) often used a *for* phrase rather than compounds. Examples include "shoes for water ice" (ice skates), "one man is clean for clothes" (dry cleaner), "in house one machine for hot" (space heater or hot air furnace), "this shoes for skiing" (ski boots), "rooms for sleep" (bedrooms).

Compounding is a powerful word-building process in English and a very common process in many languages. Nevertheless, learners often avoid or experience difficulty in learning less common compounds as they acquire the language. Part of the difficulty has to do with variability of word order within the compound.

Practice 9.2

1. Give examples of compounding in a language you know or are studying. Estimate how productive the process is. If there is a set word order for compounds, describe it. On the basis of this description, make hypotheses about how easy or difficult it might be for learners to acquire compounds in this language. Alternatively, make hypotheses about the ease with which speakers of this language might acquire English compounds.
2. Shapira (1978) includes data where a Spanish-speaking woman learning English produces errors in compounds. Examples include:

The *dry machine* no work.
The *water hot* is ready.
You know the *people Ecuador* is very nice.

How might you explain such errors in the language of beginners learning the language without instruction?

195

3. An elevator in Belgrade's Slavija Hotel is reported to have the following English instructions:

   To move the cabin push button of wishing floor. If the cabin should enter more persons, each one should press number of wishing floor.

   If you have a collection of English language directions, which have been translated from another language, such as assembly directions for products, check for strange compounds. How would you account for the errors? In writing notes in English about papers written in French, we have found we make many word order errors in our compounds. Would your explanation also hold for such errors?
4. A Japanese woman talked about a footnote story that she had heard about the royal couple. She meant gossip or a story that is going the rounds. If you know Japanese, comment on whether this innovative compound is a loan translation. If it is not, what other explanation can you offer?

Reduplication

Another additive process is that of repetition. The process of *reduplication* is not a powerful one in English, but it is in many languages of the world. We have English words like *flip flop, hush-hush,* and *honey bunny* where all or parts of the words are repeated to add quantity, intensity, or smallness qualities by repetition or elongation. Other examples are repetitions of words within a sentence context: "I'm very very sorry," "He ate lots and lots of salad," "I bought this set of teeny, tiny earrings," or "time after time." We also may lengthen (reduplicate) sounds within words to intensify or change meanings (e.g., "He's real baaad!"). Many nicknames and endearment terms are also reduplications.

Although English allows reduplication, we more typically manage the functions of intensification or endearment without repetition. We have the option of saying "It's a small, small world" but, other than in song, we are more likely to say, "It's an incredibly small world," to emphasize its smallness. We can say "She giggled and giggled," but we also have the option of saying "She had the giggles," "She giggled uncontrollably," or "She giggled and laughed." In some cases, the result of synonyms and repetition is a bit puzzling as in, "Behold, he that keepeth Israel shall neither slumber nor sleep." (Psalms 121:4) or the two-language repetitions as in the name of a baseball team called the Los Angeles Angels, or the La Brea tarpits.

In other languages, reduplication may be much more consistently used for endearment, affection, or intensification functions. Some languages also use the reduplication for other meanings. Ilocano, one of the major languages of the Philippines, uses it for plurals:

Translation	Singular	Plural
dish	piŋgan	piŋpiŋgan
field	talan	tatalan
life	biag	bibiag
head	ulo	ululo

(Data source: Gleason, 1955, p. 32; used with permission)

Vietnamese, too, uses reduplication but for a different function:

luôn luôn	often always
nhò nhò	smallish
buôn buôn	a little sad
châm châm	rather slow
chúa chúa	rather sour
cay cay	rather hot

(Data source: V. Wenzell)

Here reduplication qualifies the strength attributed to the adjective or adverb.

Reduplication is not limited to languages of southeast Asia. Reduplication is one way of forming plurals in Nahuatl (an American Indian language spoken in Mexico) although there are also certain suffix changes involved as well:

Translation	Singular	Plural
chief	tecuhtli	tetecuhtin
lord	pilli	pipiltan
hare	cihtli	cicihtin
coyote	coyotl	cocoyomeh

(Data source: F. Berdan)

Reduplication is also a strong process in American Sign Language. Reduplication can change some verbs into nouns. So the sign for the concept BOAT is a reduplication of the sign for GO-BY-BOAT. And MILK reduplicates the sign for MILK-A-COW. The sign for the noun is a reduplicated version of the verb sign.

Practice 9.3

1. Given *nuang* means carabao or water buffalo in Ilocano, what prediction can you make for the plural form? Given *trong* for *white* in Vietnamese, what prediction can you make for "rather white?" The Nahuatl data are especially interesting because all the examples are +animate. It turns out that inanimate nouns are not marked for plurality. Do

you know of any other languages where plurals are not used for inanimate objects?

2. Tagalog, the official language of the Philippines, also uses reduplication of parts of words to change the meaning of the word. Look at the following data and try to discover what is reduplicated and identify the change in meaning.

basah	read	bumabasah	reading
buhat	lift	bumubuhat	lifting
ka?ln	eat	kUmaka?ln	eating
lakad	walk	lUmalakad	walking
pasok	enter	pumapasok	entering

(Data source: J. D. Bowen)

3. In the following Hopi (American Indian) example, the colon means that the final vowel is long. What is reduplicated and what change in meaning occurs in the word?

ho'ci:	it forms a right angle
ho'cicita:	it is zigzag
wala:	it gives a slosh
walalata:	it is kicking up a sea
riya:	it makes a quick spin
riyayata:	it is whirling
hɛro:	he gives an internal noise
hɛrorota:	he is snoring
yoko:	he gives one nod of the head
yokokota:	he is nodding
ripi:	it gives a flash
ripipita:	it is sparkling

(Data source: Whorf, 1936)

4. There are some special types of reduplication in English. What does it mean when a friend says, "That's a quake quake, not an aftershock!" (when the house shook again a few hours after the 1994 Los Angeles earthquake) or friends compliment a dog, "That's a real dog dog" (in contrast to, say, a miniature purebred). You have probably heard other expressions like "a writer's writer" or an "actor's actor." List your own examples. How regular and productive is this process? That is, can any noun be duplicated and can we add a possessive to any profession to obtain this meaning?

5. There are lots of jokes based on forms of reduplication. Here, however, the repetition in meaning changes in form. Add as many examples as you can to the following list of "OK?" jokes.

Cowardice rules, if it's okay with you.
Procrastination will rule one day, OK?
Synonyms govern, all right?
Einstein rules relatively, OK?
Schizophrenia rules, OK? OK.
Amnesia rules, O.
Apathy ru.
Dyslexia lures, KO.
Anarchy no rules, Ok?
French rules, au quai.

Phrasal lexicon

Clearly, any lexicon includes a range from simple isolated words to compounds and complex words, to collocations of words and phrases to formulaic cliché phrases, to tightly bound idioms. In each case, while more and more words may be added, the meaning of the whole lexical item differs from the individual words within it and so such forms have lexical status.

Obviously it is not whether something is one word or several words that makes for a lexical unit. "Accidentally" and "by chance" have similar meanings yet different numbers of words. "Once" and "one time," "suddenly," and "all of a sudden" are synonymous but have different numbers of words. Single words in one language may have multiword correspondents in other languages. "In the meantime" becomes *entretanto* in Spanish. "Too much" is one word, *troppo,* in Italian. "By chance" is one word in German, *zufällig.*

How do we determine whether a phrase is really a lexical unit or simply a phrase made up of separate words. At one end of the continuum we might have free collocation and at the other end an unbreakable set. Think, for example, of the many words that might follow the word *read.* We can read books, lists, papers, schedules, or we can read slowly, rapidly, with difficulty, or we can read as long as there is light, in the morning, or read in the library, or on the bus. Each of these phrases goes together but the collocations are numerous and flexible. Think of words that might precede *money.* We can donate, spend, earn, invest, steal, or exchange money. Some of these seem much more tightly collocated (e.g., earn money, spend money) than others (e.g., exchange money). The number of possibilities for collocation with money are much more narrow than those with read. In each case, some collocations (e.g., read the paper, read a book and earn money, spend money) are tighter than others.

You may remember party games where one person in a circle started a sentence by saying one word, the next person added another word, and the next person, a third. The words that were uttered one after another made sense not because everyone knew what the overall sentence would be, but rather because each word suggested other words that typically occur next. So if the first word were *Let,* you might immediately think of "Let freedom ring" and supply *freedom.* If, however, it was not your turn and the next person said *me,* you might think of "Let me help you," and add *help.* If it had not been your turn and the next person supplied *tell,* you might think of "Let me tell you what I think" and add *you.* There are lots of possibilities, and each comes not from an overall established topic of conversation or script, but rather from patterns of words that typically go together.

Let us turn to combinations that are even more restricted. How many words can you think of that might precede *probability?* Bolinger (1975, p. 103) lists *high probability* as a strong collocation. We can say there is a *high probability* of rain, but if we change this to *high chance* or *high possibility,* it does not sound right. *High* and *low* go with *probability.* If you substitute *strong* or *great* and *weak* or *little, little chance* sounds much better than *low chance* and *strong chance* is better than *high chance.* The adjectives that can be used are highly predictable. When this happens they form a lexical unit in themselves. *High probability* and *low probability* can thus be thought of as single lexical units.

Collocations become set with verbs as well. Compare the collocation strength in another of Bolinger's examples. We say "to take heart/courage/fright." If we try to change these to "what he took was heart/courage/fright," the collocation no longer works. Nor does it work in the sentence frame, "The fear/heart/courage that he took was indicated by his reaction." The words are not only linked in a phrase, but the collocation is so tight that the unit cannot be broken up into its elements in normal ways.

There are many phrases where words are joined together in a set order. For example, we say "bread and butter," "this and that," "law and order," "life and death," "yes or no," "ladies and gentlemen," and "ice cream and cake." These could also be classified as tight collocations.

Sometimes whole sentences appear to consist of two lexical units, one a lexical frame and the other a single word. "Down with ____" can be completed with almost any noun. "What's the use of ____ing?" allows one to insert many different verbs in the blank, but the rest of the utterance is really one lexical unit. Some of these sentence frames have only a few options for the single word that goes in the blank. Few words can fit in the "for ____'s sake" frame, for example.

Children learning their first language and adult learners of other languages both seem to acquire lexical chunks as well as individual words. Long before they learn the meanings of the individual words, they are able to produce greetings like "How are you?" and leave-takings like

"Bye now" or "See ya later." Adults and children alike acquire such lexical chunks with facility.

It is clear that these phrases are learned as single units rather than as individual words of a phrase. Consider the adult language learner who used the lexical phrase "see ya at the pole" as a leave-taking signal. He belonged to a carpool whose members assembled for the ride home near a flagpole. Typically when they separated in the morning, someone would say, "See ya at the pole." He did not break the phrase down into its components but used the chunk as a general leave-taking even in other situations. Another adult learner, Zoila (Shapira, 1976), acquired "pick you up" as a lexical item and never seemed aware that it consisted of several units. She used it in such utterances as, "She want que I go pickyaup Sofia" and "He pickyaup seven for beach." Other learners, such as the children studied by Wong-Fillmore (1976), are able to use their many chunk utterances quite effectively for basic communication. If you think for a moment about languages you started to learn, you can probably still recall greetings, such formulas as "How do you say ____?" and politeness expressions like "That's all right." In all likelihood these phrases are as much single lexical items as any word you might be able to recall.

Becker (1975) perhaps best sums up the importance of lexical phrases: "We speak mostly by stitching together swatches of text that we have heard before; productive processes have the secondary role of adapting the old phrases to the new situations."

Because collocations reflect what is expected, we often try to violate those expectations to achieve certain effects. Poets achieve remarkable effects by constructing unusual collocations. For example, Emily Dickinson begins one of her poems with the line "Tell me the *truth* but tell it *slant,* success in circuit lies" (italics added). We expect truth to be told straight out, not at a slant. Avoidance of the expected collocation can create new images by drawing on both the expected and the unexpected at once.

Practice 9.4

1. Certain adjectives collocate with color terms (see Householder, 1971, p. 75). Try to use the word *pale* with as many color terms as you can. Which color terms can follow the word *bright*? If I say I have a pale red dress, do you visualize an unsaturated red or a pink dress? Try this experiment with color terms and adjectives in another language. Do they match your findings for English?
2. A friend exclaimed that her best friend had turned into "*an absolutely stark-raving – or is it wide-eyed? – techno*

chiphead!" meaning her friend was spending too much time at the computer. What is the difference between *stark-raving* and *wide-eyed* in terms of possible collocations?

3. Bolinger says that we can criticize someone, saying he or she is "beneath contempt." Try to combine the prepositions *above, below, beneath, near,* and *beyond* with *reproach* and *contempt.* Which ones work? How does the distribution of prepositions relate to our discussion in Chapter 5 of Clark's explanation of space and time metaphors?

4. The poetry of e. e. cummings is filled with collocations: "when *now by now* and *tree by leaf,* she *laughed* his *joy* she *cried* his *grief*" (italics added). Look at his poem "anyone lived in a pretty how town" and think about his uses and violations of collocation sets. Motion and movement of time are especially vivid in this poem because of unexpected collocations of words. List those that you feel show time's passage. How do you think this changes your reading of the poem? Or analyze Dylan Thomas's poem "Fern Hill." Because it contains so many interwoven themes, you may want to select and trace only two. Or you might try creating some unusual but vivid collocations of your own.

5. Consult the *BBI Combinatory Dictionary of English* to select sets of words which range in the degree of collocation strength. For example, "In court an *oath* is (*given, administered, put*) to you." Make up a pilot test of items where choices are available and administer it to language learners. Try to determine on what basis students make their choices.

Idioms and proverbs

Although we claim that collocations are lexical units, they are not set in cement and there are all sorts of possibilities of remaking them. Idioms are not, either, but we think of them as the set end of the continuum from loose to set collocation.

Linguists like to test whether or not ready-made, chunk utterances are really idioms. Such tests include whether or not the meaning differs from that of the sum of its words so that it is like that of a single lexical unit. The phrase "kick the bucket," meaning to die, would be an idiom. The phrase "hold your horses" would be idiomatic, but "wait a minute" would not. A second test is whether the phrase has transformation deficiencies, that is, can the words within it be separated in the utterance in the same way you might others of its type? Can "wait a minute" or "hold your horses" be separated (in "how long she waited was a minute" or "what you held were your horses") and have it mean the same thing as the original utterance? Clearly, that is not possible for "hold your horses," though it seems somewhat more possible for "wait a minute." Other less convincing cases can be made for tests that show that idioms are often not syntactically fully formed, that is, the idiom can't be used in certain grammatical patterns. If we say, "She hold*s* the horses" or "He kick*s* the bucket," the meaning changes. Another test is whether the idiom is more frequent than the literal counterpart in text. That is not the case for "hold your horses" or "kick the bucket," but it might be true for "wait a minute" or "hold it" in oral language.

Proverbs, too, are frozen phrases. They differ from idioms, however, in that they display shared cultural wisdom. Proverbs are so mutually understood, in fact, that in the appropriate situation, we may utter only the first part of the proverb (e.g., "Don't count your chickens" rather than "Don't count your chickens before they've hatched").

Although we think of proverbs as being very bound to culture, many proverbs have equivalents across many different languages.

English: Love is blind.
Spanish: El amor es ciego.

English: True love is never forgotten.
Spanish: Amor que llega a olvido, amor que nunca ha sido.

English: Out of sight, out of mind.
Arabic: Il-ba'iid 'an il-'een ba'iid 'an il-'alb.
Japanese: Saru mono wa hibi ni utoshi.
Italian: Lontano dagli occhi, lontano dal cuore.

> (Data source: C. de Neve, M. Hassan, F. El Hindawy,
> M. Shinohara, V. Chimienti)

Though we share proverbs with many different cultures, we still must be able to interpret proverbs that we encounter for the first time (see examples from Lakoff and Turner [1989] in Chapter 5). If we read the proverb in Merwin's poem:

> Cow
> parched by the sun
> pants at the moon

we try to assign meaning to it in the context in which it is offered. Proverbs are not about animals but about people and their lives, and so we assume the characteristic described for the cow are to be applied to people. We see that the cow-person has been burned once, by the sun. Now the cow-person behaves as though it will always be burned. It even pants at the moon at night.

203

If we say, "Let sleeping dogs lie," we know we are not talking about dogs. We assign the instinctual attributes and behavior of dogs (they bite, bark, whine, etc., when awake) to a person. If we bring up certain issues to someone, the person will notice them, a circumstance better avoided.

One would think that all idioms and proverbs would be transparent in meaning but they are not. An ESL or EFL student will not be able to recognize immediately the intended meaning of many idioms (that's why there are so many idiom books for language learners). Fernando and Flavell (1981) use a four-point scale for transparency of meanings in phrases:

1. opaque ("kick the bucket")
2. semi-opaque ("tarred with the same brush")
3. semitransparent ("skate on thin ice")
4. transparent–non-idiomatic; meaning derived from the words in combination ("walk by the building")

The semitransparent idioms in this classification are often metaphors ("add fuel to the fire"). The semi-opaque and opaque idioms differ in terms of intelligibility. The meanings of opaque idioms cannot be worked out from the meanings of the separate words, whereas it might be possible to do so in the case of semi-opaque idioms.

Although idioms and proverbs are not always transparent, learners are fascinated by them, just as language learners we are always intrigued with expressive, colorful language. We enjoy identifying and even using quotable or proverbial phrases in the new language. Young children seize upon such phrases as "okey-dokey," "no way, José," while older learners pick up idiomatic phrases like "in a feeding frenzy" (a current expression that refers to the media converging on a juicy news story). Idioms and proverbs provide cultural information, and in using these phrases, we feel that we are able to identify with (and perhaps show we are part of) the social group that uses them.

Practice 9.5

1. Select two expressions which you believe are idioms. Then apply Glaser's (1988) tests to determine how well each fits this linguistic taxonomy for idioms.

   a. no additions (a *very wet blanket)
   b. no deletions (hook, *[line], and sinker)
   c. no substitutions (spilled the *peas)
   d. no permutations (*sinker, hook, and line)
   e. blocks predication (sleeping partner → *partner is sleeping)

f. blocks comparative (a *wetter blanket)

g. blocks nominalization (the *playing of the waiting game)

h. blocks passives (*some beans were spilled)

If your examples do not fit all of these tests, how would you grade the degree of idiomaticity?

2. Many dictionaries for language learners list expressions such as *call up* (meaning to phone) as idioms. Since we can say, *"call Sue up"* or *"call her up,"* these do not fit the linguistic definition of an idiom. Instead, they are classified as two-word verbs or verb + particle forms. What arguments can you give for classifying such verb forms as idioms? What arguments can you give against such a classification?

3. List three examples to fit into each of Fernando and Flavell's (1981) four degrees of transparency for expressions. Scramble the order of the examples and then ask beginning, intermediate, and advanced international students for the meanings of each item. Does the accuracy of their responses agree with the degree of transparency? Are advanced students more successful in the task? Based on your findings, would you recommend that idioms and phrases be categorized and taught according to degree of transparency?

4. What is the difference between a proverb, a saying, and an idiom? Is "When the going gets tough, the tough get going" a saying rather than a proverb? Are the variants on it (". . . the tough go shopping, go fishing, go to the beach") sayings, proverbs, or idioms?

5. One of Merwin's proverbs is "Big thunder, little rain." Look for similar proverbs in English or other languages that characterize a person who makes a big fuss but never does anything.

6. Proverbs and sayings are a great source of fun for punsters. The sign on a local music store said, "Gone Chopin. Bach in a minuet." Our favorite, though, is "Though he's not very humble, there's no police like Holmes." Do you have a favorite pun? You might collect examples from your colleagues and submit a paper on the results to the WHIM conference. Luthy (1983) suggests that it may be difficult in some languages – for example, Finnish – to form such puns. Can you find examples similar to those given here in other languages?

7. Sometimes learners use idioms but err either in the form

or in appropriateness of use. In response to a lunch invitation, a nonnative speaker said, "Oh, I've cost you a lot of money and I wouldn't be seen dead in costing you more than this" (data source: Stevens, 1988). What is the idiom? What does it mean? Why can't it be used in turning down a lunch invitation? Prepare a short lesson on the form and function of this idiom for adult learners. Do you believe that idioms should be taught only for comprehension and not for production? Explain your reasoning.

How large can a lexical unit be?

We could limit the lexicon to single words, but we know that a single word for an object in one language may be several words in another (e.g., English *potato* and French *pomme de terre*). Common compounds like post office, express mail, mail box could as well be written as one word; certainly they deserve to be lexical entries in any dictionary.

Some collocations are so strong that it seems strange to list them as separate words to be combined into the collocation each time we need it. Lexical phrases such as "against my better judgment," "runaway inflation," and "state of the art" have unit meanings that differ from that of each word. Idioms and proverbs also appear to be lexical units. Proverbs and idioms were, perhaps, once actually formed by additive processes in lexical development, but it is highly unlikely that they are assembled from scratch each time they are uttered. Stereotyped utterances like "How are you," "good to see you," "sorry I'm late," and "thank you" also seem to be chunks or lexical sentences, rather than utterances made up of a words strung together anew each time they are said. Even larger chunks exist. It's unlikely that children learn the Pledge of Allegiance or other memorized pieces with an understanding of the individual words they are saying. They "pledge a legion to the flag," sing the "stars bangles banger," and of the "ramrods we washed." They ask God to bless America "with a light from a bulb," and sing of "Gladly, the cross-eyed bear."

The processes that formed these complex lexical units must, however, still be available. We say this because we can create new compounds, new collocations, new lexical phrases, new idioms, and new proverbs. And we can use them to understand new complex formations when we see or read them. However, it seems unlikely that each time we use these phrases we construct them anew by combining the words. Rather, they spring to mind and from our lips as do single words.

In acquisition studies and language attrition studies, we see the process at work. We also find that some complex items, in particular stereotyped chunks, are held in memory in special ways which seem to make them especially resistant to loss. Aphasics can often produce an entire chunk but not the words in the constituent. Foreign language learners can often recite whole dialogues they learned many years ago yet they are unable to spontaneously form sentences using the words in the dialogues.

We often think that the unanalyzed chunks of language are trite or clichéd, but the language we use is filled with them. Our greetings and our phatic communication (talk when we have little to say but wish to sustain social interaction) are comprised of chunks that we arrange and rearrange to prevent monotony. Anyone who has worked in translation realizes that much of translation has to do with knowing the "chunks" of a particular field as well as those of ordinary talk. Much of the predictability of language (and ease or difficulty of translation) has to do with these chunks.

Bolinger (1974) says that "speakers do at least as much remembering as they do putting together." That is, we string together these lexical complexes as often, if not more often, than we string together single words. The complexes vary in how chunklike they are. Some are tight and unbreakable units, others are looser and allow several words to go into slots within the complex, still others are fairly open. If we look at the full range of complex collocations, we find that they are pervasive in language. Because they are ready-made units at one moment and can be divided up into shifting combinations in another, they make the dividing line between syntax and lexicon very fuzzy indeed.

Practice 9.6

1. Eugene Ionesco's play *Les Chaises* (*The Chairs*) is made up almost entirely of formulaic utterances. Given the predictability of each phrase, closely translating the original French seems impossible. If you are proficient in French, compare the English and French versions and discuss the problems faced in the translation.

2. Critchley (1970) called the meaningless sounds with which the speaker decorates talk (in fact, y'know, actually, of course, naturally, as a matter of fact, do you know what I mean) verbal tics. Tape record a casual conversation and identify any of your own verbal tics that seem a bit obsessive. (Or read through this chapter and find ours that slipped into writing!) How easy or difficult is it to eradicate these in talk or in writing? Would you want to get rid of all of them or do some serve an important discourse function?

3. We like to think of our language use as creative and innovative, but if it were, we would not be able to process it in

> real time. Try this experiment: As you listen to a taped conversation, "shadow" each speaker as if you were simultaneously translating rather than just repeating the message. You should be able to stay with the speakers quite easily, for much of the message is predictable, made up of more complex than simple lexical items. Now repeat the process, "shadowing" a speaker giving a lecture in a technical field with which you are not familiar. If you have difficulty keeping up with the speaker, is the difficulty due to simple or complex lexical items?
>
> 4. Read Safire's (1982) essay "I led the pigeons to the flag" for examples of errors of children and adults in reciting and singing formulas such as the Pledge of Allegiance. In language acquisition, we say that comprehension precedes production. Do such errors argue against this principle? Justify your answer.

Just as we increase the lexicon by adding or joining words together, we form new words by subtractive processes where something is taken away from the original word. Subtractive processes include clipping, initialization, acronyms, and blends or portmanteau words.

Clipping

Clipping is one way in which we change words. We may shorten *dormitory* to *dorm* and thereby create a new word, or we may change *condominium* to *condo*. We use the longer term if the situation is more formal and the shorter term if the situation is more informal. However, the new term may entirely replace the longer original word. Can you tell, for example, what the original words for *psycho* or *flu* might have been?

Some fields use many clipped forms. For example, computer commands are almost always clipped terms: *del* means *delete, sho cat* means display all the files catalogued in a particular computer account, for example.

Clipping is a common feature of in-group talk and of slang. For example, English speakers in Japan have clipped *befriended* to *friended* to mark times when they assume the language teacher's role outside the classroom, as in "I was friended on the train today" when the speaker was surrounded by students who wanted to practice their English. In slang, the clipped form is often changed to end in a vowel, usually *o*, which seems to be a favorite way to end many clipped forms. We talk about *demos*, an *anthro* class, and *porno* films in everyday conversation without necessarily considering these forms slang. In Australian English,

208

clipped forms ending with o are so common that the phenomenon is often spoofed:

Thommo, a commo journo, who lived with his preggo wife from Rotto in a fibro in Paddo, slipped on the lino taking a dekko at the nympho next door. He missed out on compo, so he worked for a milko, then a garbo, and took a bit part in a panto. His wife ran off with a muso, and Thommo got dermo and gastro. When he couldn't pay his rego, he tried to shoot himself but had run out of ammo. If the Salvos hadn't found him and called the ambo, he could have ended up derro on metho.

(Servisier, quoted in Wierzbicka, 1986, 361–362)

Clipping also occurs when words are borrowed from one language to another. English words are frequently shortened when they are borrowed into Japanese. For example, *apaato* is the clipped form of the borrowed form for *apartment building, suto* is the truncated form of *sutoraiku,* the word borrowed for *strike, naitaa* is the shortened form of *night game* for baseball, and *depaato* is the abbreviated form of *department store* (data source: T. Morimoto). Gibbons (1987) study of Hong Kong English–Chinese mix includes such clipped examples as *resi* (for a member of a residence hall), and Deen gives the example of *floppy disk* being borrowed into Dutch and then clipped to *flop* for one diskette and *floppen* as the plural.

Practice 9.7

1. List all the clipped forms from one issue of your local newspaper. How many of the forms are commercial terms? How many are pop culture terms? How many have remained in the language and become terms of common usage? Would you consider *pop* as in "pop culture," or "pop art" a clipped form that has been integrated into common usage?
2. Expressions that were once phrases or compounds may later be clipped. For example, *laptop* is now used more frequently than the longer compound "laptop computer." How many of the examples you gathered for item 1 are clipped compounds?
3. Look for examples of clipped English borrowed words in another language. If these languages have few consonant clusters and open consonant + vowel syllables (as in the Japanese and Chinese examples we provided), we would expect clipping to be as much a phonological adaptation as true clipping. If you have found examples of clipped

borrowed English words in other languages, that explanation might not hold. What do your results show?

4. Language teachers sometimes include short lessons on clipped forms as a way of interesting students and motivating them to learn new vocabulary. What benefits or problems do you see in introducing such forms in your language classes?

Initialization and acronyms

Another reduction process is the use of initialization in words such as FBI, UCLA, or BYU, where each letter in the word is pronounced. Acronyms are words made up of abbreviations, too, but the result is pronounced as a word, not as a list of letters. For example, Unicef, Nabisco, Texaco, *NAFTA,* and, for linguists, even SLRF and AILA are abbreviations which have become words. The word *posh* (arguably from *p*ortside *o*ut and *s*tarboard *h*ome – the best cabin positions on the trip out to India and back) is a classic example of an acronym.

In American Sign Language, initialization has become an extremely productive process. New technical terms are being added to all languages at an alarming speed, and the deaf need to come up with signs for these. One way to do this is to initialize pre-existing signs by holding a handshape from the manual alphabet while producing a sign. So the sign THING can be initialized with an *m* to make it MATERIAL, or an *e* to form EQUIPMENT.

Deaf students sometimes use initialization to create sign jokes. L. Hunt (personal communication) gives two examples. The names of two cafeterias on the campus of NTID (an initialization, not an acronym, for National Technical Institute of the Deaf) are Grace Watson Hall and the Dining Commons. Officially, the signs for both are the initials GW and CD made at the mouth, where the EAT sign is made. Students have changed the places of articulation, making GRACE-WATSON with the G going down the throat and the W coming right back up, and DINING-COMMONS with the C around the throat as if gagging or choking.

Initialization and acronyms are not generally powerful processes for forming new words in English. Still, there are many acronyms in certain fields, particularly those with large bureaucracies. For example, after the 1994 earthquake, Los Angeles residents who hoped to find housing quickly learned that the acronym HUD was not the name of a movie but the Department of Housing and Urban Development. Those who wanted loans had to deal with SBA and FEMA, the small business and federal emergency agencies.

Practice 9.8

1. Give examples of initialization and acronyms used in the languages you teach or are studying.
2. Look at the following sets for American Sign Language. Each set has one basic sign and added initials that change the meaning. In each set, what do you think the basic sign means?

   a. *C*LASS, *G*ROUP, *T*EAM, *S*OCIETY, *W*ORKSHOP
   b. *L*ANGUAGE, *P*HRASE, *C*LAUSE
   c. *B*IOLOGY, *E*XPERIMENT, *S*TATISTICS, *C*ALCULUS, *G*EOMETRY

3. Prepare a list of the initials and acronyms used at your school. RA and TA are familiar forms at most colleges and universities for research and teaching assistants. Those for the names of buildings are local terms (a student at BYU asked, "What is this 'empty sea?' after hearing fellow students refer to a building as the MTC). Divide your list into common and local items and check to see which forms the international students know and use.
4. J. Paxton's *Penguin Dictionary of Abbreviations* includes a variety of initialized and acronym forms. Using this as a source, prepare a short lesson plan for teaching forms that would be useful for your students.

Blends

New words can also be created by blending two or more other words. For example, *brunch* came from the blend of breakfast and lunch, *flurry* from flutter and hurry, and *smog* from smoke and fog. Historically, *sparcity* came from sparseness and scarcity; *splotch* from spot and blotch. These blends (called portmanteau words by Lewis Carroll in *Alice in Wonderland*) have become part of our everyday lexicon.

Again, product advertising, the entertainment industry, bureaucracies, and technical fields seem to produce the largest number of blends. Eurail, Medicare, camcorder, and sitcom have come into the language in this way. Product names are often blends. Velveeta is a blend of velvet, eat, and cheese. The "information superhighway" will send information down a *datapike*. The *retro*active *re*pair of Los Angeles freeway overpasses by *refit*ting support columns after the 1994 earthquake became known as *retrofitting*.

When we first meet most blends, they seem quite appropriate. Others may be more difficult to process. For example, *snarky,* a combination of snide and sarcastic, is not easily deciphered. Other blends (e.g., *guesstimate, alcoholiday*) seem contrived for headlines or other more momentary uses. It is unlikely that *mummabilia* (a blend of memorabilia and mummy) will ever be used beyond the Associated Press story about a display of "long-forgotten mummies and mummabilia" (Mcquain, 1992).

Sometimes words borrowed from another language form blends via analogy. For example, the Japanese borrowed word *sukin shippu* (= skinship) is a blend of skin and kinship, meaning a relationship that is very close. Nemser (1991) collected learner errors that also demonstrate the blending process. His examples include *adjacing* from adjacent to and adjoining; *self-conceited* from self-assured or self-confident and conceited; *semiglide* from semivowel and glide. In addition, he gives examples of loan blends, where one part of the word comes from one language and the other from a second language. These blends, produced by German speakers of English, included *flutlight* for floodlight (German *Flutlicht*) and *dursty* meaning thirsty (German *durstig*).

Practice 9.9

1. Collect as many blends as you can from your local newspaper. Which seem to have just been created and which do you think are assimilated into the language? For those that are new to you, predict whether they will become ordinary words in the language and justify your prediction.
2. List as many blends in another language as you can. What similarities or differences do you see to those of English?
3. What fields do you think create the most blends? When are blends appropriate or not appropriate in this field? For example, sportscasters use a device called a *telestrator* to draw lines and circles while describing playback action. They use the term in talking with each other when they are off-camera ("Ya wanna telestrate this one?") but they do not use the term when on camera.
4. A recent newscast described the first day of President Clinton's vacation as a *Clintathlon,* a day made up of an early morning bike ride, a golf game, a discussion of social policies, a jog, a game of touch football, a visit to McDonald's, and so forth. Is this a blend of the President's name and *triathlon,* or is it a name plus the affix *-athlon*? Justify your decision.

5. If you have relevant data, add to Nemser's list of blend errors. Do you think blending is a powerful factor in explaining student errors?

The lexicon of any language is continually changing as new words are added, changed, used, and lost. In this chapter we have seen a number of ways that words are combined to create new lexical units. We have also examined ways in which word forms are reduced to create new words. It is possible that both addition and reduction will happen to the same item. For example, the lexical metaphor *flying saucer* is a compound made up of a word for its shape and a word for its attribute of flight. However, the compound *flying saucer* is easily referred to in its reduced form as a *saucer* or *UFO*. Our *language laboratory* is more often called a lab. We admire a friend's *sun tan* but may call it a *tan*. If you find *typographical errors* in your papers (or this book!), you would probably call them *typos*. And, if you are hungry, you may think about a *sub* rather than a *submarine sandwich*. The process of addition and reduction continues unabated.

Research and application

Compounding

1. Clark (1981, 1983) found that children between the ages of 2 and 6 invented new words to fill gaps in their vocabularies. Some of these were compounds (such as *plant-man* for gardener). When shown pictures, they created such compounds as *apple-knife* (a knife to cut apples) and *mouse-hat* (a hat for a mouse). Very young children, then, have no trouble in forming such constructions. Yet, as shown in the Berko study discussed in this chapter, they were not able to explain the meanings of words such as Thanksgiving in terms of its components. Read and critique this research and determine how you might investigate this discrepancy (with first or second language learners).
2. Dressler (1985) looks at the use of compounds (such as the "ice cow" example in section A) for discourse purposes in a number of different ways. Read his article and then attempt to find examples of both cataphoric and anaphoric reference accomplished by compounds in a language of your choice. You might select a number of your favorite writers and contrast their use of compounds as cohesive devices through anaphoric and cataphoric reference.

Reduplication

3. Whorf used the Hopi data in Practice 9.3.3 as one piece of evidence that we use language to organize our experience (whether languages make a distinction between blue/green is another). The Sapir-Whorf hypothesis claims that the structure of a language influences its speakers' view of the world around them. This has sometimes been misinterpreted to mean that a language forms a kind of straitjacket that forces us to view the world in certain ways. Do you believe that Hopi speakers are more likely to notice whether actions are punctual or not because of reduplication? (An English speaker can say "He jumped" or "He jumped, and jumped, and jumped," so obviously the same distinction can be made in different ways in these two languages.) The many arguments about the use of *he, chairman, mankind* in the literature on gender and language also rest in part on this claim about the connection between language and the way we view our world. State your belief about the merits of the Sapir-Whorf hypothesis (in all its many forms), and give two supporting arguments.

Lexical phrase units

4. Van Lanacker (1975) found that stereotyped phrases, which we have called lexical units, are well retrieved by some aphasia patients. She calls swear words, emotive expressions (such as "Land's sakes!" and "Oh my God!") and stereotyped phrases (such as "Well, I never," and "I don't know") *autonomous speech.* Prepare a research plan to test attrition of such phrases with foreign language learners who studied the foreign language ten or more years ago. (Decide whether you need to limit the study to adult learners ten years later or whether you will contrast children, adolescents, and adults ten years later.)

5. Kotsinas (1983) studied the vocabulary acquisition of her Swedish language students: five adult Greeks and one Polish woman. All learners acquired chunk phrases. Kotsinas especially notes those of Dimitris, who produced such utterances as *det spelar ingen roll* (it doesn't matter), *XHur mar du? Bra?* (How are you? Fine?). Other combinations include *har inne* (in here), *dar nere* (down there), *gå ut* (go out), *komma in* (come in), *gå up* (go up), *du vet* (you know), *forstar du mig?* (do you understand me?). You might want to replicate her study with your own beginning language students. What chunks do they acquire? Do they all use the same chunks? Does frequency in the input explain which chunks are used? You might

try an attrition study to see what frequent phrases are retained by learners after several years away from the language.

6. Wong-Fillmore (1976), who studied the second language acquisition of young children in classrooms, categorized their most frequently used chunk phrases by function. Consider the following categories and decide whether this would be a useful framework for categorizing lexical chunks acquired by learners you might study.

Attention callers: Oh Teacher, Hey, stupid.

Name exchanges: What'cher name? My name is X.

Greetings, leave-takings: See ya later, Take care, I gotto go, Hello, X

Politeness routines: How are you? Thank you very much, 'Scuse me, I'm sorry.

Language management: I don' understand, I don' know, How do you do this in English?

Conversation management: Ya know why? Ya know what? Guess what! Be quiet. Shaddup your mouth. OK? I gotta idea.

Comments and exclamations: How nice! I'm so lucky! Nuts to you! All right, you guys! For heaven's sake!

Questions: What's that? How much? Whatsa matter? You wanna play? Can I? You wanna X? Why do I have to?

Responses: I know. I guess so. Not me! I think so. So what? I don't care. I don't know, why? Why not?

Commands and requests: Let's go. Gimme X. Let's trade. Lemme X. Watch dese! Hurry up. Leave it 'lone. Forget it. Get outta here! Come over here! Help me! Wait a minute.

Presentatives and parallel talk: Here it is. You go like this. Not like this. Fixit up. Put it right there. One more.

Play management: I'm not playing. My turn. Your turn. Me first. I wanna be the X. Ready, set, go.

Story-telling routines: Once upon a time. One day the X was VERBing.

Explanations: Because. That's why.

Wannas and wannits: I wanna (thing). I want some more. I want dese. I don' wanna do nothing. I wanna make X. I wanna do it.

7. The Berlitz method presents learners with sets of phrases according to area of use (shopping, the hotel, and so forth). Do you think that one might learn these phrases as lexical units, memorizing and retaining them for later use? Some foreign language learners can still recite complete dialogues they had to memorize in class but cannot remember what they meant. How might one go about helping learners expand the use of chunk phrases in language

use? How might one encourage learners eventually to break up lexical phrases into their components? If you are not teaching, then imagine how you might have encouraged Zoila to use *pick-yaup* (discussed in the section titled "Phrasal Lexicon" in this chapter) more appropriately.

8. Krashen and Scarcella (1978) review the studies of acquisition of formulaic language, routines, automatic speech, or chunks in child and adult second or foreign language studies. They relate the acquisition of such chunks to "gestalt" learning and discuss the notion that routines and patterns evolve into analytic language as they are broken into smaller units so that parts of patterns are "freed" to recombine with other parts of patterns. Krashen and Scarcella see this strategy as an alternative rather than the usual route to acquisition. Do you agree or disagree with the authors on the importance and function of "phrasal lexicon" in language acquisition?

Part III Lexical classes and morphology

10 Word classification

Terms used to classify words based on their functional categories are called parts of speech, which include nouns, verbs, adjectives, and adverbs. In addition to these major classes, there are pronouns, prepositions, conjunctions, and interjections. We will discuss the major classes first.

Word class is an important feature in semantic feature analysis. In each of the following sets of words, one word does not belong. *Breakfast, talent, sing,* and *dictionary* are all common words, but *sing* is an action and therefore a verb whereas the other three items are nouns. *Happy, woman, tall,* and *thoughtful* are also common words. *Woman* is a noun while the other three items are adjectives that describe attributes of such nouns as *woman.*

The classification of the words of a language in this way is dependent on their function in communication. Nouns can occur in certain places in sentences and serve certain functions. Verbs also occur in certain places and have special functions. So, word class membership is an important lexical feature.

If we just look at a word, it is sometimes difficult to know how to classify it. For example, *book* might be used as a noun in one utterance and as a verb in another. *Can* might be a noun ("a *can* of soup"), a verb ("they *canned* the fish"), an adjective ("the *can* factory"), or a modal auxiliary ("you *can* sing"). In some cases, syllable stress helps us determine whether a word is a noun or a verb as with con'duct (verb) vs. 'conduct (noun) or re'cord (verb) vs. 'record (noun). However, this only works for a limited number of word pairs. We cannot change all nouns to verbs or verbs to nouns by changing stress patterns. So it is *use* that determines how a word is classified.

Children may begin their lexical development by using features that vary along perceptual dimensions (e.g., texture, shape, sound). Though it is fairly clear that children acquire many nouns early (in relation to early acquisition of verbs), it is not so clear when or how the child establishes word classes that are equivalent to noun or verb.

Susan's first word (i.e., recognized consistently by her parents) was /aɪ:/, a baby variant of *light.* Her parents would say "light" as they lifted her so she could assist in pulling a cord to turn on a light. Soon Susan was saying /ai:/ as she helped carry out the action. The problem is that no one was sure whether she was labeling the light itself or the action of turning it on.

Anyone who has worked with early childhood language data realizes that this is a problem. Bloom (1970) took care to annotate her child's utterances as an aid in making these decisions, or at least decisions about the functions of parts of utterances. So, for example, the utterance "no dirty soap" was said as the child pushed away a piece of worn soap, wanting to be washed with new pink soap. Yet, even with such glosses it is not always possible to classify words by parts of speech.

It may be that young children do not have a strong notion of word classes. One piece of evidence for this comes from word association studies such as those mentioned in Chapter 4. If you give adults words like *table, dark,* and *deep,* they will likely respond with *chair, light,* and *shallow,* respectively. Notice that the responses are the same part of speech as the stimulus word. Young children, however, are more likely to supply words which might continue an utterance such as *eat, night,* and *hole.* Although their responses may not show an awareness of word classes, they do show that they have a good sense of what types of words can co-occur.

Nouns

In a grammar class you may have learned that a noun refers to a person, place, or thing. In Chapter 1, we saw that nouns can be divided into subclasses. Proper nouns, like *Betsy, Ohio,* and *the Mormon Tabernacle Choir* differ from the common nouns (*woman, state,* and *choir*). Abstract nouns like *hope, understanding,* and *love* differ from such concrete nouns as *dish, table,* and *chair.* Count nouns (*books, birds,* and *pianos*) differ from mass nouns (*applesauce, gravy,* and *rice,*) which tend not to be so discrete. Group nouns (*bank, government, board, fair, club,* and *choir* also differ from other nouns that refer to people because they refer to the group as a unit (*"The choir performs* every Sunday" versus "The *singers perform* every Sunday"). We also noted that in many languages, all nouns are classified by gender whereas other languages may group them according to categories that relate to shape, texture, consistency, and so forth.

Lyons (1977, Vol. 2, Chapter 11, pp. 422–466) claims that all parts of speech have a semantic core that is language-independent. The most core-like nouns (which he calls first order) are names of people and physical objects, and entities that exist in time and space. The objects are those over which persons have privilege. Second-order nouns are observable entities which take place in time. So these would include nouns of states (e.g., *sleep*), processes (e.g., *weaving*), and events (e.g., *a crash*). Third-order entities are propositions that are truly abstract entities with no relation to time and space (e.g., *democracy*).

The more corelike the noun is, the easier it should be to learn. There is considerable evidence that words for concrete, tangible, physical objects are learned more succesfully than other types of nouns. Children acquire the names of concrete items before abstract nouns, and they use more concrete nouns in their talk than do adults. According to Camarata and Leonard (1986), children pronounce the names of concrete objects more clearly than verbs. Aphasia studies have shown that dysphasics find it easier to read common concrete nouns than abstract nouns or verbs. Even in chimpanzee studies, the words for concrete, physical objects are best learned. So, the closer to Lyons' first order the nouns are, the easier they should be to learn and retain.

Some nouns are very similar to verbs in meaning. Events such as swimming, dancing, and praying, which bring verb qualities to nouns (and have the *-ing* ending to prove it) are called gerunds. These nouns name perceptually observable events (Lyons' second-order nouns); they are less corelike as nouns. Children may comprehend some gerunds early (e.g., in phrases such as "Stop your crying" and Whining won't help"), but few gerunds appear in their early vocabulary or in that of beginning EFL/ESL learners. Abstract nouns (Lyons' third-order nouns) like *democracy, understanding,* and *responsibility* appear much later.

Nouns differ in other ways as well. Some nouns are very like adjectives in meaning. Colors and numbers illustrate this well. Numbers may be adjectives, as in "It was *thirty* years ago today" or they can be nouns as in "She's in her *thirties.*" Colors can be nouns as in *"Blue* is my favorite color," or adjectives: "I'd like a *blue* hat."

Although it is often difficult to assign word class status to words in isolation, that assignment becomes clearer once we look at the roles nouns can take in utterances. They can be subjects of sentences: *"June* has gone to Australia." They can be direct objects: "I wrote a *letter."* They can be indirect objects: "I sent the letter to *June."* They can be objects of prepositions: "I sent the letter from the *post office."* They can even be predicate nominatives: "It's a fantastic *airline."*

If we take a more functional approach, we could describe the semantic roles that nouns can have, as we noted in Chapter 7. Nouns can be agents, that is, they can carry out actions: *"Sue* biked to Malibu." They can be patients, receiving actions carried out by others: "Sue crashed her *bike."* Nouns can be dative, that is, affected by a state or action: *"Sue* felt so frustrated," *"Sue* had a headache." Nouns can be benefactive, for whom something is done: "I changed the bike tire for *Sue."* Nouns can be instrumental in helping to complete an action: *"The patch* fixed the flat tire on her bike." "I mended the tire *with a patch."* They can be recipients: "I gave the bike *to Sue." "Sue* received the award for the most flat tires." Nouns can be locatives: "*Malibu* is a great place to have a flat tire." "Sue crashed her bike *near the pier.*"

The word forms themselves do not clearly determine whether a word is a noun, verb, adjective, and so forth. The function of the word in communication determines its classification. As you can see, nouns carry many semantic roles (agent, patient, and so forth) in utterances. Their roles can also be classified in the more traditional terms of grammar roles (subject, object, and so forth).

Practice 10.1

1. Bloom's (1970) child said "Mommy sock" as she picked up her mother's sock. Later she said "Mommy sock" as her mother put the child's sock on her foot. How would you classify the role of *mommy* in each example? How would you classify each of the words in the utterance "Mommy shirts hot" said while the child's mother was ironing shirts? Is it easier to talk about semantic roles or grammar roles of the words in these three utterances?

2. According to Nelson (1973, 1979), children learn very early the words for objects that are capable of motion. (Balls roll, but tables do not move. The word *ball* is learned before *table.*) We also know that children learn words more easily for objects that they can manipulate. Yet Brown (1957) notes that 67 percent of the nouns used by children are concrete and have visual contours (compared with 39 percent in adult data). Do you think that learning is the result of manipulating objects (i.e., children manipulate balls more often than they manipulate a chair), or is it that learning is promoted because objects that can be manipulated have visual contours and are concrete? How might you research this question with young bilingual children?

3. Joan Benoit won the women's marathon in the 1984 Olympics. Determine the grammar roles of the italicized nouns in the following sentences:

   Joan Benoit won the marathon.
   Joan Benoit, *Boston's favorite runner,* won the race.
   She's a fantastic *runner.*
   They awarded *Joan* the gold medal.
   She received the medal on the *awards platform.*

   (The truncated relative clauses, sometimes called noun adjuncts, are just to see if you are paying attention!)

221

TABLE 10.1   POLISH DATA

Case	Noun form	Meaning
nominative	kobieta	woman
genitive	kobiety	of the woman
dative	kobiecie	to/for the woman
accusative	kobietę	DIRECT OBJECT the woman
locative	kobiecie	PREPOSITION (about) the woman
instrumental	kobietą	by (means of) the woman
vocative	kobieto	oh, woman

Data source: V. Wenzell, W. Whipple.

4. List the semantic roles for the italicized nouns in the following sentences:

Sheila heard shots.
Her *apartment door* was riddled by bullets.
Nobody meant to kill her with the *bullets.*
But unfortunately one bullet pierced the *door.*
Harry sent flowers to *Sheila.*
He always bought flowers for *Sheila* at the market.
Harry felt so sad, but there was nothing he could do.
Sheila was dead.

5. Many languages have special endings for case roles, which are very similar to the semantic roles discussed in this section. Slavic languages, such as Russian and Polish, have cases. Identify the semantic role (i.e., agent, patient) for each of the cases shown in Table 10.1 for the Polish word *kobieta* (which means *woman*). Since case languages are explicitly marked for semantic roles, word order can be used for other purposes. Because English does not have case marking, we must rely on word order to carry much of this information.

Verbs

Verbs are words that denote action. We said that nouns that name states, processes, and events are not as nounlike as physical objects that exist in time and space. We might also say that verbs that denote states rather than actions seem less verblike. Process verbs which have no definite end points also seem less verblike than strong actions. Vendler (1967) placed verbs into four classes: activities, accomplishments, achievements, and states. We have to think about the whole time frame, however, in order to successfully categorize verbs in this way. *Run,* for example, could be an activity or, if we *run a mile,* an accomplishment. Examples for each include:

Activities	*Accomplishments*	*Achievements*	*States*
run	paint a picture	recognize	know
walk	draw a triangle	find	love
write	run a mile	lose	have
drive a car	write a letter	understand	desire
seek	build	hear	be (tall)
listen to	kill	see	
look for	put		

Actions or activities and accomplishments seem more verblike than achievement and state verbs. So again although we think of a verb as a classification, some verbs fit or exemplify the class better than others.

We know that young children name objects in their environment especially those that are capable of motion. The first verbs they comprehend are primarily action words, such as *peekaboo, show X, clap hands,* and such formulaic warnings as *stop it, don't do it.* Brown (1957) shows this continues as children get older. They talk about actions: 57 percent of the verbs used by children are action verbs while only 33 percent of adults verbs denote action. The actions they talk about are those they observe in the here and now, transitive action words (*hug, bite*) and intransitive actions (*go, jump, run*).

We discussed a number of grammatical verb classes in Chapter 1 as we discussed semantic features. We know that there are separate verb classes for verbs that do or do not take an object (transitive versus intransitive), do not take the -*ing* form (**liking, having*), and do or do not carry stative meanings (*think, want*). In a sense, copulas or linking verbs such as *be,* seem very unverblike. In sentences like "Betsy *is* a teacher," "Betsy *is* sometimes silly," or "Betsy *is* at school," the copula *is* links the qualities in the predicate (i.e., silliness, teacherhood, and at schoolness) to the subject, Betsy. Perhaps this difference in function is why the copula is not always a verb in other languages. Nevertheless, in some languages the copula is a verb:

English: I *am* a student. We *are* students.
Spanish: Yo *soy* un médico. Nosotros *somos* médicos.
Estonian: Ma *olen* ajakirjanik. (I am a journalist.)

In other languages the copula function is carried by a pronoun:

Hebrew: Oren *hu* ha-ganav. (Oren *he* the-thief)

It can also be a particle:

Hausa: Shii sarkii *nee*
          He chief particle   (He is a chief)
          Ruwa-n tafkii *nee*
          Water-of lake particle   (It is lake water)

In other languages the copula is not represented by a form:

Russian: On student
            He student   (He is a student)   classification
            Etot stary celovek moj deduska
            This old person   my grandfather
            (This old person is my grandfather)   identification
Chamorro: Mediku si-Juan
            doctor article-John
            (John is a doctor.)   classification
                    (Data source for copula examples: V. Wenzell)

Because the copula is used for so many different kinds of sentences and has so many forms (*is, am, are, was, were*), we can predict that learners of English will experience some difficulty with it. If, in addition, the L1 of the learner differs in how the copula is represented (a verb, a pronoun, a particle, or nothing at all), the production of *be* may be particularly troublesome.

It may seem strange that a language would not have any form for the copula. Many English speakers learning American Sign Language add one (essentially changing ASL to a form of signed English by finger spelling forms of *be*). However, even native speakers of English do not always supply the copula where it seems to be required. Consider the following examples from commentary on a game:

Lakers leading 102–97.
Kareem in trouble! Look out! No harm, no foul, no blood, no ambulance!
Magic with the ball, bouncing it up and down like a yo-yo – slam dunk!
Shoots up a prayer and no answer.
Fast break! Three on four! Two points! Au-to-MA-tic!
Green, fourth year man outta Washington, looking good in there.
This game's in the refrigerator, the door shut, the light's out, and the eggs're
    coolin'.
                    (Data source: Chick Hearn, Laker commentator)

The early language of children (18–34 months) also shows little use of the copula:

That a lamb.   Man in blocks.
That a bear book.   It a my book.
Kathy in there.   Tiny balls in there.

Many colloquial dialects of English also omit the copula in certain instances. The following examples come from Labov's (1972) analysis of the speech of young black American males.

a. Before a predicate noun phrase: "She the first one started us off." He a eat-and-runner."
b. Before a predicate adjective: "You crazy." "I know, but he wild, though!"
c. Before predicate locatives: "You out the game." "We on tape."

In English, the copula has many uses. It can be used in existentials (i.e., presentatives): "*There is* a notebook in the office." It can be used with various predicates – with predicate nouns: "Betsy *is* a student"; with predicate adjectives: "The notebook *is* blue"; with locatives: "The notebook *is* in the office"; and with possessives: "The notebook *is* Betsy's." Although the copula has functions that are not shared by other verbs, we still classify it as a verb.

Auxiliary verbs are also classified as verbs. In English, this includes modals (e.g., *can, may, might, will*), auxiliary *be* (e.g., "She *is* skating;" "They *were* running"), and auxiliary *have* (e.g., "She *has* often skated." "They *had* already run"). Again, the auxiliary verbs do not fit our definition of verbs as expressing action. Nevertheless, they are traditionally included in the verb category.

As you might predict, auxiliary verbs are not acquired as early as action verbs. Those which have the clearest semantic meanings are acquired first. *Can* and *can't* in the meaning of permission and ability appear when the child begins producing three- to four-word utterances: "I *can* jump." "I *can* get down?" *Can* is the first auxiliary to appear in inverted question forms: "*Can* I?" "*Can* Heidi go?" *Will* also appears early with the semantic meaning of intention (rather than to express future tense): "I *will*! I *will*!"

We will discuss the various verb forms in more detail in Chapter 12 (morphology). To review grammar, verbs have principal parts: the infinitive (*to ring*), past (*rang*), and participle (*rung*). They are also inflected for tense (present, past, future), for voice (active, passive), and mood (indicative, subjunctive, and imperative). Let us review tense, voice, and mood in the following examples.

I *went* to the June Lake relay races.
tense: past; **voice:** active; **mood:** indicative

Our team *had hoped* to win the meet.
past perfect, active, indicative

We *have been running* well this year.
present perfect progressive, active, indicative

While Sue *was running,* she got a muscle cramp.
past progressive, active, indicative

If I *were* in better shape, we still might win.
present, active, subjunctive

Run a little faster!
present, active, imperative

The trophy *was awarded* to the Sub4 team.
past, passive, indicative

If we *had trained* hard, we would have won.
past perfect, active, subjunctive

Our coach says we *will win* next year.
future, active, indicative

He *says* that every year.
present, active, indicative

Practice 10.2

1. To account for the verbs in the on-line computer lexical
   database WordNet, Miller and his colleagues (1990) used
   15 semantic groups to classify verbs: body functions and
   care (*sweat, shiver, sleep*), change (*pacify, computerize*),
   competition (*fight, race*), consumption (*eat, drink*), contact
   (*touch, cover*), cognition (*learn, memorize*), creation (*invent, weave*), motion (*walk, run*), emotion *(fear, adore)*,
   stative (*surround, equal*), perception (*watch, spy*), possession (*take, hold*), social interaction (*charm, impeach*), and
   weather (*rain, thunder*). Which of the semantic classes
   used in WordNet would you predict would be easiest to
   learn and which would you predict would be most difficult?
   How might you test your prediction? If you develop this as
   a research project, you might also check your language
   textbooks to see whether verbs of each type appear.
2. In Chapter 9 we discussed compounds and noted that
   there are verb compounds (e.g., *make believe*). In the section on phrasal lexicon, we noted verb lexical phrases
   (e.g., *swing and sway, eat and drink*). When do you think
   children acquire such forms? Do you find any evidence
   that second language learners, children or adults, acquire
   these forms early? Can these be used with all the tense,
   voice, mood forms attributed to most verbs?
3. Rothstein's (1985) English L2 data of an adult Hebrew
   speaker show accurate use of the copula in some in-

stances and not in others. Can you classify when it is and is not used correctly? What guesses might you have about Hebrew on the basis of this difference?

Example A
It was very (long). Six month. And my father was six month. My-my brother. All the family. It's was unbelievable six month. (The war was very long. Six months. My father, my brother and my whole family were drafted for six months. It was an unbelievable six months.)

Example B
What's happen? My-my husband used to meet him one day and he ask him, "What your occupation?" (How did this happen? My husband met him one day and he asked my husband, "What is your occupation?")

Does your speculation about Hebrew hold for Arabic, given the following written data? How consistent is the alternation of copula production in present and past tenses?

My contry was lovely contry before 100 years ago it was the good contry of all contries. but now My contry is Not good because lebenon I Means My contry the Israil soldier shooting the libanes soldies and the people in My contry No just Israil and palistin and syria everyone shoot My contry. and Now Lebenon crucified on the cross.

(Data source: M. Elliott)

4. Look at these self-identification statements of callers to radio shows:

   a. I'm Betty + 47 and + have uh two teenagers?
   b. It's a pleasure uh + I'm a writer + do not write + have no trouble in uh ideas + I have plenty of 'em.
   c. Well, yes + I'm 43 + have a husband, uh 47 + been married about 21 years uh + have difficulty discussing things with him.
   d. Hello, Harry, uhh first-time caller + a Libra.
   e. Hi, I'm a Honda owner.

Does the (non)suppliance of the pronoun and copula seem natural to you? When must you supply the copula and when does it appear to be optional? Because the copula does not receive word stress, it is not always easy to hear. Record the start of several calls to radio shows. Can you be absolutely certain whether there is or is not a copula in each instance? If the copula is difficult to perceive, how easily will it be acquired by non-instructed learners? Which

227

is more important in explaining copula use – the influence of the first language or the difficulty in hearing these forms?

5. Wells (1979) notes that *can, will, won't,* and *should* are the first modals to be used by L1 children, but that they do not use them for their full range of meanings. Children use *can* to express their own ability or the possibility that they can do something, and to make requests for help. *Will* is used for intention and later for prediction. Are these the functions that are first presented in ESL and EFL class materials? Are they the functions that second language learners acquire first? If you have transcribed data of learners, check which semantic functions these modals serve for beginning language learners.

Adjectives

Adjectives are used to highlight qualities or attributes. Certain adjectives are typically used to describe particular nouns. For example, *light, dark, bright,* and *dull* are used with color names. In a sense, then, we can group adjectives in terms of semantic fields. Geckeler (1971), for example, examined the adjectives used with the concept of age in written text. In French, these include *jeune, âgé, ancien, moderne, neuf,* and *nouveau.*

In some languages, adjectives are not viewed as different from nouns. It is difficult to decide if red is a noun for a color or an attribute of something and therefore an adjective. Adjectives may also seem like verbs. *Slow* can be an adjective when we talk about "a slow race," but it could be a verb if we say, "The runner slowed after he cleared the last hurdle." Word forms ending in -*ing* may be adjectives, nouns, or verbs: "He's my traveling companion." "Traveling is supposed to be broadening." "They were traveling up the Nile." If we are looking at a word in isolation, it is difficult to classify. Once we consider function, however, the division seems more justified.

Adjectives can point out positive or negative qualities. Interestingly, young children seem to acquire positive or pleasant adjectives more readily than negative, unpleasant ones. In second language learning there is similar evidence. For example, Yoshida (1978) found that Miki, a Japanese child learning English, first acquired *long, big, new, pretty, nice,* and *happy.* He learned *big* and *little* as a pair very early (this has been noted for L1 English children as well).

One reason linguists believe that positive adjectives are learned more easily is that they are unmarked. If we ask, "How good was the movie?" we do not know whether the movie was good or bad – the value is unmarked. If we ask, "How bad was the movie?" the quality of the movie is marked. It's already known to be bad. *Good* has, therefore, a wider range of values than *bad*. It should, for that reason alone, also appear with higher frequency and with more nouns than *bad*. Unmarked terms for qualities should be acquired earlier than marked. Some cognitive linguists disagree, saying that whether a term is marked does not make it easy or difficult. Rather, our neural mechanisms always focus attention on new and pleasant attributes of stimuli and it is this focus that causes us to learn positive terms more easily. Others disagree, saying it is degree of emotional value not whether the value is good or bad. Still others would suggest that young children hear positive, pleasant words more often and that frequency should be included in any explanation.

Practice 10.3

1. In a response to an invitation to join a group for lunch, a nonnative speaker of English said, "I wish I could, but I'm broken" (example source: P. Stevens). Are both *broke* and *broken* adjectives? How would you clarify the difference between these forms?

2. In Chapter 9 we talked about collocations of adjectives and nouns. We noted that some color names seem to be tied very tightly to certain nouns – "red lips," "black-hearted," "green around the gills." Select one color, say black, and see what nouns typically collocate with this color adjective in different languages: blacklist, *Schwarzer Tag, humeur noire, pensées noires,* etc. How similar are the pairings across the languages you have consulted? How many of the collocations seem like compound units rather than adjective + noun?

3. Some culture groups associate white with death and red with joy (and the color of a wedding dress), whereas in English black is the color of funerals and red the color associated with sexuality. How important is it to teach the connotative meanings of adjectives in language classes?

4. Gross and Miller (1990) also talk about the scale or gradation of many adjectives. Here are the end points of some graded adjectives. Supply as many adjectives as you can to fill out the scale.

Size: astronomical, infinitesimal
Whiteness: snowy, pitch-black
Age: ancient, infantile
Virtue: saintly, fiendish

Value: superb, odious
Warmth: torrid, frigid

Is one end point unmarked and the other marked? Compare your examples with those of your classmates. Attempt this exercise in another language. What similarities and differences can you discover? Do you predict that first language transfer (positive or negative) will be more important than markedness in predicting the difficulty in acquiring these forms in the target language?

5. Subcategories of adjectives – those that are followed by a gerund, by an infinitive or both – are a problem for language learners and translators. Combine the following lists of adjectives and verbs to form a phrase (for example, "happy to sing," "happy singing"). Which adjectives take a gerund, an infinitive, or both?

   Adjectives: happy, wary, capable, wise, sad, suspicious, important, tired, confident
   Verbs: finish, eat, talk, put, sing

   Now translate these phrases into another language. Are there similar categories in this language? If you choose French, compare your findings to those of Flanagan (1990).

6. Gross and Miller (1990) note that some adjectives can occur both before nouns and after BE (e.g., "tall woman," "the woman is tall"). Others can only occur after BE (e.g., "asleep"). Some occur only after the noun (e.g., "daffodils galore") and some only before nouns (e.g., "former mayor"). They also include the category of adjective complements (e.g., "convinced of," "likely to") and prepositional adjectives (e.g., "on the move"). Prepare a list of adjectives that fit each category and devise a short test to see whether the placement of the adjective is easy or difficult for your students. How might you help students learn those that are difficult for them?

Adverbs

Adverbs are similar to adjectives in many ways although they typically assign attributes to verbs, to clauses, or to entire sentences rather than to nouns.

Sentential: Unfortunately, nobody wants to study Quechua at our university anymore.

Clausal: Seldom though it is, we do attract a few students.
Verb: Some study Quechua very *diligently.*

Even though they are described in terms of differences in scope, these adverbs seem quite different and we would not expect that they are all learned equally well.

Locative adverbs, like *here* and *there* are used very early by young children as ways of pointing to the location of objects. However, it is not clear when they separate them in terms of distance from the speaker. In some experiments, where children must take into account the distance of objects not only from themselves but also from other speakers, the distinction is not firm until about age 5. Even adults sometimes have problems keeping the position of speakers and hearers in mind when using these terms! For example, when talking on the telephone, it is easy to become confused about just which term to use: "Y'know it's down that road *there* – y'know the one *here* by our house? – I think it's Pallet Creek Road? You go down *there* toward the Priory." Such alternations show interesting shifts in perspective.

Time adverbs, like *now, then,* and *yesterday* are used by second language learners as an initial way to mark time. This makes it possible to clarify time meanings when more difficult verb tense has not been acquired. Schumann (1987), for example, has shown that learners will use simple time adverbs such as *now, tomorrow, always* (e.g., "And *right now* my daughter, Patricia, es 22 years old.") calendar reference (e.g., "*3 April this years* coming school") and serialization (e.g. "*coming* back in Mexico *and coming* over here") before they acquire verb tense and aspect to mark temporality.

When adverbs are used to modify verbs, adverbs like adjectives use scaled forms. Both adjectives and adverbs can be preceded by intensifiers such as *very:* ("She's a *very* talented runner. She runs *very* fast"). However, intensity can be expanded into a scale such as *slowly* to *quickly* for manner adverbs; *yesterday* to *tomorrow* for time adverbs, *here* to *there* for place adverbs, and *always* to *never* for frequency adverbs. In many cases, the interpretations of such scales shift according to context. For example, if you saw three mice outside, you might say that you saw a few mice, but if you saw them inside, you might think three a horde. If you saw two coyotes in the middle of town (we once saw two in the early morning as we biked through Beverly Hills!), you might think that would be a lot. Two coyotes would be a few if they were seen out in the desert. K. Witt (personal communication) says that when she passes a car on the freeway it is going too slow but if the same car then passes her, it is going too fast. When she drives down the freeway at night the traffic is not heavy. However if the same number of cars are there in the morning during rush hour, the traffic is light.

Practice 10.4

1. Many adjectives and adverbs, including those referring to dimensions, likelihood, numerosity, and probability, form scales. The interpretation of the value of words on the scale varies from context to context. For each of the following sets, give an example where interpretation shifts depending on context:

   all–none–many–few–some
   ordinary–common–unusual–strange–weird
   necessary–possible–improbable
   likely–unlikely
   always–sometimes–occasionally–rarely–never
   slow–fast
   tall–short
   cold–cool–tepid–warm–hot–unbearable

2. Second language learners use spatial adverbs quite readily. For example, Navajo and Koyukon pen pals whose letters were analyzed by Basham include many such examples:

   How is it thier? Is it cold? It is hot over here.
   So hows life treating you over there in Alaska, here in Kayenta, Arizona is treating me fine.

   Directional adverbs, while easily used, may not be quite so clear:

   I go swimming back at the lake.
   All the kids go back to the ball park and play.

   What explanation do you have for the use of *back* in the last two examples? Basham suggests additional information about the local Koyukon culture may be helpful here. In Koyukon, *front* is toward the river and *back* is away from the river. The Navajo children receiving these letters, however, would not know this. Can you think of similar explanations for spatial expressions in another language or culture group?

3. *No* is considered an adverb because is negates the verb rather than just qualifying it. Bloom (1970) showed that there is a semantic basis for the order in which children acquire negation. The three children in her study acquired nonexistence first, rejection second, and denial third. Examples include the following.

a. nonexistence
Eric: no more noise (*said when noise stopped*)
b. rejection
Kathryn: no dirty soap (*said as she pushed a sliver of worn soap away, wanting to be washed with the new pink bar of soap*)
c. denial
Kathryn: no dirty (*said as she picked up a clean sock*)

Are nonexistence, rejection, and denial the only functions of the negative adverbs in the following examples? If other functions are shown, what name might you assign to each?

No oil is required for this recipe.
I do*n't* mean to be inquisitive, but –
Why do*n't* you drop by some afternoon for tea?
Ca*n't* you get here on time for once!
I would*n't* do that if I were you.
I may *not* be able to get my assignment in on time.
The vector should *not* be measured in that way.
Never talk to strangers!
You're confused, are*n't* you?

4. Research on the form of negation has also been carried out for first and second language learners. There are differences in detail, but generally, negation appears in the following forms:

Child L1
a. Negation precedes or follows utterance.
no mitten   no sit there
no the sun shining   car no
b. *No* is placed before the verb; modal+neg is a chunk.
That no squirrels   he no bite you
Don't bite!   Can't catch me!
c. Essentially correct, some problems remain with negation of the *do* forms.

(Data source: Bellugi, 1967)

L2 learners (Spanish L1)
a. Negation placed before the verb, modal, or copula.
I *no* can see.   But *no* is mine.   I *no* use television.
b. Negation attached to *do,* although *don't* may be a chunk negator.
I do*n't* hear.   He do*n't* like it.   I do*n't* can explain.
c. Negation is placed after the auxiliary (*isn't, can't*).

233

d. Analyzed *do* negation (He doesn't laugh like us).
(Data source: Schumann, 1979)

Which do you think is more important in explaining problems EFL or ESL students might have with negation, the number of forms, or the range of meanings? What importance would you give the auxiliary *do* (rather than the form of the negative) in explaining the data? Do you think all L2 learners follow Schumann's stages in acquisition of negation? Give evidence in support of your answer.

Nouns, verbs, adjectives, and adverbs are considered to be the major word classes (at least for Indo-European languages). They are sometimes called open classes, which means that new nouns, verbs, adjectives, and adverbs are easily added to the language. When words are borrowed from one language to another, they almost always fit into one of these open classes. Nouns, verbs, adjectives, and adverbs are also typically content words that have semantic qualities that can be described.

In contrast, pronouns, prepositions, conjunctions, and determiners are called closed classes because new forms for these functions are infrequent. We do not, for example, create new prepositions or borrow them from other languages. Words in these classes are often called function words because their meanings show how we are to determine relations between words in utterances. Another difference between these two major divisions of word classes is that nouns, verbs, adjectives, and adverbs can be modified with a series of affixes. This does not happen with most function words since they are, for the most part, already affixlike in function – that is, they carry grammatical meanings more than content meanings.

Pronouns

Pronouns refer to nouns that have already been mentioned in the discourse or point ahead to a noun that we are about to mention. Anaphoric reference points back in the discourse to a noun that has already been established and cataphoric reference points forward to its referent. In "Enya is called the Mistress of Melody; *she* sings traditional Irish music," the pronoun is anaphoric. In "Since *it* is a mix of Mariachi and country western, Tex-Mex is yet another example of form melding in American music," the pronoun is cataphoric because it points ahead to a referent in the discourse.

If you have studied other languages, initially you may have been surprised to discover that not all languages have the same number of pronouns. It may, for example, have been difficult for you to remember to use a feminine or masculine form for *you* in another language. Or it may have been difficult to remember status or politeness conventions in choosing a plural rather than a singular *you* when talking to only one person.

We assume that all languages have some way to point to or refer to ourselves (*I*), to the listener (*you*), and to refer to someone else (*he, she, they*). This might lead us to predict that *I* and *you* would be acquired early by language learners. Child first language learning research makes different claims about this. Chiat (1986) says that *I* and *it* are acquired first and *you* second. Miller and Ervin-Tripp (1964) also list *I* as first. They say that *they* is acquired last, and *you, she,* and *he* in between. (They also note that it is easier for young children to produce pronouns in spontaneous speech than in answer to questions where the form changes between the question and the answer.)

Butterworth's (1978) data show the pronouns used by Ricardo, a teenage Spanish speaker who had just arrived in the United States from Colombia. In conversational data gathered during the first ten weeks of the school year, Ricardo produced the pronouns in these examples:

	Singular	*Plural*
	Subject	
1st	*Me* go for house.	Maybe *you me* chess speak.
	I see in Mexico.	My *father me* go.
2d	*You* teacher.	(no examples)
3rd	*He* understand a little Spanish.	*He* is *and he* is.
	Object	
1st	You tell *me*	(no examples)
2d	Me play versus *you.*	(no examples)
3rd	I look *he.*	(no examples)
	Me speak *she.*	(no examples)
	Possessive adjective	
1st	Come by *my* sister	(no examples)
2d	For *you* face.	(no examples)
3rd	For *he* clock.	(no examples)
	Possessive	
1st	No *my* (= not mine)	

There were no examples of reflexive pronouns (e.g., *myself, herself*) in these data for the first two and a half months. You will notice that there are no examples of the existential pronouns, *there* and *it.*

Existential is a fascinating term for pronouns that talk about the existence of objects. In our early lessons we teach students the forms *there is, there are* (e.g., "There is a book on the table." "There are three men in the picture"). Later on we may add *it is* (e.g., "It's hot today," "It's time for lunch"). The term for the function of these pronoun forms has changed from existentials to presentatives, an example of a new lexical item for an already rather elegant term.

Demonstratives are also used as pronouns. Again, they are usually anaphoric. They point back to some large piece of discourse:

Fashions in the 1980s and 1990s became more conservative. *This* is not surprising since fashions have always been indications of the political and social pulse.

The demonstrative here points back to the fact that fashions became more conservative. Less frequently, a demonstrative can be used cataphorically: "*This* is what I want you to work on. Page 31 then 34, ok?"

Practice 10.5

1. As a review of your grammar school pronoun identification exercises, fill in the pronouns in Table 10.2.
2. Fill in a similar chart for another language you know. Or, if you would like to try a language you don't know, ask someone who speaks that language to help you fill out such a chart. Compare the chart with the English chart. If you see differences (and you probably will), do you think the lack of complete correspondence is likely to cause difficulty for learners?
3. Here are the subject pronouns for Arabic:

	Singular	Plural
1st	ana	ihna
2d	inta (masc.)	intu
	inti (fem.)	
3rd	huwwa (masc.)	humma
	hiyya (fem.)	

   Would you find it difficult to remember to differentiate second person pronouns when speaking to male or female Arabic speakers? Why or why not? Is the distinction between masculine and feminine in second pronoun forms common in other non-European languages? What evidence do you have for your answer?
4. Young L1 children often use object pronouns as subjects: "Him did," "Her is." Notice that Ricardo, the teenager learning English used *me* as a subject pronoun: "Me go for pizza?" Why do you think this occurs?
5. Boyd (1975) looked at the order in which Spanish pro-

TABLE 10.2   PRONOUN CASE FORMS

Subject (nomin.)	Object (accus.)	Possessive (genetive)	Possessive Adjective	Reflexive Pronoun
I	me	mine	my	myself
you				
he				
she				
it				
we				
you (pl)				
they				

nouns were used by English L1 children early in a Spanish immersion program (Table 10.3). *Mio* was a form used by one very active girl. Other children quickly picked up the form and it became the classroom pronoun for first person singular at the beginning stage of acquisition. Can you think of any reason why this particular pronoun seemed so attractive to the children?

6. *He* and *she* are very difficult for many English language learners. One might think that this confusion only occurs if there is no division of the third person pronoun in the L1 of learners. When you notice students making *he/she* errors, check to see if this is the case. As an example, Arabic has *huwwa* and *hiyya* for third person and yet native Arabic speakers confuse *he* and *she* when learning English. Compile a list of the first languages of students who confuse these pronouns. What can you say about the influence of the first language in each case?

7. Many EFL books present all subject pronouns together in one lesson. Sometimes the accusative and possessive forms are in the same lesson as well. Because the forms are taught together, do you think that EFL learners acquire them all at once? How might you go about comparing the order of acquisition for EFL students versus ESL students? If you discovered that in natural, conversational data both groups of learners showed similar accuracy profiles (and these differed from the order in which they were taught), how might you account for the similarity? If they showed different orders, how would you account for the differences?

TABLE 10.3   FIVE STAGES IN PRONOUN ACQUISITION

Stage	Pronoun	Rules and examples
1.		Subject pronouns used first:
	mio	*Mio* tengo uno de estos.
	yo	*Yo* in "chunk-learned" utterances:
		Yo hablo espanol.
		Yo quiero este papel.
2.	yo	*Yo* predominates for first person
		Yo es (esta) enferma.
	mi/mio	*mi/mio* variation for pronoun adjectives:
		mi casa, *mio* casa
3.	tu	*Tu* used to address other children
4.	el	*El* before *ella*. No examples of plurals.
		Mio is now in variation with *de yo*
		(Es de *mio;* es de *yo*)
5.		Object Pronouns are added:
	a mi	(mal cosas *a mia*)
		Chunk utterances correct (da*me* los crayons)
	zero	Pronoun omitted ([zero] No quiero)

Conjunctions

There are many different types of conjunctions, but when we hear the term we usually think of *and, or, but.* These are called coordinating conjunctions. Adverbial conjunctions (*because, while, unless*) are sometimes called logical connectors because they clarify the relation between the linked clauses.

In his discussion of clause connectors, Halliday (1985) suggests that we first categorize the relation of the clauses that are to be connected – that is, do the connectors join clauses with two like elements of equal status or clauses where one modifies the other? Halliday calls these two types of relations paratactic and hypotactic. Paratactic means that the conjunction joins two clauses of equal status, for example, "I can *and* I will." The conjunction *and* connects two equal clauses in sequence. Hypotactic means that the conjunction joins two unequal clauses. One modifies the other: "I would *if* I could."

Halliday then divides the conjunctions according to whether the relation between the clauses is one of elaboration, extension, or enhancement. If we want to elaborate on one clause, we might restate it in a second equal clause, using *that is* or *at least*:

This is a paratactic relation; *that is,* the clauses are of equal status.
The clauses *are* paratactic; *at least* they seem to be equal.

If one clause modifies the other, we might use *which* or *who* with a relative clause:

The relation *that is shown here* is hypotactic.

To extend meanings by adding clauses, we might use *and, (n)or, but* (depending on whether the relation is positive, negative, or adversative). When joining a modifying clause, however, one might use *while* or *whereas.*

I want to *but* I can't. (coordinating or paratactic)
While I would like to, I can't. (modifying or hypotactic)

Enhancement includes many categories: some are spatial or temporal, others are causal or conditional, and still others have to do with manner. If we want to express cause, we might use *so, for, thus* for coordination and *because* to join a modifying clause:

I broke the toaster *so* I had to fix it. (coordinating)
Because I broke the toaster, I had to fix it. (modifying)

For conditionals, we might use *then, otherwise, though* (positive, negative, concessive) for coordination, and *if, unless, although* to join a modifying clause.

The toaster works *though* the toast still doesn't pop up.
Unless I replace the spring, the toast won't pop up.

One might wonder why there are so many different types of connectors. For example, *but* is used for contrast, but so are *however, on the other hand, rather, on the contrary,* and others. But these synonyms cannot be used interchangeably in every case (Williams, 1991).

I used to think conjunctions were simple; *but/however,* *rather,* I've changed my mind.
In Santa Monica, it is foggy all the time, *but, by contrast,* *rather* in Palmdale the sun always shines.
They said the Lakers would win, *but/in fact,* *on the other hand/* *by contrast* they are already 10 points down.

In their rhetorical structure theory, Mann and Thompson (1989) say that we place clauses next to each other to carry out many different purposes (to qualify, to clarify, to show concession, to show cause or effect, and so forth). However, the conjunctions or connectors cannot be assigned in a one-to-one correspondence to the logical or semantic goals readers or speakers have in mind when they place clauses next to each other. Mann and Thompson find that some relations are most frequently carried by a particular conjunction. *If* and *unless* express conditionality; *and* and *or* signal certain kinds of addition; *because* shows a causal relation; *even though* and *nevertheless* may be used in concessives. However, it is possible to place clauses next to each other and achieve these same effects even without the conjunction.

Many connectors used in written language are used much less frequently in speech, and some connectors used orally are not used in written language. For example, we often say *like* or *like when* if we want to give support to a previous statement we have made. We might say "Yeh? Right but – " as a challenge to a previous statement. It is unlikely that we would use any of these in writing.

We can safely assume that *and* is acquired very early and used extensively by young children. It is one of the best ways of showing that you wish to continue speaking. Children are notorious for continuing talk with "and then . . . . and then . . . ." One function of *and* is to hold the floor. It can, of course, be used to mark an entry into conversation, especially when we want to help complete a turn:

A: We wanted to help so we called (*pause*)
B: *an'* they said 'get lost', hnnn.

Well also has a special function in conversation. At the beginning of an utterance it signals that the speaker really does not agree with what the other party has said. Because disagreement is not a preferred behavior in interaction, such soft clues both mark and downgrade the threat of the projected disagreement (e.g., "Well, yerright of course, but on the news they said – "). The *well* links turns in conversation and also shows an adversative position. It can also serve to signal a readiness to end the conversation (e.g., "Well, it's been nice . . .").

A look at L1 acquisition of conjunctions shows us the kind of signals typically used in talk. Bloom et al. (1980) looked at the order of emergence for various connectors in the language of infants. *And* appeared first and somewhat later was followed by *and then* and *because*. *What*, *when*, and *so* also occurred in early childhood. Others emerged much later. It isn't always clear, however, whether children are using the conjunctions for the same purposes as adults. For example, young children often use the word *because* when they intend no causal relationship.

Use of conjunctions prior to learning their function is common in second language data as well. This may, in part, be the result of instruction. Connectors are taught, but the function of each may not have been made explicit, as in these written samples:

Tanaka, who was once prime minister in Japan, was born in 1928. *Moreover*, his family was very poor.

Although it is difficult to define culture. *But* generally culture is everything about nations received from and possess by different generations including education. *But* culture is not education.

Another example: if a man has stolen for three time his right hand must be cut off. *But* the same conditions which are required for death are mentioned in this case.

(Data source: Johns, 1980)

Similar mismatch of connector and function appears in the oral language data of both instructed and uninstructed learners.

Practice 10.6

1. Mann and Thompson (1989) list many types of relations between clauses. List one conjunction (connective) that you would use to join clauses that are related in the following ways:
   a. elaboration
   b. concession
   c. background
   d. motivation
   e. justification
   f. cause
   g. purpose
   h. conditional
   i. restatement
   j. summary

2. The data of a number of second language acquisition studies show the use of L1 connectors in L2 talk.

   Spanish conjunction *pero:*
   I wait for my cake *pero* I, I don't know ah what time is coming.
   Pero I need something, I forget in G's room last time before.
   (Source: R. Shapira)

   Piedmontese conjunction *ma:*
   The pay gotta small, *ma* I eat.
   In e coal mine I got the water. *Ma* is dirty this water.
   (Source: D. Kitsch)

   And there are examples of the use of L2 connectors in the talk of English speakers who live overseas.

   Arabic conjunction *laakin:*
   True, *laakin* (= but) it's too late now.

Why do you suppose conjunctions are a place where we unconsciously mix languages?

3. Carter (1992) notes that some connectors can carry a topic-marking function. She examined the use of *is* and *that's why* in the oral and written English of a native Mandarin speaker. *That's why* and other conjunctions may seem quite normal in the following examples; however, the very large number of such connectors point to the special function of joining topic and comment:

Example A
B: No no talking at all read jus reading.
NS: I: see
B: yea
NS: boring
B: YEA! Yea *thas a why* I hated it.
     Always a memor memorize.

Example B
NS: What did you do once you arrived in the U.S.?
B: Uh:: okay here.
     Becuz I em getting old,
     so, uh I realize.
     I realize the importance of study an education yea.
     So I try to do my best to ah study.
     Firce, force myself to study yea at least.
     I know that the education is very importan in the fu-
     ture in my future, ya.
     Thas why, I come, ah I go to school.

Example C
NS: You don't get summer break?
B: I have too much break actually before
     Before too much before
     thats why I I'm so old now. Still xxx
     Thas why
     Playing around too much
     Yea.

A number of researchers have given us examples of the overuse or strange use of the connectors *so, because,* and *that's why* by Asian learners of English. Look at the connectors your international students use in either talk or writing. Do you see any special patterns? Compare your data with that of your colleagues to see if there are definite differences across learner groups.

4. Halliday and Hasan (1976, p. 243) remark that *on the other hand* and *by contrast* emphasize an additive, though dissimilar, meaning. *Nevertheless, in fact, on the contrary, rather, in any case,* and *however* are all adversative. *However* and *in fact* are emphatic. *On the contrary* and *rather* seem to correct meaning or wording. *In any case* signals dismissal. Are these fine points included in your teaching materials for this group of conjunctions? Williams (1991) notes that they all can be replaced by *but.* Why would anyone want to learn all these forms if one will do? Why would you want to teach the distinctions (if you include them in instruction)?

5. Newmark (1988) notes that Germans use connectors in speech. *Aber, also, denn, doch, eben, schliesslich, eigentlich, einfach, ja, mal, schon, bitte,* and so forth appear three times as often in talk as in newspapers and six times as often in talk as in literature. Newmark believes the function of these connectors is partly phatic and partly to mark the talk as containing old information. Would you predict that the acquisition and use of these connectors would be difficult for German language learners? You might interview German teachers to find out whether your prediction is correct. (You might want to explore the frequency of connectors in other languages as well, using Newmark's article as a stimulus to your research.)

6. In much of our education literature, subordination is seen as somehow better than coordination. Can you explain why one type of organization should be more highly valued than another? List all the conjunctions in the examples given in this section according to whether they join clauses in coordination or subordination. Can some be used only for coordination and others only for subordination? Can some be used for both? Is there anything preferable about either set? Why do some methodologists put such high value on hypotactic, subordinate structures?

Prepositions

Prepositions are all those words that help locate items and actions in time and space. In this sense they share much with adverbs. We usually consider *above, ahead, behind,* and *underneath* as locative adverbs because they locate actions or objects or people in space in a natural way. That is, the normal way in which we see things is in terms of three reference planes: one plane is horizontal, a second is vertical, going from left to right, and the third is also vertical, from the front to the back of our visual field.

Prepositions, too, relate to these planes. Cognitive linguists (Fillmore, Clark, and Lakoff, to name but a few) have noted that prepositions also locate along these dimensions. In some cases, the location has one dimension, in others, it may locate things in two or three-dimensional space. To use Fillmore's example, if we say, "John is *on* the grass," the grass is treated as a two-dimensional space. If, instead, the utterance is "John is *in* the grass," the grass is now a three-dimensional space where John is inside with grass all around. If we say, "He is *at* the grass," grass is a one-dimensional space. The dimensions are related to *to, onto,* and *into* and *from, off,* and *out.* Paths across the space can also be traced by *via, across,* and *through.*

Catford (1968, 1969) charted these relations (Figure 10.1). We can easily fill in Figure 10.2 for these English prepositions. Because the preceding explanation is experientially based – that is, it relates to the dimensions used to locate objects around us – you might think that there would be separate terms for each cell of the box in all languages. But that is not the case. In French, all of the two-dimensional exterior spaces are covered by *sur.* According to Catford, only three markers need to be used in Malay Indonesian: *di* refers to a static position, *ka* refers to the end point, and *dari* to the start point. The other dimensions are not distinguished by prepositions.

Because young children must learn to divide up space as a cognitive task and also learn the linguistic terms for that division, there is a long history of research on the child's acquisition of prepositions. Turton (1966) collected natural production data and test data from 3- and 4-year-old children. He found the youngest children used *there* and *right there* to locate items. The 3-year olds also used *in.* By age 5, they had added *on, under,* and *by.* In tests, they came close to achieving the acquisition criterion level of 40 out of 50 items correct with *behind.* After age 5, they added some of the many meanings of *over.* These older children still substituted *by* for *between, behind,* and *in front of.* Their nonverbal comprehension tests showed they understood these terms even though they did not produce them.

From a cognitive standpoint it is not difficult to understand why *in front* and *in back* might be difficult for young children. We have said that one vertical plane in space relates to the space in front of us versus that behind us. The use of *in front* and *in back* referring to our own position should not be difficult. However, when we talk about the front and back of other objects we may become confused in terms of the spatial relation between ourselves and the object. If we are facing the back of a building and children are playing in a park between us and the building, we have a

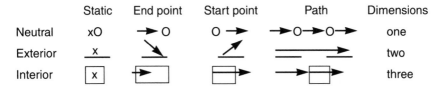

Figure 10.1   Relations charted by Catford (adapted from Catford 1968, 1969)

Static	End point	Start point	Path
at	to	(away) from	via
on	onto	off	across
in	into	out of	through

Figure 10.2   Preposition chart

choice of saying that the children are playing in the park in front of us or in back of the building. Some languages (e.g., Hausa and Djerma according to Hill [1975]), use *in front of* and *behind* in the way we refer to people in a line: z is in front of y, y is in front of x. If we picture people running in a race, we see them as moving straight ahead toward the finish line. So runners closest to the finish line are in front and those further back are behind them. This use of the prepositions is just as it is in Hausa. However, in English, French, and German, when two objects (a and b) are in front of us, we are likely to say that a is in front of us but that b is behind a (*b est derrière a, b ist hinter a*). In Hausa, the preposition would not change (*b* is *gaban a* and *a* is *gaban* the speaker).

Practice 10.7

1. Use Figures 10.1 and 10.2 to chart the spatial relations in another language. Compare your results to those of your classmates. How many languages actually have separate terms for each cell?

2. H. Clark (1973) reasoned that *at* in the Catford chart is the least complex (and therefore easiest to acquire) spatial preposition. It is one-dimensional. The more dimensions added, the more complex the preposition becomes. Clark believes the end point column prepositions are positive and the start point ones negative. Positive items are usually easier to acquire than negative items, so prepositions

245

in column 2 should be easier than those in column 3. The further the preposition is from *at* on the chart, the more difficult it should be. Do you have evidence from ESL or EFL learners to support this prediction about difficulty?

3. This ESL exercise uses prepositions that relate to time rather than space. Complete the exercise. Then, in the language you used for Practice 10.7.1, check to see whether there is an overlap of prepositions for time and space as there is for English.

The Wolf's Schedule

Morning and afternoon

6:00	Get up with the sheep.
6:30–7:30	Walk with the sheep and find grass.
7:30–5:00	Eat grass.

Evening

5:00–6:00	Go back to the town.
6:30	Drink water with the sheep.
7:30	The shepherd goes to sleep.

Night

9:30	Eat one sheep.
10:30	Go to sleep.

Assignment: Write five sentences about how the wolf spends his day. In each sentence use at least one of the following prepositions: *in, at, from . . . to, until, by.*

(Source: S. Peck)

4. Vandeloise (1987) notes that children first say that they put things *in* containers and only later *on* and *under*. This article looks at the acquisition of *devant/derrière* and *dans/sur* and uses both adult and child subjects. If you teach French, you might replicate this study with your students and compare your results and interpretation to those of Vandeloise.

5. Do you think that *in* and *under* are semantically clear? If you took an object and placed a bowl (face down) over it, would you say that the object is in or under the bowl? If instead of an object, you blew in smoke or some gas, would you say that the smoke is in or under the bowl? If you sit down at your table and stretch out your legs, are they in or under the table? If you are in a swimming pool, and you stretch out your legs, are they under the water or in the water? After you decide on the correct preposition, check to see if the *in/on* distinction works the same way in another language of your choice.

6. Jackendoff (1978) describes prepositions in a different way. He divides them into locational prepositions (those that go with the verbs *be* and *stay*) and path prepositions (those that are used with motion verbs like *go*). Location prepositions include *on, under, beside, near,* and path prepositions include *to, from, toward, around.* The path prepositions can also show extent as in *from . . . to* combinations. Prepositions can also show orientation as in *point toward* or *away from.* Would this analysis be more useful than Catford's or Lakoff's? Give examples to justify your answer.

7. English uses *in front of* and *in back of* in two ways. In the first, the object to be located may be in front or in back of another object. For example, if we left a book on the floor in front of a chair or dropped it behind the chair, the chair serves as a reference point for locating the book. It's in front of or in back of the chair. However, imagine you set the book on the floor at the side of the chair while you went to get a pencil. If you look at the chair from the side, the book is there in front of you. This ambiguity occurs in many languages. In Spanish, *delante* and *detras* works the same way. List the words for *in front* and *in back* in as many other languages as you can. Are they also ambiguous?

Articles and demonstratives

It is not difficult to sympathize with Zoila when she responds as follows to a question about why she doesn't learn function words – conjunctions, prepositions, pronouns, and articles:

Zoila: I never using this little, little words.
Rina: Like what?
Zoila: "Ah," "an" "and" "that" "/em/" "/ipidit/" y'know? "If," /bin/, /it/ sometimes xxx (*inaudible*). Well, maybe because I no study . . . never . . . an' only hear the people and . . . and talking.
Rina: Yeah, but people talk with these words.
Zoila: Yeah, pero /es, eh/ I'm hear and put more attention the big words. You know and . . . something "house." I know "house" is the "casa" for me. And /es es/ and little words is no too important for me.

We know that articles (*a, an, the*) and demonstratives (*this, that*) are important because they help us to point out objects, to bring them to the attention of our listeners. It is not surprising, then, that they develop quite early in child language. In the naming game, mothers point to objects and say, "What's this?" "What's that?" The child may or may not respond with the appropriate word and the mother continues, "That's a car. It's a car." Later the child directs the adult's attention to objects in the same way "That (pointing) car." (It is also one of the earliest pronouns used by young children.) For young children, these early demonstratives probably mean something like "notice." (It's not entirely clear whether they also use *oh-oh* for this same function or whether *oh-oh* is a vocative, a call for attention to self rather than a call to attend to an object pointed out by the child.)

We find this same naming game in data of children learning second languages. Paul, a 5-year-old Chinese child learning English, (Huang and Hatch, 1978) used vocatives and demonstratives in this same way as he elicited names for objects.

1. Vocative and demonstrative
   Paul: *Oh-oh!*
   Jim: What?
   Paul: *This (points to ant)*
   Jim: *It's an* ant.
2. Demonstrative
   Paul: *this (pointing)*
   Jim: A pencil.
   Paul: (echo) pencil
         *this+++*pencil *(falling intonation on each word)*

Notice that the child produces *this / that* in these utterances but not *a / the*. In child language, demonstratives appear before articles, and this seems to be the case for this child second language learner as well. Articles appear in language of young children, usually by the end of the third year. However, it is not clear that young children make the same distinctions between *this* and *that* or between *a* and *the* as adults. Adults usually use the definite article *the* when they can assume that the listener should already have the noun in mind. (In language classes, we tell students to use the indefinite *a* on first mention and *the* thereafter. That's a good heuristic, but it's not quite that simple!) Adults make a distinction between what is close (physically or emotionally) and what is distant in selecting between *this* and *that*. Young children may use demonstratives and articles but they do not necessarily draw these distinctions.

The English article system is difficult for students from many other language backgrounds. It is, however, a special problem for students from Asian languages that do not have such articles. International students who have problems with English definite and indefinite articles often use demonstratives or quantifiers instead as shown in parts of this paragraph written by a Vietnamese student:

Haagen Daazs ice cream has unique and special characterister. That is design of this package. Therefore, in spite of high process of this cost, the sales of it shows to increase of 25% every year.

(Data source: V. Wenzell)

Quantifiers (e.g., *some, any, one, ten*) serve many of the same functions as demonstratives and so students sometimes use these to get around the problem of article choice, as in this exam sample written by a Korean ESL student:

I will choice Job B because Job A doesn't have much salary and has too much vacation. If vacation has much time, it usually spend money too much. And Job C has high salary but hasn't much vacation. If I work too hard, I have to rest much too. I like going to vacation. If I took much vacation 6 weeks, I would hate to work. So, I decide Job B.

(Data source: B. Lynch)

Many languages do not mark nouns with articles, and some languages that use demonstratives as the predominant way of pointing out nouns. And there are languages that have only one article. In other languages, definite nouns are not marked but indefinite nouns may require a special articlelike marker.

When we look at how well second language learners acquire articles, for accuracy it is important that we look at each form and its function in both the first and second languages. (Unfortunately, many research projects lump them together under "article.") Huebner (1979), for example found that Ge, a Laotian learner of English, used *da* (the) to mark nouns as specific and known to the hearer in some cases and not in others. In many studies this information would be listed as a percent correct figure for articles. However, with a closer examination, Huebner showed that *da* was used least frequently in subject position. For example,

chainis tertii-tertii fai. bat jaepanii isa twentii eit.
(The) Chinese (man is) 35. But (the) Japanese is 28.

Why should Ge not use *da* for nouns that appear to be subjects? The explanation Huebner offers is that Ge's English, like his native language, is topic-prominent, and that topics most frequently fall in subject position. Topics typically show old information, known to the hearer. In other positions Ge used *da* more frequently to mark nouns as definite and known.

»gow howm, isa plei da gerl.
(When we) went home, (we would visit) the girls.

Thus a contrastive analysis of errors and a functional analysis as well is most useful in understanding the emerging article system in second or foreign language learning.

For English speakers, acquisition of languages with grammatical gender is perhaps just as difficult. Learners have the additional task of marking articles according to the gender of the referent, not an easy task. Eva, the 6-year-old Hungarian child acquiring French (Kenyeres and Kenyeres, 1938) was both fascinated and frustrated by grammatical gender (see Chapter 1).

Karmiloff-Smith (1979) has shown that acquisition of gender is not an easy process even for French children. She says that young children do not appear to attend to natural gender of objects but rather to the sound characteristics of the words. Young L2 Spanish learners also seem to attend to phonological characteristics in selecting articles, even though they have not been taught to do so:

Example A

Adult: Tu me dijiste que estas son las ventanas de *los* dos casas.' ¿Está
bien decir *los dos casas?
(You told me that these are the windows of the two houses. Is
it correct to say los dos houses?)

Child: Estos son *los,* es . . . estos, oh estas son *las* ventanas de ¿*los-las*
dos casas?
(Those are the, th . . . those, oh those are the windows of los-
las dos houses?)

Adult: Muy bien. ¿Y por que tenemos que decir *las?*
(Very good. And why do we have to say las?)

Child: Porque 'casa' termina con 'a' y, mmm, tiene, es 'la casa.'
(Because house ends with an 'a' and, mmm, has, is '*la* house'.)

Adult: Uhhuh.

Child: And (heh-heh) y casa, luego *las* con 's,' es *las.*
(And [*laugh*] and house, then las with an 's' is las.)

Example B

Adult: Aquí dices '*la* manzana cayó' pero aquí dices '*los* manzanas.'
¿Cuál es correcto?
(Here you say la apple fell, but here you say los apples. Which
is correct?)

Child: *Las*

Adult: Uhhuh. ¿Y por qué *las?*
(Uhhuh. And why las?)

Child: Porque manzanas termina en *a.* Yo, yo hizo este porque estaba
escribiendo rápido porque Joana no lla-lla-me llamó una uh
slow poke.
(Because apples ends in *a.* I, I did that because I was writing
fast because Joana didn't ca- ca- called me a uh slow poke.)

(Data source: S. Plann)

In each case, the child gives a "rule" that if a noun ends with an -*a*, the article must be *la* (or *las* if the noun is plural).

Perhaps one of the reasons that adults have so much difficulty with gender in the second languages they use is that they are not quite so attuned to what sounds like a masculine or feminine word.

Practice 10.8

1. Researchers have shown that young children can distinguish between *a* and *the* (in tests where they manipulate toys to act out a story line) even when they do not make the distinction in their talk. Some specialists say that children do not make the distinction in their talk because children are egocentric and so do not take the listener's knowledge into account. That is, the child will use *a* if she has just become aware of the object and not to show that the listener should bring the object to mind. (For example, the child might start a story with "The girl wants the cone," rather than "A girl wants a cone." Do you agree with this explanation? Why or why not? If you work with young children, you might want to test this with a picture book story.
2. Notice that Zoila used some articles in talking about the "little words" that were not important for her. How might you explain this?
3. Check the article use of your students. Categorize where and when articles are omitted or misused. What patterns do you see? Compare your findings with those of your classmates. What similarities or differences do you find? Can the differences be attributed to the age of the learners, their first languages, or to other causes?
4. Here are excerpts from two entrance examinations. Compare the articles in the compositions. Can you account for similarities and differences between your data in item 3 and these examples?

Chinese L1
Of three jobs offered, Job A has a leastest salary paid, hours of work, but has the most vacation and a higest job satisfaction. Which job is suitable varies from different point of view. I will accept job C. Compared with the job A and B, job C has a four times of salary paid as job A and as two and a half times of salary as a job B's –

Japanese L1
According to the graph of the number of the people over 65-year-old increase gradually. On the other hand the young people

251

under the 18 years old is getting fewer. The fact that the rate of the old people increase causes the several problem –

5. If your students use demonstratives or quantifiers in place of articles, interview them to determine whether or not this is a conscious avoidance of articles. Review articles and books on the teaching of English articles. Do they mention demonstratives and quantifiers as possible substitutes for articles?

6. Public messages and notices often use nouns without articles. For example, envelopes often have the message "Place stamp here. Post office will not deliver without postage." Collect examples (or have your students collect examples) of messages without articles. Do you or your students feel that such input makes learning of the English article system even more difficult?

7. If you teach or are studying a language which has grammatical gender, collect examples that show the ease or difficulty with which learners produce correct articles.

In this chapter we have reviewed the basic classification of words in terms of parts of speech. We began with those that carry the most content: nouns, verbs, adjectives, and adverbs. In some sources, you will find these called lexical or content words. Other words carry syntactic information and these are often called grammatical or function words. For Zoila, these are the "little words."

In the discussion of each word class we claimed that word class is determined by use. This leads to confusion in classification. Should we assign functional labels or class labels to words? Should we separate the word *can* into *four* different words: a noun, an adjective, a verb, and a modal? Should we separate the word *dancing* into two words, a verb form and a noun gerund? We can label each of these as separate nouns, verbs, adjectives, and so forth, or we can claim that some verbs can "serve as" nouns, some adjectives can "serve as" nouns. This second treatment (considering the functions for which we use words rather than any "inherent" word class) makes far greater sense especially when we move from separate words to lexical phrases.

In the discussion of conjunctions, it was difficult to limit examples to one-word conjunctions. *For example* is a very common lexical phrase connector that we cannot write as one word, but which functions like a one-word connector. We can, in fact, use many lexical phrases as if they were examples of nouns, verbs, adverbs, and so forth. *Of* is a preposition, "of the drought" is a prepositional phrase, but "because of the drought" is an adverbial phrase in the sentence "We had to conserve water because of the drought." In the same sentence, "had to conserve" is a verbal. "Had to conserve water" is a verb phrase. "Having to conserve" is a

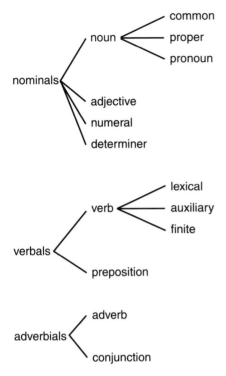

Figure 10.3   Summary of word classes (from Halliday, 1985, p. 91; used with permission)

nominal, and "having to conserve water" is a noun phrase in the sentence "Having to conserve water is no fun." When we make such changes, we often change the designation to nominal or noun phrase, to verbal or verb phrase, to adjectival or adjective phrase, adverbial or adverbial phrase, and so forth. In each case, we have shifted from a word class to a word function label.

Although it is possible to divide the traditional parts of speech into the major categories of content vs. function words, it is also possible to group them according to their three major use groups: nominals, verbals, and adverbials. Halliday (1985) displays this division in Figure 10.3. We can classify words according to the roles we give them in our talk and in our writing; however, we can rearrange words in many ways, into different groupings and, by doing so, change their roles. When we do this, we have not really changed the word but rather made it serve different purposes. The roles we assign to some words are very flexible (we can *sun* ourselves in the *sun*) while others are not. We cannot easily use prepositions as nouns except as citations (e.g., "I said *at*"). It is, perhaps, on the basis of frequency of use for different functions that a word becomes known as a noun, a verb, an adverb, an adjective, or some other part of speech.

Research and application

Nouns, pronouns, and articles

1. Several of the readings in Berko-Gleason (1993) make claims about the acquisition of subtypes of word classes. For example, Pease et al. discuss the notion of nouns of change or nouns that the child can manipulate being learned before those that are more static. They and other authors in the book talk about the acquisition of deictic terms (pointing terms such as "this" or "that"). They also note that words that refer to the here and now develop before those that are not present in the child's environment (the concurrent and present versus nonconcurrent and non-present dichotomy). If you wish to study child language development, read and critique a selection of articles in this book as the basis for your own research project.

2. Koike (1983) lists the rank order of acquisition of pronouns by three Japanese children who lived in the United States.

Rank	Pronoun	Sachiko (5 yrs)	Jun (7½ yrs)	Nobi (11 yrs)
1	I	2	1.5	1
2	you (sg)	2	3	2
3	this (sub)	7.5	4	3
4	we	5	5	4
5	my	2	1.5	5.5
6	that (sub)	10	6	5.5
7	he	10	8	9.5
8	she	5	9	7.5
9	this (det)	7.5	10	9
10	you (sg ob)	10	11.5	10
11	it (sub)	5	7	11.5
12	me	12	11.5	11.5

Koike performed Spearman rank-order correlations between each pair of children. The correlation in the order in which pronouns were acquired for Sachiko and Nobi was .61, for Sachiko and Jun, .78, and for Jun and Nobi, .84. Since the L1 for all three children was the same, why do you suppose the correlations were not higher? How does the order compare with Miller and Ervin-Tripp (1964) and Chiat's (1986) orders? You might want to read these studies as preparation for planning your own research on the acquisition of pronouns.

3. Hirakawa (1990), in a study of reflexive pronouns, tested the predictions of Universal Grammar. Grade 10, 11, 12, 13 Japanese studying English in high school were asked to identify the referent of the reflexive pronoun in five different types of sentences:

   Type A (two-clause tensed sentence): John said that Bill hurt himself.

   Type B (three-clause tensed sentence): Ted knows that John said that Bill hurt himself.

   Type C (two-clause infinitival sentence): John told Bill not to hurt himself.

   Type D (three-clause infinitival sentence): Ted thinks that John wants Bill to understand himself.

   Type E (one-clause subject-object sentence): Tom showed Bill a picture of himself.

   The test included five multiple-choice items for each type. The choices for answers were the names of the three people (John, Bill, Ted), someone else, or don't know. The means are higher for Type A and B than for C and D. Otherwise, there were no real differences across types of sentences (or proficiency levels) and so the results did not support the predictions of Universal Grammar. Read the study, critique the procedure, and then design a replication with students from another language group.

4. Tanz (1980) looked at identity and quantity in quantifiers and pronouns. She had children, aged 3 to 5, respond to such stimuli as follows.

   Identity: Make one of the pigs go in the house. Now make (a) *it* (b) *one* go in the truck. (Materials: 2 pigs, 2 chickens, house, truck)

   Quantity: There is chocolate on the table. Give (a) *it* to me; (b) give me *some*.

   Identity, plural: Drive two cars to the house. Now drive (a) *them,* (b) *two* to the edge of the cliff.

   Quantity, plural: There are flowers on the table. Give (a) *them* to me; (b) me *some*.

   You might replicate the procedure with bilingual children or use the task with both adult and child learners. How appropriate is the task across age groups? What results did you obtain with this pilot study? How might you revise the task for a study that would look at a large number of pronouns, quantifiers, articles, and demonstratives?

5. Pocheptsov (1992) notes that Russian *rjad* and *neskolko* are both translated as "more than two" yet found that speakers select

neskolko for three to four and five to six items and *rjad* for five to six to nine to ten items. He notes that we often select number terms which seem equivalent (e.g., minutes rather than hours, days rather than years and fractions rather than percentages) because they somehow sound like more, although they are really equivalent. According to Pocheptsov, we also round off numbers (e.g., "More than ten people died in the accident") as a way of "distorting facts while telling the truth." Prepare a research plan to investigate speaker preference in the use of such quantifiers as *some, several, more than* or for numerically equivalent forms (fractions vs. percentages). Do your findings support Pocheptsov's interpretations?

Adjectives and adjective agreement

6. In gendered languages, learners use gender in articles and in adjectives and must pay attention to whether the noun they are referring to is singular or plural. Early studies used longitudinal data to study the acquisition of gender agreement (see De Houwer [1987] on the acquisition of agreement for gender in the language of a bilingual Dutch and English child). Plann (1976) used a puzzle task as one of several methods of testing gender acquisition in Spanish as a second language. The puzzle pieces showed familiar objects in various colors. There were twenty-four pieces, twelve masculine and twelve feminine. Half of the puzzle pieces showed singular objects and half showed groups of objects. The child, given a puzzle frame that showed the completed picture, asked the holder of the puzzle pieces for those shown in the frame. For example, the child had to ask for the yellow dogs (*Quiero los perros amarillos*), the orange turtle (*Quiero la tortuga anaranjada*), and so forth. At all age levels, Plann found greater accuracy for masculine than for feminine forms and higher accuracy for singular than plural forms. What explanation can you give for these findings? Design a task that you might use with adult learners of a language marked for gender. Justify the appropriateness of the task and of the vocabulary that you selected for the task.

7. Magnan (1983) noted that gender errors are common in language learner speech. The question is how much importance to attach to such errors. Do they really irritate or bother the native listener? Magnan found that previous studies claimed learners' errors in gender are among the least irritating for Spanish and German native speakers. Judges listened to taped sentences which contained various types of errors (definite article, adjective agreement, prepositions between verb and infinitive, verb

morphology, clitic pronoun). The 352 judges were divided into categories by age. Adults were more forgiving of gender errors than were lycée (high school) students and lycée students also judged such errors less irritating than did C.E.S (middle school) students. For all three groups, errors involving the wrong gender with a person were judged to be more irritating than error of wrong gender with an object. (The chart on Magnan's p. 204 ranks the fifteen error types for the three groups, and gender errors are near the bottom except for *le soeur*, which is ranked fourth by CES students, eighth by lycée students, and twelfth by adults.) Why do you think that younger listeners are more critical of gender errors than are adults? If you teach French (or another language which marks gender) and your students plan to interact with young adolescents, how much emphasis would you put on gender errors?

8. Translation of poems and stories can be difficult when languages mark nouns for grammatical gender. For example, the word for grasshopper in French is feminine. The Russian word is masculine. So, typically, the French word for grasshopper is translated as the feminine *dragonfly* in Russian. The word for fir tree in German is masculine and that for a palm tree is feminine. Fir trees are feminine in Russian so, in translation of poems, the fir tree is changed to a cedar which is masculine. Why would translators bother to change the word? Isn't it more important that readers correctly identify the actual insect or tree? If you do translations across languages with gender, share your own examples of problem areas you have encountered. How did you decide whether or not to change the word?

Adverbs

9. Vendler (1984) described five types of action adverbs. These include *event adverbs* (e.g., "he rang the bell loudly," "he pulled the rope tight"), *manner adverbs* (e.g., "he danced gracefully"), a third group that include *facility* (e.g., "he solved the puzzle easily"), *moral* (e.g., "he spilled the tea accidentally"), and *timing* (e.g., "he answered quickly") adverbs, *sentence adverbs* (e.g., "stupidly he answered the question"), and *illocutionary adverbs* (e.g., "honestly, he never answered my letter"). If you teach a writing course for international students or second language learners, check to see which types of adverbs they use. If they use none or only a few of these, you might design a teaching unit and test to see whether an emphasis on type of adverb increases appropriate use of adverbs in their compositions.

Conjunctions

10. To investigate the emergence of connectors in second or foreign
    language learning, you might first review L1 studies. In addition
    to Bloom et al., look at Wells (1985) and Clancy et al. (1976) for
    comparisons across Turkish, German, Italian, and English. Tager-
    Flusberg et al. (1982) look at the types of coordination used by
    Japanese and by English speaking children. How would you
    design your own study?

Prepositions

11. Krzeszowski (1990) asked twenty-five Polish advanced learners of
    English to translate into Polish twenty senses of the preposition
    over. The cognitive descriptions and visual relations were based on
    Brugman's (1981) analysis and include relations such as those
    needed for "He jumped over the wall," "They jumped over the
    cliff," "The wall fell over," "He turned over the pages," "He rolled
    the log over," "The helicopter hovered over the town," "The power
    line stretches over my yard," "She spread the tablecloth over the
    table," "Guards are posted all over the hill," and others.
    Krzeszowski found that the most prototypic uses were consistently
    translated as *nad/ponad* in Polish and that there was much less
    agreement on translation as the uses became less prototypic. Plan a
    replication project using the same materials with another language.
    What predictions do you make regarding the outcome?
12. Morsbach (1981) administered a comprehension test of fifteen
    grammatical structures to sixty Japanese (aged 11–13 years) and
    thirty-one German (10–13 years) students living in London. As
    they listened to test sentences, the students selected the best
    picture for the sentence from a group of four pictures. Error rates
    were fairly high for pictures illustrating prepositions:

	Incorrect answers	
	Japanese Ss	*German Ss*
by	54	68
over	9	8
behind	1	8
along	0	8
up	7	8
out	6	8
down	24	0

Look at the pictures used in teaching materials to show location.
Do you think that the problem might be, as Morsbach points out

for the preposition *by*, that the differences among the prepositions are ambiguous (e.g., "The horse is [*by, in front of, behind*]
the tree")? Design a set of pictures that you think might be used
to teach or test the distinctions among these prepositions. Limit
the use to locatives. (Can you think of any explanation for the
different error rate for *down* in the two groups of students?)

13. Kalisz (1990) examined the dimension *in front of* and *behind* in
English and Polish and also discussed the metaphorical extensions of these terms. If you are studying or teach languages
which reflect a different perception of space in ways similar to
the Hausa example mentioned in the section on prepositions in
this chapter, read Kalisz's treatment of this phenomenon and
write a short report comparing these languages. How difficult do
you think these different perspectives on space might be for second language learners?

14. Weber-Olsen and Ruder (1980) studied American 5-year-olds
and adults as they learned to label spatial relationships using
four Japanese locatives that coincide or partially overlap with
into, onto, out of, and *off*. Adults learned the Japanese lexicon
faster and better than the 5-year-olds. Interference initially accounted for many of the adults' errors. *Ireru* and *oku* are similar
to *into* and *onto* and denote containment and support, respectively. However, *ireru* is used only to describe objects contained
but not physically joined to a container (e.g., an apple in a bowl)
whereas *oku* is used only when the object has superficial contact
with the reference point or support surface (e.g., putting a ring
on the palm of the hand or a pen on a table). *Hameru* is used
when objects are put in a tightly fitting relationship or in their
normative state (e.g., putting a ring on a finger, putting a cap on
a pen, putting a puzzle piece into a puzzle, screwing a bulb into
a socket). Finally, *toru* literally means to take away with the hand.
The related form *toridasu* refers to taking out with the hand but
only when the walls of a container are deep enough to encompass the object (e.g., out of cans, bottles, deep boxes but not
from shallow saucers or ashtrays). The authors suggest that
hameru, and *toru* would be more difficult for English speakers
than *ireru,* and *oku*. The authors provide the following diagrams
for *toru* and *hameru.*

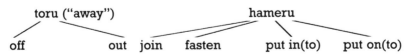

Remember that *put in(to)* refers to containment with physical
proximity to the container while *put on(to)* refers to nonhorizontal

support. Read the study and admire the training and testing procedure. In this study, object manipulation worked well with both adults and children. Redraw the diagrams using Stockwell, Bowen, and Martin's (1965) correspondence categories. Replicate the study with a group of your classmates.

11 Morphology and derivations

In Chapters 8 and 9 we discussed some of the lexical processes used to create new words – creating lexical phrases, coining new words, and borrowing and conversing. In these chapters we talked about words. In this chapter we will look at the ways we change words by adding morphology. To do this we will look at morphemes, the smallest meaningful units used in word building

Identifying morphemes

A *morpheme* is, by definition, a meaningful linguistic unit that contains no smaller meaningful units. This minimum form is called a morpheme; the meaning of the unit is called a *sememe*. The word *cats*, for example, contains two morphemes: the *lexical* morpheme *cat* and the *grammatical* morpheme *s*, which means plural.

Because morphemes have meanings, we expect that they can be defined. That is, the recurring form *-er* of *farmer, dancer, singer* means "one who" – no more, no less. The letters *e* and *r* of the word *ever* cannot be divided from the word and assigned this meaning. *Ever* is a single morpheme.

A morpheme must be internally consistent in form and meaning, which can make morpheme identification difficult. For example, *-ess* is a morpheme which means "feminine one who." Thus, the morpheme *-ess* holds two meanings within it, but it may connote even more. Consider the masculine-feminine pairs in the following list:

governor	governess
major	majorette
patron	matron
landlord	landlady
wizard	witch
master	mistress

In these word pairs, the difference is much more than just ⟨+/– feminine⟩. The change also shows a shift in level of power and seriousness traditionally assigned to the role.

Sometimes morphemes have more than one pronunciation, but the meaning of these variants does not change. For example, the plural *s* has three different pronunciations shown in the words *birds*, *breezes*, and *beets*. Even though the sound of the morpheme changes somewhat, it is still the same morpheme, and all three variants mean plural.

Two different morphemes may have the same shape. For example, when the -*s* of verbs (*learns*, *dances*, *skips*) occurs on third person singular verbs, marking them for present tense, the meaning is present tense, third person singular. The morphemes for plural and for third person singular present tense have the same form but they are separate morphemes because each has its own meaning.

It is not always possible to identify morphemes in words correctly unless we know something of etymology. For example, you might think that *hamburger* consists of three morphemes: *ham* (perhaps they were once made with ham), *burg* (maybe it has something to do with a small town), and *er* (maybe this is an -*er* that identifies a person, something like a burgher). So, *hamburger* might derive from something like *ham* that is prepared or eaten by a middle-class businessperson from a small city. If you look up *hamburger* in the dictionary, however, you will find that it refers to a sandwich first made in the city of Hamburg, Germany. It has nothing to do with ham.

We have said that the form must recur with the same meaning in order for it to qualify as a morpheme. Many morphemes have come to us from Latin and we may be unaware of their meanings. Few people stop to think of the origin of the morpheme -*voc*- in *vocation, provoke, vocabulary, vociferous, revoke, irrevocable,* and *vocalize.* Language textbooks, however, often have special exercises with Latin-based morphemes. High school science textbooks and basic medical, pharmacology, and science college texts also include such exercises. The question for our analysis, though, is whether we should consider examples like -*voc*- as separate morphemes or simply consider them part of the word stem.

Another difficulty in identifying the form of a morpheme has to do with its regularity. It is not difficult to identify the plural morpheme -*s*, and we can draw a slash to demarcate the morphemes in *boat/s, bike/s, canoe/s*. When the spelling is irregular (*copies*) we can arbitrarily place a slash before the -*s* (*copie/s*) or we can rewrite the word as *copy* + *s* to show the morpheme break. If there is no change in the word, we can rewrite the word with a zero (∅) plural morpheme (*sheep* + ∅ for plural). These problems are easily solved. However, what if the plural is not an -*s*, as in *mice*? In most cases, phonological rules describe groups of irregular plurals. (For our identification exercises, rewrite the item as *mice* = *two morphemes, mouse* + *plural*. If you were asked to do a serious linguistic description, you would, of course, change everything to phonetic script and write the phonological rules for the required changes.)

Practice 11.1

1. In each of the following sets, identify and define the shared morpheme. Using modern-day English as your guide, discard those examples which do not fit the shared meaning.

   a. unfair unwise fun unable United Nations
   b. disability dismantle displeasure distance
   c. dryness Loch Ness quickness brightness
   d. songs boys apples follows
   e. worker teacher mother paper
   f. actor lever dreamer refer
   g. mailman chairman woman lineman

2. Identify and give the meaning of two morphemes in each of the following words: dad's, teacher, walked, came, said, mailbox, untie, illness, running, repay, proudly, shapely, uniform, cattle.

3. What is the relation between a morpheme and a sound, a morpheme and a word, a morpheme and a syllable? List two morphemes that are also sounds, two that are also syllables, and two that are words.

4. What are the three variants in pronunciation of the past tense morpheme *-ed* in this list of words? What causes the change in the shape of the *-ed* morpheme?

walked	attached	danced	wished
hugged	lived	raised	judged
landed	boated	righted	loaded

5. The words in each of the following lists contain two or three morphemes. The meanings of the morphemes within each set, however, are not the same. What does each one mean?

cats (noun)	dogs (noun)	horses (noun)
cat's	dog's	horse's
cats'	dogs'	horses'
cats (verb)	dogs (verb)	horses (verb)

   All three can be used as verbs ("she cats around," "he dogged my every step," "they were horsing around"), though these are metaphorical extensions.

6. The most common affixes in science texts according to Willis (1976) are *auto-, bi-, circum-, epi-, macro-, micro-,*

mono-, peri-, pres-, proto-, supra-, ante-, demi-, di-, hypo-, mal-, meta-, poly-, retro-, -al, -ance, -ant, -ate, -ic, -ine, -itis, -ery. Check your course materials to see whether these particular affixes are included. Justify your belief that such affixes should or should not be taught in your particular program. Are these same affixes ever used to form scientific words in another language you know? If so, are the shared forms usually the prefixes rather than the suffixes? Why might this be so? Is it more important to teach the prefixes than the suffixes? Or should more importance be given to the meanings of the affixes regardless of position?

Classifying morphemes

Morphemes vary in kind and function. We can classify morphemes into several general categories: bound versus free, derivational versus inflectional, and lexical versus grammatical. Though the terms are given as clear dichotomies, there is (as always) a lot of grey area. It might be more realistic to talk about a given morpheme as being more lexical than grammatical or more lexical than another morpheme. For the sake of discussion, though, we will define each label according to its characteristics.

Bound versus free morphemes

This is the easiest distinction to define because it relates closely to English orthography. Morphemes are *free* to occur as individual words, or they may be *bound*, in which case they are always attached to another morpheme. If you divide the word *indemnity* into morphemes, you will find that each morpheme is bound. None of the morpheme units can stand alone. If we do the same with the word *nevertheless*, we find that each morpheme can stand alone; they are all free.

The free or bound quality has nothing to do with semantic meanings. For example, the same semantic meaning might be expressed in separate words or morphemes in one language and bound morphemes in another. Compare the Italian and English counterparts:

fresco	cool
freschetto	coolish
freschettino	rather coolish
freschino	sort of cool (more colloquial form)
casa	house
casetta	little house

Languages that use bound morphemes extensively are sometimes called *agglutinative*. For example, the language Kannada (as described by Aronoff & Sridhar, 1984) has number and case morphemes bound to nouns and uses multiple modification with morphemes, as in

huduga-r-ibbar-ig-oskara-vagi-yu
boy-pl-two-dat-goal-purposive-inclusive
(for the two boys, too)

Other languages, such as Chinese, are called *isolating* systems because the morphemes are all potentially free and the only morphological process is compounding.

There is a general principle in child language development that free forms are acquired before bound morphemes. For children learning English, this predicts that *not* is acquired before *-n't*, *will* before *-'ll*, *would* before *-d*, *have*, *has*, and *had* before their contracted forms, and full forms of *be* (am, is, are, was, were) before the contracted forms. Bellugi (1967) noted that even though mothers use the contracted form of *will* much more than the full form, children first use only the free form. L1 researchers admit that children produce *don't* and *can't* early, but argue that these appear only in unanalyzed chunks or memorized phrases. They are, therefore, counted as monomorphemic, free forms. Wode (1977) reports that German children use full free forms before their contracted forms. He also believes that early contracted forms, such as *wo's* and *da's* (as in the child utterance *wo's ist er* for "where is he"), are monomorphemic.

Derivational versus inflectional morphemes

Before discussing derivational and inflectional types of morphemes in greater detail, we will focus on the basic difference between the two categories.

Derivational morphemes make explicit the word class assignment of the word. Thus, they change the underlying form of the word to make it into an adjective, an adverb, or another part of speech. For example, *-ful* is a morpheme that changes nouns into adjectives (*beauty* becomes *beautiful*), *-ify* is an affix that changes nouns to verbs (*beauty* becomes *beautify*), and *-ly* is an affix that changes adjectives to adverbs (*beautiful* becomes *beautifully*).

Inflectional morphemes, in contrast, indicate the syntactic relation between words and function as grammatical markers. So, plural morphemes are inflectional morphemes that apply to all nouns, and the plural plays a syntactic role in terms of verb agreement. The third person singular present tense morpheme applies to all verbs and plays a syntactic role. The comparative morpheme *-er* applies to many adjectives and adverbs

TABLE 11.1 TYPES OF MORPHEMES

	Degrees of independence	
Kinds of morphemes	*Words*	*Affixes*
Lexical morphemes	Words incorporatable in new words by COMPOUNDING (*clam + bake →* *clambake*)	More or less productive prefixes (*un-* in "unproductive")
		Unproductive prefixes (*di-* in "digest")
	Words incorporatable in new words by DERIVATION (*push + y → pushy; mis + fire → misfire*)	More or less productive suffixes (*-able* in "orbitable")
		Unproductive suffixes (*-ose* in "verbose")
		Word fragments (*burger* in "cheeseburger")
Grammatical morphemes	Function words (*the, of, which, my, when, and, if, . . .*)	Inflectional affixes (*-s, -ed, -ing, . . .*)

Source: Adapted from Bolinger, 1975, p. 123. Used with permission.

and has a syntactic role. All of these are inflectional morphemes. Because they apply to most of the members of a class of words, inflections are much more productive than derivations.

Language Files (Ohio State University, 1982, pp. 50–52) summarizes the differences between inflectional and derivational morphemes as follows:

Inflectional	*vs.*	*Derivational*
1. Does not change meaning or part of speech of stem.		Changes meaning or part of speech of the stem.
2. Typically indicates syntactic or semantic relations between different words in a sentence.		Typically indicates semantic relations within the word.
3. Typically occurs with all members of some large class of morphemes.		Typically occurs with only some members of a class of morphemes.
4. Typically occurs at margins of words.		Typically occurs before any inflectional suffixes are added.

Lexical versus grammatical morphemes

Affixes divide neatly into two categories: derivational affixes which are more lexical in nature since they allow us to form new lexical entities, and inflectional affixes which are more grammatical in nature because they are used to show syntactic relations.

Free morphemes, however, can also be divided according to whether they carry primarily lexical or grammatical meanings. Single words like prepositions, articles, relative pronouns, are free morphemes that serve grammatical functions, just like the *-ing* or *-s* verb affixes (see Chapter 10). Thus, function words, along with inflectional morphemes, are grammatical morphemes. Table 11.1 may clarify this explanation.

Practice 11.2

1. Divide the following words into morphemes and identify each morpheme as free or bound, derivational or inflectional, lexical or grammatical.

toothbrush	debug	between
impish	daylight	repetition
closely	receive	over

2. Provide an example of your own where a morpheme may be free in one language (e.g., *little* in English) but a bound affix in another (e.g., *-ito* in Spanish).
3. Justify your choice in the following sentence: "Derivational morphemes are (always/sometimes/never) bound."
4. Which do you think that it would be easier to learn, an isolating language or an agglutinative language? What other characteristics of such languages might influence your answer? Given that Chinese languages are said to be isolating, do you think that speakers of these languages would have particular difficulty acquiring English morphology? Justify your answer.
5. Consider Table 11.1 from a curriculum standpoint. Select one type of language class (e.g., beginning grammar, ESP-science class, beginning literature class, translation class, conversation class) and estimate the importance that would be given to each area of the chart. Try to assign what proportion of class time should be spent on each area. Compare your estimates with those of your classmates. How do you account for the similarities and differences?

Derivations

In previous chapters, we have discussed many ways of creating new words from old. We can also build new words by adding derivational affixes, which do not apply regularly to an entire class of words, but only to some subset. In English, derivational morphemes are mainly prefixes and suffixes. These affixes often change the part of speech of the new, derived word from that of the stem. The affixes thereby help us to identify relationships within words. In the remainder of this chapter, we will look at how affixes produce new but derived (related) words. In Chapter 12, we will look at inflectional affixes and how they connect words within sentences.

In some languages, derivational morphology is highly regular and productive. Polish and Esperanto are two such languages. For example, the Esperanto word *bono* means good and *bona* means goodness. The endings *-o* and *-a* are always attached to the word base to change it to a noun and a verb. The system is completely regular.

English is quite different in this regard. In English, some derivational affixes are very productive and some are not. We know that *-ly* is an affix that changes adjectives to adverbs (*slow–slowly, tender–tenderly*). It is a highly productive affix. Yet it cannot be used with every adjective (*tall–tally, talented–talentedly*). We want our students to learn to use the most productive affixes, but we also want them to learn when they can and cannot be used, which is not an easy task. Some morphemes have a very limited range. For example, the affix *-ese* is not especially productive. We use it for special language registers such as *teacherese* or *TESLese*. Notice that this particular affix does not change the part of speech: *teacher* and *teacherese* are both nouns. Rather, it changes the lexical meaning of the word. Whereas a *teach*er is one who teaches, *teach*erese is the classroom register of teacher talk.

Morphemes go in and out of fashion. They may be quite productive for awhile and then virtually disappear. The *-ette* morpheme came into popularity with the word *suffragette* in the early 1900s (probably borrowed from French *-et*). It was still fairly popular in the 1950s with *usherette* and the addition of *nymphette*. By the 1980s, it had practically disappeared, although examples still pop up. On RAGBRAI (a bicycle trek across Iowa), riders stopping in a small town were served lunch by the Fire-ettes (wives of firemen). The affix *-arama* (as in *motorama*) was very popular in the 1950s and then virtually disappeared. Yet a campus newspaper announced that the students were having a *voterama*. Our supermarket advertised a *cake-arama* (cakes were on special) and a restaurant reviewer talked about a "full-service yupperama – a patisserie/ charcuterie, bistro/boulangerie, take-out, eat-in, expresso/wine bar, lunch and dinner place where cases display quiches, tartes, tortes, cerviche, and designer olive oil" (*Los Angeles Times,* October 17, 1986).

Other derivational affixes seem more lasting and productive. The affix *-able* is a case in point. It appears to be expanding its range (*workable, portable, thinkable,* and *doable*). Others have always been widely used and continue so. The *-ly* adverb affix has a very wide scope and changes many adjectives to adverbs (*happily, carefully*). It is so productive that we often apply it to words where it may not sound quite right. A friend, listening to a newscast, exclaimed, "He said that very nastily."

There may be as many as four or five competing affixes that appear to do the same work, but they are not interchangeable. Consider the prefixes for negation. We say *unable, dishonest, intolerable, nonproductive,* and *amoral.* All of these prefixes negate the morphemes that follow. If more than one can be used, the two resulting forms have different meanings or different restrictions for word collocations. This makes their acquisition very difficult. Indeed, it has led some learners, teachers, and researchers to believe that each has to be acquired as a separate word.

Nevertheless, teachers use alternate morpheme forms in teaching spelling and in giving definitions. The student who spells summary as *summery* is asked to listen to the words summary and then summarize to hear the *a.* The student who writes *histriy* may be asked to listen to *historical.* In offering definitions, teachers may elaborate using related forms. Chaudron (1982), in his study of teachers' speech in high school classes for immigrants, gives examples of teachers' attempts to clarify meanings by changing the part of speech:

miracle . . . you have anything that was miraculous?
sum up . . . summarize
revered . . . We refer to a minister as Reverend.

In practice, teachers and learners may use derivations to clarify the relation between the form and meaning of words.

Practice 11.3

1. Esperanto was created to be a universal, international language. It is Latin-based and uses many items from Romance languages. It is highly regular. Find and identify the morphemes in the following data (continues on the next page). List at least 12 morphemes and their meanings. What is the word for *instructive,* for *well,* for *porter*?

bono	goodness	instruisto	teacher
portistino	female porter	instrui	to instruct
pura	pure	bona	good

malfacila	difficult	patro	father
malbono	evil	facilo	easiness
malbone	badly	patrino	mother
facile	easily	porti	to carry
malgranda	small	instruistino	female teacher
instruo	instruction	facila	easy
granda	big	malbona	bad

(Source: adapted from Langacker, 1972, p. 82; used with permission)

Can you suggest a new morpheme that would allow speakers to talk about male and female children of the family? List your new "Esperanto" words for son and daughter. How would you form the word for "big son" or "big daughter?" Did you put the adjective affix before or after the word base? Why? Now decide how you would form "student" (one who receives instruction and is not a father or mother)? There are several possibilities for doing this. Explain why you decided on your particular form.

2. *Super* is a very productive prefix at the moment. What reasons can you give for its continued popularity? Although -*teria* seems to be used less and less, it still survives. What examples can you find for -*teria*? What does it mean? The surviving examples of -*ette* seem to have something to do with marching or dancing (e.g., Rockettes, majorette, the Cougarettes, Aggiettes). Can you think of examples where this is not the case (we found *bagelettes*, small bagels sold at a bakery)? Do you think the meaning of these affixes is becoming more and more restricted? Do you think they may eventually disappear? Justify your reasoning.

3. The newspaper reference to *yupperama* presents an interesting new word to analyze. How many morphemes would you claim it has? When did *yuppy* become popular? Why does it end with -*y*? What other forms of yuppiness have you seen in print? Do you think it occurs as frequently in talk? (Listen to National Public Radio news!)

4. Notice the prefix *mini-*. How productive is this affix? A friend of ours announced with delight that she had seen "a maxi-taxi at the mini-motel"! Are *mini-* and *maxi-* more or less productive than *micro-* and *macro-*? How do these two sets of terms differ in meaning and distribution?

5. List as many -*ese* examples as you can. Do you like the compound *teacher talk* better than *teacherese*? Does -*ese*

seem somehow pejorative? Does the pejorative quality appear in all your examples or only some? Why?

Derivational prefixes

Although derivational affixes in English are not especially regular, they still can be categorized according to their type, form, and meaning. The first major form division concerns placement: before the base (prefix) or following it (suffix). The second form distinction concerns the change in word class: nouns to verbs, verbs to adjectives, and so forth. The third has to do with the semantics of their morphology. For example, English prefixes can best be categorized according to their semantics. These include the meanings of negative (including reversible and pejorative), attitude, size or degree, locative, temporal or order, and number. There are also some prefixes that shift meaning while changing the part of speech.

Negatives

We have already noted that there are a variety of negative prefixes including *un-, non-, in-, a-,* and *dis-.* All can be added to adjectives – unimportant, nonindustrial, inescapable, amoral, displeasing – but some can also be added to nouns – nonhuman. The contrast in focus shows up in the use of more than one of the prefixes with the same word stem: inhuman, nonhuman; nonsymmetric, asymmetric. Language learners often avoid such forms in the early stages of acquisition. If they attempt to use a negative prefix, they usually supply *no* as in this example from a Spanish speaker: "For myself is no sufficient the sleep." Most linguistic books, however, do not include *no* as a negative prefix. Yet a current consumer's magazine discusses a strategy for coping with car dealers called no-haggle buying. A hardware sales catalogue lists no-heat sanders and a no-tilt shelf unit.

Some negative prefixes relate to reversibility. *De-, dis,-* and *un-* show a reversal of an action or a taking away of a quality. So, we button and *un*button clothes; we connect and *dis*connect the computer; fleas may jump on our pets but we soon *de*flea them. Marchand (1974) suggests that *un-* is used with everyday reversible verbs (undo) and reversible verbs derived from nouns (unzip). *Dis-* is used especially with verbs beginning with *en-,* or *in-* (disengage, disinfect). Marchand believes that *de-* is replacing *dis-* and is especially productive with verbs ending in *-ize* and *-ify* (declassify, demoralize). Still, where a semantic distinction exists, more than one form may be used with the same stem (unconnected, disconnected; unclassified, declassified).

When two negative affixes can be used with the same word, we have a potential for native speaker error. We easily confuse the following: unmeasurable and immeasurable; uninterested and disinterested; displace and misplace; unmoral, immoral, and amoral. In some cases, prefix errors have other causes. Lulled by the rhythm of his own phrases, President Bush responded to a question by saying he had confidence that the American people could "sort through what is fair and what is unfair, what is ugly and what is unugly" (Federal News Service, 1989). The study of slips of the tongue gives us many such delightful examples.

Algeo (1971) suggests that the negative prefix *non-* has pejorative (nonbook, nonevent) and neutral (nonobedient versus disobedient) qualities and is used as a prestige marker (nonsalaried, nonprofit) and for euphemisms (nonsuccess, nonreader). Zimmer (1964), on the other hand, believes that *non-* is neutral rather than pejorative, whereas he finds that *un-* and *in-* are judgmental (e.g., un-American versus non-American).

The pejorative category, according to Quirk and Greenbaum (1973), includes the prefixes *mis-, mal-,* and *pseudo-*. *Mis-,* meaning wrongly or astray, seems to be the most productive of the three. Quirk and Greenbaum show that it can be used with verbs (misinform), with abstract nouns (misconduct), and with participles (misleading). *Mal-* means bad(ly) and can also be used with the same types of stems: verbs (maltreat), nouns (malfunction), and participles (malfunctioning). It can also be used with adjectives (malodorous). Even though *mal-* can be added to one more class than mis-, it is less productive. *Pseudo-* has an even more restricted distribution, added to nouns and adjectives (pseudointellectual, pseudolongitudinal). It adds the meaning of false or imitation to the base word.

Attitude

Attitude prefixes are the morphemes that convey being against, with, opposite, for, or on the side of whatever stem they are added to. A good place to look for such prefixes is in bureaucractic discourse and especially in politics. Included are the prefixes *anti-, co-, counter-,* and *pro-*. News reports supply us with examples: anti-inflation, co-conspirator, counter-revolution, pro-Gore but anti-Clinton. Of course, they can be used with nonpolitical bases as well: antibiotic, coauthor, counteract, pro-bilingualism.

Size and degree

Size and degree prefixes include *arch-, hyper-, hypo-, maxi-, mini-, out-, over-, sub-, ultra-,* and *under-*. Some of these are added primarily to nouns (archrival, minivan, maxisize, supermarket), others to verbs (outdo, overheat, underestimate) or adjectives (overenthusiastic, substandard, ultraposh). As you can see, some of these prefixes can be used with several parts of speech, but in each case the meanings relate to size or degree. The choice between the prefixes *hypo-* and *hyper-* (e.g., hypoallergenic versus hyperallergenic) confuses even native speakers. President Bush used hypo in strange ways: "Those are two hypo-rhetorical questions" (*The New York Times,* 1988) and "I'm not going to hypothecate that – it may – anything goes too fast" (Muro, 1992). *Hypothecate* is a real word, but in this context he really meant he wouldn't predict an outcome.

Space and time

Spatial and temporal prefixes include *ex-, fore-, inter-, post-, pre-, re-, sub-,* and *trans-.* Spatial examples include intermountain, subway, transcontinental. Temporal or order examples include forecast, preview, postgame party, reexamine, ex-teacher.

Number

Number prefixes include *bi-, di-, mono-, multi-, poly-,* and *tri-,* as in biweekly, dichotomy, monolingual, multilingual, polyglot, and trilingual. The *bi-* prefix is especially confusing in publication statements. Is a biweekly paper put out twice a week or every other week? *Audubon* magazine states that it is published bimonthly but it is published every two months, not twice a month. Triannual reviews could be held three times a year or every third year. *Bi-* and *tri-* for other nouns are not so confusing: biathlons and triathlons are two- and three-event races held on one day.

Quirk and Greenbaum have an "other" category that includes the prefixes *auto-, neo-, pan-, proto-, semi-,* and *vice-.* Their examples for these are autobiography, neo-Gothic, pan-African, prototype, semicircle, and vice-president.

Because the prefixes can be grouped into semantic classes, we would expect that they would not be difficult to teach or learn. However, the overlap of forms even within categories makes them less regular than they seem, and we can expect students to have difficulties. In some instances, students may not know the appropriate prefix. In other cases, the prefix would be correct if the base word were different. Even native speakers sometimes make errors. The negative prefixes seem to be particularly troublesome:

1. The *no rich* people have tamales. (Spanish L1)
2. For myself is *no sufficient* the sleep. (Spanish L1)
3. Marijuana should be *illegalized.* (Chinese L1)
4. I often took myself so seriously that is *unadvantageous* for me to make friends. (Vietnamese L1)
5. Los Angeles is *overflowed* by automobiles. (Korean L1)

6. After finishing the paragraph and reading it again, I felt *unsatisfy.* (Vietnamese L1)
7. I don't have any *disillusions* about it. (English L1)
8. His writ- his works are *pseudo-right* scientifically. (English L1)
             (Data sources: #1, 2, R. Shapira; #3, 7, A. Lazaraton)

Practice 11.4

1. Two or more negative prefixes can be applied to the same word. What difference in meaning is signaled by the prefixes?

   unnconnected vs. disconnected
   unclassified vs. declassified
   un-American vs. non-American
   nonobedient vs. disobedient
   disinterested vs. uninterested

2. English speakers convert this systematicity into games with examples such as those collected by C. Campbell: "Can a skirt be depleted?" "Can the fireplace be dismantled?" "Can the addict be disjointed?" "Can the church be dismembered?" "Can a politician be devoted?" What examples can you add? Do you think Shakespeare in writing *Julius Caesar* puzzled over the line "the most unkindest cut of all" . . . most unkind . . . unkindest . . . least kind . . . least most kindest?

3. Prefixes are not highly regular, which leads to learner errors such as the following:

   The opposite of expand is inpand.
   American personality almost the outgoing but Chinese peoples is almost ingoing.

   Prepare a pilot test for such opposite prefixes. Administer the test to three language learners and three native speakers. What do your findings suggest?

4. The prefix *mini-* seems to be going out of style. We don't see examples like *minibus, miniskirt,* and *minigolf* as often as in the past, although minimarkets and minimalls are ubiquitous. Check through your local newspaper for examples of this prefix. Do you agree or disagree with our claim? Do you find many entries for *micro-?* How do *mini-* and *micro-* differ in meaning?

5. If you have access to a large database such as the Lund or Brown corpora, select one overlapping set of prefixes.

Find all the entries for these prefixes across as many different genres as you can. What do you discover?

6. If you have beginners who use *no* in the way it is used in the two Spanish L1 examples given earlier, how might you go about encouraging them to use standard negative prefixes? Do posted warning signs such as "No passing," "No refunds," "No parking," "No smoking" encourage the use of *no* as a general negator? How important is first language transfer in explaining these negation errors?

Derivational suffixes

Suffixes are much less easy to group on a semantic basis than are prefixes. Most suffixes change words from nouns to verbs, adjectives to adverbs, and so forth. We will begin with nouns, then verbs, adjectives, and adverbs.

Nouns

After suffixes are added, many nouns remain as nouns but the meaning changes. Quirk and Greenbaum (1973) list three noun-to-noun occupational suffixes: *-ster, -eer, and -er* as in *gangster, engineer,* and *New Yorker.* Four noun-to-noun diminutives or feminine endings: *-let, -ette, -ess,* and *-y, -ie* as in *piglet, cigarette, waitress,* and *cookie.* Four noun-to-noun forms have to do with status or domain: *-hood* as in *childhood, -ship* as in *friendship, -dom* as in *kingdom, -ocracy, (e)ry* as in *democracy* and *priory.* Some count nouns can be changed to mass nouns with the affix *-ing:* for example, *tops* becomes *topping, covers* becomes *covering,* and *panel* becomes *paneling.* Other count nouns can be changed to have the meaning of amount using *-ful: cup, cupful; mouth, mouthful.* If you try to find additional examples for each of these noun-to-noun derivations, you will find that they vary in terms of productivity.

Quirk and Greenbaum list five noun-to-adjective suffixes: *-ite, -(i)an, -ese, -ist,* and *-ism.* With application of these affixes, the semantic notion of a membership group is added. Examples include *socialite, Republican, Chinese, conservationist, communism.*

Verbs

There is a much larger group of affixes that change verbs to nouns. The affixes *-er, -or,* and *-ant* all have the meaning of agent or instrument: *plumber, actor, inhabitant, disinfectant.* The "one who" meaning is also shown by the *-ee* morpheme, but it is passive. That is, an employee is someone who is employed by someone else. Several endings have to do with states or actions: *-ation, -ment, -al (exploration, amazement, re-fusal)*. Others have an activity or result of activity meaning: *-ing, -age (driving, building, drainage)*.

Adjectives

Adjectives can be changed to nouns by a variety of suffixes. The forms *-ness* and *-ity* are used with states or quality as in *happiness* and *sanity*. Three suffixes transform nouns or adjectives into verbs with a causative meaning: *-ify, -ize, -en (amplify, mechanize, sadden)*. Other affixes are used to change nouns to adjectives. The suffix *-ful* gives nouns the meaning of giving or having (e.g., *helpful*); *-less* adds the meaning of without (e.g., *hopeless); -ly* and *-like* mean having the quality of *(wifely, childlike)*. We have said that the ending /i/, often spelled *-y* or *-ie*, adds a diminutive or endearing quality. Quirk and Greenbaum list it in the noun-to-noun feminine/diminutive category, but note that /i/, spelled *-y*, is also an adjective morpheme meaning like (dreamy) or covered with (muddy). The suffix *-ish* means belonging to or having the character of (Moorish, foolish).

Quirk and Greenbaum show that some adjective suffixes occur primarily in borrowed and neoclassical words: *-al* in *editorial* and *musical, -ic* in *heroic, -ive* in *attractive,* and *sensitive* and *-ous* in *virtuous* and *courteous.*

Other adjective suffixes change verbs to adjectives: *-able, -ible* as in *readable, forcible.* Above we noted that *-ish* can change a noun to an adjective, but it can also grade adjectives, as in *youngish.* The suffix *-ed* has many functions, but one is to change the phrase "having a NOUN" into an adjective. "Having a point" becomes the adjective *pointed.*

Adverbs

Adverbs can be derived from adjectives using *-ly (quickly, strangely), -ward (backward)*, or they can be derived from nouns with *-wise (lengthwise)*. The use of *-wise* to mean "as far as X is concerned" has been overused in recent years, in particular on news reports (weatherwise, budgetwise, conferencewise). It provides an easy way to signal a shift in topic in such programs.

Derivational affixes are used to form new creations all the time. Here are two new noun → verb creations. A friend who had just finished scooping out a pumpkin for a Hallowe'en jack-o-lantern, laughed and said, "I sure *pumpkinized* my hands!" Ross Perot, a 1992 presidential candidate said, "Foreign aid is not foreign policy; it's *charitizing* the world." So, although we probably never think about derivational affixes as separate from the words in which they occur, we still use such affixes to create new and original combinations.

Practice 11.5

1. In the following exercise from Yorkey's *Study Skills* (1982), students are asked to create new words from old by changing affixes. Fill in the blanks. Which entries change meanings in ways other than change of word class?

Noun	Verb	Adjective	Adverb
imagination			
		repeated	
consideration			
	succeed		
			comparatively

2. The following suffix errors are from compositions of university-level international students. In each case, supply the correct affix. Why do you think the learner made the error?

> The problem that made me suffer was no satified sentence to express my thought.   (Chinese L1)
> Today Haagen Dazs ice cream to have captured the corner on ice cream chic in U.S. because of some special unique.   (Vietnamese L1)

Note the beautiful compound "ice cream chic" and the idiomatic use of "capture the corner on," to say nothing of the poetry of *chic* and *unique*!

> There are so many rules and exceptions that are very mathematically.   (Japanese L1)
> For good notes taking, I believe we have our own way of diagrammation and symboling which we develop from experiencing and using.   (Spanish L1)

3. How would you account for the fact that native English speakers also make such errors? In the first of the following examples, a professor made the error in a lecture. In the second, the native speaker was talking about economic systems. (*Versitel* is an automatic banking system many Americans use.) The third example was a comment on Malcolm X as a role model for teenagers.

> Another way of symboling that 'er' schwa r sound –
> This may become a universital system, worldwide.
> . . . they should be that resourcive, intelligent.

4. When native speakers use incorrect forms like *pronunci-ate,* it may be that they do so on the basis of analogy (perhaps with *enunciate*) or a blend process *(pronunciation* and *enunciate).* Identify the error, list the form you would use in each case, and then see if you can think of an analogy that might be involved for the following data. The examples, collected by A. Lazaraton, are oral rather than written.

a. I'm memoried most of songs.   (Japanese L1)
b. These materials would be good for an auto mechan-ician course.   (Korean L1)
c. This year is a very activity year.   (Chinese L1)
d. Many animals want to competate to be chosen.   (Chinese L1)
e. They sat in a conventional hall.   (Thai L1)
f. It was a jubilous occasion.   (English L1)
g. I want to learn to conversate with native speakers.   (Chinese L1)
h. I was acceptant of the reality of the situa-tion.   (English L1)
i. I like exportation and importation especially. (Portuguese L1)
j. I live in a quite touristic town in southern Spain. (Spanish L1)
k. I hope my research can be applicate to eco-nomics.   (Chinese L1)

As a long-term project, you might compare the number and type of inflectional errors across L1 groups or across proficiency levels.

5. Ask three English L1 friends to rank the acceptability of each of the errors in item 4 on a five-point scale. Then ask them to rate those that appeared in signs around the world and were included in a humorous article in *Air France Bulletin* (December 1989). Why are some errors more serious than others?

The lift is being fixed for the next day. During that time we regret that you will be unbearable.   (Hungary)
Please leave your values at the front desk.   (France)
Teeth extracted by latest methodist.   (Hong Kong)
Take our tours. We guarantee no miscarriages.   (former Czechoslovakia)

Other derivational processes

In this chapter we have presented common English prefixes and suffixes that are used to derive new words from old. Other languages use other methods to achieve the same goal, or use similar processes but in different ways. We discussed prefixes as derivations, but in some languages prefixes are used for verb tense, for plurals, or (as a pronoun marker) for the person carrying out the verb action. Instead of derivations, they are inflections. Gasser (1993) gives us the Swahili example *nilikuona,* a word meaning "I saw you." It consists of four morphemes added to the verb stem *-on-.* These include three before the verb: *ni-* is the pronoun marker, *-li-* is the past tense marker, and *-ku-* is the direct object affix for second person singular. (The suffix *-a* means a neutral, not negative or subjunctive mood.) All of these affixes have syntactic (inflectional) meanings.

In some languages, morphology changes may not be carried by a morpheme but rather by a change in phonology. In Chichewa, for example, using a relatively high tone can change a verb form from present to past tense. There are even languages where something is deleted to signal a change in meaning. Martin (1988) gives us an example from Koasati where verbs have plural forms that are changed to the singular by deleting a portion of the singular form.

Root elaboration is a major process in Afro-Asiatic and especially Semitic languages. In these languages, different forms of related words are built around a common root. In Arabic, for example, the root *ktb* is used to form many related words. *Katab* means "he wrote," *maktab* is "office," *kitaab* is "book," *kutub* is "books," *kaatib* is "having written." Each vowel addition changes the root to a new word.

In English, verbs can be of almost any length. They can be short (*see*) or long (*decontextualize*). In Arabic, verbs have three basic shapes (C = consonant, v = vowel) CvCvC (as in *katab*), CvCCvC (*killim,* to speak) or CvvCvC (*saafir,* to travel). Each of these verb shapes can be further elaborated to form new words just as, in English, we can add additional affixes to verbs.

Practice 11.6

1. The root in the following Arabic data consists of three consonants. What are they and what does the root mean?

daras	he studied
darris	he taught
madrasa	school
mudarris	teacher
dars	lesson
tidrisu	you (pl) study

2. We said that verb shapes in Arabic can be changed to signal changes in meaning. Look at the following pairs. What meaning change has been signaled by changing the root shape?

daras	to study
darris	to teach
ṭala'	to rise, go up
ṭalla'	to take up, make rise
nizil	to go down, descend
nazzil	to take down
kibir	to grow
kabbar	to enlarge

Does your hypothesized meaning for the double consonants hold for the following pairs?

niḍiif	clean	naḍḍaf	to clean
maṣr	Egypt	maṣṣar	to Egyptianize
kibiir	big	kabbar	to enlarge
ṣuġayyar	small	ṣaġġar	to reduce the size
mumkin	possible	makkin	to enable, make possible.

3. There are five basic verb conjugations in Hebrew, labeled *paal, nifal, piel, hitpael,* and *hifil.* In each conjugation, the form is derived from the root in a slightly different way.

a. *piel:*	tipul	treating
	bidur	entertaining
	kinus	responding / response
	bikur	visiting / visit
	bikuš	demanding / demand
	sipur	storytelling
b. *paal:*	amira	protecting / protection
	bniya	building
	bhira	choosing / choice
	mxira	selling / sale
	sliha	forgiveness
c. *hifil:*	haakama	agreeing / agreement
	kaxlata	deciding / decision
	hafsaka	stop / stopping
	hathala	beginning
d. *nifal:*	hismrut	being protected
	hitaqiut	encountering / encounter
	himaltut	escaping / escape
	heragut	calming down

e. *hitpael:*   hithadsut   renewing
                  hitanyenut   taking an interest
                                    (Data source: R. Altman)

What are the consonant (C) and vowel (v) patterns for each group in the data? By knowing the root, the verb conjugation pattern, and the grammatical category, you can produce the correct forms in these examples. Unfortunately, this only works for some words, not for all. As with English, there is a wide variety of possible morphological shapes.

4. Compare the Hebrew example with the previous Arabic data. Would you guess that Arabic and Hebrew are related languages? In Amharic (according to Gasser, 1993) *masbar* means "to break" and *sabbar-a* means "he broke." Based on this data, would you make any predictions about the relationship among Amharic, Hebrew, and Arabic? Justify your answer.

5. Gasser (1993) divides morpheme types in language according to where they occur relative to the word stem. A morpheme can be a prefix (before the stem), a suffix (after the stem), an infix (where a morpheme is inserted between the stem and another affix), a circumfix (where part of a morpheme precedes and part follows the stem), a mutation (as in irregular plurals *mouse → mice*), a deletion (as Martin, 1988, says is done with Koasati plurals) and root elaboration (as in the Arabic and Hebrew examples presented earlier). Of these, which do you think would be the easiest to learn? Which do you think would be the most difficult? Give your rationale.

Research and application

1. Badecker and Caramazza (1989) studied the language of a 60-year-old Italian who had suffered brain damage (acute intracerebral hematoma) resulting in language deficits. His spontaneous speech showed omission or misselection of morphemes. The comparison of errors in derivational and inflectional morphemes shows many more inflection than derivation errors. One could argue that this is evidence that derivations are more lexical in nature; that is, that words are learned and stored as single units. Inflections, on the other hand, might be stored separately and put together as the sentence is produced. Read the article and consider alternative explanations for the data.

281

2. Pillon et al. (1991) discuss the language of a patient diagnosed as having Wernicke's aphasia. JPC is a 33-year-old Belgian male whose first language is French but who also knew some English, Dutch, German, and Italian. In contrast to the patient described in Badecker and Caramazza, JPC displayed large numbers of errors in derivational morphology. In picture-naming tasks, the error rate was as high as 50 percent. The authors suggest that such data can be used to address the question of whether words are constructed from stems and affixes or whether the whole word is stored and retrieved intact. Further, they tested Bybee's hypothesis that words are constructed only when they are very low-frequency items and have regular patterns of affixation. Otherwise, according to this hypothesis, they are represented and retrieved as whole words. To test this, they divided the error database into high-frequency versus mid- and low-frequency words and according to regular and irregular affixes. The findings showed that word frequency had a definite effect on the error rate while the difference between regular vs. irregular affixes was not so great.

	High frequency	*Mid/low frequency*
Regular	16.7%	54.0%
Irregular	25.9%	60.0%

The authors note that JPC often was able to retrieve the first part of a word for a pictured item correctly but not the entire word. This was shown in omissions (*noix* for *noisette, fourche* for *fourchette, mu* for *mouton*). Successful retrieval of the initial parts of words with errors in inflections were common (e.g., *palmiste* for *palmier, sucette* for *sucrier*). One solution (whether the problem is with derivations or with retrieval of the final parts of words) might be to look at derivational prefixes rather than suffixes. Bybee's hypothesis is interesting and could be further tested with adult foreign and second language learners. Whether derivational morphology is a real process for learners (or only a convenient way to describe linguistic forms) is an important theoretical issue that also has implications regarding the teaching of prefixes versus suffixes. Design a research project that would allow you to test the hypothesis.

3. Clark and Hecht (1982) have shown that children comprehend the derivational affix -*er* as an agent and as an instrument (agent: "He's a farm*er*"; instrument: "It's a cutt*er*"). Although they comprehend both uses, they use only the agent form. Derwing (1976) and Derwing and Baker (1979) investigated children's use of -*ly, -y,* and -*ie,* finding that these suffixes appear relatively late. Read these studies and prepare a pilot test to use with young second or

foreign language learners (or for adults acquiring the language). Administer your test to three learners and report the results. If your results look promising, you might want to expand this project to include a wider variety of affixes.

4. We said that -er means "one who" – no more, no less. But Randall (1988) notes that there are two types of forms for "one who" – complex forms with the -er and simple forms without the -er. So, for example, *pilot* differs from *flier, chef* differs from *baker, ballerina* differs from *dancer, soprano* differs from *singer.* Randall shows that these two types occur in different types of sentences. We say "a singer of sad songs" but not "a soprano of sad songs"; "a baker of fancy foods" but not "a chef of fancy foods." Adjectives can be used to modify both types but the meaning is different. A beautiful ballerina is a ballerina who happens to be beautiful. A beautiful dancer can mean that the person is good at dancing. Prepare a test to discover whether students (who already know the terms) can identify appropriate and inappropriate use of the simple and complex forms.

5. C. Chomsky (1970) used morphology to help children work on the spelling of problematic words. One problem area is the spelling of vowels that are said to be reduced because they do not receive word stress. For example, "dem__cratic" is difficult unless it is mentally related to *democracy.* "Comp__rable" is difficult unless it is related to *compare.* Children are asked to supply the missing vowel in such lists and then to give a related word to justify the spelling choice. This method is also used to assist children in their search for correct consonants (in examples such as medicine–medical, racial–race, gradual–grade) or to pick up silent consonants (as in muscle–muscular, sign–signature, malign–malignant). Prepare a research plan to test this technique with second language learners who might profit from such instruction.

6. McDonald's restaurant claims that the prefix *Mc* is part of its trademark. The company brought suit to stop Quality Inns from using the word *McSleep* for a chain of motels. R. Gozzi, Jr. (1992) notes that the newspaper *USA Today* is often called *McPaper.* He suggests that *Mc* means something like cheap, quick, small bites. Prepare a list of words with this prefix and administer it to speakers of different ages. Do you see patterns in the meaning and acceptability judgments for these words across speaker groups? If your results look promising, you might want to submit this as a paper to the WHIM conference, or for publication in *Verbatim.*

7. Mettinger (1990) discusses the forms and meanings of the affix -able. The affix can be attached to a verb (e.g., *breakable, eatable*) or to a noun (e.g., *marriageable, knowledgeable*). Those attached

283

to verbs have the meaning of "likely to be *Y*ed, capable of being *Y*ed" and so show modality such as possibility or necessity. Those attached to nouns have the meaning that "*Y* has already been evaluated" as positive or negative, as in knowledgeable, pleasurable, honorable. Mettinger then tries to find correspondences of the prefix *kě* in Chinese to the suffix *-able* in English. If you teach (or are learning) Chinese, read this article and comment on Mettinger's treatment of the correspondences in forms and meanings in the two languages.

8. Gasser (1993) and Gasser and Lee (1991) have developed connectionist models (computer models of learning), which make detailed predictions about the learning difficulty of particular types of morphology in languages. Gasser (1993) includes a review of connectionist experiments, beginning with Rumelhart and McClelland's (1986) classic on past tense morphemes. Connectionism challenges symbolic models of language and language learning such as those proposed by Chomsky. Read the Gasser articles and design a study to test some of the predictions in them.

12 Inflectional morphology

Inflections

Although some affixes allow us to derive new words from old, others have more grammatical functions. These inflectional endings give us information about the relation between words in sentences or utterances.

In contrast to derivational morphemes, the number of inflections is small and they apply more regularly across a larger range of items. They are more regular and productive, yet language learners still struggle with them. Perhaps for that reason, they form the basis of most grammar-based programs of language instruction.

English inflections for nouns include plural and possessive. The plural of *boy* is *boys;* the possessive of *teacher* is *teacher's.* The set of inflections for verbs include present third person singular, past, progressive, perfective (drives, drove, driving, driven). Adjectives and adverbs are inflected for comparison (larger, largest; quicker, quickest). Natural gender marks John as masculine and Joanna as feminine, so these nouns are referred to with the pronouns *he* and *she.* Pronouns are inflected for gender and case (he, him, his; she, her, hers; who, whose, whom).

Although it is true that inflectional morphology is much more regular than derivational morphology, there are irregular forms. We know that some nouns have irregular plurals (children, cherubim, alumnae) and some have a "zero" plural morpheme (deer, sheep). Others involve change of vowels in the word stem (men, geese, mice). Most nouns, other than those that refer to humans, are not marked for gender, yet some are. So *ship* is feminine at least for those speakers who refer to *ships* with the pronoun *she.*

There are a larger number of irregular forms for verbs, especially for the past tense morpheme *-ed* (took, cut, went). The perfective forms may also vary but the two most common are *-ed* and *-en* (have walked, have eaten).

The comparative inflections are *-er* and *-est* (sooner, soonest; quicker, quickest), but the grammatical function words *more* and *most* are used with longer adjectives and adverbs (more, most intelligent; more, most sensibly). If the word has two syllables, the choice depends on the word form. *Pretty* becomes *prettier,* not *more pretty; alert* becomes *more alert,* not *alerter.*

TABLE 12.1   VARIATION IN DIALECTS

Variable	Standard English	Colloquial Black English
Copula	He is going.	He goin'.
Possessive	Gene's cousin	Gene cousin
Plural	I have five cents.	I got five cent.
3rd pers sg	He lives in Miami.	He live in Miami.
Past	He walked home.	He walk home.
'If'	She asked if he did it.	She asked did he do it.
Neg	I don't have any.	I don't got none.
BE	He is always here.	He be here.
Subj	Sue moved.	Sue, she move.
Verb form	Heidi drank the milk.	Heidi drunk the milk.
Future	I will go home.	I'ma go home.
Indef Art	I want an apple.	I want a apple.
Pro form	We have to do it.	Us got to do it.
Poss Pro	His book	He book
Prep	He's over at Gene's house.	He over to Gene house.
	He coaches at Hart High	He coach Hart High.
DO for BE	No, he isn't.	No, he don't.

Source: Adapted from Baratz, 1969, and Bolinger, 1975, p. 338.

There is also variation in possessives. In most cases the -'s morpheme is used (Gene's house, the school's basketball team, the teacher's complaints). However, it is also possible to mark possessive with the preposition *of* (the leg of the table, the top of the cabinet, the back of the building, the prow of the ship).

Though there is variation, overall the system is quite regular. The system can and does vary across dialects, however. The inflection systems of American English, Australian English, Black English, British English, Egyptian English, Hawaiian English, Indian English, Philippine English, and other English dialects are not all the same. Consider the differences between standard American English and colloquial Black English adapted from Baratz (1969) and Bolinger (1975, p. 338) in Table 12.1.

In Chapter 10, we talked about the forms and functions of the English copula BE. We noted then that speakers of standard American English do not always produce a BE form in speaking. We gave examples from reporters ("Lakers leading 102–97"), from self-identification sequences in radio call-in programs ("I'm Betty + 47 and + have uh two teenagers?"). We also mentioned that many dialects of English (e.g., vernacular Hawaiian English and Black English) also omit the copula in some instances. Standard English speakers also use these forms. Many people might say, "I asked him did he do it" and we are often unsure whether to mark all plurals. Do we say six foot tall or six feet tall, a two-semester course or a two-semesters course? So there is variability even within individual ideolects.

Practice 12.1

1. For each of the following, circle and identify the inflections.

   eating   baked   pastries   sings   songs   softer
   mine   girls'   girl's   slept   pumpkins   sweetest

2. What are the past tense morphemes for each of the following verbs: take, cut, lie, go, set, am. Look at the explanations for these irregular forms in a course book. Should all irregular categories be presented at once? If not, what suggestions would you make regarding sequence?
3. Shirahata (1988) provides data from a group of thirty-one Japanese high school EFL students. Only fourteen of the thirty-one students had irregular past tense errors. The errors included: falled, catched, standed, taked, hided, speaked, weared, blowed, leaved, runned, waked. Supply the correct past tense form for each item. If you teach ESL or EFL, are these typical of errors your students make? The data were collected by asking students to tell familiar fairy tales. How might this have influenced the range of verb errors?
4. List three adjectives and adverbs and supply the comparative and superlative forms. How many use -er and -est? Form the comparative and superlative of the following positive forms.

   Adverbs: soon, lately, quietly, currently, today, here
   Adjectives: pretty, quiet, beautiful, current, daily

   Can you add -er to all color name adjectives (redder, bluer, purpler, beiger, mauver, pinker)?
5. In Table 12.1 comparing inflections in colloquial Black English and standard English, the example shows a zero plural form. However, the zero plural occurs more frequently in some cases than in others. What seems to condition the distribution of plural -s in the following examples?

   They run twenty-seven mile in the Olympics.
   You gotta carry sandwiches or pay five dollar for lunch.
   They lost they book last time but now they got new ones.
   I ain't got no car license for about three year.
   Magic he give a million dollar to his friends.

6. Table 12.1 also shows a zero form for copula and BE, which appears in some cases and not in others. What explains the variation in the following examples?

His name Magic Earvin Johnson or Earvin Magic Johnson.
He on the court every day but sometime he be sick.
He a real star. Travel all different places.
The Lakers they the champs.
We go to the Forum when they be playing.
They in the Forum. Ah man, you don' know that?
It's where they have the games, you know.
Sometimes we be waitin' outside to see them.
They got a Forum Club where they partying after every game.

What is the difference in meaning between "They in the Forum" and "They be in the Forum"? In this case, the colloquial dialect seems more precise than standard English. How would this distinction be accomplished in standard English?

Morpheme acquisition studies

As mentioned previously, Berko's (1958) famous study examined the acquisition of inflectional morphology using drawings of imaginery creatures and nonsense words (the "Wug" test). The point of using nonsense words is to be sure that learners have not simply memorized individual words with their morphological endings intact. The test consists of 27 items, each testing a particular morpheme, similar to the following examples (for exact items, see Berko, 1958).

This is a wug. Now there are two of them. There are two – ? (wugs /z/ voiced form of plural)
This is a bird who knows how to rick. It is ricking. It did the same thing yesterday. What did it do yesterday?
Yesterday it – ? (ricked /t/ voiceless form of past tense)
This is a nizz. Now there are two of them. There are two – ? (nizzes /əz/ form of plural)
This is a frog who knows how to mot. He is motting. He did the same thing yesterday. What did he do yesterday? Yesterday he – ? (motted /ɪd/ form of the past tense).
This is a little wug. What would you call such a small wug? It's a – ? (wuggy, wuglet – diminutive)
This wug lives in this house. What would you call a house a wug lives in? It's a – ? (wughouse, wug-home, wugwam – noun compounding)
This is a blick. Now there are two of them. There are two – ? (blicks /s/ voiceless form of plural)

The results showed that children had acquired plural, possesive, *-ing* continuous, past, and present. There were differences between preschool and first grade groups mainly on forms that require an additional syllable (nizzes, motted). Adults also made a few errors in deciding whether an additional syllable was needed or not (e.g., wugzez hat).

The wug test has been adapted for Spanish by Kernan and Blount (1966):

Esta es una tifa. Ahora hay otra. Hay dos de ellas. Hay dos – ?
Este es un hombre que sabe ticar. Está ticando. ¿Cómo se llama un hombre que tica?
El hombre tica. Mañana lo hará. Mañana, el – ?

Swain et al. (1972) constructed a French version of the test for Canadian children attending a French immersion kindergarten. Sample items include:

Voici un gof. Maintenant voici deux – ?
Voici un homme qui pole. Hier il a – ?
Voici une fille qui est cherte. Voici aussi un garçon qui est – ?
Voici un homme qui dape. Demain il va – ?
Voici un homme qui va tifer. Maintenant il – ?

Although the wug test has the potential of showing the order in which morphemes are accurately supplied, it has seldom been used for this purpose. Morpheme acquisition has more typically been studied using natural language data, tracking the order in which morphemes are acquired (usually 90 percent correct in obligatory instances over a two-week period is the criterion of acquisition). Brown (1973) and deVilliers and deVilliers (1973) have rank ordered the acquisition of a set of fourteen grammatical morphemes by child L1 learners. Some of these are bound morphemes and others (such as prepositions) are free. Table 12.2 shows their orders of acquisition.

We said that action words are acquired early. These words allow children to talk about actions in the here and now. Transitive actions such as hug and bite and intransitive actions such as go, sleep, sit serve this purpose. An *-ing* form of these verbs (e.g., playing, kissing, smiling) is needed to talk about the now of ongoing actions. So the *-ing* of the present progressive is acquired early. This progressive aspect morpheme shows continuing action (e.g., "She *is* swimm*ing*" shows that the action in the verb is ongoing, not completed). The semantic notion of ongoing action is transparent to most language learners. In addition, there is only one form, *-ing*, to add to the verb itself. So, it is not surprising that child L1 learners (and learners of ESL and EFL) begin using this verb form very early.

The early division between completed (past) and noncompleted actions

TABLE 12.2   L1 ACQUISITION ORDERS

Morpheme	Brown	deVilliers & deVilliers
1. Present progressive	1	2
2. *on*	2.5	2
3. *in*	2.5	4
4. Plural *-s*	4	2
5. Past irregular	5	5
6. Possessive *'s*	6	7
7. Uncontractible copula	7	12
8. Articles	8	6
9. Past regular *-ed*	9	10.5
10. Third person present *-s*	10	10.5
11. Third person irregular	11	8.5
12. Uncontractible aux	12	14
13. Contractible copula	13	8.5
14. Contractible aux	14	13

and the acquisition of *-ing* for ongoing action has led to claims that learners first acquire aspect. Antinucci and Miller (1976), among others, have argued that initially children have no real understanding of verb tense. What appears to be early use of tense is really based on the semantics of aspect, whether actions are completed or not. It may seem that children use the past tense when they are primarily attending to completion vs. noncompletion of actions. For example, they may use past tense with transitive action verbs (e.g., spill) that have a clear end result. At the same time, they will not use past tense with verbs without a clear end result (e.g., sleep, play). So, children between 1½ and 2½ say "spilled the juice" but "play Bobby house." This is sometimes called "the primacy of aspect" hypothesis in acquisition studies. Others have argued against this interpretation. Weist (1986) claims that by 20 months children refer to both past and nonpast in terms of time via tense (and not just as completed and not completed as in aspect).

Brown (1973) and the deVilliers (1973) studies of the order of acquisition in child language provided the impetus for many similar studies with L2 learners of English from many different L1 groups and age levels and from instructed as well as uninstructed learners. The first to use Brown's methodology with longitudinal data was Hakuta's (1974) study of a Japanese child learning English. The morphemes studied, examples of the 8-year-old child's production, and the order of acquisition are shown in Table 12.3. The order of acquisition is that shown in the table. Most of the studies that followed were cross-sectional where data were gathered

TABLE 12.3   MORPHEME EXAMPLES

Morpheme	Form	Example
Present progressive	-*ing*	My father is read*ing* a books.
Copula	be, am, is, are	Kenji *is* bald.
Aux (prog.)	be, am, is, are	She*'s* eating a money.
Past aux.	didn't, did	Margie *did*n't play
Prep *in*	in	Policeman is hiding *in* K's shoes.
Prep, *to*	to	He come back *to* school.
Third person irregular	has, does	She *has* mother, right?
Prep. *on*	on	Don't sit *on* bed.
Possessive	*'s*	My father*'s* teacher.
Past irregular	go, went	She *came* back.
Plural	-*s*	My hand*s* is dirty.
Articles	a, the	She's in *a* house.
Third person regular	-*s*	This froggie want*s* more milk.
Past regular	-*ed*	The policeman disappear*ed*.
Gonna aux	am, is, are	I'm *gonna* died today.

Source: Hakuta, 1974.

from a large number of subjects only once, so the order obtained is an accuracy order rather than an acquisition order. The test instruments most often used to elicit the data were Burt et al.'s (1973) Bilingual Syntax Measure and Fathman's (1976) SLOPE (second language oral proficiency test).

Krashen (1977) summarized the findings of many of these morpheme studies in his claim for a "natural" order of acquisition (Figure 12.1). Although there may be variation in orders within each box, the order between boxes should not vary.

Although the many morpheme studies have been interpreted as showing a natural order for all learners regardless of first language or age, there are also clear examples of L1 influence. We all know that the articles *a* and *the* are not as easily acquired by Asian students as students from other areas. Therefore, the order cannot be strictly the same across all learners. Indeed, if we look at the studies case by case, we find many examples that demonstrate the influence of the first language.

One interesting example is Kuwahata's (1984) study of Japanese high school students. In Japanese, the possessive construction is marked with a case marker *no,* which is placed between the possessor and the object possessed, so that "This is John's pen" might be translated as *Korewa John no pen (desu).* We might predict then that forms such as "John's pen" would be very easy: substitute the *-'s* for *no.* However, the Japanese *no* has three possible meanings. *John no hon* could mean John's book – a

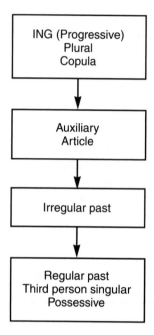

Figure 12.1   Acquisition order (from Krashen, 1977, p. 149; used with permission)

book that belongs to John, a book which was written by John, *and* a book that was written about John. The following examples show the form is not the same in the two languages:

Japanese	*Direct translation*	*English*
Yakyuu no hon	baseball's book	book about baseball
Yakyuu no senshu	baseball's player	baseball player
Minami no kuni	south's country	country in the south
Kokyo no omoide	hometown's memory	hometown memories
Ki no tsukue	wood's desk	wooden desk

In addition, Japanese has a structure *no mono* which is equivalent to the shortened form *no*. In answer to "Whose book is this?" (*Korewa dare no hon desu-ka?*), the answer would be *John no (mono) desu* ("It's John's"). Because the possessive *-'s* initially seems so similar to these Japanese structures, we can almost predict what might happen. Kuwahata's EFL learners used the possessive for the "about" meaning, transfering all the uses of the Japanese form to English. And they overused the possessive *-'s*.

Q: Is she beautiful?
A: I don't know. It depend on the *people's likeness*.

I cook *apple's pie* now.
The biggest *bed's pillow* was so big.
. . . became as *golf's good player.*
. . . dropped three *watermelon's seed.*

The students had close to perfect scores (98 percent correct) when a -'*s* form should be used, but low scores when a N *of* N was required. The result of such oversuppliance of the -'*s* is to lower the scores for the possessive (but not low enough to make it fit into the box hypothesized as the natural order). Conversely, students from other language groups may undersupply the -'*s* form. If we look only at scores, much of this information is lost.

Practice 12.2

1. If you want to use a Wug test for your own purposes, you might wish to compare the non–English-language versions mentioned in this section and those of Perez-Pereira (1989) for Spanish and Bogoyaulenskiy (1973) for Russian. What are the strengths and weaknesses of these tests for your research goals?

2. If you know Japanese, supply the direct Japanese translation of these forms produced by Kuwahata's students: guitar's school, paper's back, mountain's top, everybody's behind, college's circle, class's time. Then supply the correct English form.

3. Koike's (1983) study of three children, ages 5, 7, and 10, provides examples of both errors and correct forms for English possessives. Would L1 transfer help explain the variation in correct and incorrect forms or might other explanations be required?

   a. She's name is Lisa.
   b. Drink the lemon's juice.
   c. . . . with the tree's blossom.
   d. New York's Kennedy Airport.
   e. Washington zoo is bigger than Tokyo's zoo.

4. As you read ESL or EFL compositions, make a list of inflectional errors. Are there common patterns? Select the paper that has the most errors for any one morpheme. Calculate the percent of correct use for that morpheme in the composition. If the percent is above 80%, do you believe the errors are due to carelessness or is there some discernible explanation for whatever variability you find?

5. Shapira's (1978) friend Zoila used -*ing* forms and the base forms of verbs almost exclusively:

I no liking snow.
I no liking he liking many girl.
My family needing money.

Native English speakers talking with Zoila also adopted her -*ing* forms. Clyne (1981), too, gives examples of native speakers of English using the same -*ing* forms used by their grandmother, a native speaker of Greek:

You knowing how make baklava?
You makin' pita?
You wantin' one?
What you goin' doing?

These people did not use these forms when speaking with their grandfather. Do you think the primacy of -*ing* in their talk must be due to the saliency and frequency of these forms in the learners' talk? Or, do you think the matching is a way of showing affection and social bonding?

Errors in inflections and derivations

If you ask a native speaker to judge the seriousness of errors in morphology, they will always judge individual inflectional errors more negatively than derivational errors. Perhaps this is because we have been taught to avoid "grammar errors" at all costs. We may be thought careless or uneducated if we say, "I seen that signature on the letter," but such errors as "I saw that signaturing on the letter" may very well go unnoticed. If a native speaker says, "It was a jubilous day," it sounds charming, but if someone says, "it a grey day," it does not. These values are instilled, in part, by our educational system. There is nothing in the language system itself that says one type of error is more important than another.

Practice 12.3

1. The following composition was written by a Vietnamese student of English. Find five errors that relate to morphology. Which are more lexical and which are more grammatical in nature? Which errors seem to affect intelligibility most?

Traffic in LA

In order to solve the blocking traffic on the freeway and the air pollution problem on Los Angeles, the government suggest that each car on freeway is better carpooling. It means three or more people in a car. It will decrease the number of cars which transport in the freeway. Therefore, it will decrease the air pollution which make by the exhaust of the car and the traffic will not also slow down. If the people in Los Angeles don't decrease the number of cars which traffic in free way, they will easy get a lung congestion instead of traffic congestion.

2. Circle all the inflectional morphemes in the following composition written by an international student, a computer science major. What proportion are correct? Circle all the derivational morphemes and note what proportion are correct. Are derivational or inflectional morphemes more frequent in this composition?

Artificail Inteligient

Since computer invented, science and technology have made amaziny progress. At the beginning, people only used computer to do complicate scientifical calculation that might take human years of work. Now, not only in science and industry fields that use computer robit to replace the man power, but in supermarket they use computer detective device to fast the check out process.

The scope that interest me most is computer graphic; some people call it computer aided design or animation. It was really a exciting experience when I first time watch a video type that recorded the design of a stadium in Chicago. With a music as background we saw the stadium from every angle as we were in a halicap. It helps architect to view the result of his project before it actually builds, thus he can modivication or change it.

Some people are start to study how to make computer think as a human. Maybe someday the professor that stands at the front of the board to answer your question will not be a human being anymore but a inteligent computer.

3. Correct only the derivational morphology in the following data to make one data set. Then correct only the inflection morphology to form a second set. Ask native speakers to rate the seriousness of the errors in the data (each native speaker receives only one set). How comparable are the ratings for the two types of morphemes?

   a. She weared it on and I choosed it.
   b. I will try to conversate and speak when it is necessary.
   c. I cooking a kind of Iranian delicious last week.

  d. They try to get more children; they help the family in their aging.
  e. There is no retired income.
  f. She should never look at a foreign.
     She should be restricted only for husband.
  g. It is used communication means between others generations and the people who are remoted location.
  h. The problem that made me suffer was no satified sentence to express my thought.
  i. We have start to trade with the other countrys.
  j. From then we import the Western educational institutionals.

(Sources: A. Johns, V. Wenzell, A. Lazaraton)

Morphophonemic change

When morphemes are joined to the word base, it is quite common for changes to take place that make the new word easier to pronounce. These are called *morphophonemic* changes. The change may occur in the base or in the affix. We have already seen two examples of this phenomenon. The past tense morpheme -*ed* has three different forms: a voiceless /t/, a voiced /d/ and a syllabic /ɪd/, and the plural -*s* has three different pronunciations: a voiceless /s/, a voiced /z/ and a syllabic /əz/. In these examples, the consonant of the affix takes on the voiced or voiceless characteristics of the preceding sound in the stem. If the word stem ends in the same or similar sound, a syllabic form is used. These are examples of assimilation, a very common process in normal speech.

Three major different types of morphophonemic change – assimilation, contraction, and metathesis – occur in most languages. In assimilation, the sounds of the morpheme and of the base are changed to make them more similar to each other. Look at the following data:

illegal	immodest	irrelevant	inadmissible
illiterate	impossible	irreversible	inept
illogical	immoral	irresponsible	inequitable

If you look at the last column, you will see that the negative prefix has the form *in-*; it does not change to agree with the following vowel. In the other cases, however, the nasal *n* is pronounced at the same articulation point as the following consonant. If you observe carefully how you articulate the *in* of *inconceivable, incapable, ingratitude,* you will feel your tongue move back to the position of the velar consonants too. In the case of liquids, *l* and *r,* the quality changes from a nasal to agree with the following liquid.

Given that we have different pronunciations for this negative prefix, how can we say that it has one form with the same meaning? The key is being able to assign one form as the basic form and working out a rule that predicts what the variants of the morpheme would be. In this case, the general form is *in-* and the other forms can be predicted as assimilation to the articulation point of the following sound (and the additional change to liquid for *l* and *r*).

As affixes are added to form new words, contraction or dropping of parts of morphemes may occur. For example, in English we join *can* and *not* and drop the second vowel to yield *can't*. Contraction is also a common type of morphophonemic change. Metathesis is much less common in languages. In English, young children often say /puskɛti/ or /buskɛti/ for *spaghetti*. The consonant + vowel opening sequence, *pu-* and *bu-*, is much easier for them than the *sp* cluster. This change in order of elements is called metathesis.

Practice 12.4

1. Explain the morphophonemic rule for the three variants of *-ed* past tense morpheme.
2. Explain the morphophonemic rules for the three variants of the plural morpheme *-s*. Does this same rule apply to possessives and third person, singular present tense *-s?* How do you form the plural possessives (the Jones' house or the Joneses' house)?
3. Arabic places an article *el* before nouns. While it is always written as *il*, its pronunciation varies. Explain the morphophonemic change involved in the following examples:

il beet	the house	il gidiid	the new
il walad	the boy	il kitaab	the book
il mudarris	the teacher	il wara'	the paper
it tarabeeza	the table	it talg	the ice
id dars	the lesson	is sana	the year
in nuur	the light	iz zaayir	the visitor
ir raagil	the man	iš šanta	the briefcase
il filuus	the money	iš šimaal	the left

4. In French, contraction is especially interesting in terms of masculine and feminine adjectives:

Feminine	Masculine	Gloss
/šod/	/šo/	hot
/freš/	/fre/	fresh
/frwad/	/frwa/	cold
/movɛz/	/move/	bad
/ptit/	/pti/	little
/sul/	/su/	drunk

If you were given a French feminine adjective, how might you derive the masculine form? Given the masculine form of any adjective, could you derive the feminine form? Which is the base form?

Research and application

1. In the early stages of language learning, many learners do not use inflectional morphology, or they use one form to serve many purposes (e.g., use -*ing* or the base form for all verbs). This telegraphic form of talk has often been compared to that of agrammatic aphasics. Menn and Obler (1990) have edited a book with agrammatic aphasic data samples from fourteen different languages (with morphemic translations and English transliterations). If you teach or are studying one of these languages, consult the data to see how similar your language or that of your students matches that of these patients. (We are not saying that language learning and language disabilities are the same, only that the problems in producing or retrieving morphemes during performance in one area may shed light on similar problems in another.)

2. Results similar to those of Antinucci and Miller (1976) regarding the primacy of aspect have been reported by Ferreiro and Sinclair (1971) and Bloom et al. (1980). This claim, however, has been questioned by Weist (1986), Weist et al. (1984) and Shirai (1990b, 1993). Read and critique these papers. Is the primacy of aspect claim valid? Do you believe it also applies to the learning of other languages by children and adults?

3. Pfaff (1981) reports on the acquisition of many different inflectional morphemes and syntactic forms by German second language learners. The data for this study were elicited in individual interviews with fifty-seven children in three age groups (5–6, 9–11, 12–15). Included in this sample were speakers of Turkish, Greek, Yugoslavian, Lebanese, and American English. Features analyzed included Ø subject, gender, number, Ø article, indirect

object, Ø copula, Ø auxiliary, agreement, verb forms, negation, prepositions, Ø prepositions, Ø conjunctions, conjunction, inversion, noninversion, infinitive last, participle last, and subordinate clauses. If you are learning or if you teach German, compare the forms used by these children with those produced by adult foreign language learners.

4. Chimombo (1979) found that the order of acquisition of English morphemes for Tina, a Chichewa-English bilingual child, did not correlate with those of Brown (1973) for L1 children nor with those of Hakuta's (1974) Japanese-English child. The acquisition order obtained from the child (between 18½ months and 30½ months) also does not strictly agree with Krashen's proposal (Figure 12.1). Review the explanations Chimombo gives for this variation in acquisition order. Could one review all the morpheme acquisition studies with a bias toward difference rather than universality in orders and arrive at very different conclusions from all the studies? What languages (L1 and L2) would you want to include in order to be able to make claims for or against universality in the acquisition of morphology?

5. One criticism of the morpheme acquisition studies is that there is no clear explanation for differences in the speed of acquisition of different types of morphemes. Researchers hypothesize that input, the L1, the number of forms for each morpheme, and degree of transparency of the semantic function of morphemes, and so forth, explain the findings. Connectionist studies (Gasser, 1993; Gasser and Lee, 1991) take a different approach. Instead of collecting acquisition data from child learners, they collect data from the computer as it attempts to sense morphology patterns in input data. The computer, like humans, does not learn all forms (prefixes, infixes, suffixes, reduplication) at the same rate. If the learning patterns of computers are similar to those of second language learners, how might this new approach be used to test the hypotheses that have been proposed thus far to explain differences in acquisition?

Part IV   Vocabulary choice and discourse use

13 Variation in vocabulary choice

The lexicon is a system that we construct collectively as a social, linguistic group. We then endlessly unmake and remake it in an effort to express our individuality. Shuy (1967) is surely not the first to note that lexical choices can tell us much about a person's age (ice box vs. refrigerator), gender (lovely vs. nice), geographic origin (pail vs. bucket), education (we was vs. we were), and occupation (lexemes vs. words). We will begin this chapter with a discussion of how lexical choice reveals age, gender, occupation, and cultural and regional origin. Then we will look at the ways groups and individuals show their preferences and biases through word selection and euphemism, followed by lexical choice that relates to discourse and formality.

Geography

Linguistic fieldworkers have gathered much information on geographic variation by interviewing people from many different social groups in many different areas of the United States. The results were first compiled in *The Linguistic Atlas* (Kurath, 1939–1943). The checklist used by fieldworkers asks for the word which the person customarily uses for the defined object. Do you, for example, say *lightning bug, glow worm, firefly,* or *fire bug? Soft drink, soda, pop,* or *tonic? Sweet corn* or *roasting ears? Spider webs* or *cobwebs? Scared* or *afraid?* These choices depend in part on your geographic location. If you live in the northeast part of the United States, you are more likely to say *pail* than *bucket.* In the midwest and the South, more people use *bucket* (though *pail* is used by many urbanites living in the *bucket* area).

One area of dialect geography that is especially important for language teachers is the difference in word use among Australian, Canadian, American, and British English dialects. Among the many differences between American and British dialects are car terms like *bonnet* (hood), and *boot* (trunk), and *windscreen* (windshield), clothing terms like *jumper* (cardigan sweater), and *braces* (suspenders). To cross the street, Americans walk in the crosswalk, whereas British English pays attention to the stripes in the crosswalk and calls it a zebra zone. These differences are easily remembered. Less easy are the differences in word form correspondences such as *maths* and *math*.

Within each of these major dialects, there are, of course, regional variants of interest to linguists and teachers. Bryant (1989) prepared usage maps for variations in such terms as *slide–slippery dip* for a child's playground slide, *blood nose–bleeding nose* for a bloody nose, and *dink–double dink* (giving a passenger a ride on a bike) in Australian English. A report on a larger ongoing Australian study is given in Bryant (1991).

Dialect geography is particularly interesting when the areas analyzed have large immigrant populations. Hans Kurath (1945) and Carroll Reed (1961) worked extensively on regional dialects of Pennsylvania, showing the influence of German loanwords and loan translations on the English of the communities in which it became enmeshed. For example, the words for pancakes in much of the North Midwest area are hot-cakes in the eastern section and flannen/flannel cakes in the west. *Flannen/flannel cakes* is said to be an anglicized form of the German word *Pfannkuchen*. Of course, by now some 40 to 50 years after this research, everyone there may very well say pancakes. With the advent of television, many of these geographic differences may have disappeared.

We know that the names of people vary by geographic area. Certain names are more popular in rural areas than in urban areas. Some are more popular in the Midwest or South than on the East or West Coasts. Some people even name their children after some geographic area (e.g., a child was named Rocky Mountain National Park after his parents' favorite place). Perhaps more upsetting is the imposition of name changes that happened as families emigrated from one geographic area to another. Ellis Island immigration officials, unable or unwilling to understand the names of new citizens, changed the names of many immigrants to something more English-sounding. This also happened as people, unable to learn American Indian names, assigned them new names – often names of American military leaders who had put down Indian uprisings. Because it is common in many American Indian cultures to change one's name to mark important developments in life, the change might not seem strange, but Indian groups solved the problem by using two names, reserving their Indian name for communication within their own social groups.

Another related issue is attrition of first languages in immigrant communities. There are individual case studies, small sample studies, and studies of large immigrant populations that show the gradual shifts in forms and meanings of lexical items as they are influenced or replaced by those of the new language. We would expect the changes to be fairly rapid, especially if the community is small or dispersed and cut off by great distance from the L1 community. We see these changes at the individual level in diary studies; expatriots often comment on not being able to recall words which they once used without hesitation. Group studies show systematic changes as lexical items are attrited. Clyne (1991) comments on the L1 data he obtained from 200 German-speaking and 200 Dutch-speaking immigrants to Australia. Transfer of English lexical items into German regularly occurred in the work domain (*customer, office, college, shoppen, supervisen*) and in social and recreational domains (*beach, breakfast, watchen, relaxen*). Semantic transfer also took place, especially in cognate forms. For example, the English word *small* influenced the use of German (*schmal*) and Dutch (*smal*). English meaning patterns also appear in the immigrants' use of the Dutch word *stil* and the German word *still* (meaning silent) rather than *nog* and *noch* (meaning still).

There are fascinating patterns in L1 use in immigrant groups. Salmons (1991) found that speakers of different dialects of the same language who immigrate and live near each other may use the new language for communication with each other rather than becoming bidialectal. Language shift in such conditions is multifaceted.

Practice 13.1

1. For each of the following sets, circle the word you would ordinarily use. Compare your results with those of your colleagues or students. Can you see areal patterns in these differences? If you know other terms for the items, add them to the list and ask your colleagues if these choices are familiar to them as well. (For a more complete list of terms, see Orton, 1972.)

Household
To put a single room of the house in order: clean up, do up, redd up, ridd up, straighten up, tidy up, put to rights, slick up
Devices at the edges of the roof that carry off rain: eaves, eave spouts, eave troughs, gutters, rain troughs, spouting, spouts, water gutter
Paper container for groceries and so on: bag, poke, sack, toot, tote, tote bag

Foods
A carbonated drink: pop, soda, soda pop, tonic, soft drink
Large sandwich designed to be a meal in itself: hero, submarine, hoagy, grinder, poor-boy
Notice that these sandwiches all use a bread roll as the base. Some people use *skyscraper* or *dagwood* to refer to an oversized sandwich made with loaf-type bread. Do you use these terms too?

Games

Fast moving amusement park ride (on tracks): coaster, roller coaster, rolly-coaster, shoot-the-chutes, the ride of doom

Call to players to return because a new player wants to join: allie allie in free, allie allie oxen free, allie allie ocean free, bee bee bumble bee, everybody in free, newcomer newcomer

School

To be absent from school: bag school, bolt, cook jack, lay out, lie out, play hookey, blow school, play truant, run out of school, skip class, skip school, ditch, flick, flake school, sluff school

Drinking fountain: cooler, water cooler, bubbler, fountain, drinking fountain

Miscellaneous

Somone who will not change his or her mind is: bull headed, contrary, headstrong, ornery, otsny, owly, pig headed, set, sot, stubborn, mulish, muley

I _____ you're right: reckon, guess, figger, figure, suspect, imagine

2. When dialect differences involve inflectional morphology, we may be less forthright in saying what we say (rather than what we know to be correct). How might you get native speakers to use the word options shown as choices in the following items? Which do you say? If you sometimes say one and sometimes another, explain how context influences your choice.

   a. It (don't, doesn't) matter.
   b. They (dived, dove) (right) in.
   c. My sweater (shrank, shrunk) in the dryer.
   d. Saturday I (laid, lay) in bed all day.
   e. You (hadn't ought, ought not) to do that.
   f. Seems (like, as if) we'll never get any rain.
   g. (Like, As) I told you, I feel the same (like, as) my mom.

3. Supply the American English equivalent of the following British English words:

biscuit	chemist	tap	queue up
chips	cotton wool	tramp	roundabout
draughts	dustbin	cinema	sweet
gangway	pub	flyover	crisps

4. Give the British English equivalent of the following American English words:

baby carriage	mailman	gasoline	billion
raise (in salary)	flashlight	first floor	truck
second floor	two weeks	to mail	janitor

5. Moskowitz (1990) notes that a drinking straw is called a *popote* in Mexico City, a *pitillo* in Colombia, a *sorbete* in Ecuador, and a *caña* in Panama. Traveling in Latin America, you may find differences in the use of the word *claro,* usually said with an inbreath. In most places it functions much like the English "um-hm" or "right." That is, it is a feedback signal to let the speaker know you're listening without taking away the turn to talk. However, in Mexico, the meaning changes from "right" to something like "of course, you idiot!" From these examples and your own experience, how important do you think regional variants are for language learners? Are such regional variations covered in your teaching/learning materials?

6. Peters and Fee (1989) used Australian and Canadian magazines as a database to see the balance of British and U.S. terms such as *film/movie.* Prepare a plan to examine the use of these and other sets of terms in English magazines in another dialect region (e.g., Indian English, Egyptian English).

7. Salmons (1991) used a questionnaire approach, asking immigrants to translate fifteen English sentences into German. Free conversation on linguistic topics also formed part of the database. Variations in forty lexical items were found across the various dialect groups in his immigrant study area (Dubois County, Indiana). Compare this data collection method with the direct questionnaire method used to obtain data for the *Dialect Atlas of American English.* How might the methods be combined to obtain richer data?

8. Moskowitz (1990) developed the "box of office supplies" method to look at areal differences in language use. The box contained items including crayons, chalk, business cards, a hole punch, thumbtacks, an ink pad, and rubber bands. High school graduates in different areas were asked to name the objects. Variation was found in the use of the terms. Design a similar project to investigate geographic differences in use of terms you find interesting.

9. Are regional variants presented in your language teaching materials? Are there differences in treatment in materials for second language versus foreign language learners?

Gender

A great deal has been written about sexist terms that men and women use to refer to each other. Women have noted that there have been few parallel male words to the pejorative terms for women (chick, doll, dame, babe, skirt, and broad, to name but a few). Is this changing (jock, hunk, stud, and perhaps suit and three-piece are equivalents to skirt)? Violent terms are often used in describing women (e.g., smashing, stunning, ripping, cracking) and more rarely to describe men. The terms we use to refer to people in our writing have also come under much scrutiny as we try to make our language less sexist in nature. Although many people believe that these attempts to legislate equality through language are ludicrous, they have had some effect as seen in the response of a 7-year-old girl when she was asked one of the fundamental questions about our future, "Can man survive?" She replied, "I don't know about him, but we're working on it in Brownies."

Nilsen (1972) talks about several sexist areas of the English lexicon. Eponyms (words derived from names of people) are almost all male names. The few exceptions are those that refer to the body or to clothes (bloomer, Mae West jacket). Male and female terms reflect sexist attitudes (bachelor vs. old maid, tailor vs. seamstress). Unless they are rebels or crusaders, women are often referred to in terms of their relation to men (Mrs. John Brown, sister of). Interestingly, girls can have boys' names (Jo, Teri, Toni, Pat) but the reverse seldom happens.

Claims have been made that women and men use different words. For example, women are much more likely than men to use specific color terms like *ecru, lavender,* and *beige.* Women use *let's* more often than men to encourage cooperative action, whereas men use more direct demands. In many differences it is not clear whether the choices should be attributed to a difference in status and power or to differences in the gender of the speakers.

In some languages, the choice of terms differs much more according to the gender of the speaker. For example, in some languages men are expected to learn to use different forms of words once they reach puberty. In some languages (see Dixon's descriptions of the Dyirbal language of Australia), there are special terms that are to be used when addressing one's mother-in-law. Haviland (1979) writes about special lexical choices used in Yimidhur when addressing the parents and brothers of one's wife.

It is not difficult to understand why particular terms are used in such cases, but in other languages the choice of terms does not seem to have any special function (aside from social bonding). They have evolved through custom. There is nothing special about such terms as *pretty* or *handsome* that would account for our choice of one over the other in describing a female or male.

Practice 13.2

1. Although it is popular to talk about sexist terms, we seldom think about terms that show our views of the elderly. For each of the following pejorative terms that refer to older women, supply an endearing (or trivializing) animal term for a young woman: old bat, old biddy, battle-ax, henpeck, catty. What is an oldie, geezer, old fogey? How many positive terms can you think of that refer to older men or women? Have you noticed that we talk about "grand-fatherly advice" but we sometimes call the advice of grand-mothers "old wives' tales"? A recent newspaper column talked about a hospital as helping people of all ages, "children, adolescents, adults, and geriatrics." Is *geriatrics* an age term? If so, can we call young children pediatrics?

2. In another language of your choice, list terms for older women and men. Are they similar to the English terms from item 1? Compare your results to those of your colleagues. In which languages have you found the most positive terms for the elderly and in which have you found more negative terms?

3. The terms that we use to talk about men and women are, in a sense, linked to metaphor. We talk about peoples as objects (old battle-ax), as food (dish, peach, tomato, sugar), as animals (cat, chick, stag, fox). Note that most of the examples given here are for women. How many examples can you think of for men that fit into these categories and how do these link to the metaphors discussed in Chapter 4?

4. Kramerae (1981), Thorne and Henley (1975), Berryman and Eman (1980), and *Locating Power: Proceedings of the 1992 Berkeley Women and Language Conference* are good sources to begin researching how women and men speak and differences in the ways we speak about women and men. Tannen (1990) contains useful summaries of research on the differences in language of men and women

(and of boys and girls). Scan these sources and report an interesting finding to your class. Should this piece of information be presented to a language class? If so, when might it best be presented?

5. Visitors to the United States are sometimes surprised to hear themselves referred to as "you guys" regardless of whether they are male or female. During closing remarks at the TESOL Summer Institute, we told students, "We love you guys, we'll miss you guys." Afterward, students asked if this was correct English. Is "you guys" a typical informal "you all" for all areas of the English-speaking world? Why do you suppose "you gals" is not much used even in colloquial, informal exchanges?

6. Lexical choices of men and women in academic and technical writing are supposedly very similar. Collect a set of essays written on academic topics by your students (or your classmates). Compare the lexical choices made by males and females. Do your findings show academic writing as more standardized in this regard?

7. How important is it to teach or to learn the differences in lexical choice typical of men and women? Give examples to justify your answer. If this topic interests you, examine your language textbooks to determine whether differences are made explicit. You might also want to read Hartman and Judd (1978) for a review of ESL texts to assess the images of women and men presented to students.

Age

We have already talked about the ways in which meanings of words change and shift over time. Even within a generation, we see many differences in the ways that particular lexical items are used. In the 1940s and 1950s, people were *square, in the groove,* or *keen.* The 1960s terms were *groovy* and *cool.* In the 1980s and early 1990s teenagers used the terms *rad, awesome,* and *totally.* (*Totally* was only used ironically perhaps because it was used primarily by teenage girls, not boys. *Totally tubular,* however, seems to be used by both. Is *tubular,* meaning good, related to the old fear of being *square,* which was definitely not good?) Current slang has probably changed again. Every few years, it becomes important to separate ourselves from each other, and one way of doing that is through lexical choice. In the 1960s, teenagers were quite irate if their parents said *groovy,* and today they feel the same way when their parents say something is *down* (meaning *great*) or *bad* (meaning *good*). If you are not a member of the group, such words are not appropriate choices. By using them, you are trying to claim membership in that social group.

Much of slang is limited to words of evaluation (e.g., cool, keen, awesome), words that refer to people in an evaluative ways (e.g., nerd, square), or to school life (e.g., names of classes and dorms). The lexical choice of people of different ages is not limited to such terms. One generation talks about women friends as ladies, and the next talks about them as women. One generation invites friends over for coffee (which includes all sorts of cookies, cakes, and sandwiches), and the next asks friends to stop by or drop by (and they'll be lucky to get much of anything to eat!). Members of one generation may still call the frig an icebox, though it now has an icemaker rather than a block of ice in it. The record player may still be called a record player even though it now plays only CDs.

Like the various terms for pancakes in areas of Pennsylvania that had been influenced by German, other food terms are also markers of both differences in age and geographic area. N. Bruce says that her mother and grandmother used the terms flapjacks, griddle cakes, and johnny cakes (made with corn meal). Journeys cake were johnny cakes taken to school in a lunchpail for school lunch. These members of the older generation also use *commence* (for *begin* in such phrases as "commence to dance," "commence to clean up the room." Commence now seems much too formal a term to be used in this way.

If we look back over time, written records show that lexical choice and collocations differ from generation to generation. Here are some example sentences taken from *Ho for California! Women's Overland Diaries* (Myres, 1980).

1. Laid by on account of Mrs. C. being sick.
2. All well this morning and fixing to move on.
3. The oxen would hardly any of them drink the water.
4. We walked back to our wagons and was ready for starting when the balance came up.
5. Some of the teams came near upsetting the wagons.
6. We got 28 head of cattle drowned in the Hondo and we came very near getting some of our oxen drowned. One wagon slid down and came very near going into the creek.

But nowadays cultural change seems even more rapid, and this is reflected in our vocabulary choice. Every few years, a newspaper or magazine will run a column headed something like "Were you born before 1945?" followed by a list of changes that have taken place after the selected date. For example, there was no TV, no frozen food, no contact lenses, and no contraceptive pill. It was a time before credit cards, laser beams, and ball-point pens. In the United States, pizza, McDonald's, and instant coffee were unheard of. It was before day care centers, group therapy, fax machines, artificial hearts, and personal computers. Cigarette smoking was fashionable then, grass was mowed, pot was something you cooked in, rock music was grandma's lullaby, and nobody had walked on the moon. These are new for people born before 1945, so the vocabulary has changed in a very short time. Some people think this is why we suffer a generation gap every few years!

Practice 13.3

1. Do you suppose that your parents or grandparents ever talked about *parenting?* Will the term be used by your children when they are adults? List examples of words that you use or your parents or grandparents use that mark you as being of different generations. Why do you suppose these particular words and not others have changed?
2. Lederer's (1985) *Colonial American English* lists words and phrases of the 1600s and 1700s. Which words or phrases do you wish were still used in American English (and why)?
3. The slang of various occupational or recreational groups helps to make the group cohesive and it also varies across generations. Current motorcycle racers have special words that might be meaningless to nonracers and even to racers of another era if it were not for context. For example the expression *under the paint* means to get as close to the motorcycle as possible to reduce wind resistance, as in "Get under the paint when you take those curves." A few years ago a racer might have said "tuck in." Most people would recognize the word *bite* to talk about tire traction, but in motorcycle circles they may say *hook up* as in "It was hooking up real good until the rear tire slid out." *Traffic* is a very common word but it is currently used by speed fanatics to refer to slow motorcycles, as in "I was making time until they got me going through traffic." Select a special field and research the current slang. Ask the people who use the terms to tell you why they use these particular words rather than some of the older equivalents. If you and your colleagues obtain interesting findings, consider sharing them at the next WHIM conference or in an article for *Language in Society.*
4. The use of *real* and *really* have also varied over time. Both seem to be used as substitutes for *very,* as in "a real good

      time, he's really helpful." Still, we know that "he's really
      bad" and "he's real bad" do not mean the same thing. Col-
      lect examples of *real, really, very,* and, perhaps, *truly, gen-*
      uinely. What do your findings show about age differences
      in the use and meanings of these words?

  5. In Chapter 1 we talked about the use of *less* versus *fewer*
      with mass and count nouns (e.g., "less noise" and "fewer
      cars"). However, people often use *less* with count nouns.
      In a radio interview, a speaker talked about the decline in
      the number of art galleries, saying there are "less gal-
      leries" now than five years ago. We are also all familiar
      with supermarket checkout line signs reading "10 items or
      less." Do you think the language is changing so that *less*
      will replace *fewer*? If native speakers use *less* for *fewer*,
      should we still be concerned if language learners do not
      distinguish between the forms? Justify your answer.

Occupation

Special lexical items appear in most professions, and every field has special vocabulary to cover abstract concepts. For example, we have talked about morphology in ways that a biologist, whose field also uses this word, would find puzzling. Linguists use many terms also used by mathematicians (beta, parameters) in ways that no mathematician would recognize.

Danet (1985) lists some of the major lexical differences in legalese. Some are technical terms (real property, forfeiture), some are terms that have different meanings from those usually used (assignment, title), and some are archaic (herein, thereof, aforesaid). Legal writing also uses doublets ("cease and desist") and is more formal in register ("shall include," "does hereby convey," "assign and appoint").

The writings in many fields can be identified (even if one only sees a fragment of the writing) by such lexical choices. In some fields there are special dictionaries to help novices learn the special vocabulary. Mellinkoff (1991), for example, published a special legal dictionary that presents legal concepts in easily understood English. Sarčevič (1989) claims that legal concepts are bound to a particular national legal system and culture. French legal systems differ from Islamic law and from English law, so terms are not easily translated. For example, the French word *dettes* refers to both paid or unpaid debts, quite different from English *debts.* Sarčevič argues that specialist dictionaries for bilinguals should be based on conceptual analysis.

Terms within a field change over time as new terms become more fashionable. For example, in language acquisition, we used to talk about whether a child was prepared (or ready) to learn something in terms of having acquired a foundation for the next step in the learning process. When Vygotsky's ideas about education became well known, this next step became the *zone of proximal development*. When Krashen re-introduced the concept, it became *i plus one*. In composition teaching, we used to talk about an author's point of view but now we talk about it as *stance*. The jargon of fields change and if we do not know the current buzz words, we feel left out. We also demonstrate our lack of "currency" in the field.

The jargon of a field allows members to talk about concepts with useful shorthand forms, but it also establishes membership. If you don't know the words, you don't belong. Perhaps this is one reason why our students are often loath to ask us what we mean when we use some term. To admit that they do not know is to place themselves outside the group; they don't belong. For that reason, if no other, we should try to remember what it was like when we first encountered the subject matter that we teach – which words were not clear and need to be defined anew each time we teach a particular course.

Practice 13.4

1. List five words that are part of the jargon of applied linguistics and language education. List any examples from second language acquisition, bilingual education, literacy and reading, phonology and pronunciation, or syntax and grammar. It is possible to feel like an outsider even in our own field. List some of the jargon items that you heard at the last conference. How many of them were useful shorthand forms for you once you realized what they meant? How many were off-putting or unintelligible?

2. Select an introductory text for a university science class. List the special jargon vocabulary that the learner would be expected to acquire. Would you include these items in an ESP (English for Specific Purposes) class for international students? If so, how? If not, why?

3. Ahlswede and Evens (1988) analyzed the vocabulary of medicine, using medical admission reports on stroke victims. They found that Mel'čuk's relational model was very useful in helping to define the technical vocabulary. They list sets of words with the relation (in caps) such as *cerebellum* PART *brain, artery* TAX *blood vessel, aphasia* DYSFUNCT *speech, admission* CONVERSE *release*. They also found lexical phrases such as "doll head ma-

neuver." If you teach English for science, could you organize the technical vocabulary using the relational model? If
so, would these groupings be useful for your students as
well? If you are not sure how useful they would be with
students, how might you research this question?

4. The jargon of a particular field may also change over time
to show membership in either a very select group or to
distinguish the jargon of a field in a particular geographic
area. A computer technician talks about the futility of "wav-
ing a dead chicken." He says this means doing a doomed
repair ritual over a crashed computer system. What other
computerese examples can you add? Why do you suppose there is so much special jargon in this field? In bu-
reaucratic language? In medical language? Which fields
change jargon rapidly? Why?

Education

Literacy also influences the lexical choices available to us. As young
children, we often acquire words without knowing exactly what they
mean or, in some cases, the exact form of the word. Teachers often collect
examples of errors their students make as they begin to use new words.
Greene (1969) assembled many of these in a book called *Pullet Surprises*
(the name comes from a student's composition: "In 1957, Eugene O'Neill
won a pullet surprise"). Collectibles include such gems as, "Neptune is
always pictured with his strident," "The doctor said to take milk of
amnesia," "My dissent is unknown," and the case of the music student
who wrote a paper about "Claude W.C."

The television character Archie Bunker was a master of using big
words inaccurately. Mrs. Malaprop, in Sheridan's play *The Rivals,* has
given us the word *malaprop* for this ability. Here are a few malaprops or
bunkerisms: "I always said those two was right outta Science Friction,"
"You're invading the issue," "That man don't have one regleaming feature," "It's a proven fact that capital punishment is a known detergent to
crime." (Are the words *bunkerisms* and *malaprops* eponyms?)

It is difficult to know whether the mistakes we make in homophones
(words that are pronounced the same but have a different spelling) are
slips or not. Teachers in elementary school are forever pointing out the
difference between *there* and *their,* but many of us still type one when we
mean the other. Copy editors at newspapers allow many of these to slip
through (e.g., in a review of a novel – "his books have also peaked an
interest"; in a recipe – "kneed the bread dough"; in an ad – "have your
hair quaffed in this breezy style"; and in a popular column – "we were

offered a free desert if we weren't served in ten minutes." Public scorn greets such errors (for the latter example, "would you select the Mojave, the Sahara, or what?"); the paper, the writers, and the copy editors get their just desert.

Even when we succeed in learning to use words appropriately, we may still use certain terms in a way that reflects educational level. You may remember your teacher's admonitions and the many exercises you were required to do to distinguish *lie* from *lay* and *set* from *sit*. In addition to many other grammar rules, we were cautioned never to say "he ain't" for "he isn't" and to always use correct participles such as *has gone* rather than *has went*. English teachers prided themselves in banishing these uneducated forms from our writing and talk. Yet, our brothers and their friends continued to say "has went" whenever they were beyond the listening ears of teachers, parents, and sisters. That is, these were hallowed parts of the dialect shared especially by the boys in many areas of the country. For boys, to say "has gone" would be to disown their social group. For girls, correctness seemed more important, so we dutifully produced nondialect forms as soon as we were told that these were, indeed, the forms used by educated speakers of the language.

Practice 13.5

1. If you are a fan of British mysteries, you know that the sleuth Lord Peter Wimsey says *ain't*. Check your dictionary to see whether our English teachers were right when they said "There is no such word!" Why do you suppose different dialects and different social classes use different forms for *isn't*?

2. Many second language learners believe that the distinction between *who* and *whom* is extremely important. Others feel that it may be important in formal, written English but is not used in the spoken language. Others never use *whom*. Trace the change in use of *whom*: at what point did *whom* begin to disappear from the language? How important is it that this form be retained? Editors almost always change *which*'s to *that*'s. What is the "rule" for use of *which* and *that*? How important is it that this convention be followed?

3. The appointment secretary at our doctor's office says, "Whom may I say is calling?" if a caller asks to speak to the doctor. How do you account for such "errors"?

4. How important is it to teach homonyms to international students? Have you found any examples of homonyms in the writing of international students? Collect your own exam-

315

ples of homonym errors. Ask native speakers and language learners to locate the errors in your examples. Are learners more aware of homonyms than native speakers? How might you research this question in more detail?

5. Some of the "pullet surprises" in Greene's book are similar to Archie Bunker's errors, used in place of words that have sound similarities. Supply the correct word for each of the following teenage malaprops:

   a. Every state is permitted to send two centaurs to Congress.
   b. The tycoon raged across the island for two days.
   c. She is surreptitious about black cats.
   d. One nation under God, indivisible, with levity and justice for all.
   e. He drives a red Chivalry.

Group and individual choices

As individuals, each of us takes on a variety of roles. As our roles vary, and as we interact with other people, we change the lexical items we choose. We listen and unconsciously adjust to the language of those around us. When we move from one area of the country to another, we may find that we say *pail* instead of *bucket*. When we talk with people who are not linguists or language educators, we don't use such terms as *morphology* or *parameters*. But more important than that, we negotiate meaning in our interactions, selecting words that fit each interaction so that the outcome is one with which we feel comfortable. The range of choices we have to do that depends, at least to some extent, on our experiences, our reading, and our education.

When biases are shared across a membership group, we scarcely notice that choices have been made. For example, President Clinton was described as the next leader of the nation, our party leader, a demagogue, and a bozo during the 1992 campaign. The choice of term depends on both the setting and on political bias. When a company talks about development, environmentalists may hear it as exploitation. When a candidate talks about his program as time tested, a rival candidate may say it is out of date. Some political candidates see change as progressive, whereas others see it as crackpot extremism.

Biases are also shared in membership groups regarding what words are or are not taboo. Names of body parts are often taboo. It used to be taboo to mention the word *leg* in polite English conversation, even when you only meant the leg of a chicken. When the television commentator Ted Koppel told tennis legend Jimmy Connors that he brought hope "to every old fart in the country," everyone was aghast. In some cultures, it is quite appropriate to talk explicitly about organs involved in illness. In others it is not. In some languages, it is taboo to mention certain people by name. For example, a male Cree speaker, out of respect, does not speak the names of his sisters.

We often create new expressions when old words, while not taboo, might offend someone. For example, we may call a garbage man a sanitation engineer, or worry about a friend's facial blemishes rather than talk about pimples. This week our home improvement store has a sign saying that applications for lot engineers are being accepted. One hardly needs a degree in engineering to help people load and unload carts in a parking lot! Euphemisms are common in sales. A salesperson for carpet cleaning said he got more business if he told prospective customers that their carpets were heavily soiled. If he told them that their rugs were dirty, he almost always lost the sale. *Consumer's Guide* suggests that people wanting to sell their houses should call them *homes* and that they should list lots for sale as *home sites*.

Emotional reactions to words can be individual rather than societal. All of us are irritated by certain expressions. Sometimes that irritation is shared by others (as in the case of *badly*) and sometimes it is not. We may hate to hear people say *orientate* rather than *orient* or *summarization* rather than *summary*. We may dislike the word *reduplication* when *duplication* seems adequate. These may drive us crazy while we take special delight in finding duplications that use two languages (the Los Angeles Angels, La Brea Tar Pits, beautiful Hermosa Beach, the beach at Playa del Rey, La Puente bridge, or even pizza pie). And redundant phrases such as "the reason why is because" may also be a favorite part of our lexicon.

The popular writer Edwin Newman (1978) dislikes redundancy. Why, he asks, would something unique need to be singularly unique. He quotes President Carter as having said that a decision on a meeting time had to be made jointly by Russians and Americans. For Carter, this was a "mutual decision between us." Newman also dislikes collocations that conflict. These are called *oxymorons*. He cites a weatherman who is fond of saying the temperature will "gradually plummet."

Newman isn't alone in his concern with popular word choice. Rosen (1977), writing about "psychobabble," is especially insulted by the use of the word *freak* to mean a commitment or highly developed interest (as in Jesus freak, music freak, or computer freak). He objects that this is akin to calling a career one's chosen perversion or stimulant.

Many writers see euphemisms ("telling it like it isn't") as not only ludicrous but sinister. They see such phrases as *cost overruns* or *junior executive* as worse than misleading. They believe euphemisms show a fear to speak straight out or an effort to hide something. Although many of us

317

use such forms out of consideration for the feelings of others, others see it as the corrosion of society. The campaign against euphemism is similar to that waged against clichés in the past. Cliches, it was claimed, covered up the fact that we had nothing to say. We should strive to find words that will convey our meanings clearly and concisely. Our word choice should, as Newman says, be "eloquent where possible, playful where possible, and personal so that we do not all sound alike." Our individual lexical choices allow us to do that.

Practice 13.6

1. In another language, find out whether it is appropriate to talk about specific body parts when discussing illnesses. There are a number of guides to dangerous or taboo terms in languages; see, for example, Claire's (1980) *A Foreign Student's Guide to Dangerous English.* How helpful are such guides for learners? Does one exist for the language you used for this item?

2. J. Mitford, author of *The American Way of Death,* and E. Waugh, *The Loved One,* give a variety of euphemisms associated with death. Identify the meanings of these terms: the loved one, the bereaved, memorial park, before-need provision, funeral home. Would you include euphemism as a word-building process? Justify your answer.

3. The word *politician* can be elevated to *statesman.* Give an elevated word for each of the following terms: haggle, snoop, cheap (person), wasteful (person).

4. *Time-tested* can be downgraded to *out of style.* Give a downgraded word for each of the following terms: progressive, chic, meticulous, leader of the nation. A TV commercial for Cadillac cars mentions leather seating areas and gold ornamentation. What is the neutral term for each? How could the neutral term be downgraded? As you listen to a commercial, jot down the upgraded and downgraded terms. How might each influence a potential customer?

5. In space exploration jargon, failures are called partial successes, errors are malfunctions. When experiments fail, it is said that "the quality of results are expected to be downgraded." The names of space craft (*Jupiter, Saturn*) not only suggest space but also god-like infallability. Military jargon also assigns names such as Desert Storm to military operations. What difference would it make if we called the space craft by less "powerful" or "lucky" names? What similar terms can you find in science and govern-

ment? Are these same terms used presenting the news about these items in other languages?

6. Allen and Burridge (1991) note that we should research when and by whom euphemisms are *not* used. Select two euphemisms and determine when you would and would not use them. Check your intuitions against the responses of five other native or nonnative speakers.

Formality

The title of Joos's (1961) *Five Clocks* comes from a joke told about the Ballyhough railway station which had two clocks which disagreed by some six minutes. When a helpful traveler pointed this out to a porter, he replied, "Faith, sir, if they was to tell the same time, why would we be having two of them?" Joos decided that we have more than two choices in language. He identified five styles, five "clocks": frozen, formal, consultative, casual, and intimate. We use the consultative style in talking with strangers. In such discourse, we do not expect that all information is shared, so background information must be supplied and vocabulary is more carefully chosen. We use the casual style with friends and acquaintances who share more information with us. When we use this style to address a stranger, we signal that the person is like a friend or acquaintance. Intimate style is the language of intimate friends and the language within the family. Formal style detaches the speaker from the hearer, and frozen style, according to Joos, is the register used in print or declamation.

In Los Angeles, it is common to use *casual* style with strangers. In other parts of the country, *consultative* style is more normally used with strangers. Newcomers who move from one area to another often react quite negatively to the shift in registers. For example, a friend who moved from Los Angeles to Rochester, New York, at first thought everyone was very unfriendly. As a linguist, however, he began to notice that it was not unfriendliness but that everyone used a more formal register (while he was still using a casual style).

Beyond Joos's five levels of style, translation specialists identify much finer levels by trying to match the degree of formality, language simplicity or complexity, and emotional tone. Newmark (1988) trains translators to become sensitive to eight levels of formality:

Level	Example
Officialese	The consumption of any nutrients whatsoever is categorically prohibited in this establishment.
Official	The consumption of nutrients is prohibited in this establishment.

319

Formal	You are requested not to consume food in this establishment.
Neutral	Eating is not allowed here.
Informal	Please don't eat here.
Colloquial	You can't feed your face here.
Slang	Lay off the nosh!
Taboo	Lay off the f——— nosh.

(Newmark, 1988, p. 14)

He also expects translators to match the simplicity or complexity of the original passage in the translation. This scale has six levels: simple, popular, neutral, educated, technical, and opaque technical. Newmark's sentence for the simple level is "The floor of the sea is covered with rows of big mountains and deep pits." This sentence on the popular level is "The floor of the sea is covered with great mountain chains and deep trenches."

The third scale is emotional tone and has four levels: intense, warm, cool or factual, and cold understatement. Intense tone exhibits profuse use of intensifiers (absolutely wonderful, enormously successful). Warm tone is exemplified by such terms as *gentle, soft, heart-warming melodies.* Cool or factual tone is shown in such terms as *significant, personable,* and *considerable.* An example of cold understatement is *not undignified.* Newmark believes that a good translator will be able to match the original and the translation on each of these register or style scales.

Many linguists prefer to talk about style and formality in terms of the differences between oral and written language. If we choose the same words and phrases in speaking as we do in writing, we sound stuffy, pompous, opinionated, or preachy. This is because much of meaning is negotiated in face-to-face interaction. When we do not negotiate the interaction, we sound like someone giving a lecture. On the other hand, if we use the lexical choices for speech in written work, readers often feel the choices are inappropriate.

A second way to examine lexical choice is the unplanned-planned dichotomy. That is, the writing in journals or diaries is likely to share characteristics with talk, and a formal oral presentation in front of an audience shares the characteristics of written language. The difference is in the amount of planning and revision we do rather than in a strict talk-versus-writing dichotomy. Written or planned language has special characteristics, as does the language of spontaneous talk and unrevised, unplanned writing. In spontaneous talk, words and phrases are repeated, and words seem to touch off the use of words having similar sound sequences. In the following two examples, a client is talking to a psychologist on a radio call-in show.

Example A
C: CL nn I find this is a *w*onderful *w*ay to keep your *w*eight down.

320

Example B
C: You-you should be *n*ominated for the Nobel *P*eace *P*rize + you're so *m*arvelous + you cause *m*ore peace in *p*eople's lives than + any *p*erson I'*m* sure.

In written text, we try to use parallelism while avoiding too much repetition or too many sound touch-offs. In polishing text, we avoid repetition, searching for appropriate synonyms. The problem is to find synonyms that are appropriate, that match the level of formality of the text. This is a problem for both technical writers and journalists. For example, in writing columns about current issues, reporters cannot continually use the word *issues*. Rather, they must alternate it with *problems, concerns, difficulties,* and so forth. They cannot select a synonym from an informal register such as *bummer* or *screw-up*. When teaching writing to young children, we continually ask them to supply appropriate synonyms in revising their writing. The importance of working on synonyms for text purposes, however, seems to be a forgotten skill in most second and foreign language teaching.

We have noted in several chapters that synonyms are difficult for learners because each synonym may have different collocations. These collocations are confounded or nested within differences in style and formality. In turn, the style or formality is determined by the script within which we are communicating. To illustrate this overlap, consider Palmer's (1976) five types of synonym relations, each of which might contribute to problems in language learning. Palmer calls differences in formality the register relation. He shows this with examples such as *'orrible stink, nasty smell,* and *obnoxious effluvium.* Collocation relations also contribute to difficulty. His examples for *spoiled* are *rancid,* which collocates with *butter,* and *addled,* which collocates with *eggs.* Palmer's third synonym relation, connotation, is seen in examples like *thrifty* and *stingy.* Palmer's fourth category, synonyms that vary across dialects (*autumn* versus *fall*), may also be confusing for learners. The fifth category consists of partial synonyms like *promise* and *pledge.*

Although it is possible to categorize synonyms in this way, both the situation and the people with whom we interact in the situation set the types of collocations, types of connotations, dialect forms, and choices among partial synonyms. We use special expressions as comments about our choice of register. For example, if we want to introduce a novel term or item from another register into our discourse and get away with it, we need to comment on the register shift with expressions such as: "as they say," "so they say," "as it were," "so to speak," "in a manner of speaking," "so-called," "if you like." Without special marking, a shift in register has consequences for the social interaction.

In face-to-face communication, we can monitor how well our message is being understood and appreciated. We can change our lexical choices to make our claims stronger or weaker depending on how the interaction seems to unfold. We can modulate our statements with laughter or disfluencies (*umm, well, uhh*) or such expressions as *kinda, sorta*. In writing, we cannot say, "Oh, I didn't mean it that way" or "Well, maybe that is a bit strong," to our readers. So we use hedges, which may be changes in verb selection like *seems, suggests,* or *appears* rather than *is,* or the addition of qualifiers like *somewhat, rather,* or *possibly.* These supplement modals (*can, may, might,* and so forth) in weakening or strengthening the claims we make. Searching the text of this chapter for modals, you will find many that weaken claims. For example, in discussing the words for *pancakes* in the first section, we wrote that everyone there *may say* pancakes, rather than everyone there *says* pancakes, because we don't really want to be held responsible for that claim. You might go to Pennsylvania and find people who still say flannel cakes.

Modals are, of course, used in both spontaneous talk and in polished writing. Some writing programs urge that we eliminate all other "weasel words." However, this ignores the important discourse function that modality serves. Modality, in addition to marking our degree of certainty or the degree of possibility of the truth of statements and our attitudes of volition, permission, and obligation, is also used to establish connectedness and autonomy in face-to-face interaction or in interaction with our readers. The more distance we want to create, the more formal our choices and the more neutral and unmodulated our lexical choices. The more connectedness we hope to establish, the closer the match must be among the participants. When the match is off, we can modulate our language with the use of these special lexical markers.

As learners we want to know how to use modality and how to modify lexical choices in discourse contexts that vary from spontaneous oral interactions to that of technical writing. When we are learning a language and are exposed to a variety of registers or styles, the range of choices becomes confusing. Both first and second language learners have to learn the more formal register of academic writing, and they often begin by using language which is considered too casual. Even international students who are advanced learners occasionally use oral language expressions in formal writing.

Anyway our country have many problem seriously. But ten years ago *you know* we still a developing country.

Register differences and the use of modality to establish connectedness and autonomy are important in teaching vocabulary skills to learners at all levels.

Practice 13.7

1. Newmark (1988) says that student translators tend to use colloquial rather than informal style. Thus, they translate *de plus en plus* as "more and more" rather than "increasingly." *Surtout* is translated as "above all" rather than "particularly." In the following pairs, identify which is informal and which colloquial: job–work, recovered–got well, lots of–numerous, escape–get out of, get rid of–discard.

2. One measure of formality is said to be the preference for primarily Latinate rather than Germanic words in formal English text. Word frequency is also believed to differentiate formal and informal registers. Slang, too, is a signal of informal register. Levin and Novak (1991) asked university students to read sets of utterances and choose a probable listener (e.g., close friend, brother, sister, employer, professor, stranger). The utterances with primarily Germanic words and those with slang were thought to be informal, appropriate for friends, and the Latinate versions formal and therefore appropriate for use with strangers or persons of higher status. Here is one set from the study:

Germanic, high frequency vocabulary
Many diets work at first. Keeping the weight off is hard.

Germanic, low frequency vocabulary
Lots of diets do wonders at the start. Keeping the weight off is tougher.

Latinate, high frequency vocabulary
A number of diets are successful initially. Maintaining the weight loss is more difficult.

Latinate, low frequency vocabulary
Numerous diets accomplish weight reduction initially. Sustaining it is more laborious.

With slang vocabulary
Many diets are successful initially. Keeping the blubber off is more difficult.

Without slang vocabulary
Many diets work initially. Maintaining the weight loss is more difficult.

Ask English language learners to identify the probable listener for each of these variations. Do their responses agree with those of Levin and Novak's native speakers? Supply variants that are more and less formal for this (+Germanic, high frequency) sentence from the study: "The government cannot do everything; people must help themselves." What makes your different versions more or less formal?

3. Now that several thesaurus software programs are available, language learners have a ready source of synonyms and antonyms to consult as they write their compositions. How might you use a computer thesaurus in teaching a composition course? How does the thesaurus show choices for informal or formal registers? Is enough information given in the thesaurus so that students can select needed synonyms (or antonyms) for words used in their initial drafts?

4. The COBUILD dictionary defines *as it were* as "to make what you are saying sound less definite." Does this seem right to you? Can it also be used to show that you do not wish to identify yourself with a claim or with those who make it (especially the way they make the claim)? Do you think that *as they say* shows a willingness to identify with the claim or those who make it? Do you think that these phrases show a shift in register? How might you gather evidence to support your answer?

5. In this section, we said that modality differs in formal and informal (written versus oral and planned versus unplanned) contexts. Modality across registers, however, may not be the same for all languages. In English, for example, we use *want* or *want to* as modals that make requests more polite. We might say, "Do you want to shut the door on your way out?" to make the request less direct, or we might invite someone to join us with, "Do you want a cup of coffee?" Kato (1989) lists the Japanese word *tai* for *want,* but points out that it is not used in this way. Because the speaker should always consider the wants of the hearer, it is not polite in Japanese to ask if he or she wants something. So a Japanese person might invite one to join by asking, "Do you drink coffee?" Give examples of your own that show a contrast in use of modality to soften or strenthen requests in another language. Is the equivalent of *want* used in a way similar to English or to Japanese?

Research and application

Geographic differences

1. Anson (1990) notes that the dictionary spellings of words are not consistent (2,000 words were shown to have variant spellings). Some of these are usually attributed to differences in British and American spelling. Anson conducted a case study of spelling of *-our* words (honour, honor, colour, color) in the two dialects. Contrary to expectation, the spelling of these words has varied since 1200 in British English. In addition, the *u* is dropped in derivations of the words in British spelling (the *Oxford University Dictionary* lists *humour, humorist, humorous,* and *humourless*). Read Anson's article and check your spelling of the words listed in this group and other variant spellings which are thought to differ in British and American English.

2. Bryant (1991) outlines the initial data collection, verification, and final survey stages of an Australian English survey. Words in nineteen categories were elicited: birds, fish, animals, plants, school, children's activities, houses, food, clothing, personal items, household items, vehicles, rural terms, occupation, weather, roads and roadsides, geographic features, business and services, and miscellaneous. If you wished to conduct a survey of L1 lexical items used by an immigrant population, would you select a few items from each category or would you concentrate on only a few categories and elicit more terms? Justify your choice and prepare a list of items and a method for obtaining the data.

3. Pride (1982) and Trudgill and Chambers (1991) contain chapters on the English spoken around the world, and give information on variation across dialects of English for articles and pronouns, modals and the verb system, and adverbials. Cheshire (1991) gives English variants by area (the Pacific, West Africa, and so forth). Select one geographic area and comment on the lexical variation that would be important for a language teacher to be aware of, and how that awareness might influence the teacher's work.

4. Corson (1991) looked for area (England and Australia) and social class differences in passive vocabulary. Subjects were given forty-nine words and a key word suggesting the semantic field relevant to each target word. They were asked to form a sentence with each pair of words. Corson found no differences in word use between the two countries but did find differences across social classes. Review the methodology and materials used in the study. What adaptations would you make if you wished to replicate this study with other dialects, social or ethnic groups?

Social group differences

5. There are many dictionaries of American slang, which may, however, be specific to a particular social group. Check several entries in a general dictionary of slang against a more current or specific list (e.g., Munroe's 1991 dictionary of UCLA slang). What can such collections tell us about variation in lexical selection?
6. Shorrocks (1991) suggests that the terminology of fishing might usefully be elicited to investigate sociolinguistic variation. The subcategories would include words for tackle (*leads, floats*), water (*creek, reservoir*), bait (*spinners, worms*), activities (*casting, gutting*), fish (terms for stages of growth, esteem), natural phenomena (*beach, tide*), manmade phenomena (*pier, canal*), and sayings and proverbs. Could you collect data from TV programs on the joys of fishing? If not, what methods might you use to elicit such vocabulary? What languages, dialects and sociolinguistic variables would you want to include in the study? Why should fishing be a better choice than skiing, golfing, or other hobbies in investigating sociolinguistic variation? If you carry out this research, you might send it to *Language in Society* for possible publication.
7. Osgood (1978) discusses the talk of advertising and politics. Much of military jargon, he says, is designed to dehumanize and thus protect us from feeling moral qualms. He also lists pairs of terms used in international relations: (*exploit* vs. *aid, manipulate* vs. *advise, dominate* vs. *submit to, lead* vs. *follow, help* vs. *hinder, protect* vs. *attack*). He claims that in these fields, speakers use incantations such as "the right to self-determination," spells such as "we have a commitment," contagious magic such as "a threat to freedom in Asia, is a threat to freedom in Pearblossom, USA," and analogic magic as in "another Munich." These phrases become almost as vacuous and dissipated as terms such as socialism, capitalism, democracy. Although this article is more than 15 years old, it seems very current. If you are interested in the language of politics, the military, advertising, or other career groups, you might wish to use this article as a classic in related literature.

Formality and oral/written mode

8. In Practice 10.2, we noted that claims have been made that verbs of Greco-Latin origin are used in more formal or technical language. The pairs *begin-commence,* and *end-terminate* are synonyms that differ in formality. Check the verbs in your own academic writing. Do you select Greco-Latinate words over Anglo-Saxon equivalents? You might want to replicate Levin and Novak's

study on formality (Practice 13.7.2) with second language learners to see whether they pick the same audience for each of the utterance types. (Levin and Novak list the utterances used for the study in their appendix.)

9. Myers (1991) compared the types of lexical cohesion used in science materials written for scientists and those in popular science articles. Differences were found in use of synonyms, oppositions (antonyms, converses, and contrasting members of a taxonomy), and superordinates. Because the texts are all from the fields of science, it is surprising to find such large differences. Examine the science materials available for an EST (English for Science and Technology) course. Are the techniques for achieving cohesion more like those Myers found for science texts or for popular science materials. Do you think it is important that EST materials match those of science? If you survey several sets of materials, you might prepare an article on the importance (or lack thereof) of matching materials to those of either science or popular science.

14 The vocabulary of communication signals and speech acts

We noted earlier that single words and ready-made phrases are used for discourse purposes. In this chapter, we will reorganize that information around two different types of discourse analysis: communication signals and speech acts phrases. In conversation, participants negotiate the interaction together, and the result is a conversation. Yet, for all of our having taken part in thousands of conversations, it would be strange if each one was entirely original and new. As with scripts, a general template for the conversation is formed along with the stereotypic phrases and lexical items attached to that framework, the vocabulary of communication signals and certain speech acts. Communication requires the use (or variation on the use) of fairly stereotypic sequences of words and lexical phrases.

Communication signals

Goffman (1976) claimed that there are at least the following universal set of communication signals: open/close signals, backchannel signals, turn-taking signals, framing signals, nonparticipant constraint signals, and acoustically adequate interpretable messages following Gricean norms. We will look at the lexical signals used for each of these in turn. The actual words or lexical phrases selected will, of course, vary across languages and according to the sociolinguistic factors discussed in Chapter 13.

Open/close signals

If we were to believe many language textbooks, communication in English begins with "Hello." In real life, however, the lexical signals that we use to open communication differ according to mode (written vs. oral communication), event (party, phone call, group meeting, etc.), the projected length of the communication (conversation in an elevator, meeting in a school hallway, etc.), and the role status of the participants (your mother, your boss, etc.). For example, two men greeted each other across a tennis court with

A: *whistles to attract B's attention*
   Yo, Bill.
B: Heyyy, look who's here!
   Ready for a little game?

These men happen to be lawyers. It's unlikely that either of them would use such lexical phrases to greet each other in the courtroom.

Think for a moment about the signals you give as you meet a friend in the school entry. Some of these are nonverbal (smiles, gestures, change of walking pace) and others are verbal – either single words ("*Morning!*") or lexical phrases ("Good morning, Sue, how are you?"). These signals are responded to in kind with matching greetings ("Morning, Great"). A "How are you" or one of its variants ("How's it going") may immediately follow. A neutral reply ("Fine," "Great") allows the participants to move to an optional "noticing" because it is at this moment that the speakers can comment on anything new and noteworthy or noticeable about the other person or about other topics (such as the weather, the surroundings, last night's ball game). Compliments are often used as noticings and compliments, as we will show later, comprise a small number of lexical phrases.

The signals for telephone conversation openings and closings have been extensively studied in conversational analysis (Schegloff, 1968, Schegloff & Sachs, 1973). In American English, the sequence of predictable lexical phrases consists of summons/answer (S/A), self-identification, greeting, a how-are-you (HAY) sequence, and an optional noticing with its shift to the first topic of conversation. The following examples show lexical phrases for each of these parts. Notice that identification comes from very minimal voice cues and, in this case, Denise hears vowel elongation on Sue's "hi" greeting as uncertainty and jumps in to give a self-identification.

S/A:	*Phone rings.*
	S: Hh hello.
Greet/ID:	D: Hi, Sue,
	S: Hi:: =
	D: =It's Denise=
	S: =ohh HI, Denise.
HAY:	How are you.
	D: Fine.
Noticing:	S: Hey, I heard about your PR
	D: Hhhh
(compliment)	S: That's great.
	D: Thanks.
Topic:	D: Mmm the reason I'm calling you is . . . .

Business calls much more typically have self-identification phrases and a prompt for the reason for the call:

S/A:	*Phone rings.*
	S: This is Sue at Edmo; how may I help you?
S/A:	*Phone rings.*
	S: Kaiser Permanente; how can I route your call?

This immediate request for topic can be disconcerting to someone who is used to the more extended opening sequence of social calls:

	Phone rings.
	S: This is Sue at Edmo; how may I help you?
Greet/ID:	C: Oh hi. This is JS; I'm with uh Nortex.
	S: Uhhuh
HAY: →	C: Uhh how are you?
→	S: Fine.
	How can I help you?
	C: Uhh I wanted some information on

Nonverbal signals can be used in openings. For example, when you ask a favor of a stranger you may use nonverbal eye contact to open the request and then use a lexical phrase like "Could you please tell me *X*? to make the request. Or, a verbal call for attention such as "Excuse me" could be used: "Excuse me, but could you *X*." After an answer is given, a simple "Thanks" or "Thank you" and "You're welcome" sequence can form the closing.

In phone conversations, single word signals show that we are ready to close the conversation. An exchange of words such as *well, so, uh* show that each side is ready to stop and a close can be given.

Pre-close:	E: Okay. so::
	S: Yeah. [*slow rate*]
	E: Yeh, so I'll call yuh tomorrow then.
	S: Okay mom, talk to you later. [*normal rate*]
Close:	E: Bye.
	S: Bye.

Having given these preclosing signals, we must use additional expressions like "Oh, wait a minute!" if we suddenly decide we have one more thing to say. The preclosing segment is also the last chance to comment on anything noticeable, so although compliments are much more frequently given at the opening of the conversation, they may also appear in the preclosing segment:

Pre-close:	E: Hmm.
	J: Yeh.

	E: Well, it's been really nice talking with you.
Noticing:	Oh, and I meant to tell you I really like that dress.
	J: This?
	E: Yeh, it's just the right color.
	J: Oh thanks.
Thanks:	E: And thanks again for lunch.
	J: My pleasure.
Pre-close:	See you soon.
Close:	E: Bye.
	J: Bye.

Practice 14.1

1. What lexical phrases do you (or another teacher) use to open your class session? Are these lexical phrases or nonverbal signals also appropriate for openings of other meetings?
2. In what situations might you use the following lexical phrases without any other verbal opening? Are there equivalent phrases in another language that you teach or are learning?

   Not many people here yet, hmm?
   Did you hear the news about *X?*
   Wonderful morning, isn't it?
   How about that game last night!
   Are you a friend of *X*'s?

3. Is the sequence of lexical phrases in the opening the same in the language you teach as they are in the students' first language?

   a. Telephone: summons/answer, identification of speakers, greeting, "how are you" exchange, (noticing), bridge to first topic
   b. Conversations: greeting, how are you exchange, (noticing), bridge
   c. Letters: Time, place, date, identification of addressee, greeting (Dear June,)
   d. Request openings: Excuse me, could you – (Do you know) where's – ? When – ?
   e. Indirect openings: Whew, it's hot! Where's your dog?
   f. Social "party line" openings: Great food, hmm?

4. What greetings do you use? Because what we think we do is not always what we actually do, tape-record speakers (or yourself) in a number of situations and identify the actual lexical items and phrases used.
5. Select a dialogue from your language textbook and rewrite it to include an opening sequence. Be sure the lexical phrases are appropriate for the situational context shown in the dialogue. Depending on the proficiency of your students, you may or may not want to add a noticing. What lexical phrases did you use? How typical are these phrases as opening signals (i.e., can they be used in many similar contexts)?
6. In a language that you teach or are learning, what words or phrases do people use as pre-closers to show they are ready to close the communication channel? After the pre-closing signals are given, what lexical phrases are used to show that you have thought of something else and want to stop the closing?
7. What are the conventional closing phrases in the language selected for item 5? If you are trapped in a conversation and are in a hurry to leave, what lexical phrases might you use to escape? If your signals are misunderstood or ignored, what do you say?
8. Using the dialogue from item 5, add a preclosing and closing sequence. If appropriate for your students, as a variation, have one person trap the other in the situation and have the other escape in a tactful or more direct manner. How appropriate is your new dialogue for your students? What do you hope they will learn as a result of the modified dialogue?
9. In what situations would you use the following lexical phrases? (Is *cheerio* the name of a cereal or a closing signal for you?) After you have identified the situations, determine whether there are as many choices for closings and preclosings in another language of your choice.

Great talking with you.
Gotta go now.
Would you excuse me, I really must go.
Thanks for all your time.
Someone's at the door!
We have to get together – do lunch sometime soon.
See you soon.
Good-bye.

Can several of these be used consecutively by a
speaker? Can any of them be used by both speakers?
10. What lexical phrases of openings and closings do parents
model for their children to ensure they "behave properly"?
Do they also model the nonverbal signals that go along
with the lexical signals?

Backchannel signals

In social interaction, we expect that others will want to converse with us
and that they will value our contributions to the conversation just as we
value theirs. Backchannel signals are one way of showing that this is the
case. In American English, common backchannel signals such as
mmhmm, uhhuh, yeh, and *right,* show that we not only hear and are
listening to the message but are actively engaged in the interaction.

If we withhold backchannel signals, the speaker assumes that we are
not listening, that we are bored, or that we disagree with the message.
The talk of the speaker is timed to leave spaces during which we are
expected to offer a reassuring backchannel signal. If you try, you will find
it is very difficult to withhold backchannel signals during these pauses.
When the speaker does not receive assurance during that pause, he or she
is likely to try to fix up the trouble, sometimes even by reversing a claim.

E: I really don't like it.
   (.8 *pause*) (*no backchannel offered*)
   I mean – well, it's not so:: bad, I guess.

Or, the speaker may ask for feedback (e.g., "Does this make sense?" "Do
you understand?" "Are you listening?").

The form and frequency of backchannel signals varies from group to
group. It has been claimed that women give more supporting and encouraging backchannel signals than men. Because backchannel signals are so
automatic, it is not surprising to find that we use the signals from our first
language when speaking in other languages. Tao and Thompson (1991)
give examples where fluent English–Mandarin bilinguals use *aha, um,
yeah, uhhuh* when speaking Mandarin instead of the Mandarin *ao, a, ei,
dui/shi.*

When we use lexical items from the appropriate language, signals
which seem to us to be acceptable and positive signs of encouragement,
we or our conversational partners can still be in for a surprise. For example, it is a custom in many academic departments to welcome international guests by giving a short description of the department's program.
The chair of one such department began to do this and the international
visitor nodded and said, "interesting, interesting," as a backchannel. The
chair, taken aback by a signal which, because of the intonation sounded

333

equivalent to "boring, boring," quickly switched to another topic, offering to take the guest for a walk around the campus. The guest, looking somewhat puzzled, reluctantly agreed and then asked a question about the program.

In the classroom, teachers expect students to give them backchannel signals to show that they understand and that they find the lesson interesting or that they don't understand or that they find the lesson not worth their participation. These may be nonverbal signals (such as nods and smiles or movements of the hands and shifts in body position). When students fail to give positive backchannels, we may rephrase our message or we may make an appeal for attention (e.g., "Listen now, this is important!"). In ordinary conversations we are unlikely to tell our conversational partners to pay attention because we assume the people we talk with are interested in what we have to say. If we drift off as others speak and it is noticed, we are embarrassed and may need to offer an apology.

Practice 14.2

1. The backchannel signals you use may vary depending on many factors, among them the dialect of English you speak and your relationship with the other speaker. Check the tape that you recorded for Practice 14.1.4. What backchannel signals do the speakers use?
2. What are the words or phrases used as backchannel signals in the languages you teach or are learning? How do they vary (conversations, in class, at a performance)? What nonverbal signals are used? Are these signals presented in your language textbook?
3. What backchannel signals do teachers use in the classroom? Are different signals used to encourage boys and girls? Does the frequency of backchannel signals differ for girls? Are there differences in the frequency or form of backchannel signals directed toward adult students?
4. Do you or your students use L1 signals rather than the target language signals? Are the signals used with appropriate frequency?
5. When students or conversational partners do not appear to be listening, how do you respond? When would someone respond to negative backchanneling with lexical phrases such as:

   Am I boring you?
   Hello, hello? (*waves hand in front of partner's face*) Anybody in there?

You're not listening, are you?
Listen up, you guys!

6. Add a series of backchannel signals to the dialogue in Practice 14.1.5. Note how this shifts the amount of talk for the students. How can you fix the imbalance?

7. Plan an activity where your students tell you expressions people use as positive and negative backchannel signals. Next, ask them for phrases they might use in response to negative backchannel signals. Write these on the board and then have them divide the list into those that are and are not polite (or those they can use with anyone and those to be used only with people they know). Can some be used with both? Be prepared to tell them the phrases that can be used as a response (usually an apology) when others tell us, however politely, to pay attention.

Turn-taking signals

Ideally, the turns in a conversation are symmetric. One person or the other does not dominate without permission. There are lexical phrases that must be used to gain permission for a very long turn. The child's "You know what?" and our answering "No, what?" gets the necessary permission for an extended monologue. Adults may use such lexical phrases as, "You'll never believe what just happened" for this same purpose.

Turn-taking signals may be very subtle when the speakers know each other. The rhythm of the conversation is quickly set and each person comes in on cue according to that rhythm. One speaker cues the end of a turn by using falling intonation, stretching final vowels, or using such nonverbal signals as arm and head movements or body shifts. The gap between turns is perfectly timed if the speakers are in sync.

When there is unequal power between speakers or when one speaker is reticent and the other begins "directing," turns may be passed by asking a question (e.g., "So what do *you* think?"). The classroom is one example of unequal power discourse. The teacher controls the turns, allocating them by calling on students and responding to their answers in question-answer-evaluation sequences. The turns bounce back and forth to the teacher. In language classrooms, teachers are trained to change this natural pattern. They encourage students to call on each other and to ask each other questions, or they may use chain drills where each person responds in turn and then asks a question of the next student.

There are languages where it is quite all right to overlap turns by chiming in. These overlaps where each person is saying basically the same thing to end a turn are called *collaborative completions*. In other language or social groups, collaborating on the completion of a turn is seen not as a mark of friendship and support but rather as exceedingly rude. In some language groups, it is quite permissible to allow a long gap before responding. This is not seen as a silent signal that something is wrong in the communication, but rather that the conversation is so important that the speaker wants to take time before responding. You can imagine the problems mismatches of gap time cause in the classroom as teachers wait in vain for quick responses from students.

Involving reticient students or shy conversational partners so that the turns are symmetric is an art that we all strive to master. In learning another language, acquisition of turn-taking signals may be either easy or difficult depending on how closely they correspond with those of our first language. The social consequences of not learning them, however, make them worthy of our attention.

Practice 14.3

1. List lexical phrases that get you an extended turn at talk. Are these "monologue" signals the same in the language you are learning or teaching? Are the same lexical phrases used by men and women, by children and adults, by people of different status groups? Are these lexical phrases included in your language textbooks?

2. Are the gaps between turns the same length in your L1 and the language you are teaching or learning?

3. Do differences in gap times reflect social role differences or, perhaps, urban and rural differences? When the gaps between speakers do not match, what interpretation is put on the mismatch by each speaker (do they think the other person is pushy if the speaker overlaps their turn; do they think the other person is slow or not interested in them if it is long?).

4. Many methodologists suggest that teachers ask a question without calling on a specific student and then silently count to six so that all students have time to think of an answer. After counting to six, the teacher is then to call on an individual student. Can you vary gap time (the count to six rule)? Are there different cultural assumptions regarding gap time between yourself and your students?

5. What social interpretation is put on collaborative completions? Is the interpretation different in instructional discourse?

6. In the classroom, how are turns allocated? How might you change some of your activities to encourage more natural

turn taking among students? What lexical phrases do you use to discourage students from hogging the limelight and to encourage students who cannot get a word in edgewise?
7. Dornyei and Thurrell (1992) suggest that language students use an observation sheet to discover how turn taking works according to their textbook and also in authentic language use. How might you adapt it for use with your students? How might you see whether using the observation sheet actually improved not only their awareness of turn taking but also their performance in using appropriate signals?

Turn-taking Observation Sheet

	Text	Authentic
A speaker gives up his/her turn by		
asking a question from the next speaker		
saying something to which a reaction is expected e.g., a compliment, an offer, a request, etc.		
saying that he/she is finishing, e.g., "Well, anyway – " or "So – " or "last but not least – "		
lowering the pitch or volume of his/her voice		
slowing down his/her speech		
lengthening the last syllable		
indicating that he/she has finished by laughing		
indicating that he/she has finished by a facial gesture		
looking at someone		
There is an overlap between the turns simultaneous talk		
The speaker who takes up the turn		
starts speaking in a natural gap		
signals the wish to speak by using interjections e.g., "yeah, yeah but – ," "but listen – "		
signals the wish to speak with an audible intake of breath		
signals the wish to speak by clearing throat		
interrupts the previous speaker		

Turn-taking Observation Sheet

	Text	*Authentic*
completes or adds something to what the previous speaker said, without a pause		
indicates the wish to speak by movement e.g., leaning forward, gestures, etc.		
indicates the wish to speak with facial expression		
Other		

(Adapted from Dornyei and Thurrell, 1992, p. 25)

Acoustically adequate and interpretable messages

In order for communication to succeed, our talk must be comprehensible. When we are learning a language, that is not always the case. Sometimes we do not understand and sometimes what we say is not understandable. When that happens we use lexical phrases as well as nonverbal gestures to signal the communication breakdown.

Language students are usually supplied with lists of lexical phrases that they can use when they don't understand ("Sorry?" "I'm sorry, I don't understand." "Would you mind repeating that?" "I'm sorry, could you say that slower?"). They may also be told to repeat part of what the speaker has said with rising intonation. When students do not use these or other signals, the teacher or other speaker may use lexical phrases to check comprehension. Questions phrases "Clear?" "OK?" "Do you understand?" are typical comprehension checks.

In ordinary conversation, when we get muddled we can signal a repair with lexical phrases like "I mean," "I should say," "In other words," "That is," "Well uhhh actually," and then reformulate our talk. There is a definite preference for the speaker who is being unintelligible to repair his or her own talk. For someone else to do it seems impolite. Still, lexical phrases like "You mean – ?" "Do you mean?" "Are you saying that – ?" "I think you mean – ?" can be used. The lexical phrase "What do you mean?" must be used with care because it can be a simple appeal for help or a challenge to the speaker's veracity or point of view.

As language learners, we are not always able to organize our thoughts quickly. In order to produce interpretable messages (let alone grammatically correct messages) we need to learn the words and lexical phrases that will buy us a little time. The so-called disfluency signals (*uhh, umm, err, hmmm*) may not seem like words but they give you a minute to think of how to say something. Lexical phrases such as "Let's see," "Let me think a minute," "Ohhh just a minute" are also used for this function.

When others misunderstand us, there is also a set of lexical phrases that we can use to either apologize or to claim that the fault is not with us but with the listener: "Sorry, I'm sorry, I meant – ," "Maybe it's more like – ," "I'm really muddled, let me try again," "No, I didn't mean that," "That's not what I said," "All I was trying to say was – ."

In previous chapters we have talked about definitions but not how definitions are given in ordinary communication. We do much definition giving in classroom settings, but it is also very common in conversations as we search for the words we need to make our messages interpretable. Definition giving is also included among Tarone's (1977, 1980) communication strategies. When we cannot think of the words we need, we may try the following:

1. Message adjustment or avoidance (i.e., change the topic)
2. Paraphrasing (e.g., "that thing you look at cells" = microscope)
3. Approximation (e.g., "kinda like a prize" = lottery)
4. Mime (e.g., circular hand gestures = merry-go-round)
5. Appeal for help (e.g., "oh, what's that word that means – ")

Although meanings do get negotiated in this way, lexical phrases such as "How do you say – ?" "What's the word that means – ?" "The thing you use to – ," "The place you go to – ," "Kinda – ," "Kinda like – " carry the discourse function of showing that help is needed to make the message clear.

Teachers often worry that their messages may not be clear to students. They may simplify their vocabulary choices, restate concepts in several different ways, write words or draw diagrams and pictures on the board, or give definitions. They may also paraphrase, approximate, use mime, appeal for help, or give up and change the topic.

Practice 14.4

1. What lexical phrases are used in the language you teach or are studying to show a lack of understanding or inability to respond? Are these presented in your teaching materials? Give examples.
2. The pause fillers that help us buy time are not the same in all languages. Students often use the disfluency signals of their L1 when speaking the target language. What pause fillers are used in your target language? Are these presented in your textbook? Is it appropriate to use laughter for this function or does it only signal embarrassment at not being able to articulate the message?

3. Dornyei and Thurrell (1992) suggest the following activity: After students have performed a dialogue well, ask one of the students to pretend not to remember some of the crucial content words. Note the use of mime, types of paraphrases, and appeals for help that the student is able to use. Call these to the attention of the students and ask them to replicate this with their next dialogue (explaining why this is an important skill to develop). Do you have suggestions for further practice? How might you evaluate the effectiveness of the practice?
4. In what ways do native speakers assist learners in conversations? How often are definitions given or asked for? How helpful is simplification, restatement, remodeling, and summary in preventing communication breakdown? How could you discover whether these really help the learner?

Non-participant constraints

In communication, there have to be ways of ignoring "noise" that occurs around us. At a reception, we cannot listen and be part of one conversation and listen in and be part of another at the same time, so we shut out the communication that we are not part of. On the other hand, there have to be ways of joining or even interrupting on-going communication of which we have not been a part. Special lexical signals can be used for this.

Young children often use attention-getting signals to enter a conversation. They may call out the name of one of the participants (e.g., "Hey, Mom!") or they may use the "lookit" formula (e.g., "Lookit, hey lookit") to gain the attention of persons with whom they want to converse. Although laughter is not a lexical item, it is a communication signal. A person may approach a group, use eye contact, and join in the laughter to gain admittance to the group. We may also repeat part of what has just been said and then use a lexical phrase to explain the reason for commenting on it:

(*A is part of a group. B is walking slowly by.*)
A: . . . just another tax hike.
B: Tax hike? (*repetition*)
→   *That's interesting, I was just* talking to C. about tax hikes.
(*B joins group*)

Or we may move to participant status using lexical phrases such as "I couldn't help overhearing" and then a statement as to why we are entitled to comment.

(*A is talking to her children. B is standing nearby.*)
A: . . . because it's not good for you. (looks at B)

→ B: (*smiles*) *I couldn't help hearing you.* I agree. This stuff is terrible.

When we need to preempt communication momentarily and then leave, it is customary to ask permission or even to apologize for doing so ("Can I interrupt for a minute?" "Sorry to interrupt you," "Excuse me, could I bother you for a minute?"). Some of these lexical signals can also be used to interrupt speakers when they attempt to hog the floor or when they wander off the subject.

Practice 14.5

1. What preemption or interruption signals are there in the language you teach? How acceptable are interruptions, and are there situations in which one must not interrupt? Are the nonverbal signals of interruption the same in the L1 and the target language?
2. What lexical phrases do parents use to prevent children from inappropriately interrupting adult communication? Are these same lexical phrases used by teachers to prevent students from inappropriate interrupting?
3. Which of the following phrases are more likely to be used when the speaker simply wants to join in (move from non-participant to participant status)? Which might be used if the speaker wants to deliver a message and then leave? Which might be used when the speaker wants to interrupt to make a point or add to the point? Can some be used for more than one of these situations?

   Sorry to break in –
   Can I interrupt you for a second –
   Well, yeh but –
   Did I hear you say – ?
   I couldn't help overhearing –

4. Rewrite one of your teaching dialogues to include an interruption sequence – a sequence that gives students the appropriate signals for interrupting and entering the dialogue. How could you determine whether such practice was effective?
5. Plan an activity that gets students to practice appropriate and inappropriate interruption. Can they successfully (tactfully or otherwise) shut out inappropriate interruptions? What are the lexical phrases that they recognize and use for this function?

Gricean norms

Communication specialists offer four maxims for successful communication, called Gricean norms" after Grice (1975). The contributions of all communicating partners should be (a) relevant to the topic, (b) truthful unless noted as otherwise, (c) of appropriate quantity, and (d) the manner in which the contribution is made (i.e., clarity, lack of ambiguity, and general politeness) should allow for easy interpretation of the message. This does not mean that the maxims cannot be and are not violated. They are, but for special effect.

The maxim of relevance assumes that a topic can be identified in the communication and that the contributions of individuals contribute to that topic. One way of making sure that the topic is clear is to provide a structuring move or a statement of the topic. For example, in classrooms teachers structure the lesson for the day with such lexical phrases as "Today we're going to discuss X." The teacher may go on to identify subtopics (e.g., "that includes a, b, c") or to explain how the discussion will proceed (e.g., "first, we'll . . . then. . . . then . . . and finally, if there is time, we'll – "). The structuring move sets the topic, limits the types of contributions that will be relevant, and may set the sequence for the contributions.

In conversations, topics may be announced rather than structured: ("Did you hear about meeting at 4:00?" (contributions should be relevant to the meeting at 4:00), "Do you want to go over to Betty's?" (contributions should be relevant to going to Betty's), "We're going to have an in-service" (contributions should be relevant to having an in-service workshop). It is also possible to negotiate a topic, as shown in this fragment from a phone conversation:

> S: Oh, the Lakers' were terrible last night.
> → E: Uggg, *don't wanta talk about it.*
> S: Yeh but
> E: They won't make it to the playoff.
> S: Yeh but
> → E: *Let's talk about* that new truck D. got.
> S: Okay, what color is it? It's a '94, right?

Although contributions should be relevant to the topic, it is possible to shade the topic or shift gradually to another related topic. In the classroom, as each of the subparts of a topic are finished the teacher may mark the shift with a series of "OK?–OK" or "OK?–So" lexical transition markers. The teacher is making sure that everyone realizes that one section is finished, that everyone understands everything so far, and agrees to go. Once backchannel signals show this agreement, the teacher utters a second *okay* or *so* to show that one part is finished and the next part is to begin.

At the end of the class, the teacher may use a summary to show that the topic has been completed. In conversations, there are many lexical phrases that show we are ready to stop talking about one topic and to move on to another. Dorynei and Thurrell (1992, p. 38) have an interesting list of "proverbs and platitudes" that can be used to conclude a topic. Included on the list are such phrases as "That's the way it goes." "Makes you think, doesn't it?" "It just goes to show (you can't be too careful / you never can tell)," "What would we do without you?" "You can't win them all." (Notice that in previous chapters we talked about proverbs, idioms, and frozen lexical phrases as though they existed in a vacuum. Here we are saying that they can have definite discourse functions.) At the end of a long trouble-sharing sequence, the following proverb and frozen lexical phrase were used:

      J: I've given up. *There's no use trying.*
→ E: Yeh. *Jes goes to show you can't lead a horse.* . . .
→ J: Yeh, *I've learned my lesson. Never again.*

Having uttered such topic-closing phrases, it is up to the speakers to nominate the next topic or to begin their preclosing moves.

We have said that the Gricean norms of cooperative conversation can be violated. If a contribution is not relevant, we may interpret the person as being rude, not interested, or disruptive. Or, if the contribution is from a language learner, we may assume that the person was unable to identify the topic of conversation. Even in ordinary classrooms, teachers often have to struggle to construct relevance for the replies of students. They may restate and reform the student's utterance to make it more relevant to the announced topic.

When structuring moves and transition moves are not made explicit by the teacher (or by the leader of any other group that has met to carry out a task announced by the leader), students (or participants) are unsure how to behave appropriately – that is, how to make contributions that fit within the activity. Dorr-Bremme (1990) found that most elementary school teachers marked shifts in topics using a variety of activity formulas – lexical phrases like "Okay, let's see who's not here today" to start the attendance topic, and "Kim, go get a magic marker and let's see if you can do the calendar today" to start the calendar topic. The teachers used framing words such as "All right? Okay?–Okay" at transition points. When such phrases and words were not used, the children interpreted the lack of such structuring and transition signals to mean that it was okay for them to talk or do whatever they wished since no topic or task had been announced. They didn't need to be relevant.

The second maxim of cooperative conversation is that the contribution should be truthful. There are no special words or lexical items associated with truthfulness. However, we do use interjections like *uh, ummm, ahh,* and *uh well* when we doubt the truthfulness of something that has been said to us. We may also use words and lexical phrases such as "Really?" "Honest(ly)?" "You're kidding, right?" "You don't mean that." These responses show that we interpret obvious untruthfulness as a deliberate violation and therefore a joke.

The third maxim is one of quantity, a maxim that we have already discussed in part in talking about fairness of turn length. If our friends violate this cooperative maxim, we may do a preempt interruption to force more symmetry in turns. On the other hand, we may allow people to tell us more than we ever wanted to know about a subject because they are the teacher, the parent, or the boss.

The fourth maxim is one of manner. That is, the contribution should be clear, unambiguous, and polite. We have discussed clarity in discussing interpretable messages. The message should be clear rather than ambiguous. The politeness issue is one that spreads across all of discourse. We judge and manipulate the degree of politeness according to many of the variables discussed in Chapter 13.

Practice 14.6

1. What lexical phrases do you use in the classroom to structure activities? What structuring hints are offered in your teaching materials? Are they specific to individual lessons?
2. What lexical phrases do you use to show topic shifts (e.g., "Okay?–Okay.")? What lexical phrases do you use to show a final summary is about to take place?
3. Plan an activity where students negotiate topics in conversation. First, have them list lexical phrases they might use to say they do not want to talk about a suggested topic (e.g., "Oh no, not that again!"). Have them divide these into those to be used only with friends and those to be used with others. Then, have them list lexical phrases for suggesting another topic (e.g., "How about *X,*" "What about *X,*" "Let's") Next, have each student write a topic on a card. Shuffle the cards and let everyone draw a topic. Pair the students or have them work in small groups to practice negotiating the topics they have drawn.
4. In English we use *oh, uh, ah, uh well,* and other interjections when a contribution is not what we expect, when it is not exactly relevant, or when we doubt truthfulness. Are

similar signals used in the language you teach? Are these signals taught explicitly?

5. What lexical phrases (in addition to intonation) are used in the language you teach to show that something being said is pretense/teasing? Are these included in your teaching materials? Are responses (the equivalent of "You're kidding," "Oh, come on," "You're joking") also included in the materials. If not, plan an activity to practice violation of the truthfulness maxim.

6. Contributions should be clear rather than obscure or ambiguous. Are there any special lexical phrases that you use when you get muddled or cannot organize your thoughts?

7. Dornyei and Thurrell give an example of breaking each maxim:

A: Where are you going?
B: To buy some stamps. (*fulfills all the maxims*)
B: To the moon (*truthfulness violation*)
B: To the door, then down the stairs, then out into the street, then – (*quantity violation*)
B: Have you called your mother yet? (*relevance violation*)
B: I'm going to get something to put on a letter. (*clarity violation*)

They suggest having students work in small groups to rewrite a dialogue so that it breaks one of the four maxims. Each group then performs its version while the others listen and decide which maxim is violated. Do you have other suggestions about how you might work on the maxims with your students?

Framing or bracket signals

The final type of communication signal shows that part of the communication is not directly related to the on-going message. The *side-sequence* is marked at the beginning with lexical bracket phrases such as "Oh, before I forget it," "That reminds me," "To change the subject just for a minute," "Oh incidentally." At the end of the "side-sequence" there are signals to mark a return to the previous topic: "Getting back to – ," "Anyway," "As we were saying – ."

Nonverbal gestures often accompany these verbal signals. Body shifts, head movements, and looking up and to the right are often signals for a side-sequence. In writing, we may use footnotes or place material in parentheses.

Practice 14.7

1. Look at the following list of bracket phrases. When might
   each be used or are they all interchangeable? Can you
   produce and categorize a similar list in the language you
   teach or are learning?

   By the way – That reminds me –
   Speaking of – Talking about X reminds me
   Before I forget it – Oh, I nearly forgot –
   Oh, I just thought of something –
   This has nothing to do with what we're discussing but –
   To change the subject for a minute –

   What phrases might be used to get the communication
   back to the original topic? Are they similar to the following
   English phrases?

   As I was saying (before I so rudely interrupted myself) –
   Now, where was I?
   But let's not digress!
   Going back to –
   Let's get back to –
   Anyway –
   But let's get back to the subject.

2. Ask students to note the times that you or other speakers
   of the target language use the phrases that you have listed
   as bracket signals.

3. Write a short side sequence for one of the dialogues in
   your text. What do you hope your students will learn from
   this addition? How might you be more direct in teaching
   this function?

Communication signals form an important part of the vocabulary of the
language. The discourse meanings of many of these vocabulary items,
however, are seldom given in dictionaries. You won't find *okay* defined as
a topic transition marker, *anyway* as a bracket signal, or *so* as a preclosing signal. The emphasis placed on the acquisition of these signals, however, varies not only according to the goals and approach in language
education, but also across cultures. Studying child-rearing practices, Fernald and Morikawa (1993) found that Japanese mothers were very concerned with communication signals, the rituals of social exchange while
American mothers were very concerned with helping their children learn
the names of objects. In playing with their children, American mothers
labeled toys and identified their parts ("That's a car. See the car? You like
it? It's got nice wheels"). The Japanese mothers in their study often used

onomatopoeia (*buubuu–vroom-vroom* for car, truck, and an animal noise *wanwan* [woof-woof] for dog) and used these unlabeled objects to engage infants in social routines: *Hai buubuu* (Here! It's a vroom-vroom) *Choo-dai* (give me). *Hai arigatoo* (yes, thank you).

Many parents feel that social formulas, meaning appropriate openings and closings, turn taking, non-interruption of others, giving relevant responses, talking the appropriate amount of time, and politeness formulas, can best be learned by a combination of explicit teaching and their own modeling. In language classes, we see a wide range of opinions. Some teachers apparently feel they are of little importance, using the signals of the L1 rather than the target language for classroom management. Others believe these can easily be acquired without explicit instruction. As teachers, they model the signals in the target language and believe that students can acquire them in this way. The third position is one to which we subscribe. Communication signals are a very important part of the vocabulary of a language and the system, the words, and the lexical phrases should be explicitly taught.

Practice 14.8

1. Can you or your students learn the vocabulary (and the system) of communication signals of a new language without explicit instruction? How much opportunity will you or your students have to observe these signals being used by fluent speakers of the language? Give evidence to support your contention regarding the need or lack of need for explicit instruction.
2. Are all of the communication signals discussed in this section included for explicit instruction in your language teaching materials? How accurate are the materials? Do they show what speakers really do in the dialect of the language you want to learn or teach?
3. If you believe that the teacher needs to use the first language to carry out many communication signals discussed in this section because of the students' proficiency level, at what point do you think a shift to the target language should begin? Is there any particular sequence that might be used for this shift (i.e., should the first shift be for openings and closings)?
4. You will have noticed that many of the signals are not precisely words (e.g., *uhh, umm*), some are words (e.g., *wow!, hi!*), and others are phrases (e.g., "I know what you mean," "How's it going?"). Which do you think would be the easiest to learn or to teach? Justify your answer.

5. Would it be possible to learn the lexical phrases and words used as communication signals and very little else and still be able to carry on a conversation? Would it be possible to learn many lexical phrases and words but none that are used as communication signals and still carry on a conversation? Give evidence to support your answer.

The lexicon of speech acts and speech events

Speech act research draws on the work of Searle, Austin, Halliday, and Wierzbicka, among others. The overall goal of the research is to discover whether it is possible to identify some limited number of functions for which we use language. The speech act categories used by American linguists usually include:

Directives (ask others to do or to not do something)
Examples: Pick up your shoes! Let's go to the mall.

Commissives (promises or refusals for action)
Examples: Yes, I will. I already gave at the office.

Representatives (factual information)
Examples: The class meets at 1:00. Maybe it's kinda blue.

Declaratives (bring about a change or new state of being)
Examples: I find you guilty as charged. I pronounce you husband and wife.

Expressives (statements of feeling)
Examples: What a great day! Oh, I'm so sorry!

The Council of Europe used speech-act theory as a basis for the notional-functional approach to language teaching. Communicative language teaching shares much with this approach. The instruction hopes to produce students who are able to use language to carry out functions such as those listed above in communication.

In language education, speech act research has been important for it seeks to understand whether speech acts have universal categories and whether within each language they are performed in a way that reflects the social norms and assumptions of the culture. We will return to this issue after we have discussed basic functions and some of the typical lexical phrases used for each.

Teachers and methodologists differ over whether or not the lexicon of speech acts should be taught. Many believe they will be learned automatically, without explicit teaching, as students use the language. Perhaps this is true, but our position is that explicit teaching can make that learning more efficient.

It is impossible in the space remaining to discuss each of the functions and typical lexical phrases for each. Rather, we will discuss the functions identified in the Threshold Level (*le niveau seuil*) of syllabus design. These differ somewhat from the functions of Austin and Searle, but we present them here because they are so widely used in syllabus design and materials development.

Identification of functions

The functional approach works with six basic functions: Imparting and seeking (1) *factual* information, (2) *intellectual* information, (3) *emotional* information, (4) *moral* information, (5) suasion, and (6) social routines. We will look at the first five of these functions in more detail since social routines have already been discussed in the section on communication signals.

When we ask for factual information from someone we do not know well, we are likely to use softened lexical phrases, such as "Would you . . . ?" "Could you . . . ?" "Do you mind telling me . . . ?" "Could you give me some information?" "Could you find out about . . . ?" Notice the use of the modals *could* and *would* that make the request more polite. Among friends we are more likely to use a direct question, such as "What's a . . . ?" "Know anything about . . . ?" "Where do you keep the . . . ?" "What's the name of that . . . ?"

Language teachers are trained to give students as much practice in asking information questions as possible. Students are, however, more likely to practice the forms used with strangers than those used with close friends.

The first response learned for factual questions is often "I don't know." In very informal situations, the inability to offer factual information can be expressed in such lexical phrases as, "Don't have a clue." As with all communicative language teaching, students will need to be helped to understand the register appropriateness of various forms.

Practice 14.9

1. In a language of your choice, what question forms are used when the speaker does not know the person from whom information is to be received? Are they softened through modality, or are other lexical politeness formulas used?

2. When might you ask for information with "Got any idea about . . . ?" "Know anything about . . . ?" "Have you heard anything about . . . ?" "Is this the way to . . . ?" "Where do you keep the . . . ?" What are the parallel forms in the lan-

349

guage you teach? At what level would it be appropriate to present these forms? Do students hear these forms in your class during other activities?

3. When we are asked for information we cannot supply, we may use lexical phrases like "Sorry, I don't know." What kinds of lexical phrases do you use when you do not know how to answer a student's question? How do students respond to questions when they do not know the answer?

4. When might a speaker reply "Don't have a clue," "Don't ask me," or "No idea"? What parallel forms are there for these lexical phrases in the language you teach or are learning?

5. Examine your language learning dialogues for information exchanges. What question forms are used? If you vary the dialogue so that the asker and answerer are acquaintances (perhaps the clerk and customer are friends), how would the questions and answers change? Have students vary the dialogue drawing attention to the changes.

6. Dornyei and Thurrell (1992) suggest the following activity: Devise a "mystery" scene. In each group, one or two students get to be the detective and ask lots of questions. The other students are the suspects who must answer the questions. If students are advanced, some can be willing answerers and others can use the 'no idea, don't have any idea' type responses. How might you determine whether this "game" promotes the acquisition of lexical phrases for seeking and imparting factual information? Why is it important to practice expressing one's inability to give factual information?

Expressing and discovering intellectual attitudes

The intellectual function includes asking about or stating our attitudes toward information. Do we agree or disagree with the information? Do we consider the information possible or impossible, logical or illogical, certain or uncertain? In many notional-function texts, this function also includes asking and giving permission, offering and either accepting or rejecting invitations, which we will discuss in the section on suasion.

Common lexical phrases used to ask for other's opinions are "What do you think?" "What would you say about X?" Common lexical phrases to express one's own opinion are "I think," "In my opinion," "If you ask me." Lexical formulas such as "I agree" or, in teenage talk, "for sure, for sure" are used to show agreement. It is much more difficult to tell someone that you disagree with their opinions. In political debates, it is common to hear "I disagree" but in ordinary conversation we are less direct, using such phrases as "umm," "maybe," and "Do you really think so?" to express disagreement.

Common lexical phrases express whether we think something is (im)possible (e.g., "I'm sure, It's possible/probable/impossible"). Less common phrases, such as "Can't prove it by me," "Why ask me?" or "Don't know" not only show we do not know but also that we do not perhaps even like to be asked.

Expressing certainty or uncertainty is an especially important function in academic environments. In some fields it is quite proper to express strong to weak certainty, using such words and phrases as *without doubt, clearly, arguably*. In other fields, one never expresses certainty about information, and one cannot say something proves or causes something else. Instead, such lexical phrases as "it appears," "it suggests," "it may be," "x supports (does not support)" are used. In classrooms, however, teachers and students may report uncertainty with lexical expressions such as "I'm not sure, but . . . ," "We still have not determined" (decided) . . . ," or "There is much argument about . . ." Only the brave will joke, "I was absent that day," to show inability to respond to a teacher's question.

Practice 14.10

1. When would you use "I think . . ." or "Do you know what I think? I think . . ." or "If you ask me . . ."? Are there parallel forms for these phrases in the language you teach? Are these presented in your teaching materials? If they are not, do you use them in classroom interactions?
2. How do you vary the strength of the opinion in the language you teach? What parallel forms are there for "I'd say . . . ," "It seems to me . . . ," "As near as I can tell . . . ," "I'm pretty sure that . . . ," "It appears . . . ," "It's quite clear that. . . ." Which are used in academic discourse? Are these included in your teaching materials?
3. Adverbs of certainty are a little tricky (for the linguist if not for language learners). The word *positive* seems to show more confidence than *sure* or *certain* as shown in the exchanges:

A: Are you sure?
B. I'm positive.
A: Are you positive?
B: Well, I'm (pretty) sure.

Does the following list reflect your understanding of which terms carry the most or the least certainty?

Most certain   definitely
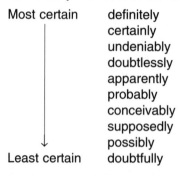
                certainly
                undeniably
                doubtlessly
                apparently
                probably
                conceivably
                supposedly
                possibly
Least certain   doubtfully

In what sorts of discourse might speakers or writers use these forms? If you teach technical writing, how frequently are these used and do they carry the same certainty value in all fields?

4. Select a basic dialogue and add phrases for expressing opinions and agreement with opinions. Dornyei and Thurrell (1992) suggest writing some of the lexical phrases on cue cards and giving them to students. First, have them perform the dialogue in its original form. The second time they must add in the phrases on their cards. Another variation is the "silly Sam" game where "Sam" agrees with whatever anyone says. Students make all sorts of nonsensical claims and the student who is "Sam" must agree.

5. Change the dialogue again so that opinions are expressed and the other person disagrees. (This will be much more difficult.) Try to vary the dialogue so that students first practice polite disagreement and then disagreement with a close friend. Devise a "Disagreeable Dan" game where "Dan" disagrees with every statement. Students can trick "Dan" into a disagreement when he wants to agree.

Expressing or inquiring about emotional attitudes

The expressive function allows us to show our own or inquire about another's interest, surprise, hope, fear, worry, preference, intention, want, or desire. The function includes expressing gratitude, sympathy, and compliments.

We use backchannel signals to express our interest and support of the speaker and to encourage the speaker to continue his or her message. Such expressives as "wow!" "really!" "I can't believe it!" "Can you imagine!" show a heightened interest, surprise, or fear. Expressives, however, can be the central topic of conversation (e.g., "I'm so worried about the exam!").

Advice-seeking and troubles-sharing are typical types of discourse where emotional attitudes become the focus of attention. Lexical phrases like "I'm so worried," "I'm so upset," and "I'm so angry" lead to narratives about what is wrong. Troubles-sharing assumes that sympathy will be offered (e.g., "That's too bad," "That's just not fair," "Poor you") and a negotiation of possible solutions (e.g., "Why don't you just . . . ," "I'd just . . . ," "But I can't just . . . ," "Maybe you should . . ."). These are likely to be followed by some sort of platitude or consolation phrase like "We'll just have to wait and see what happens," "I'm sure everything will turn out for the best," or "Oh, for heaven's sake, just shape up or ship out!"

In American English, the most common expressions of gratitude are "thanks" and "thank you." To make this stronger, we may add *so* or *very.* "Thanks very much" is used by both men and women and in both formal and informal settings. The expression "Thank you very much indeed" sounds very formal (although it's often used on BBC broadcasts to thank the expert who has answered questions about the news of the day).

We noted that expressions of sympathy (or empathy) occur in troubles-sharing (e.g., "that's too bad," "that's really too bad"). The expression of sympathy at a death in a family is somewhat different. In such cases, it is difficult to know what will comfort the family. "I'm so sorry" seems to be the basic expression used.

Compliments come in only a few forms. Manes and Wolfson (1981) found that over half of the 686 compliments they collected fit the lexical phrase formula "X is/looks (really) ADJ" ("Your hair looks really great!" "That blouse is really nice!"). Two more lexical phrases – "I really like/ love X" ("I really love those shoes!") and "PRO is (really) a ADJ X" ("This was really a great meal!") – allowed them to account for 85 percent of the compliments. Four less common lexical formulas complete the set: "You have a ADJ X" ("You have a great voice!"), "What a ADJ X" ("What a great shirt!"), "ADJ X" ("Great tie!"), and "Isn't X ADJ" ("Aren't you incredible!").

Compliment responses differ according to all the variables discussed in the previous chapters. American men often ignore compliments, whereas women are more likely to respond with thanks. Compliments often occur as "noticings" in the opening and closing sections of conversations, where they seem to be used as a kind of social bonding. When compliments occur elsewhere (as in praise of someone's work or performance), the compliment may be taken more seriously and its truth value negotiated in a series of responses following the compliment.

Compliments and responses may vary greatly across languages. Olshtain (1993), for example, notes that in Hebrew the reactions to compliments are much more varied and relate to the content of the compliment. In contrast, she found that approximately 90 percent of the responses in English were "Thank you."

Language learners often report their inability to use expressives in the target language. They feel uncomfortable in not knowing how strong or how modified their expressives should be. They may be unsure which lexical phrase is appropriate for use in certain situations or with specific people. They may feel uncomfortable receiving compliments that they may feel are insincere (but for the American English speaker are simply expressions of friendship). Although the native speaker can get away with outrageous expressives if they are said with a laugh (which shows they may not be meant the way they sound), learners may feel safer using neutral phrases or by not expressing their feelings at all. This is a shame, because friendship includes fluency in using the lexical phrases that show emotional attitudes.

Practice 14.11

1. What lexical phrases are there in the language you teach to show surprise? Are the same surprise signals used by both males and females? Are the frequency of such signals the same for men and women?

2. When and by whom might the following expressions be used?

   Really? No, it can't be!
   Gosh! Wow! Oooh!
   What! Incredible! Amazing! Fantastic!
   I don't/can't believe it!

3. Dornyei and Thurrell (1992) use the following lists of lexical phrases for expression of pleasure and displeasure. Prepare an equivalent contrasting list of lexical phrases for the language you teach or are learning. How might students practice those that are appropriate for their age group?

Oh, good!	Oh, come on!
I'm so glad!	Are you sure?
Good for you!	Really!
(Hey) (that's) great/	What!
fantastic wonderful/	
brilliant!	Are you pulling my leg?
I'm really pleased to hear	I don't/can't believe it!
that.	You're kidding/joking,
Well, isn't that great/	aren't you?
wonderful.	

4. Prepare a list of statements (e.g., "I left my books on the bus!" "I really messed up on the exam!" "My boyfriend won't take me to the party!" "I got an A!" "I'm going to Hawaii!") and have students reply with either positive (e.g., Hey, great!) or negative lexical phrases (e.g., That's terrible!) If your students like to joke, they may use the wrong ones (e.g., "You failed the exam? That's great!") and then you can teach the "What do you mean! It's terrible!" responses.

5. In what circumstances would the following lexical phrases be used? Are different phrases used by men and women? Give a few examples that show the phrases cannot be used in all circumstances.

   I know the feeling!
   You poor thing! Poor you!
   I'm so sorry.
   That must have been horrible!
   You must be very sad/unhappy/upset.

   What other expressions can you think of? What corresponding phrases are there in the language you teach or are learning?

6. In what dialects of English is the word *right* used in compliments instead of *very*? For example, do you say "I'm right proud of you!" rather than "I'm very proud of you!" If you use *right,* can you also use it in other expressives (e.g., "That's right good news!"). Do you also use *just* (e.g., "That's just marvelous!"). Do you use *real* and *really* in expressives ("That's real / really kind of you.")? Do you think the use of *right* as an intensifier for expressives is related in any way to the expression "Right on!"?

7. Are the lexical phrases for giving and accepting compliments similar in the language you teach or are learning? Do they appear in the same places and with the same frequency as they do in American English? Do they serve the same social functions?

Expressing or questioning moral attitudes

At some time, we do something we wish we had not and we then must apologize or request forgiveness. There are also times when we need to express approval or disapproval of the actions of others. In some syllabi, appreciation, regret, and indifference are included in this function group.

In our discussion of scripts, we said that evaluation is an important part of all communication. We constantly evaluate the actions of others, judge the appropriateness of the actions, and may or may not express that evaluation. Some roles, for example, teacher, parent, and supervisor require that evaluation be made explicit through praise (e.g., "Good job! You're doing great!") or criticism (e.g., "Try it this way!" "I'm disappointed that you . . ." "Maybe you could . . ." "Well of all the nerve! How could you?"). For these roles, at least, it is only in frustration that we offer a last resort expression of indifference – "I don't care WHAT you do! Do anything you want!" – meaning that we care very much and hope the behavior will change.

Gripes and complaints are meant to contrast what *is* with what *ought* to be. Brown and Levinson (1978) classify direct complaints as "face-threatening acts" – acts that may disturb the relationship between the complainer and the person responsible for the complaint. Perhaps that is why it is so much easier to complain about a person's behavior to someone else.

Brown and Levinson say we have three options in expressing complaints: decide not to complain at all, use "off-record" strategies like hints and rhetorical questions, or use bald "on-record" strategies such as direct, clear statements of complaint. If speakers decide to use on-record strategies, they have two choices. They may use a "positive politeness" form, where the complaint focus is on how the behavior harms the one who has misbehaved (e.g., "I'm worried about your health. Cigarettes can be very bad for you") or a "negative politeness" form, which focuses on the well-being of the person making the complaint (e.g., "We don't allow smoking here"). Brown and Levinson classify language/culture groups as preferring one form over the other. English is said to be a "negative politeness" language.

In research on complaints, data from Americans show the use of negative politeness forms, but the complaints are softened with hedges (e.g., "Uhh, any chance of your maybe keeping the noise down a little bit or something, maybe just turning it down a notch?"). Nash (1983) found that Taiwanese Chinese speakers used positive politeness forms. The translated complaints about a guest who stayed out late and made a lot of noise on returning to the house included expressions of worry about health ("it's too hard on you staying out so late. Your health is important") and safety ("If something were to happen to you . . . in the middle of the night, nobody would know"). The Americans and Chinese in this study did have in common the fact that they seldom said that the behavior bothered only them. Instead they used *we* or shifted the complaint locus to someone else (e.g., "My wife . . . ," "It's the kids, you know . . ."

"There are people . . . ,"). Many people avoid complaint situations altogether because it is difficult to complain and still preserve the social relationship.

If a complaint is accepted as legitimate, an apology and, perhaps, an expression of forbearance may be called for. In American English, common lexical phrases of acknowledgment include "I didn't realize . . . ," and "I just wasn't aware . . ."). A denial of responsibility may be expressed with lexical phrases like "Why tell me? It's not my fault." Apology lexical phrases include "I'm sorry," "Sorry," "Please forgive me." Common acceptance of apology expressions are "That's okay," "That's all right," "Never mind, it's okay." The formality of the setting and the degree of misbehavior determine whether the speaker will use a strong or weak form. A simple slight, apologized for with "Sorry," may be responded to with "No problem." A more serious infraction requires a more elaborate apology and response. "I'm so very sorry" followed by a promise of forbearance (e.g., "I'll be sure it doesn't happen again") or a request for forgiveness (e.g., "Will you please forgive me?") completes a formal expression of regret. Such an apology might be responded to with a reassuring "I'm sure you didn't mean to," or "Of course, it wasn't really that bad."

Practice 14.12

1. It is easier to express approval than disapproval of the behavior of others. What common phrases are there for each in the language you are teaching or are learning?
2. How do you express approval or disapproval of the behavior of your students, or how do your teachers express their approval or disapproval of your actions? Some teachers always use the student's first language for these functions. Would you argue for or against using the target language for this purpose? Justify your choice.
3. In griping we are more likely to use bald "on-record" strategies than we do in direct complaints. Is this the case in the languages you teach or study? Would you classify these languages as positive or negative politeness languages? Give lexical phrases of complaints to support your answer.
4. What are the lexical formulas for apology in a language of your choice other than English? Are these included in your language textbook? What acceptance of apology phrases are included in your language textbook? Are there a variety of situations used to show how forms for apology giv-

ing and apology acceptance vary in strength and
formality?

5. Olshtain (1993) discusses five "semantic formulas" for
complaining:

   a. Vague hint of the offense.
   b. Disapproval without direct mention that the hearer is
   responsible.
   c. Direct complaint with explicit reference both to the violation and the hearer's responsibility.
   d. Stronger complaint, expressing accusation and
   warning.
   e. A straightforward threat.

   Give an example of a lexical formula that might be used
   for each type. Then, give lexical formulas of responses to
   the complaint. Repeat the activity in another language of
   your choice. How similar are the types of phrases used in
   the two languages?

Suasion

There are many ways in which we can influence the actions of others. We
can suggest, request, invite, instruct, advise, or warn someone to (not) do
something. There are also a variety of ways to offer or request assistance
so that we can complete tasks.

Some of the most commonly presented lexical phrases in ESL/EFL
textbooks do the following:

Suggest a course of action: Let's; We could
Advise others to do something: Why don't you; I can recommend
Warn to refrain: Be careful; Look out
Offer or request assistance: Can you help me? Can I help you?

The lexical phrase "I can recommend" does not seem to be very common
in our experience, although waiters use it as they make suggestions to
customers on what to order!

Research on gender issues has shown that girls use *let's* frequently in
their interactions as they make plans for an activity or in carrying it out.
Boys, on the other hand, use many more direct imperatives (e.g., "Don't
touch that!" "Hit it!"). Girls and boys also use different noncompliance
responses. Boys, for example, are more likely to use the phrase "No way,
man" than are girls. However, one girl in a classroom we observed was
just as determined to *not* do whatever anyone told her to do. Her response was a stubborn "Won't!"

Not surprisingly, suasion (in all its many forms) makes up the bulk of the language addressed to preschool children. Suasion doesn't stop, though, when children enter school. Teacher talk also contains a very large amount of suasive speech. These range from direct to indirect forms (e.g., "Open your books to page 213." "Write your name in the upper right hand corner of your paper." "Could you please speak a little louder?" "I'd like you to help me, but I know your reading teacher is probably waiting for you right now.").

Offers and the acceptance or rejection of offers also belong with suasion because they are requests that the addressee do something – to accept what is being offered. Offers and acceptance of offers do not seem to be particularly difficult for students studying English as a second or foreign language. Rejecting offers, however, can be problematic for both native speakers and learners of the language because rejection may damage the social relation with the person making the offer. When invitations are offered, it is expected that they will be accepted. To avoid outright rejection, we may use lexical phrases as preliminaries to invitation. If someone says "What are you doing this weekend?" or "Are you doing anything special this weekend?" we know that an invitation is on the way. It is possible, though admittedly difficult, to reject the invitation at this point by replying as though the preliminary was really an information question. For example, one might say, "We've planned a really special weekend. We're going to . . ." The invitation may then be made in a modified form (e.g., "Oh, too bad. We hoped you'd join us for . . .") which can be rejected (e.g., "Oh, I'm sorry. If I'd known. But perhaps we can do that another time"). If the original response is "I'm not sure" or "Nothing, why?" we have indicated that we will accept the impending invitation. Lexical phrases of invitation include: "We were wondering if you would like to . . . ," "We'd like you to come . . . ," "We're having a . . . hope you can come. Come on over." To reject the offer after that would be difficult. Of course, we can always say we have to check with other members of the family first.

Practice 14.13

1. Supply two English lexical phrases for each of the four suasion subcategories: Give two examples for each from the languages you teach or are studying. How similar are the lexical phrases? At what level would you suggest presenting the forms you have supplied?

   Suggest a course of action
   Advise others to do something
   Warn to refrain
   Offer or request assistance

2. What lexical phrases do you use in class to ask and receive permission to do something? Are these phrases included in your course materials?
3. Arrange the following suasion phrases in terms of strength. Do you need more than the four categories in item 1 to classify them?

These X need (to be) VERB
These potatoes need mashing.

Would (could) you (please) VERB
Would you please pick up your shoes?

Could we have X done?
Could we have the salt passed?

Let's VERB
Let's give him a higher dosage, nurse.

Are there any (do you have any) NOUN
Do you have any matches?

Have some/another NOUN
Have another cookie.

May I have a NOUN
May I have a salad, please.

Gimme
Give me a cookie!

I want (I don't want) NOUN/VERB
I want a clean pair of socks, hon.

Seems kinda/awful ADJ
Seems kinda cold in here.

Ervin-Tripp (1972) suggested that the phrases used for suasion vary according to whether the person addressed is a subordinate, a familar subordinate or equal, an unfamiliar person, a person who differs in rank or who is physically distant, someone who is in his or her own territory, someone whose willingness to comply is in doubt, someone who might not comply or when there is an obstacle to compliance, and family members, people who live together, and work groups. Can you identify which of the phrases presented in this exercise you would use in addressing each of these addressees?

4. Is the distribution of direct (e.g., "move it!") and indirect (e.g., "let's move it over here") suasion influenced by gen-

der in the language you teach? Is this difference illustrated in your teaching materials? Should it be?

5. List lexical expressions of compliance and noncompliance that vary from formal to informal in the language you teach (e.g., "I'd be glad to," "Happy to," "Sure," "No problem," "Okay, if I have to"). Then match these to the types of requests that might have evoked them (e.g., "Would you please," "Do it!" "Kindly *X*," "Do you think you could possibly *X*?"). Which of these are appropriate for your teaching syllabus?

6. What lexical phrases are used for invitations and acceptance and rejection of invitations in the languages you teach or are studying. Are these presented in your text? How much attention is paid to rejection of offers and invitations? What other activities could be used to practice acceptance and rejection of offers?

Socializing

We have already discussed communication signals that ease social interaction and allow communication to be negotiated among the participants. But lexical phrases for a number of other social acts – introducing, proposing a toast, offering congratulations, beginning (and closing) a meal – also need to be acquired.

The lexical phrases commonly used in American English for introductions are "*X*, this is" (my friend, colleague, the person I've been telling you so much about) + *Y*'s name, then, "*Y*, this is *X*." In response to the introduction, each of the newly introduced people may express their pleasure at being introduced with words and lexical phrases that vary according to the age, sex, status of the participants, and social setting: "Hi," "Hello," "Glad to meet you." "Nice to meet you." The "pleased to meet you" lexical phrase seems to be used primarily by older people or in formal situations.

American English has no obligatory lexical phrase to call persons to the table for a meal. However, there are phrases that vary from formal (e.g., "Shall we have dinner?" "Shall we all sit down to dinner?") to a neutral announcement (e.g., "Dinner's ready!") to the informal (e.g., "Soup's on!" "Chow time!"). Some family groups offer a grace or thanksgiving upon being seated; others do not. There is no special lexical phrases like "bon appetit" to be said by the parent or host or hostess. During the meal, there are many offers (suasion) such as "Have another *X*," "Would you please pass the *X*." At the end of the meal, it is common to thank the person who prepared the food or who invited everyone to the table. Again, these thanks may vary in degree of formality (from "This was a wonderful meal, X, thanks very much" to "Yum, Mom, you did it again!") and the acknowledgment of the thanks may serve as a closing signal to the meal, allowing everyone to leave the table.

Practice 14.14

1. Does your language text include instruction on introductions? What lexical phrases are used? Are there special phrases used to describe each of the participants? For example, after the basic introduction, does the person doing the introduction then comment on something about each person as a way of giving them a topic for conversation (e.g., "John's been telling me about the work he's been doing in Mojave. You've been doing some exploration, too, haven't you?")

2. Do your materials include lessons in both self and other introduction? Are the rules of introduction the same in English and the language you teach? Do your materials limit the types of introductions to be practiced (e.g., age, role, status, sex, situation). How much information is given about the person being introduced?

3. What lexical phrases are used to begin a meal in the language you teach? Are these modeled in your teaching materials? Are there special lexical phrases to use in offering, accepting/rejecting offers of food and drink? What lexical phrases are used to end the meal?

4. In American English, there are no special lexical phrases that we are aware of for offering toasts. Toasts are given on special occasions (e.g., To the bride and groom! at weddings) and even at some less special times (e.g., To the cook!). The toast on special occasions is often proceeded by a short anecdote that explains why the person offering the toast is entitled to make it. How comparable is this to the offering of toasts in the languages you teach or are learning?

5. Look once again at Wong-Fillmore's (1976) list of lexical phrases used by bilingual children in an immersion class in California. How many of the phrases have a clear discourse function? How do you account for the accuracy of these phrases (because they were not taught) compared with the perhaps less "correct" use of other parts of the language?

   Attention callers: Oh, Teacher, Hey stupid
   Name exchanges: What'cher name? My name is X.

Greetings, leave takings: See ya later, Take care, I gotto go, Hello *X*.

Politeness routines: How are you? Thank you very much, 'Scuse me, I'm sorry.

Language management: I don' understand, I don' know, How do you do this in English?

Conversation management: Ya know why? Ya know what? Guess what! Be quiet. Shaddup your mouth. OK? I gotta idea.

Comments and exclamations: How nice! I'm so lucky! Nuts to you! All right, you guys! For heaven's sake! That's not okay!

Questions: What's that? How much? Whatsa matter? You wanna play? Can I? You wanna *X*? Why do I have to?

Responses: I know. I guess so. Not me! I think so. So what? I don't care. I don't know, why? Why not?

Commands and requests: Let's go. Gimme *X*. Let's trade. Lemme *X*. Watch dese! Hurry up. Forget it. Get outta here! Come over here! Somebody help me! Wait a minute.

Presentatives and parallel talk: Here it is. You go like this. Not like this. Fixit up. Put it right there. One more.

Play management: I'm not playing. My turn. Your turn. Me first. I wanna be the *X*. Ready, set, go

Story-telling routines: Once upon a time. One day the *X* was VERBing.

Explanations: Because. That's why.

Wannas and wannits: I wanna(thing). I want some more. I want dese. I don wanna do nothing. I wanna make *X*. I wanna do it.

How might you assess your students' proficiency with these lexical phrases compared with vocabulary that is less discourse bound?

Research and application

Communication signals

1. Godard (1979) describes the telephone openings in business and personal calls in French as compared with American English. In the French openings, callers identify the phone number within the sequence. Compare phone openings of other languages with those for French and English. In what ways are they similar and how do they differ? Answering machines also use set scripts of-

ten containing predictable lexical phrases. Collect data on these as well. How might you use the information you have collected in planning activities to teach the forms to students?

2. Tao and Thompson (1991) found that Mandarin speakers used relatively fewer backchannels than English speakers. Although the backchannel signals of English speakers may overlap the speaker's talk or fit very closely to it, Mandarin speakers have a perceptible gap between the speaker's talk and the backchannel. They also argue that the backchannels in Mandarin are used less to encourage the speaker than to show understanding of or agreement with the speaker. How might this information be useful in planning a lesson on backchannel signals for Chinese learners of English or for English-speaking learners of Mandarin?

3. Fernald and Morikawa (1993) compared the language addressed to 6-, 12-, 19-month-old children playing with toys at home. Thirty Japanese and thirty American (white, middle-class, some college) mothers and their children participated in the study. The researchers found that American mothers labeled objects more frequently and consistently. Japanese mothers, in contrast, used objects to engage infants in social routines. Fernald and Morikawa suggest that Korean mothers may emphasize the same rituals of social exchange as those of the Japanese mothers in this study. Because all groups use culturally appropriate child-rearing behaviors, consider replicating the procedure with another group of mothers or with children who are somewhat older. What do mothers emphasize: the vocabulary of reference (names that refer to things) or communication signals and the lexical phrases of speech acts?

Lexical phrases of speech acts

4. The goal of the Cross-cultural Speech Act Realization Patterns (CCARP) project (Blum-Kulka & Olshtain, 1984) is the development of data-elicitation methods and data analysis methods that would allow researchers to compare speech act performance across many language groups. Blum-Kulka, House, and Kasper (1989) express similar goals. After reading through these publications, draw up a plan for carrying out similar research with speakers of another language group but shift the emphasis to a comparison of the lexical phrases used by each language group.

5. In *Conversational Routines* Coulmas (1981) offers a collection of research that compares the performance of particular speech acts by different language groups. Survey this volume and select

one article. What speech act was compared in this article? What lexical phrases were used by each group? How were the data collected (i.e., do you think the lexical phrases used by participants in the study are those they use in natural, unobserved conversation)? How were the data analyzed? What conclusions can you draw about teaching of the lexicon of this particular speech act based on the findings of this article?

6. Wolfson (1981, 1989) notes that bilinguals sometimes use the lexical phrases of a speech act from the first language when speaking the second. For example, a Farsi speaker complimented his mother's cooking saying, in English, "It was delicious, Mom. I hope your hands never have pain." In another example, an Iranian responded to his friend's compliment, "Your shoes are very nice," with, "It is your eyes which can see them which are nice." If you are from a bilingual family, it may be possible for you to collect data on the use of translated lexical phrases for a variety of speech acts. Consider submitting your findings to the *Journal of Pragmatics.*

7. When Cook (1981) asked students to ask directions or request the time, their performance did not differ much from that of native speakers, but the heavy use of modals in their lexical phrases made them sound more polite. They also used idiosyncratic lexical expressions such as "Thank you I very gratitude you" or "Be so kind of saying the shortest way to the bus station." The overall structure of the communication patterns were correct but the lexical phrases were less so. After reading Cook's research, plan a replication with speakers of other language groups.

8. D'Amico-Reisner (1981) analyzed the forms of disapproval expressions collected within family units or in conversations among people who were well acquainted. Two major patterns accounted for 86% of the data.

Requests for which responses were expected (45 percent)
What are you eating? Why are you putting more syrup?
Why (the hell) did you, hon?
You gonna go or not? You coming?
Do you always read people's mail?

Declaratives (41 percent)
This bathtub is filthy!
You look a mess.
Dishes should be emptied.
(Hey hon) those socks are dirty.
(Lookit) I've been standing here 20 minutes.

After you have read this article, explain why these forms are so different from those discussed in this chapter (or those presented in most language textbooks). Is it important to include these forms in teaching English complaints? If so, what kinds of activities might you do to practice them?

9. Harlow (1990) compared the French of American students with that of native speakers in three speech acts: requesting information, apologizing, and thanking. Harlow varied sociolinguistic factors such as the age, sex, and closeness of relationship with the addressee. How could you use the results of this research in teaching French to Americans?

10. Scarcella (1979) used role plays of party invitations to study pre-invitation, invitation, and acceptance or rejection by adult students of English. Examples such as "I forgot to tell you but I have a party this weekend." "Okay, you'll be one of the members" show that the lexical phrases for such speech acts need to be practiced. Devise a short lesson to teach pre-invitation phrases, invitations, and responses. How might you evaluate the effectiveness of your lesson?

11. Our attitudes toward factual information are carried by verbs that group together as "believing" verbs and "doubting" verbs. Lehrer (1974) compared the types of syntactic structures that can be used with the verbs *assume, presume, postulate, posit, presuppose, suppose, take (it) for granted, guess, know, believe, think, doubt.* The analysis also includes the adverbs mentioned in Practice 14.10.3. Lehrer concludes that an inventory of lexical items is a beginning point, but that to understand the meaning and use of words, one must go far beyond constructing taxonomies or lists of words. This article is a good place to start for further research on attitudes toward intellectual information as a speech act. Do you agree or disagree with Lehrer's conclusion regarding the usefulness of lists of terms and the value of arranging them in hierarchies?

12. In this chapter, we have emphasized the vocabulary of lexical phrases used as communication signals and as speech acts. Specialists in discourse analysis object, and quite rightly, to an emphasis on lexical phrases because these phrases are useless unless they are correctly placed in negotiated discourse. Read Chapters 1, 2, and 4 of Hatch (1992), or Atkinson and Heritage (1984). How might you support explicitly teaching the discourse meanings of lexical phrases?

Part V Vocabulary learning and vocabulary teaching

15 General vocabulary learning and learner strategies

While knowing more about semantics and the lexicon produces insights in us as language educators, most of us are principally interested in knowing how to translate that knowledge into practice or understanding of what learners do or should do and of what teachers do or should do to aid the process of language learning. Chapter 16 will deal with teachers and materials developers and the strategies they use to help learners learn and comprehend vocabulary. This chapter deals directly with learners' strategies for learning vocabulary and compensating for vocabulary that they do not know. We will look first at some of the general issues or questions that arise in discussions of vocabulary learning. Then we will discuss five steps that seem essential for students in their vocabulary learning. Finally, we will examine compensation strategies used by learners when they don't know or can't retrieve particular vocabulary items.

General issues

Discussions of vocabulary learning are often divided between intentional learning and incidental learning. We define intentional learning as being designed, planned for, or intended by teacher or student. We define incidental learning as the type of learning that is a byproduct of doing or learning something else. There is general consensus among L1 vocabulary experts (e.g., Calfee & Drum, 1986; Stahl & Fairbanks, 1986; Beck, McKeown, & Omanson, 1987; Chall, 1987; Drum & Konopak, 1987; Graves, 1987) that intentional learning, in particular instruction, does aid in the learning of words. However, several studies have shown how few words are learned or taught by direct instruction compared to how many students need to know. For example, Nagy and Anderson (1984) and Nagy and Herman (1987) were able to show that even the most ambitious vocabulary teaching programs in the first language (in their case, English) did not teach more than a few hundred words per year. This in spite of the fact that there are more than 450,000 entries in *Webster's Third International Dictionary* and that claims are made that university students in the United States know at least 200,000 of them. We are quite sure that not all 200,000 have been intentionally taught.

In a second language the contrasts are just as vivid. According to

Ramsey (1981), a 12-year-old in Spain knows approximately 135,000 vocabulary words in the first language. High school students studying English in Spain are introduced to 800–1,000 English words in first year EFL classes, 1,700–2,000 more in second year classes, and another 2,500–3,000 in third year. So, in three years they might acquire, at most, 6,000 words in English. If they continued at the same rate for 12 years (to make the comparison to the 12-year-old fair), they would still know only about 24,000 words.

Because there is a definite gap between what is taught and what is known, more attention needs to be given to the issue of incidental vocabulary learning. Most of the work with incidental learning has focused on the vocabulary which is learned through reading. Saragi, Nation, and Meister (1978) looked at the learning of vocabulary by adults who read Burgess's *A Clockwork Orange,* which contains 241 words in an invented language called "nadsat." Saragi et al. designed a multiple-choice test containing 90 of the nadsat words and administered it to native English-speaking adults who had just read the book. The scores on the test ranged from 50 to 96 percent correct with an average of 76 percent correct, suggesting that the adults had learned about 70 words incidentally with just one reading of the book. Likewise, Nagy, Herman, and Anderson (1985), using 1,000-word passages and 57 eighth-grade students, have shown that incidental learning accounts for a large proportion of L1 vocabulary growth by school-age children.

Yun (1989) did a study similar to that of Saragi et al., using 32 intermediate ESL learners reading a simplified version of *Tom Sawyer.* Yun devised a test of 60 words which teachers had selected as ones students were likely not to know. She pre-tested her subjects and then tested them after they had read the book. She concluded that students learned incidentally approximately 16 percent of all unknown words with just one reading of the book. From scores on the pretest, she calculated that approximately 19 percent of the words in the book would have been unknown and, therefore, that, on the average, 106 words would have been learned from just the one reading.

This incidental learning of words from reading in particular is apparently quite powerful also in the foreign language (rather than the second language) environment. In fact, after one study with French learners in the United States, the researchers, Dupuy and Krashen (1993) estimated that the learners who participated in reading and watching a film (in this case *Très hommes et un couffin*) in class acquired approximately five to ten words per hour from incidental learning from a quite difficult text. The research did not test words that could have been learned from regular classroom interaction, so it is possible that students actually acquired even more words incidentally.

Besides the division between intentional learning and incidental learning often discussed with regard to vocabulary learning, there is also the division between receptive vocabulary and productive vocabulary. Some people say the division is between "passive" and "active" vocabulary rather than between receptive and productive vocabulary. Belyayev (1963) criticizes the passive/active terms, arguing that reading and listening should not be considered passive skills and that, therefore, the vocabulary needed for those skills should not be considered passive, either. Linguists and teachers since then have generally accepted the receptive/ productive dichotomy, defining the two terms in much the same way as Haycraft (1978): receptive vocabulary is "words that the student recognizes and understands when they occur in a context, but which he cannot produce correctly," and productive vocabulary is "words which the student understands, can pronounce correctly and use constructively in speaking and writing" (p. 44). We sense that there is not really a dichotomy between receptive and productive but rather a continuum of knowledge, as Crow and Quigley (1985) have surmised. They suggest that learners may learn core or basic meanings of words sufficiently to understand what they hear or read without knowing enough about the syntactic restrictions, register appropriateness, or collocations to be able to produce the words on their own.

Furthermore, the discussions of dichotomy between receptive and productive vocabularies do not seem to take into account personal choice. We understand multitudes of words in our native language that we may never use. For example, we may understand terms used by our parents or grandparents, but never produce those terms, although we could. Likewise, we may recognize the meaning of nonstandard words such as *ain't,* or taboo words, but studiously avoid saying them because we are concerned about other people's views of us. This also suggests that the division between receptive vocabulary and productive vocabulary is not always real; lack of production may be due to choice and not simply lack of knowledge.

The most important point of the receptive/productive discussion is that it suggests that there are different ways to "know" a word, that what is considered sufficient knowledge under one circumstance will probably not be sufficient under others. In previous chapters we have talked about some of the things that speakers know and about lexical processes they use to come to this knowledge: semantic fields and features, core meanings and prototypes, lexical relations, universals, loan words and cognates, figurative language and metaphors, scripts or domains, word borrowing and coining, incorporation, word building, lexical classes, morphology, and social "markings" on words for location, gender, age, occupation, education, group, and formality.

The specificity of any individual's knowledge about a word depends on the person and his or her motivation, desires, and needs for the word.

Acquisition does not appear to be a simple throwing of a switch between knowing and not knowing; rather, there seems to be a continuum of knowledge about any word and a learner can be anywhere along the continuum. For example, it has been shown that children can recognize and list several color terms before they can identify the colors to which the terms apply. In a similar way, we may know that waistcoat, muffler, bermudas, housecoat, and Birkenstocks refer to items of clothing without being able to identify the items.

Furthermore, knowledge about words may include information that may cause learners to choose not to produce them. For example, we may understand terms used by speakers of other dialects, but never choose to use them. Likewise, we may recognize such nonstandard and slang expressions as "done deal" or "no way," but studiously avoid saying them for social or other reasons. Thus, it appears that the receptive/productive division is not a simple dichotomy nor a simple knowledge continuum, but is probably related to both a knowledge continuum and a "self-image" continuum. Knowing vocabulary may, therefore, also consist of knowing enough to use words which represent the image we wish others to have of us. Any theory or model of vocabulary learning must account for these different levels of knowledge about and use of words.

Practice 15.1

1. Read the first chapter of a textbook on any subject on which you are not an expert. Write down any terms which are new to you or seem to be used in a new way. How many of those terms are explicitly defined in the chapter? How many do you think you could define even though they are not defined in the chapter? What can you say about the strength of intentional and incidental teaching and learning on the basis of this exercise? How much of learning a subject seems to be learning the vocabulary of that subject?

2. Select two lessons at random out of each book in a textbook series for a language you hope to teach. How many words does each teach explicitly (intentionally)? If learners learned every word taught explicitly, how many words would they know once they had finished one year of the series? The entire series?

3. Read Saragi, Nation, and Meister's (1978) study using *A Clockwork Orange,* or Pitts, White, and Krashen's (1989) replication with L2 learners, or Yun's (1989) study using *Tom Sawyer.* Try replicating one of these with ESL learners you are acquainted with.

4. In a game called Category, the leader names a category –
flowers, furniture, items of clothing, jazz singers, etc. – and
then at a particular point in a rhythmical clapping each person in the circle in turn has to name some thing or some
person which fits in the category (rose, daisy, petunia, etc.,
for the category "flowers"). Try playing this game with
some friends using categories that do not include names
of persons or other proper nouns. How many of the item
names do you recognize readily as fitting in the category
without knowing enough to distinguish them completely
from other items in the category? How many of the items
do you know thoroughly so you could pick them out of the
group of everything named?

5. Ask individuals if they can think of any words in their native language that they never use. Ask them what reasons
they have for not using these words. How many of the reasons relate to a possible lack of knowledge? How many of
them relate to the image the person is trying to portray?
Are there other reasons people choose not to use words
productively? Do you think the receptive/productive dichotomy is real for native speakers? Now ask individuals who
speak a second language to think of any words in the second language that they never use. Are their reasons for
not using the words the same as the ones native speakers
give? Is the issue of receptive and productive vocabulary
the same for second language learners as it is for native
speakers?

Five essential steps in vocabulary learning

Teachers have always been naturally interested in how learners go about
learning vocabulary. If we know more about learner strategies and what
works and what does not work well, we can help learners acquire more
profitable strategies. Intuitively, we have always given advice about how
to learn vocabulary. Some teachers even make assignments for this purpose. For example, "Write down every new word you encounter in a
notebook. Try to guess what it means in the context in which you heard
it." Or, "Try to use any new words you learn as soon as you learn them.
In fact, I want you to write me ten sentences tonight using new words you
have learned."

Payne (1988) made a more formal study of vocabulary learning strategies used by ESL students. She began by asking seventeen ESL students
randomly selected from an intensive English program what strategies they

used to learn vocabulary. All but the highest level students were interviewed in their native language in order to be sure that students could
explain their strategies as they desired. The answers to this open-ended
question were transcribed and Payne devised a questionnaire containing
thirty-two statements, each of which described a strategy mentioned by
the students who had been interviewed. This questionnaire was then
administered to more than 100 ESL students asking them to rate how
effective they thought each described strategy was for them. Using Payne's
data, Brown and Payne (1994) did an analysis that resulted in a very clear
model where the strategies fall into five essential steps: (1) having sources
for encountering new words, (2) getting a clear image, either visual or
auditory or both, for the forms of the new words, (3) learning the meaning
of the words, (4) making a strong memory connection between the forms
and meanings of the words, and (5) using the words.

Although the steps identified by Brown and Payne may possibly be
divided into smaller components, it appears to us that each represents
something learners must do, at least at some minimal level, to come to a
full productive knowledge of words. (It may be that step 5 is not absolutely essential if the goal is purely receptive knowledge.)

The steps might be seen as a series of sieves as illustrated in Figure 15.1.
If learners or teachers can do anything to move more words through any
of the steps, the overall result should be more vocabulary learned. The
five processes are described in more detail below.

Encountering new words

The first essential step for vocabulary learning is encountering new
words, that is, having a source for words. The student strategies here
included "learning new words by reading books," "listening to TV and
radio," and "reading newspapers and magazines" (Payne, 1988, p. 33).
As far as incidental learning of vocabulary goes, this step is obviously the
most vital. Because incidental learning of vocabulary must occur if second
language learners are to approach a vocabulary that compares with that
of native speakers, this step is crucial.

How many words make it past this step may vary because of many
learner factors. For example, natural learner interest or motivation may
cause learners to pay more attention to some words than others. As
discussed in Chapter 3, Yoshida's (1978) subject, Miki, learned many
words in an area which was of interest to him, finding ways to encounter
and learn all kinds of words for vehicles, wild animals, and outdoor
objects, but very few for other very common items such as dress, skirt,
ring, lamp.

In addition to interest, actual need may make a difference in whether
encountered words are learned. We seem to learn words more quickly if

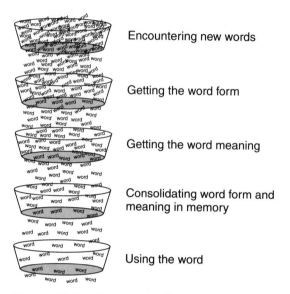

Encountering new words

Getting the word form

Getting the word meaning

Consolidating word form and
meaning in memory

Using the word

Figure 15.1   Five essential steps to learning new words

we have felt a need for them in some way. LaPorte (1993) looked at
words learned by students engaged in dialogue journal writing with their
teacher. In several instances students had to use their native language
word or a circumlocution to express a concept. When the teacher supplied the second language words for the concept, the students readily
picked them up, as the following excerpts from the journals show (the
numbers indicate the number of the entry in the journal):

Student 10

S7: He is living in a pension. The lady encharged of it had a trouble
with her heart and he had to take her to the hospital –

T8: I have to tell you that I got a little confused with the story about
your boyfriend's landlady and your relationship in it.

S9: I see you were little confused about the story of my boyfriend's
landlady and our relationship.

S9: the problem was that have decided to meet that night but as the
landlady felt bad my boyfriend took her to hospital very late at
night.

S9: The landlady's husband was out and knew what happened very
late.

Student 11

S4: There most of his family brothers, nieces, nephews, etc. were
celebrating this day. Some were dancing cueca and others were
doing empanadas and rescoldo which is made of the mass [Spanish

masa means "dough"] of the bread and is put in the hot coals
covered with ashes.
T4: Do you put the bread dough directly on the coals and cover it with
ashes, or is the dough in some container that you then put on the
coals?
S5: Rescoldo is like an omelet and the bread dough is put directly on
the coals and is covered with ashes and with coals, too.

Another indication that encountering words may be more effective
under some circumstances than others has been found in work with
interactive video materials. When students have seen an object or an
action, their desire to know the label (word) for it may increase so that,
when the word for it is encountered, it is learned very quickly. This
appeared to be the case in Brown's 1993 study where learners were using
an interactive version of *Raiders of the Lost Ark*. Learners had seen some
objects or actions in the video so they had a visual image of them but did
not hear or see the vocabulary items until later. Later in the video script or
the instructional exercises, the words were supplied for what the learners
had seen. These vocabulary items were learned significantly faster than
other words in the script or exercises.

The number of times that a word is encountered may also affect
whether it is learned. It appears logical that the need learners feel for a
word would increase as they continued to encounter it. There is some
evidence that learners are sensitive to the frequency with which they
encounter both familiar and unfamiliar words. They say such things as "I
don't know what that word means, but I've seen it a lot," or "I've never
seen that word before."

Nagy and Herman (1987) have argued that "even a single encounter
with a word in context" might help increase learner's knowledge about
that word and its meaning. Likewise, in first language learning, Jenkins
and Dixon (1983) have argued that between six and twelve encounters
with a word were necessary to ensure that the word would be learned.
However, Brown (1993) found no connection between the words that
were acquired and the number of occurrences of those words in the
source text. Instead, there was a small (.20) but important correlation
between the words acquired and their general frequency (as given in
Francis & Kučera, 1982). Learners may need various encounters with the
same word in multiple sources rather than in just one source.

Reading is not the only way in which learners encounter words. The
learners in Payne's study frequently mentioned watching television and
listening to the radio as good ways to learn vocabulary. Living with
speakers of the language one is trying to learn is also important. As
teachers of second (not foreign) languages, we are continually amazed at
the vocabulary questions which come from our college students living in

the dormitories. Also, we have known learners with the personal strategy to go out and speak with native speakers until they have encountered a certain number of new words every day.

Other strategies may not be as personally interactive and interesting, but they do serve learners. For example, textbook or teacher-assigned word lists are sources where learners may encounter new words. Lehr (1984) claims that the word list is probably the most widely used approach to vocabulary development in formal settings, and most textbooks, particularly those used in foreign language settings, provide chapter word lists, end glossaries, or both.

Dictionaries are also sources where new words and new uses for old words can be encountered. Recent work in progress in Hong Kong by Yongqi Gu followed the reading and dictionary use of students and found that the better learners used the dictionary extensively to learn not just the words they originally started to look up but also related words or words nearby in the dictionary.

Other teachers have suggested that students be encouraged to generate their own word lists. Such lists are very easily compiled by students learning a language but may not be quite as easily generated in foreign language environments. As students notice where they encounter foreign words, they can begin to see some of the issues related to variation in lexical choice. In Japan, for example, many French words are found in fashion ads, and English words abound in music- and entertainment-industry-related products. Students would also learn that words encountered on t-shirts may differ from the words encountered on food product or technological instrument labels and instructions.

Continued work with sources may clarify what sources or characteristics of sources are most desirable, but for now it is quite clear that learners have to encounter words in textbooks or out before they can learn them.

Practice 15.2

1. Have classmates or friends list two topics of great interest to them and two topics in which other people have interest but they do not. Then give them a few minutes to write down as many words as they can on each of the topics. Are there differences in the quantity of words they write about the topics they are interested in and those they are not? Ask how they learned the words about the topics which interested them. Then try the same thing with your language learners having them write words for the topics in the language they are learning. How different are their lists for the topics of interest and the topics without inter-

est? How did they learn the words for their topics of interest?

2. Ask some of your language learners if they know of times when they wanted to express a particular idea or concept for which they did not have the words. What did they do, if anything, to get the words? Do any of them recount stories of circumlocuting on the spot and then finding the words they needed later? Do any of them have ideas or concepts for which they still don't have the second language words? Can you tell why? Can you think of sources where they might have learned the words they want?

3. Using a word frequency list such as that of Francis and Kučera (1982) for English, choose twenty words that come from twenty different levels of frequency in another language of your choice. Give the list (without any marking of frequency) to native speakers of the language and ask them to rank them in order from the most frequent to the least frequent. Give the same list to nonnative learners of the language and have them do the same thing. How accurate are both groups? For items which seem to be quite out of order, ask your subjects why they ranked them as they did.

4. Make a list of all possible sources for encountering new target language words which your learners might use in a second language environment and rate them for which ones you think would be best in terms of quantity of words encountered. Then, do the same thing for encountering target language words in the foreign language environment. How do the two lists differ? Now, ask your learners about where they encounter most of the words they learn. Are there some sources they are not using that you could teach them to use profitably? Are there some sources they are using which you could suggest to other learners?

5. Open your dictionary at random and read a definition for a word. Do you also automatically glance at nearby words to see what new and interesting other words you might learn? If learners who use dictionaries also look at words around the word they have looked up, would it be better if these nearby words were semantically related to the word they had first looked up? The *Oxford Advanced Learners' Dictionary* (Hornby) and the *Longman Lexicon of Contemporary English* (McArthur) group related words under semantic headings. How might you determine whether such groupings are helpful for learners who like to browse after looking up a word?

Getting the word form

The second step essential to vocabulary learning appears to be the getting of a clear image – visual or auditory or both – of the form of the vocabulary item. This step was shown in comments such as "associating new words with words that sound similar in my native language," "writing the sounds of words using sound symbols from my native language," "associating words that are similar to words in other languages I have studied," "associating a word with a similar sounding English word I know," and "seeing a word that looks like another word I already know" in this step.

The importance of having a clear image of the "form" of a word becomes apparent when we think about what happens when we try to retrieve words. The classic study in this area was done by Brown and McNeill (1966). Definitions of words with very low frequency were read to the participants and the participants were asked to write down what they thought the word might be. When they could not think of the word, they were asked to write down what they could remember. When the target was a "flat-bottomed boat used in rivers along the coast in Southeast Asia," responses including saipan, Siam, Cheyenne, sarong, sympoon, sanching, houseboat, barge, and junk were supplied. Many of these share sounds and the two-syllable length with *sampan,* the target-word. Brown and McNeill concluded that initial sound, final sound, and number of syllables were all aspects used to retrieve words from memory. A similar study done by Brown (1983) with second language learners had similar results. Learners also seemed to give a higher than average number of guesses with the correct initial sound, final sound, and number of syllables for words that were on the tip-of-the-tongue. There were also indications that the form of native language words affected the search for the target language words.

The importance of getting the form of the word also appears when students are asked to give definitions for words. Beginning students are particularly likely to make mistakes that are obviously related to confusions of the form of one word with the form of other words. In one experiment students were given an English sentence with one word underlined and were asked to write their native language translation of the word. Their translations were then backtranslated to English. Table 15.1 shows some of the words for which the students were attempting to give translations and what the backtranslations of their words were (the persons who did the backtranslation had not seen the original sentences nor test words).

Many of the errors seem to be caused by, or related to the confusing of words similar in form either to a native language word or to another English word.

TABLE 15.1   BACKTRANSLATIONS OF LEARNERS' NATIVE LANGUAGE
DEFINITIONS

English word	Backtranslation	Native word
happened	happy	felices (Sp.)
shouts	shots	tiros (Sp.)
worth	word	palabra (Sp.)
then	than	que (Sp.)
recently	recipe	receta (Sp.)
still	style	estilo (Sp.)
path	patio	patio (Sp.)
	peace	paz (Sp.)
each	which	dono (Jap.)
script	scriptures	escritura (Sp.)
	description	byoshya (Jap.)
bronze	blouse	buraus? (Jap.)
incurred	include	fukumu (Jap.)
prominently	average	promedio (Sp.)
rope	closet	ropero (Sp.)
	clothes	ropa (Sp.)
intoxicated	intelligence	interi (Jap.)
explosion	explanation	setsumei (Jap.)
	experiment	jikken (Jap.)

The use of word form can also be seen in a study by Huckin and Bloch (1993), in which three native Chinese-speaking subjects were given two English texts to read. Twenty-seven words from the texts had been chosen as "test" words, which the learners were less likely to know, and the subjects had been pretested on these words. The subjects were then asked to translate the texts into Chinese while "thinking aloud" in either English or Chinese about what they were doing. Huckin and Bloch found that the learners were able to use context to define and translate correctly twenty-five of the possible forty-four words they did not know (twenty-seven words by 3 students minus the words already known on the pretest). They were unsuccessful in their guessing nineteen out of the forty-four times, and nine of those times "they apparently mistook the word for another that resembles it (e.g., pillars for appliers)" (p. 160). All of these errors indicate that learners are often led astray in their attempts to understand words because they confuse the form of the word with another form.

Problems for learners arising from words similar in form have been identified as a major problem for language learners and given the name *synophones* by Laufer (1981). In a lexical error analysis, Teemant (1988) also found form confusion to account for about one fourth of all errors. In this study, the language background of the students was an important factor. Spanish and Portuguese native speakers had many more form confusions than Japanese native speakers. Teemant felt that this aspect of vocabulary learning was harder for the learners whose languages used the Roman alphabet because of confusions with words and spellings in their native language. Japanese words were so different in form that fewer written form confusions resulted. Whatever the reason for the confusion of the learners, it is obvious that learning the form is important. Almost all learners seem to have strategies, such as those listed above, that they automatically use to help them remember the form of foreign language words.

Practice 15.3

1. As you teach a foreign language class, identify lexical errors that your students make. Record each error and its context. Then also record your best guess as to what the learner was trying to communicate. If possible, find out what the lexical item would be for that concept in the learner's native language. What percentage of the errors can be attributed to a confusion with a similar looking or sounding word in the target language? What percentage can be attributed to a confusion with a similar looking or sounding word in the native language? What kind of teaching strategies might help your students?

2. Researchers into the reading processes in the first language looked at word identification issues in the late 1960s and early 1970s. Read Kenneth Goodman's (1969 or 1973) work on miscue analysis or Frank Smith's (1969 or 1988) work on word identification. Then, record a group of your friends or students reading aloud a passage in your target language. Listen to the reading and identify occasions when the readers either say a wrong word or start to say an incorrect word and then backtrack and correct the word. How many of the mistakes seem to be caused by the grammatical structure? How many of them seem to be caused by mistaking one word for a similar looking word? What do Goodman's and Smith's findings and methodology and your own study teach you about the influence of form on how students identify words in context?

3. Read Ringbom's (1987) work or Nash's (1978) work discussed in Chapter 6, and Singleton and Little's experiment discussed in Chapter 4. What evidence is there in

these works that word form affects vocabulary learning and use? Would you predict that word form would have more or less effect on vocabulary learning for your students than it had for the Swedish, Finnish, and Spanish users of English and the English learners of French that these works discuss?

4. The tip-of-the-tongue experiments show that we use phonological cues (i.e., it starts with a *k-*, it sounds something like, it's a long word) in attempting to retrieve words. Baker (1974) asked participants to do a retrieval task based on the sounds of words by listening to a word and trying to match it. We will try the task with printed words instead. As soon as you read the word, try to think of as many like words as you can that have the same initial, medial, or final sound.

Group 1: same vowel sound as the word given
        bone   tick   cake

Group 2: same initial consonant
        boy   fan   cone

Group 3: same final consonant
        rim   mass   cab

Group 4: same number of syllables
        survival   hippopotamus desk

Group 5: same medial consonant
        ladder   mileage   final

Group 6: same part of speech
        sit   yellow   quick

Group 7: same last syllable
        hunter   photo   lesson

Stress and rhyme probably influence the number of words you think of in many of the categories. In order to get the same medial consonant, and the same vowel, you probably relied on rhyme with the test word. Again, what happened to the medial parts of words in your attempts to supply words?

5. Haynes (1993) reports that in a study where students were supposed to guess the meaning of unknown words in context, one of her subjects mispronounced the word *waves* and then guessed that it meant "the opposite of 'husbands'" (p. 54). Look at the words given in Table 15.1 and those that you collected for item 1. Are there any in which mispronunciation may have played a role? What might be

said about the relationship of pronunciation and vocabulary learning?

6. In *Pullet Surprises* (Green, 1969), randomly select ten to twenty of the items. What forms did the writers really want for each? In what ways do these form confusions resemble those made by language learners? Are there any differences? Are the native speakers who confused the forms just acquiring these vocabulary words? What other reasons might there be for the confusions? Do any of these reasons apply to second language learners?

Getting the word meaning

The third essential step in the learners' reported strategies is the one which is most often associated with the idea of vocabulary learning: getting the word meaning. This step includes such strategies as "asking native English speakers what words mean," "asking people who speak my native language the meaning of new words," "making pictures of word meanings in my mind," and "explaining what I mean and asking someone to tell me the English word."

The specificity of the meaning that learners need may vary. For example, if someone asks, "What's an azalea?" we may reply, "a type of flower," or, more specifically, "a type of honeysuckle," or "the kind of flower or bushes like those pink ones in front of Aunt Mary's house." If we are in a botany class, however, the definition might be as specific as "a genus of flowering shrubs with funnel-shaped corollas and deciduous leaves. They are from the heath family and related to rhododendrons. There are three commonly cultivated native American species: *Azalea nudiflora, Azalea viscosa,* and *Azalea lutea.*"

The level of distinctions that must be made in word definitions seems to vary both with the requirements of the task or situation and also with the level of the learner. Although beginning learners seem satisfied with quite general meanings, more advanced learners often need more specific definitions in order to differentiate between near synonyms. Similar characteristics are seen in the definitions which mothers supply to children learning their first language. Anglin (1977, 1978) found that adults used general names for objects, such as *money* in place of *nickel* or *dog* instead of *collie*, when talking to 2-year-olds. Likewise, Mervis and Mervis (1982) found that mothers sometimes gave their 13-month-old children general, but slightly incorrect (by adult standards) labels for objects. For example, the mothers might call a toy leopard a *kitty-cat* or a toy tow truck a *car*. Berko-Gleason (1993) observes that these kinds of parental definitions seem to follow what Rosch, Mervis, Gray, Johnson, and Boyes-Graem (1976) have called basic-level categories (see the discussion of basic categories in Chapter 3).

The kinds of definitions given by adults to children change, however, with the age of the children and the words to be learned. Callanan (1985) found that mothers of 2- to 4-year-olds used a lot of pointing to teach basic level words, but gave lists of objects to teach superordinate terms (e.g., "a car and a bus and a train. All of them are kinds of vehicles").

Language learners may also need different kinds of definitions and distinctions depending on the words being learned and the reasons for needing them. Advanced learners may find thesauruses more appropriate than dictionaries in supplying the finer distinctions in meaning that they need. Table 15.2 shows some of the errors advanced ESL learners made with native language translations for English words (the errors in Table 15.1 came from the same set of data, but generally from lower level students.)

Learners often get close to the meaning of the English words, choosing meanings that have some of the features (see Chapter 1) of the test word, but not all. For example, a windshield is a window, but it is a particular kind of window. *Upon,* as used in the test sentence, does relate to time but it does not mean *since, after, once,* or *by* in this context. *Strong* and *hard* share some features with *heavy,* but are also distinct in several ways. Likewise, a path is not a footbridge, an entrance, nor a road, but it shares some characteristics with those things.

The data in Table 15.2, which come mainly from intermediate or more advanced learners, indicate that the learners know some things about the vocabulary, but they also seem to indicate the need to refine meanings for words, to make finer distinctions, which thesauruses generally do better than regular dictionaries. Doing feature analyses might help learners in their attempts to get the meaning of the words they are learning.

Most teachers know, however, that learners assume that dictionaries are one of the main sources of word definitions. After all, language learners carry around dictionaries, not grammar books. If learners carry dictionaries, however, it would seem wise for them to have the best possible dictionary. Oskarsson (1975) carried out experiments to see what kind of glossaries (and, hence, dictionaries) were most helpful to students. He found that students receiving bilingual glosses (oral or written) scored consistently higher on vocabulary tests (both written cloze tests and oral interviews about texts which had been read) than students who received monolingual glosses. In one experiment, the scores of students using a monolingual glossary were only 78 to 84 percent of scores by those who received bilingual glosses. There seems to be natural progression in the type of dictionaries or glosses that learners prefer. They seem to go from picture dictionaries, to bilingual dictionaries, and then to monolingual dictionaries and thesauruses.

TABLE 15.2 MEANINGS FOR ENGLISH TEST WORDS GIVEN BY SPANISH AND
JAPANESE ESL STUDENTS

Test word in context	*Student meaning given for test word*
The *windshield* was clean.	shutter, window, window frame
They think the best *course* is –	reason, result, procedure
The box of books was *heavy*.	strong, hard
The *path* was beautiful.	entrance, footbridge, road, street
Upon hearing the news –	since, after, for, once, by
We need a *rope*.	string or ribbon, pipe
The real *worth* of the book isn't . . .	meaning, significance
They loved their *idol*.	important thing, pretty thing
Please hand me the *script*.	handbook, scriptures, documents
I had the *honor* of introducing –	responsibility, authority, credit

Another way of getting definitions is simply by having a bilingual friend or a teacher explain. Research into ways in which teachers present academic information in classes for native speakers and classes in "sheltered English" (where international students as a group take an academic content class) has shown that native speakers naturally make adjustments and supply clarifications and definitions for nonnative speakers. The usefulness of these clarifications is not always certain, however. Chaudron (1983, 1988) has shown that learners are sometimes more confused than helped by such explanations. We will discuss this further in Chapter 16.

Finally, one very popular (with language pedagogues at least) way and practically the only way in incidental learning for learners to get the meaning of words is through context. Learners guess the meaning of words from the situation, discourse, and/or context in which they are used, and from the structure of the words themselves. Haynes (1993) found that "guessing" was one of only two principles urged in all of the reading textbooks she examined. In order to see the effectiveness of such guessing, Haynes had ESL students read passages and guess at the meaning of unfamiliar words. Each passage contained two nonsense words which replaced all occurrences of two real words. The nonsense words were included in order to ensure that students would encounter words they could not have known from any other source. The only way they could tell what the words meant would be through context and word structure. The meaning of one of the nonsense words in each passage could be guessed from the clues just within the sentence in which it occurred (Haynes calls this "locally constrained"). Guessing the meaning of the other nonsense word required synthesizing information from throughout the passage (Haynes calls this "globally constrained").

Haynes found that all the learners were much more successful at guessing the meaning of locally constrained words than the globally constrained words. She also found that guessing success depended a great deal on the number of other unfamiliar words in the passage.

Although the depth of definition needed may vary and the sources from which meaning can be extracted may be quite different, all learners must get the meaning of words in some manner, or the words can never be considered truly learned.

Practice 15.4

1. There are arguments about what role pictures (and other visual aids) have in promoting vocabulary acquisition. Try using a pictorial gloss for a selection of words with one group of your students and a bilingual gloss with another. Which group do you think will retain the meanings longer? (This project might be done as an over the summer attrition project.) Which of the many picture dictionaries do you think is most useful? Justify your choice of pictures and use your survey of dictionaries as part of the literature review for your project (or prepare an article giving your evaluation of the dictionaries).

2. Using tapes that you recorded previously in language classes, identify words for which teachers give explicit definition or clarifications. What, if any, indications are there on the tapes that these clarifications helped the students? Are there any indications that some of the clarifications may have caused more confusion? Can you see any characteristics that make one type of clarification more helpful than another?

3. Whiskeyman (1990) developed interactive videodisc materials where students could stop the flow of information to find meanings of words or phrases. The "helps" in this program are in the target language not in the students' L1. The first help layer gives information on the meaning of the word. The second help is a sound or graphic illustration. The third might be more graphics or an animated sequence. Students click on the question mark symbol in order to get the helps. For example, the help in the first help cue might be:

   a. A synonym: igual = los mismo   (*Equal = the same*)

    b. A definition: Pana es una tela de algodón. (*Corduroy is a cotton material.*)

    c. An explanation: Un paraguas es para la lluvia. (*An umbrella is for the rain.*)

    d. A simile or metaphor: Una blusa es como una camisa pero es para una mujer. (*A blouse is like a shirt, but for a woman.*)

    e. A category: Un saco es un artículo de ropa. (*A suitcoat is a piece of clothing.*)

The help in the second help cue for this last item might be a picture of a suitcoat and the help in the third might be an animated sequence showing a man buying a suitcoat.

    Select a short article from the popular press in a language you are studying or teaching. Mark the words or phrases where you or your students could use a help button. Then consider the kinds of helps that would be most useful and include this information. If you use Hypercard or Supercard or Toolbook, you might want to prepare a short computer lesson using your materials.

4. Choose a passage you want your students to read. Starting with the second sentence, mark every *n*th (tenth, fifteenth, or twentieth) word. Then re-examine the passage looking for any context cues which might give hints to the definitions of the marked words. For how many words can you find context cues? Which would you consider locally constrained cues and which would you consider globally constrained cues? If students knew all of the words in the passage except the ones you marked, what percentage of the marked words do you think they would be able to guess from context? What would happen to the ability of students to use contextual cues if they knew only about 60 percent of the other words?

5. *Pullet Surprises* (Green, 1969) shows that students are often trying to figure out the meanings of words based on their forms. For example, the word *risibility* sounds like *visibility* and some students defined it as "how far an aviator can see." But others defined it as the "ability to rise in the world." A student who thinks bronchitis is saddle soreness uses both processes – the sound similarity with bronco and the knowledge that *itis* has to do with illness. In the following quiz, match a student definition from the second column with a word in the first column. Then explain your choice.

a. aspirant   1. study of mapping roads
b. bibulous   2. to miss again
c. antithesis   3. two tribes combined
d. stalemate   4. one using aspirin to excess
e. pathology   5. a paper disproving another
f. diatribe   6. slang for Mongolian
g. immutable   7. knowing the Bible well
h. insipid   8. unable to be silenced
i. remiss   9. not fit to drink
j. monger   10. one of the older officers on a ship

Consolidating word form and meaning in memory

The fourth necessary step revealed by Brown and Payne's analysis requires the consolidation of form and meaning in memory. Many kinds of vocabulary learning drills, such as flashcards, matching exercises, crossword puzzles, etc., strengthen the form-meaning connection. Almost all of the ten memory strategies that Oxford (1990) mentions consolidate the connection between word form and meaning in memory. Oxford divides these strategies into four general categories: (1) creating mental linkages, (2) applying images and sounds, (3) reviewing well, and (4) employing actions. Nine specific memory strategies Oxford mentions, along with the general categories in which they fall, are:

1. Grouping language material into meaningful units (category 1)
2. Associating new language information to concepts already in memory (category 1)
3. Placing new words into a context, such as a meaningful sentence, conversation, or story (category 1)
4. Using semantic mapping (category 2)
5. Using keywords with auditory and/or visual links (category 2)
6. Representing sounds in memory in such a way that they can be linked with a target language word in order to remember it better (category 2)
7. Reviewing the target language material in carefully spaced intervals (category 3)
8. Acting out a new target language expression (category 4)
9. Using mechanical techniques, such as writing words on cards and moving cards from one stack to another when a new word is learned (category 4)

Many of these strategies specifically mention vocabulary, expressions, or words. Those that do not mention vocabulary explicitly still can be applied to vocabulary study, for example, reviewing at carefully spaced intervals.

Mnemonic devices and their uses have been studied extensively by researchers (see, for example, Cohen and Aphek [1981]). One method in particular, the keyword method, has received great attention. This method calls for the word to be learned in a sentence that gives contextual cues to the meaning of the word while relating the form to forms the learner already knows. Jenkins and Dixon (1983) describe the method as having two stages: In the first, students are taught to link an unfamiliar word with an acoustically or visually similar word (e.g., persuade – purse). Next the students are shown a picture which contains both concepts in an interactive display. For instance: Two women are pictured in a store. One states, "Oh, Martha, you should buy that purse (pointing to a purse), and the second replies, "I think you can persuade me to buy it." Beneath the picture is the statement "Persuade (Purse) – when you talk someone into doing something" (p. 242). Supposedly the story or sentences with or without the picture will make the meaning of *persuade* clear. The pronunciation of the word is remembered because of its association with the known word, *purse*. If all of the learners in a language class have the same L1, the keywords can be done in the L1, as in the following example for native English speakers learning the Spanish word *pato* (adapted from Cohen, 1987):

1. Students are shown a picture of a duck with a pot over its head.
2. Students hear, maybe see, and learn the sentence, "The duck has a pot over its head."
3. Because the image is a silly one, and the sentence contains the equivalent sounding English words for the Spanish word (English pot o——— = Spanish pato), the learner may more easily recall the phonetic form and the meaning of the Spanish word and be able to produce it.

If the class has a heterogeneous language background, the keywords and sentences must be in the L2. In addition to deciding which language to do keywords in, learners or teachers may need to decide whether verbal or visual (imagery) mnemonics are more effective and whether learner-generated or teacher-supplied mnemonics are more helpful. With regard to verbal or visual mnemonics, Cohen (1987) cited mixed results depending on whether the words to be learned represented concrete or abstract items (verbal mnemonics were better for abstract items), on the age of the learner (younger children could not seem to generate visual images as easily), and on learner fluency (more fluent learners benefit more from verbal mnemonics).

With regard to whether mnemonics should be generated by the learner or the teacher, Cohen cited studies which generally showed that either method worked equally well. Cohen did point out, however, that almost all experiments had used words for which keywords were easy to generate.

The difficulty of generating keywords may discourage learners, or they may simply opt for more traditional ways of consolidating word forms with word meanings. Probably the most traditional way of doing this is to memorize words and their meanings from lists. There are variations on this method – using flashcards, covering one side of the paired lists (words and their meanings) and trying to guess the other, drawing lines between words in one list and their meanings in another list with a different order – but many cultures or educational systems simply call for students to memorize a list with the word and its meaning paired. Although this method may not be as entertaining as others, there are sufficient persons who have learned languages in this way so that the method should not be discounted.

Which method learners use for this step does not seem to be as crucial as that they do it. The more words learners can get through this step, the more words they will know overall.

Practice 15.5

1. Ask a group of your students or your classmates what mnemonic or memory devices they have used in learning second language vocabulary. Do all of them connect the form and the meaning in some way? Compare what your students say with the kinds of strategies in Oxford (1990). Does Oxford include any strategies that your students are not using? Do your students include any strategies that Oxford has not listed?

2. After you have compiled a list of at least 10 strategies in item 1 from many people, show the list to people (either the people from whom you got the original ideas for the list or a completely new group) and have them categorize the strategies into four categories: (a) those they have thought of before and tried, (b) those they have thought of before but never tried, (c) those they had not thought of before and want to try, and (d) those they had not thought of before and do not want to try. Have them rank the techniques they place in categories (a) and (c) in order from most useful to least useful. Ask them to give reasons for their ranking and for why they have not or would not want to try the techniques in categories (b) and (d).

3. Compile a list of ten words you would like to learn or would like your students to learn. See if you can invent keyword sentences in English to help remember the words and their meanings. What problems or successes do you encounter with the method?

389

4. Use the same list you compiled in item 3, but this time try to invent keyword sentences in another language you are familiar with. What problems or successes do you now encounter with the method? What are the differences between the use of L1 and L2 keyword sentences?

5. Have your language students read a newspaper article, short story, or article in the target language, circling all of the words they do not know for sure. After reading, have the students use any method they prefer for finding the meaning of the circled words. Teach them how to invent keyword sentences for their words and then let them try the method for half of their circled words. How well do the students invent the keyword sentences? Wait a month or so and then test the students on all of the words they had circled. Compare their scores on the words for which they invented keyword sentences with their scores on the words for which they did not invent keyword sentences. Is the difference worth the time used in inventing the sentences?

6. Get a classmate or friend who speaks a language you do not know to write a list of twenty common items and their meanings in that language. See how quickly you can memorize the list and then get your friend to test you to be sure that you know the words. Were some words on the list easier to learn than others? Why? Did you find that you used any kind of mnemonic devices as you learned the words? If so, which devices did you use? Why?

Using the word

The final step in learning words is using the words. Some would argue that this step is not necessary if all that is desired is a receptive knowledge of the word. Such an argument can apply to many of the other processes as well, since a great amount can be comprehended in context even if a reader or listener knows nothing about many of the words being used. However, if the goal is to help learners move as far along the continuum of word knowledge as they can, word use is essential. Furthermore, use seems to provide a mild guarantee that words and meanings will not fade from memory once they are learned.

Possibly because the use of a word tests the learner's understanding of the word, learners feel more confident about their word knowledge once they have used a word without undesired consequences. Use of the word may simply be a form of hypothesis testing, allowing learners to see if the knowledge gained in the other steps is correct. Sugawara demonstrated this fact in her 1992 study in which she pretested the vocabulary knowledge and confidence about that knowledge of ESL subjects. In the study, Sugawara had students view a video and then complete one of three tasks: write short paragraphs answering questions about the video trying to use certain specified words in the answers; complete a cloze exercise where the video script was the text and a list of possible words (the same specified words as in the first task) were supplied as options for filling in the blanks; write a short essay about the video in their own language (students who completed this task were considered the "no treatment" group).

When all the students had completed one of the three procedures, Sugawara gave them three posttests which were the same as the pretests they had completed before seeing the video. One was a test of confidence, where students marked how confident they felt about knowing the words being tested. The other two were a receptive (multiple-choice) vocabulary test and a productive test. The group who actually used the word in answering questions about the video did better than the other two groups on all three tests. Sugawara concluded that having students use the new words at least once was likely to lead to increased use of the words eventually because of the greater confidence which the students had in their word knowledge.

In addition to increasing confidence and receptive knowledge, use of words seems to be necessary for students to test their knowledge of collocations, syntactic restrictions, and register appropriateness as discussed in the chapters in Part III. Crow and Quigley (1985) have suggested that learners may not know such things when they have only a receptive knowledge of vocabulary.

In this section, we have discussed five essential steps which learners take in vocabulary learning. Although there is a broad range of activities, strategies, or techniques that individuals use at each step, the necessity of the steps seems more constant. Learners need all five in order to have a full knowledge of the words they want to learn.

Practice 15.6

1. Examine textbooks for a language you are trying to teach or learn to see what kinds of vocabulary exercises they contain. What use of the words being learned do the exercises require students to make? How helpful would the exercises be in helping students acquire collocational knowledge, syntactic restrictions, and register appropriateness for the words? What other aspects of word knowledge might be influenced by these exercises?

2. Haggard (1980) found that people were more likely to remember learning words when they had had a strong (usually negative) emotion associated with the word.
Frequently the emotion was embarrassment because of a
mistake with the word or because the word was obscene.
Other times the emotion associated with the use of the
word was one of "belonging" because the word was considered "adult" or a marker of group identity of some sort.
Poll your students and friends to see what words they remember learning in their native languages and why they
remember learning them. Do their memories about learning words have strong emotional attachments? Are there
any differences in memories about learning first languages
besides English? Now, poll your students and friends
about what words they remember learning in their second
language and why they remember learning these words.
How do the second language memories match those in
the first? How are they different? How many of the memories are related to use of the word and how many are only
related to the hearing or seeing of the word?

3. Record your students in conversation with native speakers
of the language they are trying to learn. Listen to the conversations and identify lexical errors that your students
make. How many of them do the native speakers correct?
How many of the corrections are recognized or acknowledged by the nonnatives? What types of refinement in
word knowledge are possible from the corrections which
are made? What kinds of refinement are not possible?

Learner compensation strategies

Selinker (1972) coined the term "interlanguage" and discussed how
learners had *communication strategies* that they used to make up for
what they sometimes lacked in linguistic knowledge. This section
discusses how these communication strategies or *compensation strategies,* as Oxford (1990) calls them, are used when learners do not have the
vocabulary they need at a particular moment.

Using a picture description task, Tarone (1977, 1980) collected data
and examined the communication strategies which her Mandarin-, Span-
ish-, and Turkish-speaking ESL learners used. After eliciting the descriptive data, Tarone asked the learners to review their performance on the
task by listening to a recording. As they went over the task again, they

gave retrospective comments on their strategies. Based on the data, Tarone devised an initial typology of strategies. The strategies include avoidance, paraphrase, conscious transfer, appeal for assistance, and mime. Avoidance was shown in topic avoidance and also by message abandonment. Tarone listed approximations (pipe for waterpipe), word coinage (airball for balloon), and circumlocution as types of paraphrase. Conscious transfer categories included literal translation from the L1, and language shift. Although some of these strategies might also fall under the category of the vocabulary learning processes (e.g., appeal for assistance), the majority are principally ways of coping when the learner does not have the necessary vocabulary (or grammar) for production.

Glahn's (1980) study shows somewhat different strategies. In this study, learners of French described eight pictures to each other. The learners were then asked to listen to their performance, stopping the tape whenever they wished to comment. The strategies revealed in their comments included waiting for the term to appear, appealing to formal similarity, retrieval by semantic field analysis (where they said aloud words from the same field in an attempt to retrieve the word), searching other languages, consulting the learning situation (mentally looking up the place they encountered the word such as the chapter on French cooking to find *mouton*), and sensory procedures (such as staring at the floor to find a word for ground).

In previous chapters we have given numerous examples where learners struggle to find the right term in the new language. In conversational analysis, these searches are often negotiated between learners, between native speakers, or between native speakers and learners. The emphasis in these studies is on the interactive building of meanings (and the nature of repair – that is, of self correction and other correction). Yet if we look at examples from such studies we can see many of the learner strategies discussed here. In the following example, Mari and Hamid are talking about an amusement park, and Mari seems to be searching for the word *ferris wheel*:

```
Mari:   . . . for junior high school? or adults because
                              |claps hands
            that's uh many kind |of
        |looks up and flutters eyelids, purses lips
        |uhh (1.0) mmmmm
        |closes eyes, grits teeth |opens hands, looks at H.
        |(1.5)                    |example Jet Corso?
        |looks away, hands in lap |hands up
        |and uh mmmm              |Water Shoot?
        |looks back at H. |closes eyes, fingers moving
        |very, very mmmm |(1.0) ve:ry
```

Hamid: inter ⌈esting⌉
Mari: ⌊yeah ⌋   interesting and
        ⌈fingers in circle motion ⌈iconic gestures
        ⌊huh huh huh   ⌊Jet Corso is uh very fast.
Hamid: Yeah like merry-go-round
Mari: Not- not merry-go-round because (.2)
        ⌈gestures over shoulder
        ⌊we are- we are (.2) opposite.

(Data source: Schwartz, 1980, pp. 143–144)

Notice Mari's heavy use of mime to make the meaning clear. She gives the names of two other related rides but indicates that these are not quite right. Hamid then supplied the name of a related ride, merry-go-round, but it, too, is rejected with gestures to show that the ride Mari is thinking of entails sitting across from one another. This example, then, shows data similar to Glahn's category (c), semantic field analysis, and Tarone's category of mime.

Haastrup (1991) also used a discourse analysis perspective in analyzing the "think-aloud" (introspection) and "retrospect" data obtained from paired Danish learners of English. Each pair discussed test words in reading passages. The following record of a think-aloud conversation illustrates the many ways learners guess at meanings. The passage is about a military leader with insatiable political ambitions.

Test word: *insatiable*
A: Able mans being able to – insane – ins
B: I think it is a positive word – something with extremely great
A: What does sati mean
B: Satanic
B: There is also a negation – it is something with in – they couldn't be calmed down
A: Why do you think it is a negation?
B: It usually is with in – I mean the prefix
A: He sounds as if he is rather single-minded
A: In-sa-ti- okay – in- is something with
B: It is a negation – it is something with u-
B: This is a good word – oh by the way sati is related to satisfy
A: Yes he has not yet been satisfied.
(They agree on) not satisfied.

(Haastrup, 1991, p. 127)

The learners use morphological information (e.g., *-able* means being able to; *in-* means negation), sounds or forms of the lexical item (e.g., *sati-* might be related to satanic or satisfy), semantics (e.g., it is a positive word), and the discourse or text (e.g., he sounds rather single-minded). The learners do not try one strategy – for example, morphology – and once that is complete, turn to examine the lexical form. Rather, they use all sources of information simultaneously.

As illustrated earlier, there are a wealth of studies of the compensatory strategies learners use when they do not know a word in the L2. The studies show that beginners are more likely to use L1-based strategies and appeals for assistance, whereas more advanced learners are more apt to use approximation and circumlocution. Turian and Altenberg (1991) studied whether the same compensatory strategies occur during attrition of the L1. They describe the attrition data of the Russian-English child, Joseph. Initially a dominantly Russian speaker, he shifted dominance to English when, at age 3½, the primary language of caretakers and the environment became English. The data include examples of code switching, lexical borrowing (adapting the English word *basement* to Russian *besmInter*), innovation (forming an equivalent to the English *baby bear* by combining *medvedi,* meaning bears, and *deti,* meaning children, as *medvedeti*), approximations, avoidance, and appeals for help. These strategies are similar to those found in most adult second language acquisition studies.

A parallel study exists in Thompson's (1989) analysis of the lexical search strategies used by twenty-four adult learners of Russian (during ACTFL testing sessions). Thompson divides the strategies into L1-based, L2-based, and cooperative strategies. L1-based strategies include language switching (Congress *mog veto*), literal translation (*vysokuyu shkolu,* tall school, for high school), and Russification (adding Russian case endings to English words). L2-based strategies include paraphrase, generalization, coinage, and self-repair (self-correction). Cooperative strategies include requests for help, requests for feedback, and admissions of ignorance. Beginning learners used primarily L1-based strategies and advanced learners used more L2-based strategies. All learners used approximately the same number of cooperative strategies.

From these and many other studies, we know that learners and native speakers alike have many ways to compensate for gaps in vocabulary or vocabulary retrieval problems. At points these compensation strategies overlap with the necessary processes for vocabulary learning, and we can speculate about the relative usefulness of the various compensation strategies in terms of both the communication success and the vocabulary learning that they might promote.

Practice 15.7

1. Galvan and Campbell (1979) wondered whether child L2 learners would use the strategies Tarone found for adults. Data were obtained as English-speaking children in a Spanish immersion class were asked to serve as transla-

tors for Spanish-speaking parents who came to enroll their children in school. If you can record similar data with more advanced L2 learners (or learners of a different L2), replicate this study and compare the results.

2. Meisel (1977) lists the following features of German spoken by foreign workers:

   a. Use of foreign words, not necessarily of the speaker's native language (e.g., amigo, capito, compris)
   b. German words used in a different sense (e.g., *viel* [much] used in the sense of very in *viel gut* and the special kind of negation using *nix* for *nicht* as well as *kein* (*nix geld* for no money)
   c. Formal address *Sie* is replaced by informal address *du*
   d. Lexical material which is semantically least marked is preferred (e.g., use of *machen* [to do] for more specialized verbs)
   e. Analytical paraphrases replace what are intuitively judged to be complex expressions
   f. Decomposition of predicates (e.g., *ganze mafioso, mache kaput drei mensche* "much mafioso, make kaputt [dead] three men" meaning, "he is a real mafioso, he killed three men")
   g. Missing elements, in particular articles, prepositions, copula, auxiliaries, and personal pronouns
   h. Omission of inflectional endings on verbs, adjectives, and nouns
   i. Use of subject pronouns in the imperative
   j. Word order errors
   k. Few complex sentences, and complementizers and relative pronouns may be omitted.

   Which of these features of learner language relate to lexical compensation strategies? Identify which of the five essential steps the learners seem to have missed so that compensation strategies are necessary.

3. Have pairs of students read a story or article which is challenging but not overwhelming for them. Ask them to mark words for which they are not sure of the meaning. Then have the pairs try to figure out the meaning of the words they have marked. Record their conversations as they do this task. Which strategies do your learners seem to use most? Which strategies seem to help them the most (result in correct guesses being made) and which seem to

help them the least (result in incorrect guesses being made)?

4. Review the categories used in taxonomies of compensatory strategies of learners (see Turian and Altenberg [1991] for an excellent bibliography). Which categories are the most useful (and why)? How would you recategorize these strategies in terms of what they might contribute to the steps of vocabulary learning?

5. Review Thompson's (1989) search categories discussed in this section. How might the use of some of these strategies lead to shifts in lexical forms and meanings in immigrant populations? Check with friends who have lived among immigrant populations. Can they give examples of second language learners who have done the kinds of things Thompson discussed? Can they give examples of differences from the standard target language that the entire immigrant group seems to have adopted?

When language learners have gaps in their lexical knowledge in the language they are learning, they basically have two options (if they do not completely ignore the gap): they can find words to fill the gaps and then go through the five steps of learning them, or they can compensate for the lack of knowledge in a number of ways. Some activities can fit under both of these choices, for example, an appeal for help (which is a compensation strategy) can also be an appeal for someone to supply the meaning of a word. Furthermore, some of the strategies tie significantly to what others do. The next chapter deals with how teachers and other pedagogues can help learners overcome their gaps in lexical knowledge.

Research and application

1. Sternberg and Powell (1983) noted eight basic kinds of context cues used by high school students when they read and encountered unfamiliar L1 words: temporal, spatial, physical properties, functional properties, worth or affect, causal, class membership, and equivalence. These researchers found that these eight types of cues and several moderating factors (such as frequency of word occurrence) accounted for 72 and 92 percent of the variance in deriving definitions from context. They did not test the relative effect of the different kinds of cues, but they did suggest that multiple contexts increased the number and kind of cues available to students. Design two experiments, one to test the relative effect of the different kinds of cues and one to test whether multiple con-

texts increase the number and kind of cues available to learners. If you have sufficient students, carry out one of the studies. What do you expect to find?

2. Parry's (1993) subject, Yuko, recorded all the new words she encountered in her reading for her anthropology course. Yuko recorded 168 words and guessed at the meaning of 148 of them. Thirty-three percent of her glosses were completely correct, and 36 percent were partially correct. Parry categorized the partially correct glosses into superordinates of the words being glossed, hyponyms of the words being glossed, members of the same superordinate category, part for whole, and whole for part, subtracting meaning from words being glossed, adding meaning to words being glossed, and both adding and subtracting aspects of meaning to the meaning of the words being glossed. Replicate this experiment with students you have who are enrolled in academic classes where they are required to read in the L2 they are learning. How do the percentages of your subjects' correct and incomplete glosses compare with Yuko's? Can you categorize their partially correct glosses into the same categories that Parry used? Would the addition of relational information (such as that discussed in Chapter 4) make the categorization easier?

3. Cohen and Aphek (1981) studied the specific strategies learners reported using to increase memory. They had native English-speaking students use whatever means they desired to learn self-selected unfamiliar words in a Hebrew text. Learners were asked to describe any kind of association used to learn the words. The learners reported using the following nine types of associations:

   a. Associating L2 words to L1 words with a similar sound (e.g., *memaher* – "he hurries" to hare).
   b. Associating L2 words with other L2 words by sound (e.g., *rehov* – street to *rehok* – far).
   c. Associating one part of a word to an L2 word by sound and meaning, and the other part to an L1 word by sound and meaning (e.g., *benatayim* – "meanwhile" with *ben* associated with Hebrew *beyn* – "between" and *tayim* with English *time*).
   d. Associating an L2 word to an L1 phrase by sound and meaning (e.g., *benatayim* – "meanwhile" to English *been a long time*).
   e. Associating an L2 word by meaning to a word in a third language (e.g., *tox* – "inside" to Yiddish *tuchus* – "backside").
   f. Associating the word with another L2 word according to structure (e.g., *lifney* – "before" to *lifamim* – "sometimes").
   g. Associating by one or more letters (e.g., *masa'it* – truck – because names of vehicles often begin with *m* in Hebrew).

h. Associating the word with a frequently seen sign (*la'atsor* – "to stop" with the sign *atsor* – "stop" seen in buses).

i. Creating a mental image of the word's referent.

All of the associations except (i) in some way connect word form or some part of it with word meaning. Design your own research plan to investigate the effectiveness of mnemonics that connect form and meaning. How would you select the vocabulary for the project? Would illustrations from picture dictionaries help you in preparing the associations? How might you pilot your materials and methods prior to carrying out the project?

4. Pressley, Levin, and Delaney (1982) surveyed almost fifty studies looking at the use of mnemonic (memory-aiding) devices, in particular the keyword method, and concluded that the method definitely helped vocabulary learning and that it was superior to many other common techniques, such as using pictures, doing rote repetition of words, or simply placing words in meaningful sentences and author adjustments in vocabulary use with learners. Use this article as the basis for your own research. How might you collect data from students about what methods they themselves use (rather than methods the teacher asks them to use)? If the methods that "work" do not match the methods used in independent study, what suggestions would you have?

5. Palmberg (1990) talks about "potential" vocabulary as vocabulary that learners may not yet have encountered but that they would understand. Palmberg also believes that some items may jump directly into active use once they are encountered. In a sense, then, potential vocabulary might jump from step 1 to step 5 without much learner effort. It may also be the case that some words are easily encountered and meanings attached to them but that much effort is needed to move them through steps 3 and 4 to accurate and productive use in step 5. Palmberg suggests that words linked by derivational morphology might fall into this category, using different steps. How might you investigate the notion that some words can be ready for use quickly whereas others take a long time? How might you identify which types of words are quickly recognized and quickly brought to use or which types of words are very slowly and often inaccurately used?

6. The importance of vocabulary use for vocabulary retention is discussed by Obler (1982) who compared the naming ability of monolingual aphasics, polyglot aphasics, demented senior citizens, and healthy senior citizens. Obler found that content words are far more susceptible to loss than function words. Proper nouns are more difficult to retrieve than common nouns, and nouns

are more difficult to retrieve than verbs. However, strongly emotional words and phrases (e.g., "Help!" or "I love you.") are especially impervious to loss. Obler concluded that language use is the key element that facilitates retention in the speech of the elderly and that it is crucial in the treatment of aphasic patients. If the gerontological issues interest you, review this work and also Riegel's (1970) relational semantics model on the loss of types of lexical items in the aging process. Develop a research plan for investigating first language loss of elderly bilinguals in your community.

16 Vocabulary pedagogy and teacher strategies

Just as Chapter 15 dealt with what learners do and/or should do to learn vocabulary, this chapter deals with what teachers and other language pedagogical specialists do and should do to help learners. The chapter is divided into two sections – one on unplanned vocabulary adjustments and teaching and one on planned vocabulary adjustments and teaching. In the first section, we will discuss spontaneous vocabulary adjustments that teachers make in order to help students understand vocabulary. Then we will discuss some ways that teachers can turn such spontaneous encounters with unfamiliar vocabulary into "on-the-spot" vocabulary teaching. In the section on planned vocabulary adjustments and teaching, we will look at vocabulary adjustments that materials developers make in order to help learners understand texts or acquire vocabulary. Then we will discuss specific principles for guiding the classroom strategies and techniques of planned formal vocabulary teaching and give examples of how the principles can be applied to judging the value of various vocabulary teaching approaches, methods, or techniques.

Unplanned vocabulary adjustments and teaching

Teachers' adjustments in vocabulary

Learners are not the only ones who make adjustments when their vocabulary is limited – we as teachers and communicators with the learners often make adjustments, too. Persons studying motherese or caretaker speech have examined the vocabulary adjustments that are made for L1 learners, finding that caretakers had a tendency to use more general terms with children such as calling a leopard a *kitty-cat* or labeling a tow truck by the more general term *car*.

In language classrooms, teachers appear to automatically monitor their vocabulary choice, selecting high frequency words, using little slang, and few idioms. They offer definitions either explicitly (e.g., "This means X," "It's a kind of X") or implicitly by intonation (e.g., "a triangle?" "It's got three sides?"). In their definitions they sometimes use morphology frames (e.g., "sum up – summarize"), give more common terms (e.g., funds or money, industrious and busy), and add semantic relation information (e.g., HASA relation: "a database, it has a lot of examples in it"). Or, LOC relation as in, routed, like at the postoffice. As mentioned earlier, Chaudron's (1982) studies show that vocabulary adjustments are a major component of teacher talk. The relative usefulness of each type of adjustment has not been clearly demonstrated, however. Chaudron showed that many of the definition adjustments that teachers made could result in greater confusion rather than less, some because they broke the natural discourse, others because learners were not able to tell if the teacher's elaboration was a new word or referent or another way to refer to a previous word as the following underlined examples demonstrate:

. . . the beaver is known as a very *industrious* and busy, uhm, *hard-working* animal.
. . . Canada was a – *booming* – and *expanding* and economically rich – ,
. . . because of the *Depression,* because of the *economic situation,* because of the society –

(Chaudron, 1982, p. 176, italics added)

Adjusting vocabulary choices and offering definitions at the spur of the moment are not examples of intentional vocabulary instruction. Rather, these adjustments are made in order to make the message clear or to keep the flow of conversation going. They do, however, serve as a possible source for vocabulary learning.

Practice 16.1

1. Obtain a copy of transcripts of language classrooms. See if you can identify instances when teachers are making definition adjustments for students. How many of these adjustments have the potential to result in greater confusion rather than less? Categorize these "poor" adjustments according to whether they broke the natural discourse or caused confusion because learners were not able to tell if the teacher's elaboration was a new word or referent or another reference to the previous word. Are there other reasons the adjustments seem unhelpful? Compare your conclusions and findings with those of your classmates.

2. Mannon (1986) tape-recorded a teacher lecturing (on sound waves) to a class of native speakers and to a class of international students. Do you think that the teacher's use of synonyms or paraphrases following the problematic word would be helpful or confusing for the students? Justify your opinion.

   a. . . . the louder the sound you produce, the more *perturbation or movement* we have.

b. . . . difficult to hear *reliably.* To *really be sure* what we're hearing.

c. So it's *convenient very useful* to have a way –

d. There is in effect a *rippling out, a wave* of each set of air particles.

e. *larynx* sometimes called in English the *Adam's apple.*

f. . . . the vocal cords and they *vibrate or buzz.*

3. Mannon asked other groups of international students to listen either to the taped lecture for native speakers or to the lecture for international students and then answer a set of information questions based on the lecture. The group that listened to the lecture meant for international students answered more questions on the content correctly. Mannon concluded that the adjustments resulted in improved comprehension but she was less sure whether students actually learned vocabulary (or anything else about the language). How might you redesign this study to address the issue of whether the learner acquires more vocabulary when these adjustments are made.

Unplanned vocabulary teaching

Seal (1991) divides vocabulary teaching into planned and unplanned activities. Unplanned vocabulary teaching happens when the student requests a meaning for a vocabulary item during a lesson or when the teacher realizes that a word that has just come up needs to be clarified. The teacher must improvise on the spot. We are not all equally good at improvising in a way that would promote learning. However, Seal suggests a method he calls the three C's for use in such situations. First, the teacher *conveys* the meaning, perhaps via mime, synonyms, or an anecdote. Second, the teacher *checks* that the meaning is understood, perhaps by a series of questions. Third, the teacher *consolidates* the information by trying to get the students to relate the word to another context or personal experience. To illustrate, Seal uses the example word *boring.*

Convey meaning
Teacher: When you go to the movies sometimes the movie is not very interesting, it makes you want to go to sleep. (*T puts hand to mouth and yawns.*) The movie is very boring. Or sometimes you have a teacher who speaks very slowly and who never makes you laugh and whose lessons make you go to sleep. The teacher is so boring.

Check meaning
Teacher: (*to S1*) Do you like boring teachers? (*to S2*) Is this lesson boring? (*to*

S3) Is this book boring? (*to S4*) Are you a boring person? (*to S5*) Am I a boring teacher?

Consolidate meaning

Teacher: Turn to the person next to you and ask them if they had a boring weekend. If they say "yes," find out why. (*General hubbub*) Now ask the person next to you what television shows they think are boring.

No teacher would take this much time away from the lesson without first deciding that the word was important and worth teaching. If the word is low frequency or too specialized, it is better to give a brief definition or none at all. If it is worth teaching, Seal argues that it is worth carrying out all three steps.

If we think of this three C's technique in terms of the vocabulary acquisition sequence discussed in Chapter 15, we can see that the first and second steps deal with the getting of the meaning of the word, and the third step clearly involves the using of the word. The first process, encountering the word, must also have occurred as this is the very trigger that Seal suggests for the implementation of the three C's technique. What is not handled explicitly in this method is the getting of the form of the word and the connecting of the form and the meaning permanently in memory. The teacher might approach the former by writing the word on the blackboard, asking students to say the word, or perhaps spelling the word. The latter step may be more crucial for vocabulary that the teacher intends that the students learn. It would be helpful but perhaps difficult to do well in spur-of-the-moment vocabulary teaching.

Practice 16.2

1. Observe several language classes for learners at different levels of proficiency. For each, note the specific vocabulary items about which students ask questions. As you observe each class, try to think of how you would answer the questions asked and note how the teacher answers the questions. Can you tell if the answers are satisfactory to the learners who asked the questions? Are there any characteristics of answers which you can identify as being more helpful? Compare your notes with those of your classmates. Does the proficiency level of the students make a difference in what kinds of answers are helpful?

2. Examine some of the classroom recordings which you have made on previous occasions for times when teachers give what appear to be spur-of-the-moment helps with vocabulary. Analyze the spontaneous teaching in terms of Seal's three C's. How many times are all three steps

used? Which step seems to be present most often? Which seems to be missing most often? Why do you think this is so? What, if anything, should teachers do in the classroom in order to give greater spontaneous help with vocabulary?

3. In a textbook you are using in one of your classes, have a partner randomly pick a word being used on any page in the textbook and ask you to define it the way you would do it if the question came up in your class. How difficult is it to come up with spontaneous definitions? Are there any types of words that are more difficult than others to define?

Planned vocabulary adjustments and teaching

Materials developers' selections and adjustments in vocabulary

Although teachers must make spontaneous adjustments in vocabulary use and improvise teaching in the classroom, they are also able to take advantage of deliberate adjustments which have been made by textbook authors and editors to help learners. Skierso (1991) notes that "most teachers tend to follow the text's sequence, methodology, pacing, and vocabulary to the letter" (p. 432). It is important for educators to know what kind of vocabulary adjustments are made by these materials developers – to know how vocabulary is selected and in what context it is introduced and reinforced in language teaching materials.

The main issue in materials development is deciding what words are basic for language learners. Are these always the simplest, least idiomatic forms? Are they the basic (not the superordinate or subordinate) level terms? As one way to solve this problem, textbook writers often adopt a basic vocabulary list from some sourcebook such as the old West (1936, reprinted in 1953 and revised in 1971) General Service List, the Thorndike and Lorge (1944) list, or some more up-to-date list based on frequency. Although such sourcebooks contain the most frequent vocabulary in some cross-section of written discourse, they seldom include oral language sources, which can limit their usefulness.

Current popular language teaching methods have influenced and produced other methods or reasons for the choice of vocabulary used and presented in general language textbooks. In the 1950s and 1960s audiolingual textbooks used a set plan for selecting and limiting vocabulary. In addition to a frequency criterion, vocabulary was selected according to an expanding scope for the learners. The lessons began with vocabulary of the classroom, then school, home, community, and work. Later, the list was enlarged to include common vocabulary about the state and the

405

nation. Finally, the scope became communication around the world. This concentric circle approach to theme and vocabulary selection still appears in many ESL and EFL textbooks.

In addition to this expanding scope, writers of audiolingual materials believed that the number of vocabulary items per lesson should be kept to the minimum so that learners would concentrate on pronunciation and grammar. Since contrastive analysis was important during this era, vocabulary was also selected to show contrasts. Many false cognates were highlighted for extra practice.

During the late 1960s and early 1970s, ESL teaching in the United States turned to more communicative materials and to more directly usable English with such approaches as Survival English, Contextual English, and Situational Reinforcement. Survival English materials, usually produced by school districts, were designed for the immigrant student family. In all of these approaches, the contexts in which the learner would use English were identified and sequence priority was given to contexts that would be crucial for survival purposes in the new country. Vocabulary was selected to match these basic English units, including units on such scripts as obtaining housing, doing banking, shopping, getting a driver's license, and filling out job applications. These approaches are still frequently used in adult education, Amnesty, and citizenship courses.

Theme-based approaches, still part of the continuing communicative movement and similar to those of Contextual English, go beyond "newcomer" themes to those that the teacher or textbook writers believe are not only important for practical use but also exploitable for teaching purposes. The selected vocabulary relates to such social or global issues as world peace, the environment, world communication and technology, space exploration, AIDS, world health, and human rights.

A third communicative approach is the notional-functional syllabus (discussed in Chapter 14). This approach provides teachers and program development specialists with a list of the basic functions of language and the vocabulary related to different notions within functions. The major functions identified in van Ek (1975), listed here along with related vocabulary domains, are:

1. Exchanging factual information
   Vocabulary domains: identify, ask, report, say, think X, etc.
2. Exchanging intellectual information
   Vocabulary domains: agree, disagree, know, remember, etc.
3. Exchanging emotional attitudes
   Vocabulary domains: surprise, hope, disappointment, fear, worry, preference, gratitude, sympathy, want, desire, etc.

4. Exchanging moral attitudes
   Vocabulary domains: apology, forgiveness, approval, disapproval, appreciation, regret, indifference, etc.
5. Suasion
   Vocabulary domains: suggest, request, invite, instruct, advise, warn, offer or request assistance, etc.
6. Socializing
   Vocabulary domains: greetings, leave-takings, holiday sayings, toasts, etc.

Notions are different from functions. The major notions identified for the threshold level in this approach are similar to the themes used in survival English courses. The threshold level as described by van Ek (1976) lists the following notions for inclusion in a basic curriculum: personal identification; house and home; trade, profession, occupation; free time, entertainment; travel; relations with other people; health and welfare; education; shopping; food and drink; services; places; foreign languages; and weather. Thinking of the possible scripts involved in each of these notions will give you a good idea of the vocabulary needed for each. This list of functions and notions provided a basis for what is called threshold level language. The list gives materials development experts a framework for planning materials and lessons with appropriate vocabulary.

Communicative approaches have continued in the 1980s and 1990s with an increasing focus on authentic materials – materials prepared for native speakers of the language. In beginning language classes, where these materials may primarily supplement other course materials, they may include menus, labels, advertisements, various types of forms to be filled out, taped news broadcasts, or soap operas. In more advanced classes, content-based instruction has become important. In these classes, the subject matter of the language course is the subject content of another course. For example, English for Business Purposes may accompany regular business courses. In some cases, these courses are "sheltered" in that only language learners take the content course. In other cases, students attend the content class with native speakers and then take an adjunct language class that uses the content material as the basis of language instruction.

In authentic language approaches, the vocabulary materials ideally reflect the needs and interests of the students and their teachers. If the approach is "pure," neither the vocabulary nor the language structures are simplified or sequenced in any way. There is variation in content-based programs in that some teachers believe that it is acceptable to adapt the content materials (adaptation usually resulting in simplification), whereas others argue that any form of adaptation means the materials are no longer authentic. Madsen and Bowen (1978) argue that adaptation is inevitable when materials are used in the classroom. Teachers constantly change materials to match the needs and interests of their students, just as they often simplify the vocabulary, provide numerous definitions, examples, paraphrases, and synonyms, and even do some improvised vocabulary teaching in the process.

With the growing use of computers in language instruction, the selection of vocabulary to be learned has been placed increasingly in the hands of the learner. Programs such as Hypercard or Toolbook allow teachers to prepare "hypertexts," which are texts linked to other texts, such as dictionaries, thesauruses, or pictures, within the computer. The journal *CALICO* is filled with articles that show how teachers can use such programs to encourage students to work with authentic language materials. The students using these programs decide when and where they need help with vocabulary. When a student clicks on a word or touches the key indicated in the program, a pop-up dictionary gives the meaning, or grammar or cultural information, or simple translation information related to the word. With computer access to the dictionary, a thesaurus, or large database, the student can search for meanings with ease. Collocational information can also be provided, as in the COBUILD language course and the BBI Combinatory Dictionary computer programs.

In a more traditional vein, many publishing companies have continued to produce readers (usually called guided or structured readers) for language learners. Generally, the publishers use very controlled vocabulary or specifications for ways in which materials should be adapted for learners. The *Heinemann Guided Readers Handbook* (Milne, 1977), for example, suggests that beginner-level texts have approximately 600 basic words (that is, "not peculiar to the story and fully explained in the text, or illustrated or appearing in the Glossary"), elementary-level texts have 1,100, intermediate-level texts have 1,600, and upper-level texts have 2,200. The basic vocabulary is not given in any particular word list or because of any particular frequency count. The handbook also suggests that writers of the guided readers use "an intuitive, commonsense attitude to the control of vocabulary" (p. 16). Also, the writers are advised to use "the occasional unfamiliar word," especially if they structure the readers so that the meaning of such words is made clear by a "well-chosen illustration" or a gloss of the word in the context of the story – "that is [they] have used the word in a situation where it is possible for the student to make an intelligent guess at its meaning" (p. 16). The guidelines explain that at beginner and elementary levels, authors have had to use more illustrations since they found that "the language needed to gloss the word in a Glossary was more difficult than the language used in the text itself."

William Collins and Sons (1979) used a slightly different approach to vocabulary adjustments in its guided readers. Collins' six levels of readers have 300, 600, 1,000, 1,500, 2,000, and 2,500 headwords (with singular/plural and regular verb tense variants counted together as one), respectively. Their instructions include eight guidelines for deciding what these headwords would be:

1. frequency (based on a comparison of nine frequency counts)
2. range (with "terms that denote classes of objects" being more used "than terms that denote members of that class" producing hierarchies such as "food [1], meat [2], lamb [4], roast lamb [5]")
3. communicative need
4. lexical sets ("words that commonly go together are included together" such as *knife, fork,* and *spoon*)
5. known words (international terms borrowed from English or other languages and basic classroom items)
6. new words (such as *astronaut* or *hijack*)
7. style ("Words like dawn, dusk, blaze and blossom are included because they are simple, concrete, expressive and pleasing.")
8. idiom ("a group of words whose complete . . . meaning cannot be deduced from the sum of its parts. Examples: by the way, get up, inside out.")

Other publishers have similar guidelines that they give to authors of guided readers. Because the rationale behind specific criteria is not always stated, Bunker (1988) decided to test several guidelines to see which adjustments actually made materials easier for learners.

Bunker examined seven sets of writing guidelines used by publishers or by organizations preparing materials for nonnative speakers, particularly nonnative speakers who were also newly literate. All of the guideline sets advocated some kind of vocabulary control or adjustments. Six vocabulary guidelines seemed to be almost universally advocated. Bunker divided them into two major classes of adjustments: selection and control. The four general selection guidelines called for use of short terms, use of common or familiar terms, consistent use of the same word for the same concept, and use of precise terms (specialized terms) relevant to the topic. The two general control guidelines called for a number of word repetitions for new words and for contextual definitions of terms.

Bunker then found authentic materials on health, social, and economic issues that had been adjusted on-site for newly literate and low-level English learners. The materials preparers had not followed specific guidelines, but had simply made adjustments until they were sure that the users of the materials could understand them. Bunker had a group of very low-level ESL learners in the United States read and rate the difficulty of the materials and then she correlated those ratings with vocabulary characteristics of the texts. Bunker found no significant correlation between word length (both as measured in number of letters in the words and number of syllables) and text difficulty. However, she did find a definite negative correlation between reading difficulty and the percent of words that appeared within the 500, 750, and 1,000 most frequent words in the Brown University corpus (Francis & Kučera, 1982). In other words, the more words in the materials which were among these most common and frequent words, the easier the reading materials.

Next, token/type ratios (the number of total words divided by the number of unique words) were calculated for the materials and the ranking of these ratios was compared with the difficulty ranking to determine if consistent vocabulary made a difference. Bunker found a very high correlation (.83), suggesting that consistency makes a difference. In a second study of consistency, she checked a random sample of 10 percent of the words from each document (set of materials) to see how each content word was used. She then used a thesaurus to find synonyms for these content words and rechecked the documents to see how many of these synonyms appeared in the documents. There was no significant correlation between the average number of synonyms per word used and the difficulty of the text.

The proportion of technical words to total words correlated positively with the difficulty ranking, suggesting that more technical terms make materials more difficult. The correlation between the percentage of technical words defined in the context (either by a direct definition or a clearly identifiable example) and the difficulty ranking was also significant, but in this case the correlation was negative. In other words, the more technical terms that were defined, the easier the materials were to read.

When Bunker looked at the effect of word repetition, she found that the easiest text repeated about 33 percent of its words more than five times, the second easiest had about 20 percent of its words repeated at least five times, the third easiest a little more than 14 percent, the fourth easiest about 19 percent, the fifth easiest a little more than 14 percent, and the most difficult a little less than 14 percent repeated five times. The correlation between these figures and the difficulty ranking was −.80, suggesting that the higher the percent of terms repeated more than five times (a number suggested by several sets of guidelines), the easier the texts were to read.

Overall, Bunker found that the following lexical characteristics contributed to the ease with which materials could be understood.

1. Use of common and familiar words.
2. Consistency in use of terms.

3. More than five repetitions of words.
4. Definitions of words in context.

The following vocabulary adjustments did not seem to contribute to understanding:

1. Use of short words.
2. Use of fewer synonyms.
3. Repetitions of words fewer than five times.

Even though these vocabulary adjustments made materials easier to understand, there is no proof that they make vocabulary easier to learn.

In addition to general textbooks and readers, there are several other kinds of books for oral and aural practice that have specific kinds of vocabulary information. For example, Tillitt and Bruder's *Speaking Naturally* and Jones and von Baeyer's *Functions of American English: Communication Activities for the Classroom* offer practice activities to help students learn the vocabulary of speech acts (how to complain, how to apologize, how to ask for information, and so forth). The Fragiadakis *All Clear?* series (with cassettes and computer software) gives students practice with conversational interactions on a variety of scripts (ordering fast food, leaving messages on answering machines, and so forth). Such materials give students additional practice working with script vocabulary and especially with lexical phrases. Schecter's *Listening Tasks* is designed to teach listening and focuses on listening to telephone exchanges, natural conversations, and short public address announcements. The use of materials of this sort would give students more awareness of the vocabulary of communication signals.

Unlike general textbooks, readers, and textbooks such as those just discussed, which have many language teaching purposes in addition to vocabulary development, some textbooks are designed specifically to teach vocabulary. The rationale for what vocabulary is taught in these textbooks sometimes but not always follows the rationale for vocabulary selection in general texts. A vocabulary text that might follow word frequency guidelines is the *Advanced English Vocabulary* series by Barnard. The words in the course are based on several frequency lists including West's General Service list and counts made "of non-technical vocabulary in university science and social science textbooks" used in Hyderabad, India, and Victoria University in Wellington, New Zealand.

Other familiar approaches used by vocabulary textbook writers for selecting vocabulary to teach are focus on situations, domains, or scripts in which the words might be used. For example, Seal's *American Vocabulary Builder* volumes have chapters on such topics as housework, sports, party time, money, and space. The Janus Survival Vocabulary Series has separate books with such titles as *Banking Language, Clothing Language, Credit Language, Medical Language,* and *Restaurant Language.* Burgmeier, Eldred, and Zimmerman's *Lexis: Academic Vocabulary Study,* focuses on vocabulary in history, biology, business, and psychology, among others.

Other vocabulary texts, such as Trump, Trechter, and Holisky's *Walk, Amble, Stroll,* examine words used in particular domains such as the "walk" domain or the "happy–sad" domain, while still others, such as *The Words You Need* and *More Words You Need* by Rudzka, Channell, Putseys, and Ostyn use a semantic field approach to words much like that discussed in Chapter 2. Key words that appear in the news articles or readings used as context are listed in "grids" with similar words. Thus, words such as *reach, accomplish, achieve, attain,* and *gain* are examined in one grid in a chapter about the human animal and how it compares to other animals, and words like *secret, clandestine, secretive, furtive, stealthy, underhand, underhanded* are examined in a section of another chapter dealing with hidden romantic relationships.

Other vocabulary textbooks select items to teach in ways not usually followed in more general textbooks. For example, numerous ESL vocabulary textbooks (e.g., Dixson, *Essential Idioms in English;* Feare, *Practice with Idioms;* McCallum, *Idiom Drills;* Reeves, *Idioms in Action;* Genzel, *Getting the Hang of Idioms and Expressions;* Adams and Kuder, *Attitudes through Idioms;* McPartland, *Take It Easy: American Idioms;* Collis, *Colloquial English*) treat idioms and phrasal verbs. It is possible that these vocabulary items are selected because of difficulty. They are often not syntactically full formed (e.g., We say, "She hit the ceiling," or "She'll hit the ceiling," but not generally "She is hitting the ceiling"), so the points where there are exceptions to rules need to be learned. Many of them are also frozen, with little allowance for variation (e.g., We say, "He's in over his head," but not "He's in over his hair" or "over his nose," or "over his mouth"), so the words making up the idiom have to be learned precisely. However, the main reason so many books choose to treat these vocabulary items is probably not just their difficulty, but also because students find them so interesting and pervasive. They are highly figurative and analogical and they share characteristics with other kinds of word play, so they become fun. Furthermore, they are everywhere, so language students find them vital for understanding.

Other vocabulary textbooks (e.g., Yorkey, *Checklists for Vocabulary Study;* Keen, *Developing Vocabulary Skills;* Sheeler and Markley, *Words Words Words: A Guide to Formation and Usage;* Hymanson, *Connections and Contexts*) seem to select vocabulary on the basis of word parts or morphemes (roots, suffixes, and affixes). These books seem to help students learn particular words and strategies for figuring out the meanings of other words as well.

412

Practice 16.3

1. Review a general textbook for the language you teach. On what basis has the vocabulary been chosen? If the choice is based on frequency, what frequency list was used? If it is based on scripts, which scripts were chosen and why? If the organization is theme-based, what themes were selected? If it is a communicative approach that emphasizes the notional-functional approach, do the textbook writers explain which functions were selected and how the vocabulary is linked to functions? If the materials are based on authentic language materials, have the writers adapted the original? To what extent?

2. If you can obtain textbooks from different eras or espousing different approaches to teaching (e.g., audiolingual, Survival or Contextual English, notional-functional), look at how vocabulary is handled. How was vocabulary selected for inclusion or focus? What categories of vocabulary are included? What, if any, kinds of vocabulary exercises are in the book? Are there any similarities about the way vocabulary is handled regardless of approach? Which approaches seem most different in their handling of vocabulary? What approach does your current textbook seem to use?

3. Teachers in content-based courses spend a great deal of time planning ways to teach vocabulary within authentic contexts (for examples, see Brinton, Snow, & Wesche, 1989). They may use the texts to teach ways of defining, the uses of synonyms and antonyms in context, and the ways that lexical cohesion works. To investigate lexical cohesion in the following paragraph, underline the words that relate to the notion of perception or vision. In which cases is equivalence of meaning clear? What other problems do you see in using this piece of authentic text with second language readers?

   It is as though we – or the people of any other society – grow up perceiving the world through glasses with distorting lenses. The things, events, and relationships we assume to be "out there" are in fact filtered through this perceptual screen. The first reaction, inevitably, on encountering people who wear a different kind of glasses is to dismiss their behavior as strange or wrong. To view other peoples' ways of life in terms of our own cultural glasses is called ethnocentrism.

   (Source: Brinton, Snow, and Wesche, 1989, p. 172)

What is ethnocentrism? Can you supply an antonym for this word? Do you think that learners would be able to define the term after reading the paragraph? If possible, ask three international students to read the paragraph and give a definition for this term.

4. It's unlikely that you would supply perceptual screen as a synonym for distorting lenses. Are *balloting* and *voting* synonyms? What about *assertions* and *statements?* Cohen et al. (1988) found that students in their case studies were not always sure about synonyms and paraphrases in the texts they read. And they sometimes thought that terms were synonymous when they were not. For example, one reader thought *repair mode, repair processes,* and *repair scheme* might refer to the same thing since they all start with the same word. Select a passage that contains synonyms and paraphrases. How close are the synonyms in meaning? How adequate are the paraphrases? Then ask an international student to read a passage and respond to your questions about the selected words. Does the use of either synonyms or paraphrases create a problem for the student?

5. See if you can replicate Bunker's study with materials that you are using. Select five to seven texts and have your students read them and rank them for difficulty. Then try doing some of the tests that Bunker did. What kinds of vocabulary tools (frequency lists, thesauruses, etc.) do you need to carry out this study? Do you have access to such tools in the language you are teaching? How would you test which vocabulary adjustments relate to vocabulary learning and not just understanding?

6. Choose a text in your target language that you would like to use with your learners but find too difficult for them. Try to make the adjustments in the text according to the four guidelines that Bunker found to be helpful. Use your adapted materials with a group of your learners. Do they find them any easier? Which of the adjustments do you find to be the hardest to make? Why?

7. Bunker (1988) found that having more than five repetitions of a word made materials easier for ESL learners, whereas Brown (1993) found no correlation between the number of times a word was used in a specific context and the learning of the word. How would you explain this contradiction?

8. If possible, find a textbook specifically designed to teach vocabulary that you would consider using. Without reading the preface, forward, or notes to the teacher, look at the chapters or lessons and see if you can tell how words were selected for inclusion in the text. Does the reason for choosing the vocabulary match the reasons for including vocabulary in the more general textbook you might use? What advantages and disadvantages do you see to matching and not matching? Do the advantages and disadvantages you see match those of your classmates or colleagues?

Planned vocabulary teaching

We have considered the types of vocabulary adjustments that are used to make language accessible to learners. We noted that the language addressed to learners, whether by teachers or other native speakers of the language, is unconsciously adjusted to the level they believe is appropriate for the learner. They do this adjusting in order to make their messages understood and to allow the discourse interaction to continue with as few breakdowns as possible. The aim is not that of teaching the learner. Learning, therefore, is incidental. In this section we will discuss issues that relate to intentional vocabulary instruction.

There are numerous types of approaches, techniques, exercises, and practice that can be used to teach vocabulary. The dilemma teachers often face is in deciding which among these numerous types would be best for their students and their circumstances. We have found several principles that can inform such decisions.

One principle that we have found useful in all methodological decisions is the principle of time-effectiveness. How much preparation time does the method require of the teacher? How much time does it require of the learner? Does the benefit received match the time spent?

Another principle for judging methods is that of content. When the learners are finished using the method, what do they have in the way of content? Will the method help learners acquire the words they want or need? Furthermore, what aspects of words will be known or enhanced as a result of using the method? Will learners see the features, the fields, the core meanings, the prototype structures, or the relations of the words because of the method? Will they be sensitive to the words' potential as figurative language or aware of their differences across cultures? Will they know what scripts, communication signals, or speech acts the words are used in? Will they recognize and use the morphological features of the word correctly? Will they understand any register restrictions the words may have and, thus, be able to use them in appropriate ways and contexts? Some activities will give greater knowledge in some of these areas and some will give greater knowledge in others.

Another way to look at content is to judge what steps in the vocabulary acquisition process – encountering new words, getting the word forms, getting the word meanings, consolidating word form and meaning in memory, or using the words – the method might contribute to. What additional instruction would be necessary in order to have all of the acquisition steps covered and the words fully learned?

Furthermore, methods can be judged by what additional value or learning they bring to the learners: Will the learners just know a limited number of new words or will they also know how to learn words better? Will they have transferrable strategies and techniques for learning that can be used with other vocabulary? Maybe even more important, will they want to continue learning words?

Following are evaluations of the merits of two rather general approaches to vocabulary techniques or exercises, chosen because one is considered a traditional method and the second is considered a more recent development. The evaluations are carried out using the principles just listed as evaluation guidelines.

The first approach to be discussed, which seems decidedly product-focused, and also closely connected to the first step of vocabulary learning (encountering new words), is that of using word lists. The basic technique is to give students a list of words to be learned. Such lists have not been as strong a component of communicative language approaches as they were of audiolingual and grammar translation methods. Yet, Huff (1992) found vocabulary lists in all of the current university foreign language texts (seven in Spanish and ten in German) he examined.

The time-effectiveness of the word list method can be enhanced depending on how we handle several variables. For example, what learners will have in the way of content depends on what words we include in the lists. Lists taken directly from a book may or may not be what learners want or need depending on the topics the book treats. A more likely way to get word lists that match learners' desires and needs is to have the learners make their own lists from materials they use. Students will learn the vocabulary of fields that interest them. For children, this may mean finding picture books with all sorts of vehicles, or buildings, or foods. If students are interested in some particular field of study, there are English for specific purposes materials on business, banking, tourism, hotel management, and a variety of other topics, each with its own specialized vocabulary. Although students may be motivated to seek out the vocabulary that is needed in their areas of interest, the teacher can facilitate self-study by making such materials available. In Chapter 15, we noted that students thought television and radio broadcasts were an excellent way to encounter new vocabulary. You may want to encourage acquisition of such materials for your school and encourage students to make their word lists as they use the materials. The *ABC News ESL Video Library* is a series of authentic broadcast materials on timely topics that may be appropriate. Lee (1994) found that video clips of TV commercials proved very helpful in teaching Chinese vocabulary (and other language aspects) to native English speakers. All materials would need to be previewed to be sure they are appropriate for your students. Another possibility would be to use ideas and techniques like those offered by Dornyei and Thurrell (1992) that will help students to first discover and then practice the lexical phrases needed for successful speech act performance. Working with such materials, students have opportunities not only to list, learn, and use appropriate words and lexical phrases, but also to develop an awareness of and sensitivity to the vocabulary of particular speech acts.

Ashton-Warner's book on teaching among the Maoris, *Teacher* (1963), shows clearly how letting students choose their own words to learn enhances learning. Ashton-Warner tells of using this technique with the children who were learning to read. Each day she encouraged them to bring words that they wanted to learn. She found that the learners came to have a genuine eagerness to learn the new words and that their motivation level was much higher with this technique than with any other she had previously tried.

If computers are available, you can try a more modern version of the word list method. Classes or individuals can build their own word lists or even complete dictionaries using do-it-yourself computer programs. Entries placed in these lists or dictionaries can then be programmed into a variety of computer word games or multiple-choice activities (Choicemaster is a good program for this latter work). Using the program, students can monitor their work and you can keep track of their progress.

Word lists by themselves are not particularly good for helping learners learn other content features of words such as semantic networks or fields, figurative potential, or morphology. If all of the words on the word lists are given in context, however, there are possibilities that learners will get some of the other information. Contexts larger than single sentences are usually more helpful. Having words in such contexts can also help learners increase their abilities to use the process of guessing meanings from context cues.

Huff (1992) also found that manipulating the arrangement of words in a word list could enhance the learning of some features. In his study, he compared the word learning of students who used a list of Russian words in random order to that of students who used a list containing the same words presented in order by part of speech. He found that the second group (those who received the words listed by part of speech) were able to internalize that information along with the meaning of the words.

417

Sometimes native language translations (a bilingual gloss) or second language synonyms for the words are provided with word lists. When word lists are coupled with glosses, either L1 or L2 glosses, or when learners are encouraged to use context to guess meanings, another step in vocabulary learning – getting the word meaning – has already been taken for the learners. The kinds of activities teachers assign to be done with the word lists may bring in the other steps in the vocabulary acquisition process. In Suggestopedia, a language teaching method, where learners often deal with very long lists of new words, sometimes the lists are presented orally or by the teacher with varying types of pronunciation. For example, the teacher might repeat the words several times varying vocal qualities such as volume (whispers and shouts), pitch (very high and very low), intonation (altering ups and downs), and speed (very fast and very slow). The results have a tendency to stick in memory so that learners remember the word form. Suggestopedia techniques also call for the use of background music, which relieves anxiety and enhances memory. The use of such techniques with the word list helps teach a technique or strategy that learners can use with subsequent vocabulary.

If learners are required to match words with their meanings given in another list (not in the same order as the word list), the activity helps consolidate word forms with word meanings, another essential vocabulary learning step. In a common variation on this technique, a word from the word list is on one card and its meaning is on another. Students then find matches in some kind of game, like Concentration, where all cards are placed face down in random order and then students take turns turning over two cards trying to match word and meaning. If no match is found, the two cards are put in their regular places face down again and the next person turns over two cards. These kinds of activities, of course, help students see other strategies that they might use in trying to learn words they may encounter later.

Activities can be added which also take students through the final step of vocabulary acquisition – using the word. Written activities can be as simple as asking students to write a sentence for each word studied. Sugawara (1993) found that having students answer questions that necessitate use of the word in the answer also helped students learn words and feel confident in their use. Such questions might be based on information found in natural databases. Levy (1990) gives us a description of English language databases of differing sizes (the Brown corpus, the Survey of the English Language, the Lancaster-Oslo-Bergen corpus, the Australian Corpus Project, COBUILD) and those developed for specific-purpose vocabulary (e.g., English for Business Courses, Corpus of Academic Texts). Students can use concordances to search these databases for information about word use. Concordance programs are becoming more and more readily available (most college campus computer centers have at least WordCruncher and MicroConcord). More and more databases are also being released on other languages (for a description of a French database, see Morrissey, 1993). Furthermore, student roleplaying and responding to oral questions using words from the word list are good ways of encouraging oral use and ensuring a more complete knowledge of the words.

A traditional vocabulary learning method (word list learning, in this case) thus may or may not be time-effective, depending on what activities and techniques are included as part of the method. Particular activities and techniques can enhance motivation, interest, word usefulness, knowledge of word features and functions, and acquisition of vocabulary learning strategies. In short, the overall choice of approach may be less significant in what is learned or how fast it is learned as are the many small choices of details within the overall approach.

The second method we will evaluate using our guideline principles is something generally considered a more modern way of teaching vocabulary: semantic domains. With this method, words in the same semantic field, such as words for cooking, or loving, or walking, and so forth, are taught together. Most of the instruction with the domains approach consists of giving information about the differences between words. For example, in *Walk, Amble, Stroll: Vocabulary Building Through Domains Level 2* (Trump, Trechter, & Holisky, 1992) the following information can be found for the BUILD domain:

Verbs like *establish, found, set up,* and *organize* are used to describe the first step in starting a new company, an organization, or even a country.

Some words in this domain give the idea of people working on a building, a bridge, or some other physical structure. Some verbs like this are: *build, construct, erect,* and *put up.*

The verbs *make, produce,* and *manufacture* are general words that describe the whole process of making a new thing.

(pp. 48–49)

Exercises following the instructions in this book require learners to substitute one word from the appropriate domain for another, for example, *construct* for *build,* or to choose between two possible words to fill a blank in a given sentence, e.g., "Paper was first _____ in China" (*manufactured, constructed*). Then students may answer questions on the founding of their own country and about a reading about Thomas Edison. After these exercises have been completed, students are introduced to related forms for the concepts: nouns where words have been introduced as verbs, or verbs where words have been introduced as nouns. The exercises following have students recognize and/or use the new forms introduced.

Although not all domain approaches are as thorough as the one in

419

Walk, Amble, Stroll, it raises the issue of the cost-effectiveness of such exercises. With regard to content, once again the domains' usefulness to students and their desires to learn the words depends entirely upon their individual experiences. Although students could produce their own domain lists, this could take considerable time if done thoroughly. However, it is possible to compromise between handing students a list of words in a domain and expecting them to come up with the words on their own by giving students paragraphs or longer segments of discourse on a single topic. If the passages use several words from the same domain in order to avoid repetition of terms, students could be taught to look for such related words and to make their own small domain lists which could be expanded through dictionary or thesaurus work.

This method can be used to address other aspects of content although they are not necessarily part of it. For example, you and your students can identify core meanings or prototypes within the domain, or potential scripts, registers, and contexts where the different words might be used. These elements often appear naturally as part of the information given in the instructions differentiating words within the domain. Notice, for example, how the instructions given above for the BUILD domain suggest spheres (such as an organization, company, or country) when a particular word might be used.

As with the word list approach some necessary vocabulary acquisition steps are naturally included with the domain approach, and others may require conscious inclusion through accompanying activities. For instance, the domain method automatically provides for encountering specific words listed in the chosen domain, the first step to acquisition. As with word lists, there is little natural focus on the acquisition of form, although, as above, this could be improved with the addition of Suggestopedia techniques. The third step, getting the meaning of the word, is handled explicitly in the domain method with the myriad of instructions for differentiating one word from another. In fact, the information given in this regard appears to be precisely the kind of information which learners need in order to differentiate between words that are similar in meaning, a common problem for more advanced learners (see Table 15.2 in Chapter 15).

Just as with word lists, there are no specific ways for consolidating word form and meaning in memory in the domain approach, although many of the possible exercises for the word list approach could serve this purpose with the domain approach. Flashcards and matching games are also possible in this approach although they are more difficult because differences between words are smaller within a particular domain.

Using words, the final necessary acquisition step, comes naturally in the domain approach. If contexts are given in which different words appear, it is natural to ask written or oral questions about the subject matter of the context, leading to natural use of the words to be learned. Roleplaying also provides opportunities for learners to use new words orally.

As with the word list method, the domain method should help students to pick up vocabulary learning strategies that can be used in other situations. Making a domain list is a strategy that could help students in the future. The habit of searching a semantic field for related terms develops a strategy they can continue to use. Getting used to making fine distinctions in meaning can also prepare students to use thesauruses and even dictionaries better. Processes that will help students learn better in the future may also be taught, whether intentional or not, in the activities and exercises related to working with domains.

Each of these two distinct methods neither motivates nor demotivates learners necessarily. Rather, motivation depends on many accompanying activities and intangible qualities, including teacher enthusiasm and preparation and individual student enjoyment of the activities. As mentioned previously, the choice of words also makes a difference, and teachers can facilitate these choices and activities by seeing that appropriate materials are available.

All of this may sound almost impossible if you are just setting up a program or if you teach languages other than English. Fortunately, there are many new materials on the market for a variety of languages. Check current publishers' catalogs for these and subscribe to the *Athelstan Newsletter on Technology and Language Learning* (2476 Bolsover, Suite 464, Houston, Texas 77005; e-mail: barlow@ruf.rice.edu). The group that puts out this publication tests and evaluates a wide variety of computer-assisted instruction programs for most languages taught in colleges and universities. Their survey of software includes programs for English, Spanish, French, Japanese, Arabic, Italian, German, Russian, and Chinese. The publication also has a "concordancing corner," CD-ROM news, resources (including computer clearing house information), and ads for new products.

If your school does not have the variety of materials nor the funding needed to support your instructional program, you can still begin to build your own small collection. In many countries, young people are required to do public service as a way of paying for their own education. Such aides can help find and organize materials for a learning center even if it has to be in one corner of your classroom. In visits to language classrooms in very poor schools, vocabulary posters and posters of lexical phrases organized around greetings, invitations, and other speech acts are prepared by the students themselves and proudly posted in the hallways. Not only do these decorate sometimes unattractive buildings, but they also reinforce the vocabulary the students have learned. Each time students pass by, they may point out the words they contributed and study those contributed by their classmates. The effectiveness of such materials and activities may be very high with little time or money spent.

The key in all vocabulary teaching is to keep motivation high while encouraging students to develop strategies that they can continue to use once they leave the classroom. The effectiveness of these strategies for individual teachers and learners depends on many factors, and language educators must approach decisions about methods and materials systematically, using principles to help us make wise decisions.

Practice 16.4

1. Select fifty words that you would like your students to learn in a second language. Now list ten different methods that you have seen used by teachers or in textbooks for teaching vocabulary. Make a chart in which you can show which methods you think are most effective for each of the fifty words. Which words would be hard (or easy) to learn by any method? Which method do you perceive to be the most useful for the words you have chosen? Which method do you perceive to be the least useful? Can you isolate what characteristics cause a method to be more or less effective? Try various methods with your learners and assess their effectiveness.

2. If you encounter unknown words in a language you are studying, do you stop and look them up, guess from the context, or continue reading with the hope that the meaning will become clear? Would it help if the teacher presented words before you began a reading? What kinds of clues might a teacher give about meaning that would help you understand the text?

3. Krantz (1991) investigated three questions about learning vocabulary in a foreign language: (a) Does vocabulary learning take place in reading words in context? (b) Does vocabulary learning take place by both reading words and looking them up in a dictionary? (c) Which is more efficient, a bilingual or monolingual dictionary? How might you replicate this study but also test the effect of explicit vocabulary teaching as well? What other questions would you like to ask about the effectiveness of teacher techniques (rather than the effectiveness of particular teaching materials)?

4. What other methods and techniques, in addition to the ones listed here, have you used? With students you teach, try out some of these methods and others previously

discussed in this book. Assess the amount of time it takes for you to prepare to use the method, how much time it takes for the students to use the method as designed, how well you feel your students have learned the words they were trying to use, what aspects of the words the students seem to have learned, what vocabulary learning strategies the students have learned, and how they seem to enjoy the method. What factors are most important in your deciding what methods to use?

5. Make a list of vocabulary learning strategies that have been discussed in this chapter that you can teach your students. Are there any strategies that may not work with the language you are teaching? With your classmates or fellow teachers, devise plans for how to present the strategies. What kinds of tests would you use to see if your teaching makes a difference? Test the effectiveness of your plans.

Research and application

1. Huff (1992) examined where and how vocabulary was presented in seven widely used university Spanish textbooks and in ten prominent university German textbooks. All of them had vocabulary lists, but the point in the chapter in which they were presented had changed over the years. Three of the texts Huff looked at (and only one written after 1970) had the vocabulary at the front of the chapter like older grammar-translation-type textbooks. In five the vocabulary was only in the middle of the chapter; in five others it was only at the end of the chapter; and in four it was both in the middle and at the end of the chapter. Most methodologists believe that it is better to "prime" vocabulary learning by presenting the words to be learned in a lesson first, asking students if they have encountered the words before, asking for their guesses on definitions, and asking for words they think might be related. This prepares students to encounter the words in the lesson and check the accuracy of their guesses. How might you test the effectiveness of vocabulary placement and the use of planned preliminary activities vs. planned vocabulary teaching following lessons?

2. When Gipe (1979) looked at four different methods of vocabulary instruction with children, she found that a treatment consisting of definitions and instructional sentence contexts was better than one where the children just studied the words with their definitions. Both of these treatments were better than one in which unfamiliar words and familiar words similar to them in meaning were paired

423

on one list and mixed on another list, and students were asked to categorize the words. The definitions and instructional sentence contexts were also better than a treatment in which the children looked up the words, wrote the definitions they found, and then composed original sentences using the words. Levin, McCormick, Miller, Berry, and Pressley (1982) did a similar study and found no significant advantage for the instructional context sentence group over a group who studied words and their definitions for an equivalent amount of time. Examine the methods of both studies. Whose findings do you find the most convincing? How would you go about doing a similar study with methods for teaching second language vocabulary?

3. Jenkins and Dixon (1983) criticized Gipe's (1979) study on methods of teaching word meanings because she did not control for time. Rank the methods you listed in Practice 16.4.1 according to the amount of time each would take to learn one word. Why would it be important to think about the amount of time each would take? How would you design a study to test time-effectiveness of different methods? If you can, carry out your study with students and see what conclusions you can draw.

4. Jenkins, Matlock, and Slocum (1989) looked at two approaches to vocabulary instruction – teaching individual word meanings and teaching how to derive word meaning from context. Not surprisingly, these researchers found that the first method resulted in students' having knowledge of specific words and that the second method taught students how to use contextual clues. What general principles about research can be discovered from these findings? Do learners always do better the thing that they practice doing? How would you test these ideas?

5. Beck and colleagues (Beck, McCaslin, & McKeown, 1980; Beck, Perfetti, & McKeown, 1982) combined several vocabulary instruction practices including "defining tasks, sentence generation tasks, classification tasks, oral production tasks, game-like tasks completed under timed conditions, and tasks that take advantage of the semantic or affective relationship among target words and previously acquired vocabulary" (1980, p. 13). The 104 target words were grouped into semantic categories consisting of eight to ten words (e.g., people – accomplice, rival, virtuoso; eyes – gape, spectator, binoculars) and each category was taught for 30 minutes a day over a period of five days. A subset of words from each semantic category was reviewed two or three days after the words had been taught to see if greater familiarity with the words would produce greater "automaticity" of recognition under timed conditions.

424

Beck et al. found that students receiving the combined activities treatment performed better than students receiving no special vocabulary treatment. They also found that the reviewed words were recalled better than the nonreviewed words and that students performed faster for the reviewed words on a sentence verification test than they did for the nonreviewed words. What was surprising was that the students who had received the combined-activities treatment did better than the no-treatment group on a vocabulary test that contained words that had not been studied in the treatment. Beck and her colleagues speculated that the explicit instruction on vocabulary may have made the students more word conscious and, thus, have had a more important effect than the simple learning of the words studied over a five-month period. Read the study and see what was discovered in terms of product and process. Devise a similar study, looking at both product and process results.

6. Although the domain method of instruction is fairly new in second language learning, it has been tried for other verbal learning tasks. Higa (1963) found learning interference when words on lists to be learned were too related. He found that learning of such related words was slower than learning of completely unrelated words. Tinkham (1993) found that students had more difficulty learning new words when they were presented in semantically related groups than when they were presented in unrelated groups. It is unclear if Higa and Tinkham looked at whether the words in the two groups (related and unrelated) were learned to the same depth of knowledge. The unrelated words were never presented or tested in any way that requires making distinctions among closely related terms. How would you design a study to test how initial presentation in related groups or unrelated groups affects the eventual ability to differentiate both unrelated and related terms and the time to reach that attainment?

Conclusion

In this book we have looked at a variety of ways in which linguists, psychologists, anthropologists, cognitive scientists, and teachers describe the systems that are included in vocabulary, semantics, and language education. The goal of discovering system is one that is shared by most fields of inquiry. Each of the methods gives us one way of thinking about how words and meanings are related and how they are used in our everyday activities.

Whenever we search for system, we immediately find variation. We have demonstrated the types of variations that exist in the ways that speakers of different languages use words to convey meanings. While there certainly are underlying primitive or universal meanings, the ways these are expressed differ across language and culture groups. Vocabulary selection varies across dialects and across the full range of sociolinguistic variables, which are constantly shifting as we play out our parts in interactions with each other. These variations are as important, and as interesting, as the basic systems that underlie them.

Glance at each of the objectives listed in the introduction to see how well you have met the goals we set for you. If you selected other objectives, check to be sure that you have met them as well. We hope we have given you sufficient practice to connect the objectives of this course and the related information in the text to practical application of that information to the kinds of everyday issues learners and teacher confront in their classrooms.

We also hope that this introduction to vocabulary, semantic, lexical, and morphology systems will serve as a guide for your teaching, materials development, research, and testing projects. An introduction, however, is only that. We urge you to continue your study of this field of language research, and to feel free to contribute to the field by sharing your ideas, your data, and the outcome of your teaching and research projects. From your work will come better descriptions of the invisible semantic and lexical systems of language. You can also contribute by applying what you have learned to our understanding of how we learn and use these systems in other languages and in cross-cultural communication not discussed here.

References

Acharya, J. (1990). Lexical modernization in Nepali: A study of borrowing. *Georgetown Journal of Languages and Linguistics, 1,* 3, 267–290.

Ackerman, B. (1983). Form and function in children's understanding of ironic utterances. *Journal of Child Psychology, 35,* 487–508.

Adams, T. W., and Kuder, S. R. (1993). *Attitudes through idioms.* 2d ed. New York: Heinle & Heinle.

Ahlswede, T., and Evens, M. (1988). A lexicon for medical expert systems. In M. Evens (Ed.), *Relational models of the lexicon* (pp. 97–111). Cambridge: Cambridge University Press.

Aitchinson, J. (1987). *Words in the mind: An introduction to the mental lexicon.* Oxford: Basil Blackwell.

Albert, M., and Obler, L. (1978). *The bilingual brain.* New York: Academic Press.

Algeo, J. (1971). The voguish uses of *non-. American Speech, 46,* 87–105.

Allen, K., and Burridge, K. (1991). *Euphemism and dysphemism, language used as shield and weapon.* Oxford: Oxford University Press.

Altman, R. (1985). Subtle distinctions: *Should* versus *had better.* Research Note, *Studies in Second Language Acquisition, 8,* 1, 80–89.

Ameka, F. (1990) The grammatical packaging of experiences in Ewe: A study in the semantics of syntax. *Australian Journal of Linguistics, 10,* 139–181.

Andersen, E. (1975) Cups and glasses: Learning the boundaries are vague. *Journal of Child Language, 2,* 79–103.

Anderson, J. (1983). *The architecture of cognition.* Cambridge, Mass.,: Harvard University Press.

Andrews, J., Rosenblatt, E., Malkus, U., Gardner, H., and Winner, E. (1987). Children's abilities to distinguish metaphoric and ironic utterances from mistakes and lies. In J. Van Dormael, M. Spoelders, and T. Vandamme (Eds.), *Metaphor* (pp. 9–25). Ghent: Communication and Cognition.

Anglin, J. (1977). *Word, object, and conceptual development.* New York: Norton.

Anglin, J. (1978). From reference to meaning. *Child Development, 49,* 969–976.

Ankist, I. (1985). Incorporated meanings: Conversions of nouns into verbs in English. M.A. thesis, Applied Linguistics, University of California, Los Angeles.

Anson, C. (1990). Errours and endeavors: A case study of English orthography. *International Journal of Lexicography, 3,* 1, 35–63.

Antinucci, F., and Miller, R. (1976). How children talk about what happened. *Journal of Child Language, 3,* 167–189.

Apresjan, J. (1969). Semantics and lexicography: Towards a new type of unilingual dictionary. In F. Kiefer (Ed.), *Studies in syntax and semantics.* Dordrecht: D. Reidel.

Ard, J., and Homburg, T. (1983). Verification of language transfer. In S. Gass and L. Selinker (Eds.), *Language transfer in language learning* (pp. 157–176). Rowley, Mass: Newbury House.

Aronoff, M. (1985) Automobile semantics. In V. Clark, P. Eschholz, and A Rosa. (Eds.) *Language: Introductory readings* (pp. 401–421). 4th ed. New York: St. Martin's Press.

Aronoff, M., and S. Sridhar (1984). Agglutination and composition in Kannada verb morphology. In D. Testen, V. Mishra, and J. Drogo (Eds.), *Lexical semantics* (pp. 3–20). Chicago: Chicago Linguistic Society.

Ashton-Warner, S. (1963). *Teacher.* New York: Simon & Schuster.

Atkinson, J., and Heritage, J. (1984). *Structures of social action: Studies in conversational analysis.* Cambridge: Cambridge University Press.

Ayto, J. (1989). *The Longman register of new words.* Harlow, Essex: Longman.

Backhouse, A. (1981). Japanese verbs of dress. *Journal of Linguistics, 17, 1,* 17–29.

Badecker, W., and Caramazza, A. (1989). A lexical distinction between inflection and derivation. *Linguistic Inquiry, 20, 1,* 108–116.

Baker, L. N. (1974). The lexicon: Some psycholinguistic evidence. *University of Califormia Working Papers in Phonetics, 26,* iv–132.

Baldinger, K. (1980). *Semantic theory.* New York: St. Martin's Press.

Bantu, F. (1981). Teaching German vocabulary: The use of English cognates and common loan words. *Modern Language Journal, 65, 2,* 129–136.

Baratz, J. (1969). A bidialectal task for determining language proficiency in economically disadvantaged negro children. *Child Development, 40,* 90–100.

Barnard, H. (1975). *Advanced English Vocabulary. Books 1–3B.* Rowley, Mass.: Newbury House.

Barsalou, L. (1983). Ad hoc categories. *Memory and Cognition, 11,* 211–227.

Barsalou, L. (1985). Ideals, central tendency and frequency of instantiation as determinants of graded structure in categories. *Journal of Experimental Psychology, 11, 629–654.*

Battig, W., and Montague, W. (1969). Category norms for verbal items in 56 categories. *Journal of Experimental Psychology,* Monograph 80.

Beck, I., McKeown, M., and Omanson, R. (1987). The effects and uses of diverse vocabulary instructional techniques. In M. McKeown and M. Curtis (Eds.), *The nature of vocabulary acquisition* (pp. 147–163). Hillsdale, N.J.: Lawrence Erlbaum Associates.

Beck, I. L, Perfetti, C. A., and McKeown, M. (1982). The effects of long-term vocabulary instruction on lexical access and reading comprehension. *Journal of Educational Psychology, 14, 3,* 506–521.

Beck, J., McCaslin, E., and McKeown, M. (1980). *The rationale and design of a program to teach vocabulary to fourth-grade students.* Pittsburgh: University of Pittsburgh, Learning Research Center.

Becker, J. (1975). The phrasal lexicon. In R. Schank and B. Nash-Webber (Eds.), *Theoretical issues in natural language processing* (pp. 38–41). ACL Workshop, Cambridge, Mass. June, 1975.

Beeching, C. (1989). *A dictionary of eponyms.* London: Library Association.

Bellugi, U. (1967). *The acquisition of the system of negation in children's speech.* Ph.D. diss., Harvard University.

Belyayev, B. V. (1963). The receptive, reproductive, and productive command of a foreign language. In *The psychology of teaching foreign languages* (pp. 176–193). New York: Macmillan.

Benson, M., Benson, E., and Ilson, R. (1986). *BBI combinatorial dictionary of English*. Amsterdam and Philadelphia: John Benjamins.

Bentahila, A. (1975). The influence of the L2 on the learning of L3. M.A. thesis, Bangor University.

Berkeley Women and Language Group. (1992). *Locating power: Proceedings of the 1992 Berkeley Women and Language Conference*. Berkeley, Calif.: University of California.

Berko, J. (1958). The child's learning of morphology. *Word, 14,* 150–177. Reprinted in S. Saporta (Ed.). 1966. *Psycholinguistics* (pp. 359–375). New York: Holt, Rinehart and Winston.

Berko-Gleason, J. (1993). *The development of language*. 3d ed. New York: Macmillan.

Berko-Gleason, J., and Weintraub, S. (1976). The acquisition of routines in child language. *Language in Society, 5,* 137–151.

Berlin, B., and Kay, P. (1969). *Basic color terms and their universality and evolution*. Berkeley: University of California Press.

Bermudez, A., and Prater, D. (1990). Using brainstorming and clustering with LEP writers to develop elaboration skills. *TESOL Quarterly, 24,* 3, 523–528.

Berryman, C., and Eman, V. (Eds.) (1980). *Communication, language and sex*. Rowley, Mass.: Newbury House.

Billow, R. (1981). Observing spontaneous metaphor in children. *Journal of Experimental Child Psychology, 31,* 430–445.

Block, D. (1992). Metaphors we teach and learn by. *Prospect 7,* 3, 42–55.

Bloom, L. (1970). *Language development: Form and function in emerging grammars*. Cambridge, Mass.: MIT Press.

Bloom, L., Lahey, J., Hood, L., Lifter, K., and Feiss, K. (1980). Complex sentences: Acquisition of syntactic connectives and the semantic relations they encode. *Journal of Child Language, 7,* 235–261.

Bloom, L., Lifter, L., and Hafitz, J. (1980). Semantics of verbs and development of verb inflection in child language. *Language, 56,* 386–412.

Blum-Kulka, S., House, J., and Kasper, G. (1989). *Cross-cultural pragmatics: Requests and apologies*. Norwood, N.J.: Ablex.

Blum-Kulka, S., and Olshtain, E. (1984). Requests and apologies: A cross-cultural study of speech act realization patterns (CCSARP). *Applied Linguistics, 1,* 1, 1–18.

Bogoyaulenskiy, D. (1973). The acquisition of Russian inflections. In C. Ferguson and D. Slobin (Eds.), *Studies of child language development* (pp. 284–294). New York: Holt, Rinehart and Winston.

Bolinger, D. (1965). The atomization of meaning. *Language, 41,* 4, 555–573. Reprinted in L. Jakobovits & M. Miron (Eds.), *Readings in the psychology of meaning* (pp. 432–448). Englewood Cliffs, N.J.: Prentice-Hall, 1967.

Bolinger, D. (1974). *Meaning and memory*. Paper presented at Brown University Linguistics Colloquium. Providence, R.I.

Bolinger, D. (1975). *Aspects of language*. New York: Harcourt Brace Jovanovich.

Boyd, P. (1975). Second language learning: The grammatical development of Anglo children learning through Spanish. *TESOL Quarterly, 9,* 2, 125–136.

Brinton, D., and Gaskill, W. (1978). Using news broadcasts in the ESL/EFL classroom. *TESOL Quarterly, 12,* 4, 403–413.

Brinton, D., Snow, M., and Wesche, M. (1989). *Content-based second language instruction.* New York: Newbury House.

Brown, C. (1993). Factors affecting the acquisition of vocabulary: Frequency and saliency of words. In T. Huckin, M. Haynes, and J. Coady (Eds.), *Second language reading and vocabulary learning* (pp. 263–286). Norwood, N.J.: Ablex.

Brown, C. (1983). Some principles of mental organization of the second language lexicon. In C. Campbell, V. Flashner, T. Hudson, and J. Lubin (Eds.), *Proceedings of the Los Angeles Second Language Research Forum.* Vol. II. Los Angeles: ESL Section, English Department, University of California, Los Angeles.

Brown, C., and Payne, M. E. (1994). Five essential steps of processes in vocabulary learning. Paper presented at the TESOL Convention, Baltimore, Md.

Brown, P., and Levinson, S. (1978). Universals of language usage: Politeness phenomena. In E. Goody (Ed.), *Questions and politeness* (pp. 56–324). Cambridge: Cambridge University Press.

Brown, R. (1957). Linguistic determinism and the part of speech. *Journal of Abnormal and Social Psychology, 55,* 1–5. Reprinted in S. Saporta (Ed.), (1966) *Psycholinguistics: A book of readings* (pp. 503–509). New York: Holt, Rinehart, and Winston.

Brown, R. (1965). *Social psychology.* New York: Free Press.

Brown, R. (1973). *The first language: The early stages.* Cambridge, Mass.: Harvard University Press.

Brown, R., and McNeill, D. (1966). The tip of the tongue phenomenon. *Journal of Verbal Learning and Verbal Behavior, 5,* 325–327.

Brownell, H. (1988). Appreciation of metaphoric and connotative word meaning by brain-damaged patients. In C. Chiarello (Ed.), *Right hemisphere contributions to lexical semantics* (pp. 33–46). Berlin and New York: Springer-Verlag.

Brugman, C. (1981). Story of *over.* M.A. thesis, University of California, Berkeley. Available from the Indiana University Linguistics Club.

Bruner, J. (1966). *Towards a theory of instruction.* Cambridge, Mass.: Harvard University Press.

Bryant, P. (1989). The south-east lexicon usage region of Australian English. *Australian Journal of Linguistics, 9,* 85–134.

Bryant, P. (1991). A survey of register usage in the lexicon of Australian English. In S. Romaine (Ed.), *Language in Australia* (pp. 289–303). Cambridge: Cambridge University Press.

Buckingham, H., Jr. (1980). On correlating aphasic errors with slips-of-the-tongue. *Applied Psycholinguistics, 1,* 199–220.

Bunker, E. L. (1988). Toward comprehensive guidelines for the preparation of materials in English for EFL adults with limited education. M.A. Thesis, Linguistics Department, Brigham Young University. Provo, Utah.

Burgmeier, A., Eldred, G., and Zimmerman, C. B. (1991). *Lexis: Academic vocabulary study.* Englewood Cliffs, N.J.: Prentice-Hall Regents.

Burt, M., Dulay, H., and Hernandez, E. (1973). *Bilingual syntax measure*. New York: Harcourt Brace.

Butterworth, G., and Hatch, E. (1978). A Spanish-speaking adolescent's acquisition of English syntax. In E. Hatch (Ed.), *Second language acquisition: A book of readings* (pp. 231–245). Rowley, Mass.: Newbury House.

Calfee, R., and Drum, P. (1986). Research on teaching reading. In M. Wittrock (Ed.), *Handbook of research on teaching* (pp. 804–849). New York: Macmillan.

Callanan, M. A. (1985). How parents label objects for young children: The role of input in the acquisition of category hierarchies. *Child Development, 56,* 508–523.

Camarata, S., and Leonard, L. (1986). Young children pronounce object words more accurately than action words. *Journal of Child Language 13,* 1, 51–66.

Campbell, L., and Mithun, M. (1979) *The languages of Native America*. Austin: University of Texas.

Carter, E. (1992). Strategies in the oral and written English of a native Mandarin speaker. Unpublished paper, University of Southern California.

Casagrande, J., and Hale, K. (1967). Semantic relations in Papago folk definitions. In D. Hymes and W. Bittle (Eds.), *Studies in Southwestern ethnolinguistics* (pp. 165–196). The Hague: Mouton.

Catford, J. (1968). Contrastive analysis and language teaching. *Monograph Series on Language and Linguistics, No. 21.* Washington, D.C.: Georgetown University.

Catford, J. (1969). Learning a language in the field: Problems of linguistic relativity. *Modern Language Journal, 53,* 5, 310–317.

Cazden, C. (1972). *Child language and education*. New York: Holt, Rinehart and Winston.

Celce-Murcia, M. (1978). The simultaneous acquisition of English and French in a two-year-old child. In E. Hatch (Ed.), *Second language acquisition: A book of readings* (pp. 38–53). Rowley, Mass.: Newbury House.

Chaffin, R., and Herrmann, D. (1988). The nature of semantic relations: a comparison of two approaches. In M. Evens (Ed.), *Relational models of the lexicon* (pp. 289–334). Cambridge: Cambridge University Press.

Chaika, E. (1985). Discourse routines. In V. Clark, P. Eschholz, and A. Rosa (Eds.), *Language: Introductory readings* (pp. 429–458). 4th ed. New York: St. Martin's Press.

Chall, J. (1987). Two vocabularies for reading: Recognition and meaning. In M. McKeown and M. Curtis (Eds.), *The nature of vocabulary acquisition* (pp. 7–17). Hillsdale, N.J.: Lawrence Erlbaum Associates.

Channell, J. (1990). Vocabulary acquisition and the mental lexicon. In J. Tomaszczyk and B. Lewandowska-Tomaszczyk (Eds.), *Meaning and lexicography* (pp. 21–30). Amsterdam and Philadelphia: John Benjamins.

Chaudron, C. (1982). Vocabulary elaboration in teachers' speech to L3 learners. *Studies in Second Language Acquisition, 4,* 2, 170–180.

Chaudron, C. (1983). Foreigner talk in the classroom – An aid to learning. In H. Seliger and M. Long (Eds.), *Classroom oriented research in second language acquisition* (pp. 127–145). Rowley, Mass: Newbury House.

Chaudron, C. (1988). *Second language classrooms: Research on teaching and learning*. New York: Cambridge University Press.

Cheshire, J. (Ed.), *English around the world*. Cambridge: Cambridge University Press, 1991.

Chiat, S. (1986). Personal pronouns. In P. Fletcher and M. Garman (Eds.), *Language acquisition*, 2d ed. (pp. 339–355). Cambridge: Cambridge University Press.

Chimombo, M. (1979). An analysis of the order of acquisition of English grammatical morphology in a bilingual child. *Working Papers on Bilingualism.* Ontario Institute for Studies in Education, Toronto, Ontario, Canada. *18,* 201–230.

Chomsky, C. (1970). Reading, writing and phonology. *Harvard Educational Review, 40,* 287–309.

Chomsky, N. (1981). *Lectures on government and binding*. Dordrecht: Foris.

Chukovsky, K. (1968). *From two to five*. Berkeley: University of California Press.

Claire, E. (1980). *A foreign students' guide to dangerous English*. Rochelle Park, N.J.: Eardley.

Clancy, P., Jacobsen, T., and Silva, M. (1976). The acquisition of conjunction: A crosslinguistic study. *Papers and Reports on Child Language Development, 12,* 71–80. Linguistics Program, Stanford University.

Clark, E. (1973). What's in a word? On the child's acquisition of semantics in his first language. In T. Moore (Ed.), *Cognitive development and the acquisition of language* (pp. 65–110). New York: Academic Press.

Clark, E. (1980). Here's the "top": Nonlinguistic strategies in the acquisition of orientational terms. *Child Development, 51,* 329–338.

Clark, E. (1981). Lexical innovations: How children learn to create new words. In W. Deutsch (Ed.), *The child's construction of language*. New York: Academic Press.

Clark, E. (1983). Meanings and concepts. In J. Flavell and E. Markman (Eds.), *Cognitive development*. Vol. 3 of P. Mussen (Ed.), *Handbook of child psychology* 4th ed. (pp. 787–840). New York: Wiley.

Clark, E., and Hecht, B. (1982) Learning to coin agent and instrument nouns. *Cognition, 12,* 1–24.

Clark, H. (1973). Space, time, semantics, and the child. In T. Moore (Ed.), *Cognitive development and the acquisition of language* (pp. 65–109). New York: Academic Press.

Clark, H., and Clark, E. (1977). *Psychology and language: An introduction to psycholinguistics*. New York: Harcourt Brace Jovanovich.

Clyne, M. (1981). Second generation "foreigner talk" in Australia. *International Journal of the Society of Language, 28,* 69–80.

Clyne, M. (1991). German and Dutch in Australia: Structures and use. In S. Romaine (Ed.). *Language in Australia* (pp. 241–248). Cambridge: Cambridge University Press.

Cohen, A. D. (1987). Verbal and imagery mnemonics in second- language vocabulary learning. *Studies in Second Language Acquisition, 9,* 1, 43–62.

Cohen, A. D., and Aphek, E. (1981). Easifying second language learning. *Studies in Second Language Acquisition, 3,* 221–236.

Cohen, A., Glasman, H., Rosenbaum-Cohen, P. R., Ferrara, J., and Fine, J. (1988). Reading English for specialized purposes: Discourse analysis and the use of student informants. In P. L. Carrell, J. Devine, and D. E. Eskey (Eds.), *Interactive approaches to second language reading* (pp. 152–167). New York: Cambridge University Press.

Collins, A., and Quillian, M. R. (1972). How to make a language user. In E. Tulving and W. Donaldson (Eds.), *Organization of memory* (pp. 310–354). New York: Academic Press.

Collis, H. (1981). *Colloquial English: How to shoot the breeze and knock 'em for a loop while having a ball.* New York: Regents.

Conde, M. (1977). *Dicho ciertos y ciertos dichos.* Mexico: B. Costa- Amic Editor.

Cook, V. (1981). Language function in second language learning and teaching. Paper presented at AILA, Lund, Sweden.

Corson, D. (1991). Social class differences in lexicon. In S. Romaine (Ed.). *Language in Australia* (pp. 349–361). Cambridge: Cambridge University Press.

Coseiu, E. (1967). Zur Vorgeschichte der strukturellen Semantik. In *To Honor Roman Jakobson* (pp. 489–498). The Hague: Mouton.

Coulmas, F. (1981). *Conversational routine.* The Hague: Mouton.

Crane, L., Yeager, E., and Whitman, R. (1981). *An introduction to linguistics.* Boston: Little, Brown.

Critchley, M. (1970). *Aphasiology and other aspects of language.* London: Edward Arnold.

Crow, J. T., and Quiqley, J. R. (1985). A semantic field approach to passive vocabulary acquisition for reading comprehension. *TESOL Quarterly, 19,* 3, 497–513.

Cruse, D. (1986). *Lexical semantics.* New York: Cambridge University Press.

Curran, S. (1983). Transfer and topic prominence in Korean-English interlanguage. M.A. thesis, Applied Linguistics Department, University of California, Los Angeles.

D'Amico-Reisner, L. (1981). Expressions of disapproval. Unpublished paper, Department of Educational Linguistics, University of Pennsylvania.

D'Andrade, R. (1987). A folk model of the mind. In D. Holland and N. Quinn (Eds.), *Cultural models in language and thought* (pp. 113–145). Cambridge: Cambridge University Press.

Danesi, M. (1985). *Loanwords and phonological methodology.* Toronto: Didier.

Danet, B. (1985). Legal discourse. In T. Van Dijk (Ed.), *Handbook of discourse analysis,* Vol 1. (pp. 273–299). New York: Academic Press.

De Houwer, A. (1987). Nouns and their companions. *Belgium Journal of Linguistics, 2,* 55–73.

Demers, A., and Farmer, A. (1986). *A Linguistics Workbook.* Cambridge, Mass.: MIT Press.

Derwing, B. (1976). Morpheme recognition and the learning of rules for derivational morphology. *Canadian Journal of Linguistics, 21,* 38–66.

Derwing, B., and Baker, W. (1979). Recent research on the acquisition of English morphology. In P. Fletcher and M. Garman (Eds.), *Language acquisition* (pp. 209–223). Cambridge: Cambridge University Press.

De Villiers, J., and de Villers, P. (1973). A cross-sectional study of the acquisition of grammatical morphemes in child speech. *Journal of Psycholinguistic Research, 7,* 3, 189–211.

Dillon, G. (1977). *Introduction to contemporary linguistic semantics.* Englewood Cliffs, N.J.: Prentice-Hall.

Dineen, A. (1990). Shame/embarrassment in English and Danish. *Australian Journal of Linguistics, 10,* 2, 217–230.

Dittmar, N. (1984). Semantic features of pidginized learner varieties of German. In R. Andersen (Ed.), *Second languages: A cross-linguistic perspective* (pp. 243–270). Rowley, Mass.: Newbury House.

Dixon, R. (1968). Noun classes. *Lingua, 21,* 104–125.

Dixon, R. (1972). *The Dyirbal language of North Queensland.* Cambridge: Cambridge University Press.

Dixon, R. (1982). *Where have all the adjectives gone?* Berlin: Walter de Gruyter.

Dixson, R. J. (1994). *Essential idioms in English.* New ed. Englewood Cliffs, N.J.: Regents/Prentice Hall.

Dole, R. (1983). Types of L1 interference on L2. *Bulletin of the Canadian Association of Applied Linguistics, 52,* 143–155.

Dornyei, Z., and Thurrell, S. (1992) *Conversation and dialogues in action.* New York: Prentice-Hall International.

Dorr-Bremme, D. (1990). Contextualization cues in the classroom: Discourse regulation and social control functions. *Language in Society, 19,* 379–402.

Downing, P. (1984). *Japanese numeral classifiers: Syntax, semantics and pragmatics.* Ph.D. diss., University of California, Berkeley.

Dressler, W. (1985). Morphology. In T. Van Dijk (Ed.), *Handbook of discourse analysis, Vol. 2* (pp. 79–86). London: Academic Press.

Drum, P., and Konopak, B. (1987). Learning word meanings from written context. In M. McKeown and M. Curtis (Eds.), *The nature of vocabulary acquisition* (pp. 73–87). Hillsdale, N.J.: Lawrence Erlbaum Associates.

Duffy, P., Henly, E., Maurice, K., McPartland, P., and Stempleski, S. (1993), *ABC News ESL video library.* Regents/Prentice-Hall and ABC News.

Dunn, L. (1959). *Peabody Picture Vocabulary Test.* Circle Pines, Minn.: American Guidance Service.

Dupuy, B., and Krashen, S. D. (1993). Incidental vocabulary acquisition in French as a second language. *Applied Language Learning, 4,* 1/2, 55–63.

Durrell, M. (1988). Some problems with contrastive lexical semantics. In W. Hüllen and R. Schulze (Eds.), *Understanding the lexicon* (pp. 230–251). Tübingen: Max Niemeyer Verlag.

Eisenberg, A. (1993). Eponymous science. *Scientific American,* December 1993, 144.

Enani, M. (1993). Interpretation of metaphor and irony in literature with special emphasis on poetry. In M. Abousenna (Ed.), *Creativity in translation.* Cairo: CDELT, Ain Shams University.

Erickson, T., and Mattson, M. (1981). From words to meaning: A semantic illusion. *Journal of Verbal Learning and Verbal Behavior, 20,* 540–551.

Ervin-Tripp, S. (1972). On sociolinguistic rules: Alternation and co-occurrence. In J. Gumperz and D. Hymes (Eds.), *Directions in sociolinguistics* (pp. 213–250). New York: Holt, Rinehart and Winston.

Evens, M. (1988). Introduction to M. Evens (Ed.), *Relational models of the lexicon* (pp. 1–37). Cambridge: Cambridge University Press.

Evens, M., Litowitz, B., Markowitz, J., Smith, R., and Werner, O. (1980). *Lexical-semantic relations: A comparative survey.* Carbondale, Ill., and Edmonton, Canada: Linguistic Research.

Fathman, A. (1975). The relationship between age and second language production ability. *Language Learning, 25,* 2, 245-254.

Feare, R. E. (1980). *Practice with idioms.* New York: Oxford University Press.

Federal News Service. (1989). Press conference with President George Bush, November 7, 1989. Washington, D. C.: Federal Information Systems Corporation.

Fellbaum, C. (1990). English verbs as a semantic net. *International Journal of Lexicography, 3*, 4, 278–301.

Fernald, A., and Morikawa, H. (1993). Common themes and cultural variations in Japanese and American mothers' speech to infants. *Child Development, 64*, 3, 637–656.

Fernando, C., and Flavell, R. (1981). *On idiom: Critical views and perspectives*, Vol. 5. University of Exeter: Exeter Linguistic Studies.

Ferreiro, E., and Sinclair, H. (1971). Temporal relations in language. *International Journal of Psychology, 6*, 39–47.

Fillmore, C. (1971) Verbs of judging. In C. Fillmore and D. Langendoen (Eds.),*Studies in Linguistic Semantics* (pp. 273–290). New York: Holt, Rinehart & Winston.

Fillmore, C. (1977). The case for case reopened. In P. Cole and J. Sadock (Eds.), *Syntax and semantics, 8* (pp. 59–82). New York: Academic Press.

Fishman, J., Cooper, R., and Ma, R. et al. (1971). *Bilingualism in the barrio, Vol. 3*. The Hague: Mouton.

Flanagan, M. (1990). Subclassification of English adjectives for French to English machine translation. *Georgetown Journal of Languages and Linguistics, 1*, 3, 291–296.

Fonagy, L. (1963). *Die Metaphern in der Phonetik*. The Hague: Mouton.

Foster, S. (1990). *The communicative competence of young children*. London and New York: Longman.

Fowler, R. (1985). Power. In T. van Dijk (Ed.), *Handbook of discourse analysis. Vol. 4: Discourse analysis in society* (pp. 61–82). London: Academic Press.

Fragiadakis, H. (1993). *All clear! Idioms in context*, 2d ed. New York: Newbury House.

Fragiadakis, H., and Statan, L. (1993) *All clear! Computer-assisted software*. New York: Newbury House.

Francis, W. N., and Kučera, H. (1982). *Frequency analysis of English usage: Lexicon and grammar*. Boston: Houghton, Mifflin.

Frawley, W. (1988). Relational models and metascience. In M. Evens (Ed.), *Relational models of the lexicon* (pp. 335–372). Cambridge: Cambridge University Press.

Fromkin, V. (1971). The non-anomalous nature of anomalous utterances. *Language, 47*, 27–52.

Fromkin, V. (Ed.) (1973). *Speech errors as linguistic evidence*. The Hague: Mouton.

Frost, R. (1969). *Robert Frost's Poems*. New York: Washington Square Press.

Galvan, J., and Campbell, R. (1979). An examination of the communication strategies of two children in the Culver City Spanish immersion program. In R. Andersen (Ed.), *The acquisition and use of Spanish and English as first and second languages* (pp. 133–150). Washington, D.C.: TESOL.

Gardner, H., Winner, E., Bechhofer, R., and Wolf, D. (1978). The development of figurative language. In K. Nelson (Ed.), *Children's language*, Vol. 1 (pp. 1–38). New York: Gardner.

Gaspar de Alba, A. (1987). Beggar on the Cordoba Bridge, *Three times a woman*. *Bilingual Review, 14*, 1/2, 5.

Gasser, M. (1975). A stage in the acquisition of Amharic by an adult. Abstract in E. Hatch (Ed.) *Second language acquisition: A book of readings.* (p. 450). Rowley, Mass: Newbury House.

Gasser, M. (1988). A connectionist model of sentence generation in a first and second language. Ph.D. diss., University of California, Los Angeles.

Gasser, M. (1993). *Learning words in time: Towards a modular connectionist account of the acquisition of receptive morphology.* Technical report, Computer Science and Linguistics Departments, Indiana University, Bloomington.

Gasser, M., and Lee, C. (1991). A short term memory architecture for the learning of morphophonemic rules. In R. Lippmann, J. Moody, and D. Touretzky (Eds.), *Advances in neural information processing systems, 3* (pp. 605–622). San Mateo, Calif.: Morgan Kaufmann.

Geckeler, H. (1971). *Zur Wortfelddiskussion: Untersuchungen zur Gliederung des Wortfeldes "alt-jung-neu" in heutigen Französisch.* Munich: Fink.

Genzel, R. B. (1991). *Getting the hang of idioms and expressions.* New York: Maxwell-Macmillan.

Gernsbacher, M. (1991). Comprehending conceptual anaphors. *Language and Cognitive Processes, 6,* 2, 81–105.

Gibbons, J. (1987) *Code-mixing and code choice: A Hong Kong case study.* Clevedon, Avon: Multilingual Matters.

Gillis, S. (1987). Words and categories at the onset of language acquisition. *Belgium Journal of Linguistics, 2,* 37–53.

Gipe, J. (1979). Investigating techniques for teaching word meanings. *Reading Research Quarterly, 14,* 624–644.

Glahn, E. (1980). Introspection as a method of elicitation in interlanguage studies. *Interlanguage Studies Bulletin* (Utrecht) *5,* 119–128.

Glaser, R. (1988). The grading of idiomaticity as a presupposition for a taxonomy of idioms. In W. Hüllen and R. Schulze (Eds.), *Understanding the lexicon* (pp. 264–279). Tübingen: Max Niemeyer Verlag.

Gleason, H. (1955). *Workbook in descriptive linguistics.* New York: Holt, Rinehart and Winston.

Glucksberg, S., Gildea, P., and Bookin, H. B. (1982). On understanding non-literal speech: Can people ignore metaphors? *Journal of Verbal Learning and Verbal Behavior, 21,* 85–98.

Godard, D. (1979). Same setting, different norms: Phone call beginnings in France and the United States. *Language in Society, 6,* 2, 209–219.

Goffman, E. (1976). Replies and responses. *Language in Society, 5,* 3, 254–313.

Goodman, K. S. (1969). Analysis of oral reading miscues: Applied psycholinguistics. *Reading Research Quarterly, 5,* 9–29.

Goodman, K. S. (Ed.). (1973). *Miscue analysis: Application to reading instruction.* Urbana, Ill.: ERIC Clearinghouse on Reading and Communication Skills.

Gozzi, P., Jr. (1992). McMetaphor. *Etc., 49,* 4, 447–474.

Graham, C., and Belnap, R. (1986). The acquisition of lexical boundaries in English by native speakers of Spanish. *International Review of Applied Linguistics, 24,* 4, 275–286.

Graves, M. (1987). The roles of instruction in fostering vocabulary development. In M. McKeown and M. Curtis (Eds.), *The nature of vocabulary acquisition,* (pp. 165–184). Hillsdale, N.J.: Lawrence Erlbaum Associates.

Green, J. (1991). *Neologisms: New words since 1960.* London: Bloomsbury.

Greenberg, J. H. (1987). *Language in the Americas.* Stanford, Calif.: Stanford University Press.

Greene, A. (1969). *Pullet surprises.* Glenview, Ill.: Scott, Foresman.

Greenough, J., and Kittredge, G. (1901). *Words and their ways in English speech.* New York: Macmillan.

Grice, H. (1975). Logic and conversation. In P. Cole and J. Morgan (Eds.), *Syntax and semantics 3: Speech acts* (pp. 41–58). New York: Academic Press.

Gross, D., and Miller, K. (1990). Adjectives in WordNet. *International Journal of Lexicography, 3,* 4, 265–277.

Gruber, J. (1967). Look and see. *Language, 43,* 937–947.

Haastrup, K. (1991). Developing learners' procedural knowledge in comprehension. In R. Phillipson, E. Kellerman, L. Selinker, M. Sharwood Smith, and M. Swain (Eds.) *Foreign/Second language pedagogy research* (pp. 120–133). Clevedon, Avon: Multilingual Matters.

Haggard, M. (1980). Vocabulary acquisition during elementary and post-elementary years: A preliminary report. *Reading Horizons, 21,* 1, 61–69.

Hakuta, K. (1974). A report on the development of the grammatical morphemes in a Japanese child learning English as a second language. *Working Papers on Bilingualism, OISE, 3,* 18–44.

Hall, R. A., Jr. (1964). *Introductory linguistics.* Philadelphia: Chilton Books. The chapter "Pidgin languages" is reprinted in *Readings from Scientific American. Human communication: Language and its psychobiological bases* (1981, pp. 72–79). San Francisco: W. H. Freeman.

Halliday, M. (1975). *Learning how to mean: Explorations in the development of language.* London: Edward Arnold.

Halliday, M. (1985). *An introduction to functional grammar.* London: Edward Arnold.

Halliday, M., and Hasan, R. (1976). *Cohesion in English.* London: Longman.

Harkins, J. (1990). *Shame* and *shyness* in the Aboriginal classroom: A case for "practical semantics." *Australian Journal of Linguistics, 10,* 2, 293–306.

Harlow, L. (1990). Do they mean what they say? Sociopragmatic competence and second language learners. *Modern Language Journal, 74,* 328–351.

Harris, J. (1975). Metaphor in technical writing. *Technical Writing Teacher, 2,* 2, 9–14.

Harris, J. (1986). Shape imagery in technical writing. *Journal of Technical Writing and Communication, 16,* 1/2, 55–61.

Hartman, P., and Judd, E. (1978). Sexism and TESOL materials. *TESOL Quarterly, 12,* 4, 383–393.

Hasselmo, N. (1976). *Swedish America: An introduction.* New York: Swedish America.

Hatch, E. (1978) *Second language acquisition: A book of readings.* Rowley, Mass.: Newbury House.

Hatch, E. (1992). *Discourse and language education.* Cambridge: Cambridge University Press.

Hatch, E., and Hawkins, B. (1991). Narratives of "at risk" children. Paper presented at Second Language Research Forum, University of Southern California, Los Angeles, California.

Haugen, E. (1950). The analysis of linguistic borrowing. *Language, 26,* 210–231.

Haviland, J. (1979). Guugu Yimidhirr brother-in-law language. *Language in Society, 8,* 3, 365–393.

Haycraft, J. (1978). *Teaching vocabulary. An introduction to English language teaching* (pp. 44–54). London: Longman.

Haynes, M. (1993). Patterns and perils of guessing in second language reading. In T. Huckin, M. Haynes, and J. Coady (Eds.) *Second language reading and vocabulary learning* (pp. 46–64). Norwood, N.J.: Ablex.

Henley, N. (1969). A psychological study of the semantics of animal terms. *Journal of Verbal Learning and Verbal Behavior, 8,* 176–184.

Hernandez, H. (1987). *Refranes y dichos populares.* San Jose, Costa Rica: Editorial Alma Mater.

Higa, M. (1963). Interference effects of intralist word relationships in verbal learning. *Journal of Verbal Learning and Verbal Behavior, 2,* 170–175.

Hill, C. (1975). Variation in the use of "front" and "back" by bilingual speakers, *Berkeley Linguistics Series, 1,* 196–206.

Hirakawa, M. (1990). A study of the second language acquisition of English reflexives. *Second Language Research, 6,* 8, pp. 60–85.

Holisky, D., Trump, K., and Trechter, S. (1992). *Walk, amble, stroll: Vocabulary building through domains, Level 2.* Boston: Heinle and Heinle.

Hornby, A. (1989). *Oxford advanced learners' dictionary.* 4th ed. Oxford: Oxford University Press.

Householder, F. (1971). *Linguistic speculations.* London and New York: Cambridge University Press.

Huang, J., and Hatch, E. (1978). A Chinese child's acquisition of English. In E. Hatch (Ed.), *Second language acquisition: A book of readings* (pp. 118–131). Rowley, Mass.: Newbury House.

Huebner, T. (1979). Order of acquisition vs. dynamic paradigm: A comparison of methods in Interlanguage research. *TESOL Quarterly, 13,* 21–28.

Huckin, T., and Bloch, J. (1993). Strategies for inferring word-meanings in context: A cognitive model. In T. Huckin, M. Haynes, and J. Coady (Eds.) *Second language reading and vocabulary learning* (pp. 153–178). Norwood, N.J.: Ablex.

Huff, R. (1992). Effects of grammatical category on the acquisition and use of Russian vocabulary. M.A. thesis. Language Acquisition (Russian) Department, Brigham Young University, Provo, UT.

Hymanson, M. C. (1981). *Connections and contexts: A basic vocabulary.* New York: Harcourt Brace Jovanovich.

Ilson, R., and Mel'čuk, I. (1989) English BAKE revisited: BAKE-ing an ECD. *International Journal of Lexicography, 2,* 4, 325–343.

Iris, M. (1984). A lexical/semantic analysis of Navajo children's lexicons. In D. Testen, V. Mishra, and J. Drogo (Eds.), *Lexical semantics* (pp. 143–149). Chicago: Chicago Linguistic Society.

Iris, M., Litowitz, B., and Evens, M. (1988). Problems of the part-whole relation. In M. Evens (Ed.), *Relational models of the lexicon* (pp. 261–288). Cambridge: Cambridge University Press.

Itard, J. (1962). *The wild boy of Aveyron.* Translated by G. and M. Humphrey. New York: Appleton-Century-Crofts.

Jackendoff, R. (1978). Grammar as evidence for conceptual structure. In M. Halle, J. Bresnan, and G. Miller (Eds.), *Linguistic theory and psychological reality* (pp. 201–228). Cambridge, Mass: MIT Press.

Jackendoff, R. (1985). *Semantics and cognition.* Cambridge: Cambridge University Press.

Jakobson, R. (1972). *Louvain lectures.* Edited by M. van Ballaer as *Aspects of the theories of Roman Jakobson.* Monograph. Leuven: Katholieke Universiteit.

James, C. (1980). *Contrastive analysis.* London: Longman.

Janus Survival Vocabulary Books. (1980). Hayward, Calif.: Janus.

Jarmul, D. (1981). *Plain talk: Clear communication for international development.* Mt. Rainier, Md.: Volunteers in Technical Assistance.

Jenkins, J., and Dixson, R. (1983). Vocabulary learning. *Contemporary Educational Psychology, 8,* 237–260.

Jenkins, J. R., Matlock, B., and Slocum, T. A. (1989) Two approaches to vocabulary instruction: The teaching of individual word meanings and practice in deriving word meaning from context. *Reading Research Quarterly, 24(2),* 215–235.

Jespersen, O. (1938). *Growth and structure of the English language.* 9th ed. Excerpt reprinted in C. Laird, and R. Gorrell (Eds.) 1971. *Readings about language* (pp. 124–129). New York: Harcourt Brace Jovanovich.

Johns, A. (1980). Cohesive error in the written discourse of nonnative speakers. *CATESOL Occasional Papers, 8,* 65–70.

Jones, L., and von Baeyer, C. (1983). *Functions of American English: Communication activities for the classroom.* New York: Cambridge University Press.

Joos, M. (1961). *The five clocks.* New York: Harcourt Brace Jovanovich.

Jordens, P. (1977). Rules, grammar intuitions and strategies in foreign language learning. *Interlanguage Studies Bulletin, 2,* 2, 5–76.

Kachru, B. (1978). Toward structure code-mixing: An Indian perspective. *International Journal of Sociology of Language, 16* (Aspects of Sociolinguistics in South Asia), 24–47.

Kalisz, R. (1990). A cognitive approach to spatial terms represented by "in front of" and "behind" in English, and their metaphorical extensions. In J. Tomaszczyk and B. Lewandowska-Tomaszczyk (Eds.), *Meaning and lexicography* (pp. 167–179). Amsterdam and Philadelphia: John Benjamins.

Karmiloff-Smith, A. (1979). *A functional approach to child language: A study of determiners and reference.* Cambridge: Cambridge University Press.

Kastovsky, D. (1990). Semantic and formal structures in the lexicon. In J. Tomaszczyk and B. Lewandowska-Tomaszczyk (Eds.), *Meaning and lexicography* (pp. 75–91). Amsterdam and Philadelphia: John Benjamins.

Kato, A. (1989). A discourse analysis of "want" as an indirect directive in comparison to Japanese directives. M.A. thesis, Applied Linguistics Department, University of California, Los Angeles.

Katz, J., and Fodor, J. (1963). The structure of a semantic theory. *Language, 39,* 2, 170–210. Reprinted In L. Jakobovits and M. Miron (Eds.), *Readings in the psychology of language* (pp. 398–429). Englewood Cliffs, N.J.: Prentice-Hall, 1967.

Katz, A., Paivio, A., and Marschark, M. (1985). Poetic comparison: Psychological dimensions of metaphoric processing. *Journal of Psycholinguistic Research, 14,* 365–383.

Keen, D. (1994). *Developing vocabulary skills.* 2d ed. Boston: Heinle & Heinle.

Kellerman, E. (1977). Towards a characterization of the strategy of transfer in second language learning. *Interlanguage Studies Bulletin, 2,* 58–145.

Kellerman, E. (1978). Giving learners a break: Native language intuitions as a source of prediction about transferability. *Working Papers on Bilingualism, 15,* 59–92.

Kelly, K. (1989). A Turkish metaphorical description of anger and love. M.A. thesis, Applied Linguistics Department, University of California, Los Angeles.

Kenyeres, A., and Kenyeres, E. (1938). Comment un petite Hongroise de sept ans apprend le français. *Archives de Psychologie, 26,* 104, 322–366.

Kernan, K., and Blount, B. (1966). Acquisition of Spanish grammar by Mexican children. *Anthropological Linguistics, 89,* 1–14.

Kimura, M. (1989). The effect of loanwords on the acquisition of the correct range of meanings of English words. M.A. thesis, Linguistics Department, Brigham Young University, Provo, Utah.

Kitsch, D. (1982). The English Interlanguage of a native speaker of Piedmontese. M.A. thesis, Applied Linguistics Department, University of California, Los Angeles.

Koike, I. (1983). *Acquisition of grammatical structures and relevant verbal strategies in a second language.* Tokyo: Tai shu Kan.

Kolers, P. (1963). Interlingual word associations. *Journal of Verbal Learning and Verbal Behavior, 2,* 291–300.

Korfeld, J. (1975). Some insights into the cognitive representation of word meanings. In R. Grossman, L. San, and T. Vance (Eds.). *Papers from the parasession on functionalism* (pp. 271–275). Chicago: Chicago Linguistics Society.

Kosko, B., and Isaka, S. (1993). Fuzzy logic. *Scientific American, 269,* 1, 76–81.

Kotsinas, U. (1983). On the acquisition of vocabulary in immigrant Swedish. In H. Ringbom (Ed.), *Psycholinguistics and foreign language learning* (pp. 75–100). Publications of the Research Institute of the Abo Akademi Foundation, no. 86. Abo: Abo Akademi.

Kovecses, Z. (1986). *Metaphors of anger, pride, and love.* Philadelphia: John Benjamins.

Kovecses, Z. (1988). *The language of love: The semantics of passion in conversational English.* Lewisburg, Pa.: Bucknell University Press.

Kramerae, C. (1981). *Women and men speaking: Frameworks for analysis.* Rowley, Mass: Newbury House.

Krantz, J. (1991). Learning vocabulary in a foreign language: A study of reading strategies. *Gothenburg Studies in English, 63.* Gothenberg: Gothenberg University.

Krashen, S. (1977). Some issues relating to the Monitor Model. In H. Brown, C. Yorio, and R. Crymes (Eds.), *On TESOL '77: Teaching and learning English as a second language: Trends in research and practice* (pp. 144–158). Washington, D.C.: TESOL.

Krashen, S., and Scarcella, R. (1978). On routines and patterns in language acquisition and performance. *Language Learning, 28,* 2, 282–300.

Kroeber, A. (1909). Classificatory systems of relationships. *Journal of the Royal Anthropological Institute, 39,* 77–84.

Krzeszowski, T. (1990). Prototypes and equivalence. In J. Fisiak (Ed.), *Further insights into contrastive analysis* (pp. 29–46). Amsterdam and New York: John Benjamins.

Kuczaj, S., and Maratsos, M. (1975). On the acquisition of "front," "back" and "side." *Child Development, 46*, 202–210.

Kurath, H. (1939–1943). *The Linguistic Atlas.* Providence, R.I.: Brown University.

Kurath, H. (1964). Interrelation between regional and social dialects. *Proceedings of the Ninth International Congress of Linguists* (pp. 135–143). The Hague: Mouton. Reprinted in H. Allen and G. Underwood (Eds.), *Readings in American dialectology* (pp. 365–374). New York: Appleton-Crofts, 1971.

Kuwahata, M. (1984). The negation system in the interlanguage of a Japanese speaker. M.A. thesis, Applied Linguistics Department, University of California, Los Angeles.

Labov, W. (1972). *Language in the inner city.* Philadelphia: University of Pennsylvania Press.

Labov, W. (1973). The boundaries of words and their meanings. In J. Fishman (Ed.), *New ways of analyzing variation in English* (pp. 340–373). Washington, D.C.: Georgetown University Press.

Lakoff, G. (1987). *Women, fire, and dangerous things: What categories reveal about the mind.* Chicago: University of Chicago Press.

Lakoff, G., and Johnson, M. (1980). *Metaphors we live by.* Chicago: University of Chicago Press.

Lakoff, G., and Turner, M. (1989). *More than cool reason: The power of poetic metaphor.* Chicago: University of Chicago Press.

Langacker, R. (1972). *Fundamentals of linguistic analysis.* New York: Harcourt, Brace, Jovanovich.

LaPorte C. (1993). From receptive to productive vocabulary: A study using dialog journals. M.A. thesis, Linguistics Department, Brigham Young University, Provo, Utah.

Laufer, B. (1981). A problem in vocabulary learning – synophones. *ELT Journal, 33*, 3, 294–300.

Laufer, B. (1991). Words you know: How they affect the words you learn. In J. Fisiak (Ed.), *Further insights into contrastive analysis* (pp. 573–593). Amsterdam and New York: John Benjamins.

Lederer, R. M. (1985) *Colonial American English.* Old Lyme, Conn.: Verbatim.

Lee, F. Y. (1994). The effect on listening comprehension of using television commercials in a Chinese as a second language class. M.A. thesis. Department of Language Acquisition (Chinese). Provo, Utah, Brigham Young University.

Legaretta, D. (1979). The effects of program models on language acquisition by Spanish-speaking children. *TESOL Quarterly, 13*, 4, 521–534.

Lehmann, D. (1977). A confrontation of *say, speak, talk, tell* with possible German counterparts. *PSiCL, 6*, 99–109.

Lehr, F. (1984). Promoting vocabulary development. *Journal of Reading, 27*, 656–658.

Lehrer, A. (1969). Semantic cuisine. *Journal of Linguistics. 5*, 1, 39–55.

Lehrer, A. (Ed.). (1974). *Semantic fields and lexical structure.* Amsterdam: North-Holland.

Lehrer, A. (1974). Belief predicates (Some hard words). In A. Lehrer (Ed.), *Semantic fields and lexical structure* (pp. 131–149). Amsterdam: North Holland.

Lehrer, A. (1983). *Wine and conversation.* Bloomington: Indiana University Press.

Leondar, B. (1975). Metaphor and infant cognition. *Poetics, 4,* 273–287.

Leopold, W. (1939). *Speech development of a bilingual child. Vol 1. Vocabulary growth in the first two years.* Evanston, Ill.: Northwestern University Press.

Levenston, E., and Blum, S. (1977). Aspects of lexical simplification in the speech and writing of advanced adult learners. In S. Corder and E. Roulet (Eds.), *The notion of simplification, interlanguages, and pidgins and their relation to second language pedagogy.* Proceedings of the 5th Colloque of Applied Linguistics. Neuchâtel: Faculté des lettres.

Levin, B. (Ed.) (1985). *Lexical semantics in review.* Cambridge, Mass.: Center for Cognitive Science, MIT.

Levin, H., and Novak, M. (1991). Frequencies of Latinate and Germanic words in English as determinants of formality. *Discourse Processes, 14,* 389–398.

Levin, J. R., McCormick, C. B., Miller, G. E., Berry, J. K., and Pressley, M. (1982). Mnemonic versus nonmnemonic vocabulary-learning strategies for children. *American Educational Research Journal, 19,* 121–136.

Levy, M. (1990). Concordances and its integration into a word-processing environment for language learners. *System, 18,* 2, 177–188.

Lewandowska-Tomaszczyk, B. (1988). The increment values of predicates in the semantic lexicon. In W. Hullen and R. Schulze (Eds.), *Understanding the lexicon* (pp. 137–147). Tubingen: Max Niemeyer Verlag.

Lewandowska-Tomaszczyk, B. (1990). Meaning, synonymy, and the dictionary. In J. Tomaszczyk and B. Lewandowska-Tomaszczyk (Eds.), *Meaning and lexicography.* Amsterdam and Philadelphia: John Benjamins.

Lewis, M. (1951). *Infant speech.* London: Routledge and Kegan.

Luria, A. (1968). *The mind of a mnemonist.* New York: Basic Books.

Luthy, M. (1983). Linguistic limitations on cross-cultural humor. In C. Brown (Ed.), *Proceedings of the DLLS Symposium.* Linguistics Department, Brigham Young University, Provo, Utah.

Lyons, J. 1977. *Semantics.* Vol. 2. Cambridge: Cambridge University Press.

MacKey, D. (1986). Prototypicality among metaphors: On the relative frequency of personification and spatial metaphor in literature written for children versus adults. *Metaphor and Symbolic Activity, 1,* 2, 87–107.

Mackey, W. (1965). *Language Teaching Analysis.* London: Longmans, Green & Co., Ltd.

MacLeod, C. (1976). Bilingual episodic memory: acquisition and forgetting. *Journal of Verbal Learning and Verbal Behavior, 15,* 347–364.

Madsen, H., and Bowen, J. D. (1978). *Adaptation in language teaching.* New York: Newbury House.

Magnan, S. (1983). Age and sensitivity to gender in French. *Studies in Second Language Acquisition, 5,* 2, 194–212.

Manes, J., and Wolfson, N. (1981). The compliment formula. In F. Coulmas (Ed.), *Conversational routine.* The Hague: Mouton.

Mann, W., and Thompson, S. (1989). *Rhetorical structure theory: A theory of*

text organization. Los Angeles, Calif. University of Southern California Information Science Institute.

Mannon, T. (1986). Teacher talk: A comparison of teacher's speech to native and
non-native speakers. M.A. thesis, Applied Linguistics Department, University of California, Los Angeles.

Marchand, H. (1974). *Studies in syntax and word formation.* Munich: Fink.

Markowitz, J. (1988). An exploration into graded set membership. In M. Evens
(Ed.), *Relational models of the lexicon* (pp. 239–260). Cambridge: Cambridge University Press.

Marmaridou, A. (1989). Proper names in communication. *Journal of Linguistics,
25,* 355–372.

Marti, E. (1987). First metaphors in children: A new hypothesis. In J. Van Dormael, M. Spoelders, and T. Vandamme (Eds.), *Metaphor* (pp. 65–74).
Ghent: Communication and Cognition.

Martin, J. (1988). Subtractive morphology as dissociation. In H. Borer (Ed.),
Proceedings of the Seventh West Coast Conference of Formal Linguistics
(pp. 229–240). Palo Alto, Calif.: Stanford Linguistics Association.

McArthur, T. (1981). *Longman lexicon of contemporary English.* London:
Longman.

McCallum, G. P. (1983). *Idiom drills for students of English as a second language.* 2d ed. New York: Harper & Row.

McCawley, J. (1970). Where do noun phrases come from? In R. Jacobs and P.
Rosenbaum (Eds.), *Reading in English transformational grammar.* New
York: Ginn.

McCawley, J. (1975). Lexicography and the count-mass distinction. *Proceedings
of the First Annual Meeting of the Berkeley Linguistic Society* (pp. 314–
321). Berkeley: Berkeley Linguistic Society.

McCloskey, M., and Glucksberg, S. (1979). Decision processes in verifying membership statements: Implications for models of semantic memory. *Cognitive
Psychology, 11,* 1–37.

McLaughlin, B. (1984). *Second language acquisition in childhood.* Vol. 1: Preschool children. 2d ed. Hillsdale, N.J.: Lawrence Erlbaum Associates.

McLaughlin, J. (1970). *Aspects of the history of English.* New York: Holt,
Rinehart and Winston.

McPartland, P. (1981). *Take it easy: American idioms.* Englewood Cliffs, N.J.:
Prentice Hall Regents.

Mcquain, J. (1992, August 10). On language: Sweet talk. *The New York Times*
(Late Edition – Final), sec. 6, p. 10, col. 3.

Meara, P. (1978). Learners' word associations in French. *Interlanguage Studies
Bulletin* (Utrecht), *3,* 1, 192–211.

Meara, P. (1982). Word associations in a foreign language: A report on the
Birkbeck Vocabulary Project. *Nottingham Linguistic Circular, 11,* 2, 29–
38.

Meara, P. (1990). A note on passive vocabulary. *Second Language Research, 6,* 2,
150–154.

Meisel, J. M. (1977). Linguistic simplification: A study of immigrant workers'
speech and foreigner talk. In S. P. Corder and E. Roulet (Eds.), *The notions
of simplification: Interlanguages, and pidgins and their relation to second
language pedagogy* (pp. 88–113). Geneva: Droz.

Mel'čuk, I. (1981). Meaning-Text models: A recent trend in Soviet linguistics. *Annual Review of Anthropology, 10,* 27–62.

Mel'čuk, I. (1984). *Dictionnaire explicatif et combinatoire du français contemporaine.* Montreal, Quebec: University of Montreal Press.

Mel'čuk, I., and Zholkovsky, A. (1970). Towards a functioning "meaning- text" model of language. *Linguistics. An International Review, 57,* 10–47.

Mel'čuk, I., and Zholkovsky, A. (1984). *Explanatory combinatorial dictionary of Modern Russian: Semantico-syntactic studies of Russian vocabulary.* Vienna: Wiener Slawistischer Almanach. Sonderband 14.

Mellinkoff, D. (1991). *Mellinkoff's dictionary of American legal usage.* St. Paul, Minn.: West.

Menn, L., and Obler, L. (Eds.). (1990). *Agrammatic aphasia: A cross-language narrative sourcebook.* 3 volumes. Amsterdam and Philadelphia: John Benjamins.

Mervis, C. B., and Mervis, C. A. (1982). Leopards are kitty-cats: Object labeling by mothers for their thirteen-month-olds. *Child Development, 53,* 267–273.

Mettinger, A. (1990). Comparing the incomparable? English adjectives in -able and their rendering in Modern Chinese. In J. Fisiak (Ed.), *Further insights into contrastive analysis* (pp. 422–432). Amsterdam and New York: John Benjamins.

Miller, G. (1972). A case study in semantics and lexical memory. In A. Melton and E. Martin (Eds.), *Coding processes in human memory* (pp. 349–363). New York: Wiley.

Miller, G. (1991). *The science of words.* New York: Scientific American Library.

Miller, G., Beckwith, R., Fellbaum, C., Gross, D., and Miller, K. (1990). Introduction to WordNet: An on-line lexical database. *International Journal of Lexicography, 3,* 4, 235–244.

Miller, G., and Charles, W. (1991). Contextual correlates of semantic similarity. *Language and Cognitive Processes, 6,* 1, 1–28.

Miller, G., Johnson-Laird, P. (1976). *Language and perception.* Cambridge, Mass.: Harvard University Press, Belknap Press.

Miller, W., and Ervin-Tripp, S. (1964). The development of grammar in child language. In U. Bellugi and R. Brown (Eds.), *The acquisition of language.* Monographs of the Society for Research in Child Development, *29,* 9–34.

Milne, J. (1977). *Heinemann guided readers handbook.* London: Heinemann Educational Books.

Mitford, J. (1978). *The American way of death.* New York: New Fawcett Crest.

Morimoto, T. (1983). Japanese students' semantic interpretation of English loanwords in Japanese. M.A. thesis, Applied Linguistics Department, University of California, Los Angeles.

Morrissey, R. (1993). Texts and contexts: The ARTFL database in French studies. *Profession 93.* (Modern Language Association), 27–33.

Morsbach, G. (1981). Cross-cultural comparisons of second language learning: The development of comprehension of English structures by Japanese and German children. *TESOL Quarterly, 15,* 2, 183–188.

Moskowitz, A. (1990). A box of office supplies: Dialectological fun. *Georgetown Journal of Language and Linguistics, 1,* 3, 315- 344.

Mufwene, S. (1984). The count/mass distinction and the English lexicon. In D. Testen, V. Mishra, and J. Drogo (Eds.), *Lexical semantics* (pp. 200–221). Chicago: Chicago Linguistic Society.

Munroe, P. (1991). *Slang U.* New York: Harmony Press.

Muro, M. (1992, June 29). Wayward words. *The Boston Globe* (City Edition), p. 39.

Myers, G. (1991). Lexical cohesion and specialized knowledge in science and popular science texts. *Discourse Processes, 14,* 1–26.

Myres, S. (1980). *Ho for California! Women's overland diaries from the Huntington Library.* San Marino, Calif.: Huntington Library.

Nagy, W. E., and Anderson, R. (1984). The number of words in printed school English. *Reading Research Quarterly, 19,* 304–330.

Nagy, W. E., and Herman, P. A. (1987). Breadth and depth of vocabulary knowledge: Implications for acquisition and instruction. In M. McKeown and M. Curtis (Eds.), *The nature of vocabulary acquisition* (pp. 19–36). Hillsdale, N.J.: Lawrence Erlbaum Associates.

Nagy, W. E., Herman, P. A., and Anderson, R. C. (1985). Learning words from context. *Reading Research Quarterly, 20,* 2, 233–253.

Nakao, K. (1989). English-Japanese learners' dictionaries. *International Journal of Lexicography, 2,* 4, 294–314.

Nash, R. (1978) Don't molest me now, I'm busy. In R. Andersen (Ed.). *Acquisition and use of Spanish and English as first and second languages* (pp. 33–42). Washington, D.C.: TESOL

Nash, T. (1983). American and Chinese politeness strategies: "It sort of disturbs my sleep" or "Health is important." *University of Hawaii Working Papers, 2,* 2, 23–39.

Nehls, D. (1991). The designation of spherical objects in five European languages: An essay in contrastive semantics. In V. Ivir and D. Kalogjera (Eds.), *Languages in contact and contrast* (pp. 329–334). Berlin and New York: Mouton de Gruyter.

Nelson, K. (1973). Structure and strategy in learning to talk. *Monograph of the Society for Research in Child Development, 38,* 1–2, serial 149.

Nelson, K. (1979). Explorations in the development of a functional semantic system. In W. Collins (Ed.), *Children's language and communication.* Minnesota Symposia on Child Development, Vol. 12. Hillsdale, N.J.: Lawrence Erlbaum Associates.

Nemoianu, A. (1980). *The boat's gonna leave.* Amsterdam: John Benjamins.

Nemser, W. (1991). Language contact and foreign language acquisition. In V. Ivir and D. Kalogjera (Eds.). *Languages in contact and contrast* (pp. 345–364). Berlin and New York: Mouton de Gruyter.

Newman, E. (1988). *I must say! On English, the news, and other matters.* New York: Warner Books.

Newmark, P. (1988). *Textbook of translation.* New York and London: Prentice-Hall.

The New York Times. (1988, September 26). The presidential debate: Transcript of the first TV debate between Bush and Dukakis. *The New York Times,* sec. A, p. 16, col. 1.

Nilsen, A. (1972). Sexism in English: A feminist view. In N. Hoffman, C. Scott, and A. Tinsley (Eds.), *Female studies VI: Closer to the ground* (pp. 102–109). Old Westbury, N.Y.U.: Feminist Press.

Nilsen, D., and Nilsen, A. (1975). *Semantic theory.* Rowley, Mass.: Newbury House.

Nilsen, D., and Nilsen, A. (1982). Language play. In P. Eschholz, A. Rosa, and V. Clark (Eds.), *Language awareness.* 3rd ed. New York: St. Martin's Press.

Obler, L. (1982). Neurolinguistic aspects of language loss as they pertain. In R. Lambert and B. Freed (Eds.), *The loss of language skills.* (pp. 60–79) Rowley, Mass.: Newbury House.

Ohio State University Linguistics Department (1982). *Language files.* Reynoldsburg, Ohio: Advocate Publishing Group.

Oliver, J. 1983. *Refranero Español.* Madrid: Sena Editorial.

Oller, J., and Ziahosseiny, S. M. (1970). The contrastive analysis hypothesis and spelling errors. *Language Learning, 20,* 2, 183–197.

Olshtain, E. (1979). The acquisition of English progressive: A case study of a seven-year-old Hebrew speaker. *Working Papers on Bilingualism, 18,* 81–102.

Olshtain, E. (1986). The attrition of English as a second language with speakers of Hebrew. In B. Weltens, K. De Bot, and T. van Els (Eds.), *Language attrition in progress* (pp. 187–204). Dordrecht and Providence: Foris.

Olshtain, E. (1993). Language in society. In A. Omaggio Hadley (Ed.), *Research in language learning* (pp. 47–65). Lincolnwood, Ill.: National Textbook Company.

Ornstein, J., and Gates, W. (1964), *The ABC's of languages and linguistics.* Philadelphia: Chilton.

Orton, H. (1972). *Questionnaire for the investigation of American regional English: Based on work sheets of the linguistic atlas of the United States and Canada.* Knoxville: University of Tennessee.

Osgood, C. (1967), Semantic differential technique in the comparative study of cultures. In L. Jacobovits and M. Miron (Eds.), *Readings in the psychology of language* (pp. 371–397). Englewood Cliffs, N.J.: Prentice-Hall.

Osgood, C. E. (1978). Conservative words and radical sentences in the semantics of internal "politics." In B. Kachru (Ed.), *Linguistics in the seventies: Directions and prospects.* Special issue of *Studies in the linguistic sciences, 8,* 2, 43–62.

Oskarsson, M. (1975). On the role of the mother tongue in learning foreign language vocabulary: An empirical investigation. *ITL Review of Applied Linguistics, 27,* 19–32.

Oxford, R. (1990). *Language learning strategies: What every teacher should know.* New York: Newbury House.

Paivio, A., and Clark, J. (1987). The role of topic and vehicle imagery in metaphor comprehension. In J. Van Dormael, M. Spoelders, and T. Vandamme (Eds.), *Metaphor* (pp. 95–115). Ghent: Communication and Cognition.

Palermo, D. (1986). From the marble mass of language: A view of the developing mind. *Metaphor and Symbolic Activity, 1,* 1, 5–23.

Palermo, D. (1989). Knowledge and developing a theory of the world. *Advances in Child Development and Behavior, 21* 269–295.

Palmberg, R. (1990). Improving foreign language learners' vocabulary skills. *RELC Journal, 21,* 1, 1–10.

Palmer, F. (1976). *Semantics: A new outline.* Cambridge: Cambridge University Press.

Pany, D., and Jenkins, J. R. (1978). Learning word meanings: A comparison of instructional procedures and effects on measures of reading comprehension with learning disabled students. *Learning Disability Quarterly, 1,* 21–32.

Pany, D., Jenkins, J. R., and Schreck, J. (1982). Vocabulary instruction: Effects on word knowledge and reading comprehension. *Learning Disability Quarterly, 5,* 202–215.

Parish, P. (1988). *Amelia Bedelia's family album.* New York: Greenwillow Books.

Parker, L. (1985). Teacher influences on second language development: A study of how teachers define vocabulary during reading lessons (a pilot study). Paper presented at University of California Chancellor's Conference on Bilingualism, Lake Tahoe, Calif.

Parry, K. (1993). Too many words: Learning the vocabulary of an academic subject. In T. Huckin, M. Haynes, and J. Coady (Eds.) *Second language reading and vocabulary learning* (pp. 109–129). Norwood, N.J.: Ablex.

Patterson, F., and Cohn, R. (1990). Language acquisition by a lowland gorilla: Koko's first ten years of vocabulary development. *Word, 41,* 2, 97–144.

Pavlovitch, M. (1920). *Le langage enfantin: Acquisition du Serbe et du Français par un enfant Serbe.* Paris: Champion.

Paxton, J. (1991). *Penguin dictionary of abbreviations.* London: Viking Press.

Payne, M. E. (1988). Vocabulary learning strategies used by ESL students and their relationship to perceptual learning style preferences. M.A. thesis, Linguistics Department, Brigham Young University, Provo, Utah.

Pearson, B., Fernandez, S., and Oller, D. K. (1993). Lexical development in bilingual infants and toddlers: Comparison to monolingual norms. *Language Learning, 43,* 1, 93–120.

Pease, D., Gleason, J., and Pan, B. (1993). Learning the meaning of words: Semantic development and beyond. In J. Gleason (Ed.), *The development of language.* 3d ed. (pp. 115–149). New York: Maxwell Macmillan.

Perez-Pereira, M. (1989). The acquisition of morphemes: Some evidence from Spanish. *Journal of Psycholinguistic Research, 18,* 3, 289–312.

Peters, E. (1985). *The mummy case.* New York: TOR (Tom Doherty Associates, Inc).

Peters, P., and Fee, M. (1989). New configurations: The balance of British and American English features in Australian and Canadian English. *Australian Journal of Linguistics, 9,* 135–147.

Pfaff, C. (1981). Incipient creolization in Gastarbeiterdeutsch? An experimental sociolinguistic study. *Studies in Second Language Acquisition, 3,* 2, 165–178.

Phillips, S. (1974). The invisible culture: Communication in classroom and community on the Warm Springs reservation. Ph.D. diss., University of Pennsylvania.

Phillips, S. (1983). *The invisible culture: Communication in classroom and community on the Warm Springs Indian Reservation.* New York: Longman.

Piaget, J. (1928). *Judgment and reasoning in the child.* London: Routledge and Kegan.

Pillon, A., dePartz, M., Raison, Z., and Seron, X. (1991). L'orange, c'est le fruitier de l'orangine: A case of morphological impairment? *Language and Cognitive Processes, 6,* 2, 137–167.

Piotrowski, T. (1990). The Meaning-Text Model of language and practical lexicography. In J. Tomaszczyk and B. Lewandowska-Tomaszczyk (Eds.). *Meaning and lexicography* (pp. 277–286). Amsterdam and Philadelphia: John Benjamins.

447

Pitts, M., White, H., and Krashen, S. (1989). Acquiring second language vocabulary through reading: A replication of the *Clockwork Orange* study using second language acquirers. *Reading in a Foreign Language, 5,* 271–275.

Plann, S. (1976). The Spanish-immersion program: Towards native-like proficiency or a classroom dialect? M.A. thesis, University of California, Los Angeles.

Plann, S. (1979). Morphological problems in the acquisition of Spanish in an immersion classroom. In R. Andersen (Ed.), *The acquisition and use of Spanish and English as first and second languages.* Washington, D.C.: TESOL.

Pocheptsov, O. (1992). Mind your mind: Or some ways of distorting facts while telling the truth. *ETC. A Review of General Semantics, 49,* 4, 398–406.

Politzer, R. (1978). Paradigmatic and syntagmatic associations of first-year French students. In V. Honsa and M. Hardman-de-Bautista (Eds.), *Papers on Linguistics and Child Language: Ruth Hirsch Weir Memorial Volume* (pp. 203–210). The Hague: Mouton Press.

Potter, S. (1971). Word creation. In C. Laird and R. Gorrell (Eds.), *Reading about language* (pp. 119–123). New York: Harcourt Brace Jovanovich.

Pressley, M., Levin, J. R., and Delaney, H. (1982) Mnemonic keyword method. *Review of Educational Research, 52,* 1, 61–91.

Pride, J. (1982). *New Englishes.* Rowley, Mass.: Newbury House.

Quackenbush, E. (1974). How Japanese borrows English loanwords. *Linguistics: An International Review, 131,* 59–75.

Quackenbush, H. (1977). English loanwords in Japanese. *Journal of the Association of Teachers of Japanese, 12,* 2/3, 149–173.

Quinn, N. (1987). Convergent evidence for a cultural model of American marriage. In D. Holland and N. Quinn (Eds.), *Cultural models in language and thought* (pp. 173–192). Cambridge: Cambridge University Press.

Quirk, R., and Greenbaum, S. (1973). *A concise grammar of contemporary English.* New York: Harcourt, Brace Jovanovich.

Ragevska, N. (1979). *English lexicology.* Kiev: Vysca Skola Publishers, Head Publishing House.

Ramsey, R. (1981). A technique for interlingual lexico-semantic comparison: The lexigram. *TESOL Quarterly, 15,* 1, 15–24.

Randall, J. (1988). Of butchers and bakers and candlestick-makers: The problem of morphology in understanding words. In A. Davison and G. Green (Eds.), *Linguistic complexity and text comprehension* (pp. 223–245). Hillsdale, N.J.: Lawrence Erlbaum Associates.

Reed, C. (1961). Double dialect geography. *Orbis, 10,* 308–319. Reprinted in H. Allen and G. Underwood (Eds). *Readings in American dialectology* (pp. 273–284). New York: Appleton- Crofts, 1971.

Reeves, G. (1985). *The new idioms in action.* New York: Newbury House.

Riegel, K. (1970). The language acquisition process, a reinterpretation of selected research findings. In L. Goulet and P. Baltes (Eds.), *Life-span developmental psychology, research and theory* (pp. 357–399). New York: Academic Press.

Ringbom, H. (1987). *The role of the first language in foreign language learning.* Clevedon and Philadelphia: Multilingual Matters.

Rips, S. (1975). Inductive judgments about natural categories. *Journal of Verbal Learning and Verbal Behavior, 14,* 665–681.

Rips, I. J., Shoben, E., and Smith, E. (1973). Semantic distance and the verification of semantic relations. *Journal of Verbal Learning and Verbal Behavior*, 12, 1–20.

Robinett, B. (1965). *Language Teaching Analysis*. Bloomington: Indiana University Press.

Romaine, S. (1986). The syntax and semantics of the code-mixed compound verb in Punjabi/English bilingual discourse. In D. Tannen and J. Alatis (Eds.), *GURT '85. Languages and Linguistics: The Interdependence of Theory, Data and Application* (pp. 35–49). Washington, D.C.: Georgetown University Press.

Ronjat, J. (1913). *Le developpement du langage observé chez un enfant bilingue*. Paris: Champion.

Rosch, E. (1973). On the internal structure of perceptual and semantic categories. In T. Moore (Ed.), *Cognitive development and the acquisition of language* (pp. 111–144). New York: Academic Press.

Rosch, E. (1983). Prototype classification and logical classification: the two systems. In E. Scholnick (Ed.), *New trends in cognitive representation* (pp. 73–86). Hillsdale, N.J.: Lawrence Erlbaum Associates.

Rosch, E, and Lloyd, B. (Eds). (1978). *Cognition and categorization*. Hillsdale, N.J.: Lawrence Erlbaum Associates.

Rosch, E., Mervis, C., Gray, W., Johnson, W., and Boyes-Graem, P. (1976). Basic objects in natural categories. *Cognitive Psychology, 8*, 382–439.

Rosen, R. D. (1977) Psychobabble. In G. Goshgarian (Ed.), *Exploring Language* (pp. 344–355). Boston: Little, Brown.

Rothenberg, J. K. (Trans.). (1982). In beauty may I walk. In S. Heaney and T. Hughes (Comps.), *The rattle bag: An anthology of poetry* (p. 208). London: Faber and Faber.

Rothstein, G. (1985). The expression of temporality in the English interlanguage of a native Hebrew speaker. M.A. thesis, Applied Linguistics Department, University of California, Los Angeles.

Rudzka, B., Channell, J., Putseys, Y., and Ostyn, P. (1981). *The words you need*. London: Macmillan.

Rudzka, B., Channell, J., Putseys, Y., and Ostyn, P. (1985). *More words you need*. London: Macmillan.

Ruhlen, M. (1987). *A guide to the world's languages, Vol. 1: Classification*. Stanford, Calif.: Stanford University Press.

Rumelhart, D., Lindsay, P., and Norman, D. (1972). A process model for long term memory. In E. Tulving and W. Donaldson (Eds.), *Organization of memory* (pp. 198–248). New York: Academic Press.

Rumelhart, D., and McClelland, J. (1986). On learning the past tense of English verbs. In J. McClelland and D. Rumelhart (Eds.), *Parallel distributed processing, Vol. 2* (pp. 216–271). Cambridge, Mass.: MIT Press.

Sachs, H., Schegloff, E., and Jefferson, G. (1974). A simplest systematics for the organization of turn-taking for conversation. *Language, 50, 5*, 696–735.

Safire, W. (1982). I led the pidgeons to the flag. In P. Eschholz, A. Rosa, and V. Clark (Eds.), *Language awareness* (pp. 279–283). New York: St. Martin's Press.

Salmons, J. (1991). Register evolution in an immigrant language: The case of some Indiana German dialects. *Word, 42, 1*, 31- 56.

Saragi, T, Nation, I. S. P., and Meister, G. F. (1978). Vocabulary learning and reading. *System, 6,* 72–88.

Sarčević, S. (1989). Conceptual dictionaries for translation in the field of law. *International Journal of Lexicography, 2,* 4, 177–293.

Scarcella, R. (1979). Watch up! Prefabricated routines in second language acquisition. *Working Papers on Bilingualism* (Toronto: OISE), *17,* 79–88.

Scarcella, R. (1983). Discourse accent in adult second language performance. In S. Gass and L. Selinker (Eds.), *Language transfer in language learning* (pp. 306–326). New York: Newbury House.

Schank, R. (1984). *Conceptual information processing.* Amsterdam: North Holland.

Schank, R., and Abelson, R. (1977). *Scripts, plans, goals, and understanding.* Hillsdale, N.J.: Lawrence Erlbaum Associates.

Schegloff, E. (1968). Sequencing in conversational openings. *American Anthropologist, 70,* 6, 1075–1095.

Schegloff, E. & Sacks, H. (1973). Opening up closings. *Semiotica, 8,* 4, 289–327.

Schlue, K. (1976). An inside view of Interlanguage. M.A. thesis, Applied Linguistics Department, University of California, Los Angeles.

Schumann, J. (1979). The acquisition of English negation by speakers of Spanish: A review of the literature. In R. Andersen (Ed.), *The acquisition and use of Spanish and English as first and second languages* (pp. 3–32). Washington, D.C.: TESOL.

Schumann, J. (1987). Acquisition of temporality in basilang speech. *Studies in Second Language Acquisition, 9,* 21–42.

Schwartz, J. (1980). The negotiation of meaning: Repair in conversations between second language learners of English. In D. Larsen-Freeman (Ed.), *Discourse analysis in second language research* (pp. 138–153). Rowley, Mass.: Newbury House.

Seal, B. (1990). *American vocabulary builder.* Vols. 1 & 2. White Plains, N.Y.: Longman.

Seal, B. (1991). Vocabulary learning and teaching. In M. Celce-Murcia (Ed.), *Teaching English as a foreign or second language* 2d ed. (pp. 296–312). New York: Newbury House.

Selinker, L. (1972). Interlanguage. *IRAL: International Review of Applied Linguistics, 10,* 3, 209–231.

Shanon, B. (1991). Faulty language selection in polyglots. *Language and Cognitive Processes, 6,* 4, 339–350.

Sharpe, P.A. (1989) Pragmatic considerations for an English-Japanese dictionary. *International Journal of Lexicography, 2,* 4, 315–323.

Shapira, R. (1976). A study of the acquisition of ten syntactic structures and grammatical morphemes by an adult second language learner. M.A. thesis, Applied Linguistics Department, University of California, Los Angeles.

Shapira, R. (1978). The non-learning of English: Case study of an adult. In E. Hatch (Ed.), *Second language acquisition: A book of readings* (pp. 246–256). Rowley, Mass.: Newbury House.

Sheeler, W. D., and Markley, R. W. (1981). *Words words words: A guide to formation and usage,* Book 1. New York: Regents.

Shibatani, M. (1990). *The languages of Japan.* New York: Cambridge University Press.

Shiffrin, D. (1987). *Discourse markers.* Cambridge: Cambridge University Press.

Shirahata, T. (1988). *The learning of English grammatical morphemes by Japanese high school students.* M.A. thesis, University of Arizona.

Shirai, Y. (1990a). Putting PUT to use: Prototype and metaphorical extension. *Issues in Applied Linguistics, 1,* 1, 78–97.

Shirai, Y. (1990b). *On the primacy of aspect.* Ph.D. diss., Applied Linguistics Department, University of California, Los Angeles.

Shirai, Y. (1993). Inherent aspect and the acquisition of tense-aspect morphology in Japanese. In H. Nakajima and Y. Otsu (Eds.), *Argument structure: Its syntax and acquisition* (pp. 185–209). Tokyo: Kaitakusha.

Shorrocks, G. (1991). Towards a survey of angling terminology: An untapped source of traditional and dialectal usage. *Transactions of the Philological Society, 89,* 2, 123–130.

Shuy, R. (1957). *Discovering American dialects.* Urbana, Illinois: National Council of Teachers of English.

Shyu, S. (1989). An analysis of Chinese metaphors of anger and love. M.A. thesis, Applied Linguistics Department, University of California, Los Angeles.

Singleton, D., and Little, D. (1991). The second language lexicon: Some evidence from university-level learners of French and German. *Second Language Research, 7,* 1, 61–81.

Skierso, A. (1991). Textbook selection and evaluation. In M. Celce-Murcia (Ed.), *Teaching English as a second or foreign language.* 2d ed. (pp. 432–453). New York: Newbury House.

Smith, E., Shoben, E., and Rips, L. (1974). Structure and process in semantic memory. *Psychological Review, 81,* 3, 214–241.

Smith, F. (1969). The use of featural dependencies across letters in the visual identification of words. *Journal of Verbal Learning and Verbal Behavior, 8,* 215–218.

Smith, F. (1988). *Understanding reading: A psycholinguistic analysis of reading and learning to read.* 4th ed. Hillsdale, N.J.: Lawrence Erlbaum Associates.

Snell-Hornby, M. (1990). Dynamics in meaning as a problem for bilingual lexicography. In J. Tomaszczyk and B. Lewandowska-Tomaszczyk (Eds.), *Meaning and lexicography* (pp. 209–226). Amsterdam/Philadelphia: John Benjamins Publishing Company.

Snow, C., Barnes, W., Chandler, J., Goodman, I., and Hemphill, L. (1991). *Unfulfilled expectations: Home and school influences on literacy.* Cambridge, Mass.: Harvard University Press.

Söderman, T. (1993). Word associations of foreign language learners and native speakers: The phenomenon of a shift in response type and its relevance for lexical development. In H. Ringbom (Ed.), *Near-native proficiency in English.* English Department Publications 2, Abo Akademi University, Abo, Finland.

Sonoda, K. (1975) A descriptive study of English influence in Modern Japanese. Ph.D. diss. New York University.

Southworth, F., and Daswani, C. (1974). *Foundations of linguistics.* New York: The Free Press.

Stahl, S., and Fairbanks, M. (1986). The effects of vocabulary instruction: A model-based meta analysis. *Review of Educational Research, 56,* 72–110.

Stanlaw, J. (1982). English in Japanese: Communicative strategies. In B. Kachru (Ed.), *The other tongue: English across cultures.* Urbana: University of Illinois Press.

Sternberg, R., and Powell, J. (1983). Comprehending verbal comprehension. *American Psychologist, 8,* 878–893.

Stevens, P. (1988). Saying "No!" cross-culturally and pragmatic failure: Some strategies of Arab learners of English. Paper presented at TESOL, Chicago, Ill.

Stevens, P. (1991). Conflicting pragmatic norms between English and Arabic speakers in Egypt. In H. Guidi (Ed.), *Essays in honour of Saad Gamal El Din* (pp. 97–114). Cairo: Cairo University Department of English Language and Literature.

Stockwell, R., Bowen, J. D., and Martin, J. (1965). *Grammar Structures of English and Spanish.* Chicago: University of Chicago Press.

Stoffel, H. (1991). Common features in the morphological adaptation of English loanwords in migrant Serbo-Croatian. In V. Ivir and D. Kalogjera (Eds.). *Languages in contact and contrast* (pp. 416–429). Berlin and New York: Mouton de Gruyter.

Sugawara, M. (1992). The effect of productive-use vocabulary exercises on confidence in vocabulary knowledge and receptive and productive vocabulary acquisition. M.A. thesis. Linguistics Department, Brigham Young University.

Swadesh, M. (1972). *The origin and diversification of language.* London: Routledge & Kegan Paul.

Swain, M., Naiman, N., and Dumas, G. (1972). Some aspect of the learning of French by English-speaking five-year-olds. In E. Hatch (Ed.), *Second language acquisition: A book of readings* (pp. 297–312). Rowley, Mass.: Newbury House.

Szalay, L., and D'Andrade, R. (1972). Scaling versus content analysis: Interpreting word association data from Americans and Koreans. *Southwestern Journal of Anthropology, 28,* 1, 50–68.

Tager-Flusberg, H., de Villiers, J., and Hakuta, K. (1982). The development of sentence coordination. In S. Kuczaj. (Ed.), *Language development.* Vol. 1: *Syntax and semantics* (pp. 201–243). New York: Academic Press.

Talmy, L. (1980). Lexicalization patterns. Semantic structure in lexical form. In T. Shopen (Ed.), *Language typology and syntactic description,* Vol. 3: *Grammatical categories and the lexicon* (pp. 57–149). New York: Cambridge University Press.

Tannen, D. (1990). *You just don't understand: Women and men in conversation.* New York: Morrow.

Tanz, C. (1980), *Studies in the acquisition of deictic terms.* Cambridge: Cambridge University Press.

Tao, H., and Thompson, S. (1991). English backchannels in Mandarin conversations: A case study of superstratum pragmatic "interference." *Journal of Pragmatics, 16,* 3, 209–223.

Tarone, E. (1977). Conscious communication strategies in interlanguage. In H. D. Brown, C. Yorio, and R. Crymes (Eds.), *On TESOL 1977* (pp. 194–203). Washington, D.C.: TESOL.

Tarone, E. (1980). Communication strategies, foreigner talk and repair. *Language Learning, 30,* 417–431.

Teemant, A. (1988). Lexical errors in ESL compositions. M.A. thesis, Linguistics Department, Brigham Young University, Provo, Utah.

Terban, M. (1990). *Punching the clock: Funny actions idioms.* New York: Clarion Books.

Thompson, I. (1989). Lexical search strategies in L2: A developmental analysis. In J. Alatis (Ed.), *Georgetown University Round Table on Languages and Linguistics 1989: Language teaching, testing and technology.* Washington, D.C.: Georgetown University Press.

Thornbury, S. (1991). Metaphors we work by: EFL and its metaphors. *English Language Teaching Journal, 45,* 3, 193–200.

Thorndike, E., and Lorge, I. (1944). *The teacher's wordbook of 30,000 words.* New York: Columbia University Press.

Thorne, B., and N. Henley (Eds.) 1975. *Language and sex: Difference and dominance.* Rowley, Mass: Newbury House.

Tillitt, B., and Bruder, M. (1985). *Speaking naturally: Communication skills in American English.* New York: Cambridge University Press.

Tinkham, T. (1993). The effect of semantic clustering on the learning of second language vocabulary. *System, 21,* 3, 371–380.

Tomlinson, B. (1986). Cooking, mining, gardening, hunting: Metaphorical stories writers tell about their composing processes. *Metaphor and Symbolic Activity, 1,* 1, 57–79.

Trudgill, P., and Chambers, J. (Eds.). 1991. *Dialects of English: Studies in grammatical variation.* London: Longman.

Turian, D., and Altenberg, E. (1991). Compensatory strategies of child first language attrition. In H. Seliger and R. Vago (Eds.), *First language attrition* (pp. 107–226). Cambridge: Cambridge University Press.

Turton, L. J. (1966). The status of ten prepositions in the verbal and non-verbal response patterns of children during the third and fourth years of life. Ph.D. dissertation. Lawrence, Kansas: The University of Kansas.

Twain, M. (1971). *The diaries of Adam and Eve.* New York: American Heritage Press. Originally published in *Harper's Magazine,* December, 1905.

Tyler, S. (1978). *The said and the unsaid: Mind, meaning and culture.* New York: Academic Press.

Ulijn, J., Wolfe, S., and Donn, A. (1981). *The lexical transfer effect of French knowledge in the acquisition of English by native Vietnamese speakers.* Report 6, Foreign Language Acquisition Research THE, Eindhoven University of Technology.

Vandeloise, C. (1987). Complex primitives in language acquisition. *Belgium Journal of Linguistics, 2,* 11–36.

Van Dijk, T. (1985). Semantic discourse analysis. In T. van Dijk (Ed.), *Handbook of discourse analysis,* Vol. 2 (pp. 103–136). London: Academic Press.

Van Ek, J. (1975). *The threshold level.* Strasbourg: Council of Europe. Also published in 1980 as *Threshold level English.* Oxford: Pergamon.

Van Ek, J. (1976). *The threshold level for modern language teaching in schools.* London: Longman.

Van Lanacker, D. (1975). Heterogeneity in language and speech: Neurolinguistic studies. *Working Papers in Phonetics, 29,* Linguistics Department, University of California, Los Angeles.

Van Oostendorf, H., and de Mul, S. (1990). Moses beats Adam: A semantic relatedness effect on semantic illusion. *Acta Psychologica, 74,* 1, 35–36.

Vendler, Z. (1967). *Linguistics in philosophy.* Ithaca, N.Y.: Cornell University Press.

Vendler, Z. (1984). Adverbs of action. In D. Testen, V. Mishra, and J. Drogo (Eds.), *Lexical semantics* (pp. 297–307). Chicago: Chicago Linguistic Society.

Vihman, M., and McLaughlin, B. (1982). Bilingualism and second language acquisition in preschool children. In C. Brainerd and M. Pressley (Eds.), *Verbal processes in children: Progress in cognitive development research* (pp. 35–58). Berlin: Springer.

Visser, A. (1990). Learning vocabulary through underlying meanings: An investigation of the interactive technique. *RELC Journal, 21*, 1, 11–28.

Vital Speeches of the Day. Published annually. New York: City News Publishing Company.

Von Raffler-Engel, W. (1977). The nonverbal adjustment of adults to children's communicative style. In B. Laria and D. Gulstad (Eds.), *Papers from the 1977 Mid-American Linguistic Conference* (pp. 3–28). Columbia: University of Missouri.

Walsh, M. (1993). Quebecers accused of French-frying the language. *Los Angeles Times,* Feb. 16, p. H3.

Waugh, E. (1947). *The loved one.* Boston: Little, Brown.

Waugh, L. (1976). *Roman Jakobson's science of language.* Lisse, Netherlands: Peter De Ridder Press.

Weber-Olsen, M., and Ruder, K. (1980). Acquisition and generalization of Japanese locatives by English-speakers. *Applied Psycholinguistics, 1*, 183–198.

Weekley, F. (1912). *Romance of words.* London: John Murray.

Weinreich, U. (1969). Problems in the analysis of idioms. In J. Puhvel (Ed.), *Substance and structure of language.* Berkeley: University of California Press.

Weist, R. (1986). Tense and aspect. In P. Fletcher and M. Garman (Eds.), *Language acquisition.* 2d ed. (pp. 356–374). Cambridge: Cambridge University Press.

Weist, R., Wysocka, H., Witkowska-Stadnik, K., Buczowska, E., and Konieczna, E. (1984). The defective tense hypothesis: On the emergence of tense and aspect in child Polish. *Journal of Child Language, 11*, 347–374.

Wells, G. (1979). Learning and using the auxiliary verb in English. In V. Lee (Ed.), *Language development: A reader* (pp. 250–270). London: Croom Helm.

Wells, G. (1985). *Learning through interaction: The study of language development, language at home and at school: 1.* Cambridge: Cambridge University Press.

Werner, O., Manning, A., and Begishe, K. (1983). A taxonomic aspect of the traditional Navajo universe. In A. Ortiz (Ed.), *Handbook of North American Indians.* Washington, D.C.: Smithsonian Institution.

West, M. (1936). A general service list of English words. London: Longman. (Reprinted 1953).

Whorf, B. (1936). The punctual and sementative aspects of verbs in Hopi. *Language 12*, 127–131.

Whorf, B. (1966). Science and linguistics. In S. Saporta. (Ed.), *Psycholinguistics* (pp. 460–468). New York: Holt, Rinehart and Winston.

Wierzbicka, A. (1980). *Lingua mentalis.* New York: Academic Press.

Wierzbicka, A. (1986). Does language reflect culture? *Language in Society, 15*, 3, 349–373.

Wierzbicka, A. (1990a). Introduction. *Australian Journal of Linguistics, 10,* 133–138.

Wierzbicka, A. (1990b). The semantics of emotions: *Fear* and its relatives in English. *Australian Journal of Linguistics, 10,* 2, 359–376.

Wierzbicka, A. (1990c). *Cross-cultural pragmatics.* Berlin: de Gruyter.

Wierzbicka, A. (1991). Semantic rules know no exceptions. *Studies in Language, 15,* 2, 371–398.

Wilkins, W. (1988). Thematic structure and reflexivization. In Wilkins, W. (Ed.), *Syntax and semantics, 21* (pp. 191–213). San Diego: Academic Press.

Wilkins, W. (1994). Lexical learning by error detection. *Language Acquisition, 3,* 2, 121–157.

William Collins and Sons. (1979). *A guide to Collins English library.* London: William Collins.

Williams, H. (1991). Logic of contrastive adverbs. Ph.D. qualifying paper supervised by M. Celce-Murcia, Applied Linguistics Department, University of California, Los Angeles.

Williams, K. (1991). Radial structuring in the Hausa lexicon: A prototype analysis of Hausa "eat" and "drink." *Lingua, 85,* 321–340.

Willis, M. (1976). Affixation in English word formation and applications for TESL. M.A. thesis, Applied Linguistics Department, University of California, Los Angeles.

Wilson, F. (1970). *The Oxford dictionary of English proverbs.* 3rd ed. Oxford: Clarendon Press.

Wode, H. (1977). Free vs. bound forms in three types of language acquisition. *Working Paper 19,* English Seminar of Kiel University.

Wolfson, N. (1981). Compliments in cross-cultural perspective. *TESOL Quarterly, 15,* 2, 117–124.

Wolfson, N. (1989). *Perspectives: Sociolinguistics and TESOL.* New York: Newbury House.

Wong-Fillmore, L. (1976). The second time around: Cognitive and social strategies in language acquisition. Ph.D. diss., Stanford University.

Wu, Y. (1990). The usages of kinship address forms amongst non-kin in Mandarin Chinese: The extension of family solidarity. *Australian Journal of Linguistics, 10,* 61–88.

Yamada, J. (1981). Evidence for the independence of language and cognition: Case study of a "Hyperlinguistic" adolescent. *Working Papers in Cognitive Linguistics* (Linguistics Department, University of California, Los Angeles), *3,* 121–160.

Yamamoto, M., and Swan, J. (1989). Connotative differences between foreign and Japanese English teachers in Japan. *Journal of Multilingual and Multicultural Development, 10,* 3, 233.

Yorkey, R. (1981). *Checklists for vocabulary study.* New York: Longman.

Yorkey, R. (1982). *Study skills for students of English.* 2d ed. New York: McGraw-Hill.

Yoshida, M. (1978). The acquisition of English vocabulary by a Japanese-speaking child. In E. Hatch (Ed.), *Second language acquisition: A book of readings* (pp. 91–100). Rowley, Mass.: Newbury House.

Yun, Z. (1989) The effect of part of speech on the acquisition of vocabulary from context. M.A. thesis. Linguistics Department. Brigham Young University.

Zernik, U. (1987). Strategies in language acquisition: Learning phrases in context. Ph.D. dissertation, Computer Science, University of California, Los Angeles.

Zimmer, K. (1964). Affixal negation in English and other languages. *Word, Monograph 5*, 20, 2, supplement, 3–101.

Zubin, D. & Svorou, S. (1984). Perceptual schemata in the spatial lexicon: a cross-linguistic study. In D. Testen, V. Mishra, & J. Drogo (Eds.), *Lexical semantics* (pp. 346–358). Chicago: Chicago Linguistic Society.

Index

Index

authentic materials, 407, 409
auxiliaries (auxiliary verbs), 171, 218, 224, 233–234, 298, 396
avoidance, 194, 201, 252, 339, 393, 395
Ayto, 176

backchannel signals, 328, 333–335, 342, 352, 364
Backhouse, 132
Badecker and Caramazza, 281, 282
Baker, 177, 282, 283, 381
Baldinger, 59, 154
Bantu, 183, 184
Baratz, 286
Barnard, 411
Barsalou, 46, 62
basic level, 53–57, 383
Battig and Montague, 61, 62
Becker, 201
Beck, McCaslin, and McKeown, 424, 425
Beck, McKeown, and Omanson, 368
Beck, Perfetti, and McKeown, 424, 425
Bellugi, 233, 265
Belyayev, 370
benefactive, 220
Bentahila, 143
Berko, 193, 213, 288
Berko-Gleason, 382
Berko-Gleason and Weintraub, 148
Berlin and Kay, 116, 122, 123
Bermudez and Prater, 165
Berryman and Eman, 308
bilingual dictionaries, 75, 131, 142, 383
Billow, 99
blends, 123, 129, 208, 211–213, 278
Block, 109, 310
Bloom, 219, 232
Bloom, Lahey, Hood, Lifter, and Feiss, 240, 258, 298
Bloom, Lifter, and Hafitz, 249, 258, 298
Blum-Kulka and Olshtain, 364
Blum-Kulka, House, and Kasper, 364
Bogoyaulenskiy, 293
Bolinger, 21, 28, 29, 58, 200, 202, 207, 266, 286
borrowing, 131, 138, 170–175, 182–189, 209, 210, 212, 234, 261, 268, 276, 370, 395, 409
bound morphemes, 264–267, 289
Boyd, 236
bracket signal, 346. *See also* communication signals
Brinton, 167, 413
Brinton and Gaskill, 167
Brinton, Snow, and Wesche, 413
Brown and Levinson, 356

Brown and McNeill, 378
Brown and Payne, 373, 387
Brown, C., 375, 378, 414
Brown Corpus, 168, 274, 410
Brown, R., 34, 221, 223, 289, 290, 299, 375, 378, 414, 418
Brownell, 114
Bruner, 23
Bryant, 303, 325
Buckingham, 32
Bulgarian, 183
Bunker, 409, 410, 414
bunkerisms, 314, 316
Bush, 97, 272, 273
Butterworth and Hatch, 36, 195

Calfee and Drum, 368
Callanan, 383
Camarata and Leonard, 220
Campbell, 274
Campbell and Mithun, 187
Carter, E., 242
Carter, J., 317
Casagrande and Hale, 85
case (grammar), 159, 167, 168, 222, 223, 237, 265, 395
cataphoric reference, 213, 234
Catford, 244, 245, 247
causative, 69, 276
Cazden, 23, 122
Celce-Murcia, 129
Chaffin and Herrmann, 84
Chaika, 155
Chall, 368
Chamorro, 223, 224
Channell, 71, 412
Chaudron, 22, 57, 269, 384, 402
Cheshire, 325
Cheyenne, 378
Chiat, 235
Chichewa, 279, 299
Chimombo, 299
Chinese, 44, 59, 62, 81, 84, 96, 98, 105, 112, 150, 151, 185, 209, 248, 249, 251, 265, 267, 273–275, 277, 278, 284, 356, 364, 379, 417, 421
Chomsky, C., 283, 284
Chomsky, N., 158–160
Chukovsky, 100
Chumash, 177
chunks, 200–202, 206, 207, 214–216, 233, 237, 265
circumfix, 281
circumlocution, 57, 374, 393, 395
Clancy, Jacobsen, and Silva, 258
clang responses, 65, 68, 71, 80, 83

Index

Index

Mitford, 318
mix languages, 125, 242
mnemonics, 89, 388–390, 399
mnemonist, 118
modality, 284, 322, 324, 349
modals, 218, 225, 228, 233, 252, 322, 324, 325, 349, 352, 365
monolingual dictionaries, 383
mood, 225, 226, 279
Morimoto, 173, 187, 209
morpheme acquisition and morpheme acquisition studies, 288–294
morphemes and morphology, 225, 256, 261–299, 305, 312, 316, 370, 394, 399, 401, 417, 426
morphophonemic change, 296–297
morphophonemic rules, 297
Morrissey, 419
Morsbach, 258
Moskowitz, 306
motherese, 401
motivation, 241, 370, 374, 417, 419, 421, 422
Muro, 273
Myers, 327
Myres, 310

Nagy and Anderson, 368
Nagy and Herman, 368, 375
Nagy, Herman, and Anderson, 369
Nahuatl, 197
Nakao, 120
names, 14, 39, 45, 56, 78, 113, 116, 117, 156, 166, 170, 175–179, 187, 193, 210, 211, 219, 220, 228, 229, 248, 255, 303, 307, 310, 316–318, 346, 364, 372, 382, 394, 398
Nash, 90, 130, 183, 356
National Public Radio, 176, 270
natural semantic metalanguage, 139, 143
Navajo, 26, 79, 82, 85, 91, 103, 232
negative adverbs, 233
negatives, 20, 271
Nehls, 120, 121
Nelson, 221
Nemoianu, 18
Nemser, 194, 212
Nepali, 171, 173, 174
networks, 77, 145, 146, 153, 163, 417
Newman, 317–318
Newmark, 193, 243, 319, 320, 323
Nilsen, 307
Nilsen and Nilsen, 139, 161, 165
Nixon, 104
nonverbal, 101, 149, 244, 329–331, 333–335, 338, 341, 345

Norwegian, 53
noticings, 329, 353
notional-functional approaches, 406–407
nouns, 14–16, 21, 24–28, 30, 31, 55, 57, 66, 73, 74, 80, 117, 123, 130, 141, 159, 160, 177, 179–181, 189–193, 197, 198, 200, 218–222, 223, 225, 228–230, 234, 237, 248–254, 256–257, 263, 265, 268, 271–277, 283–285, 288, 297, 312, 360, 372, 396, 399, 419
number, 265, 271, 273, 298

objects of prepositions. See prepositions
object pronouns, 236, 237
Obler, 399, 400
offers, 50, 66, 70, 98, 113, 116, 122, 128, 152, 249, 359, 361, 362, 364
Olshtain, 56, 195, 353, 358, 364
Omanson, 368
onomatopoeia, 347
openings, 329–333, 347, 363. See also communication signals
oral (vs. written) language, 21, 55, 104, 203, 241, 242, 278, 291, 320, 322, 324, 326, 328, 384, 405, 411, 419, 420, 424
Ornstein and Gates, 59
Orton, 304
Osgood, 155, 326
Oskarsson, 383
overextensions, 17, 62
Oxford, 387, 389, 392
oxymorons, 90–91, 163, 317

Paivio and Clark, 113
Palermo, 101
Palmberg, 399
Palmer, 321
Papago, 85
paradigmatic, 68, 71, 83
paradox, 90, 91
paraphrase, 115, 116, 339, 393, 395
paratactic, 238, 239
Parish, 112
Parker, 81, 82
Parry, 398
participle, 225, 298
part–whole relations, 67–68, 70, 89, 398
passive (vs. active) vocabulary, 77, 325, 370. See also productive (vs. receptive) vocabulary knowledge
passive voice, 225–226, 275, 325
patient, 66, 70, 146, 152, 158–160, 221, 222, 282
Patterson and Cohn, 192
Payne, 372–373
Peabody Picture Vocabulary Test, 56, 157

Index

466